Judaism for
Everyone

ALSO BY RABBI SHMULEY BOTEACH

Judaism for
Everyone

Renewing Your Life
Through the Vibrant Lessons
of the Jewish Faith

Shmuley Boteach

BASIC
BOOKS

A Member of the Perseus Books Group

Published by Basic Books,
A Member of the Perseus Books Group.

A CIP catalog record for this book is available from the Library of Congress.
ISBN 0-465-00794-5

Set in 10-point Stone Serif by the Perseus Books Group
FIRST EDITION

02 03 04 05 / 10 9 8 7 6 5 4 3 2 1

To my grandmother Ida Paul,
who ensured that I had a Jewish education

To Shneur Zalman Fellig,
without whose inspiration, influence, and
friendship I would not have become a Rabbi

To Michael Heinhardt,
whose love for all things Jewish
has given me inspiration

And to the Lubavitcher Rebbe,
Rabbi Menachem Mendel Schneerson,
of blessed memory, who inspired generations
of young Jewish men and women
to become spiritual leaders

May the same wonder-working Deity who, long since delivering the Hebrews from their Egyptian oppressors, planted them in the promised land—whose providential agency has lately been conspicuous in establishing these United States as an independent nation—still continue to water them with the dews of Heaven and to make the inhabitants of every denomination participate in the temporal and spiritual blessing of that people whose God is Jehovah.

—PRESIDENT GEORGE WASHINGTON,
in a letter to Congregation Mikve Israel
in Savannah, Georgia, 1789

I have heard from my father and mother all the answers that faith in God could offer to those who doubt and search for the truth. In our home and in many other homes the eternal questions were more actual than the latest news in the Yiddish newspaper. In spite of all the disenchantment and all my skepticism I believe that the nations can learn much from the Jews, their way of thinking, their way of bringing up children, their finding happiness where others see nothing but misery and humiliation.

—ISAAC BASHEVIS SINGER

Contents

Preface

Let not the wise man glory in his wisdom, the mighty man in his might, let not the rich man glory in his riches; but let him that glories glory in that he understands and knows Me.

—JEREMIAH 9:22–23

MY JEWISH FAITH HAS ALWAYS BEEN my greatest love and inspiration. Knowing that millions of Jews, throughout history, have laid down their lives rather than relinquish the faith of their ancestors has given me considerable pause in undertaking the composition of this book. In the end it was entirely due to the request and encouragement of Robin Baird-Smith, original publisher of *Kosher Sex* and friend, as well as Joann Miller, my editor at Basic Books, that this book was written. It is my attempt to offer traditional Judaism to a modern Jewish and non-Jewish audience in a rational, intelligible, and inspiring light. The book incorporates the insights of many of the old giants of Jewish history as well as more contemporary Jewish thinkers. Foremost on this list are my great teacher and mentor, the Lubavitcher Rebbe, Rabbi Menachem Mendel Schneerson, of blessed memory; Rabbi Samson Raphael Hirsch; Rabbi Joseph Dov Soloveitchik; and Rabbi Abraham Joshua Heschel. Other scholars whose ideas appear here include Rabbi Dr. Norman Lamm, my dear friend Dennis Prager, and Yeshayahu Leibovitz.

In my other books I have thanked my wife, Debbie, for being my greatest pillar of support, without whom none of my projects would have achieved fruition. In this book I thank her, not for supporting me, but for inspiring me. Judaism has long maintained that women possess a higher innate spirituality than men. My wife demonstrates this with her absolute love and devotion to God, people, and Judaism. Nothing that her Jewish faith requires is ever a burden to her, and nothing it demands fails to show her its immediate inner beauty. I also wish to thank my children, who are my joy and the lights of my life. Imparting to them my passion for the Jewish faith has been the foremost responsibility of my life.

I also thank Jo Ann Miller, Executive Editor at Basic Books, for her belief in this material and her enthusiasm for my ideas. I hope that her steadfast support will not prove misplaced. I extend my hearty gratitude to my agent and friend Lois Delahabay, who served as a wonderful matchmaker for this book. And finally, I offer humble thanks to my extremely wise friend Ron Feiner, who gives me profound advice on all aspects of life, both personal and professional, without which I would be significantly more impoverished.

As always, I thank Almighty God for granting me the strength to complete this task. I can only hope that I have done His great law some measure of justice.

Readers acquainted with my writings know that at the age of eight I experienced the trauma of my parents' divorce, which split my family in two. My mother moved with me and my siblings to Miami, and my father remained in Los Angeles. We had always been an Orthodox Jewish family that celebrated the Sabbath, kept a kosher home, and observed the Jewish festivals, and we children attended a Jewish day school. As young boys, my brothers and I wore yarmulkes always, both at home and in public. But we partook fully in the modern world as well. My siblings and I consumed copious quantities of television and participated in all the adolescent fads that characterized mid-1970s America. We skated in roller rinks on Saturday nights, sang Bee Gees songs, and went to endless showings of *Grease* and *Rocky*. But there was a void in my heart that could not be filled. I began to lag behind the rest of my class and became, like some of my siblings, a troublemaker at school. Although my pranks made me popular among my classmates, I felt aimless and lost. With my father 3,000 miles away, I had no full-time authoritarian figure to exert any real influence over me, and my mother selflessly worked two jobs to support her five children.

When I was ten, my life took a vastly different course. My mother could not afford to send my brothers and me to a mainstream Jewish summer sleep-away camp. But the worldwide Hassidic Jewish movement, Chabad-Lubavitch, was opening an eight-week overnight camp in the blistering and mosquito-infested Homestead, Florida, and she signed us up. For the first time in my life, I was immersed in a completely Hassidic Jewish environment, and I found myself in my element. I was a popular camper, and for three consecutive summers I won the competition for learning by heart the most Mishnah, the ancient rabbinic oral code of law. The young rabbinical students who served as my counselors became surrogate fathers to me, and I continued to enjoy a close relationship with them during the year, attending virtually all the weekly classes and programs they ran for Jewish children in South Florida.

At the time of my Bar Mitzvah, the principal Lubavitch figure in my life was Shneur Zalman Fellig, a young rabbinical student who exerted spirited influence on me, was my surrogate older brother, and is one of the people to whom I have dedicated this book. He somehow finagled a meeting between myself and the Lubavitcher Rebbe, Rabbi Menachem Schneerson, the foremost Rabbi and Jewish spiritual leader of his time. I met the Rebbe at three o'clock in the morning, in his tiny Brooklyn office, while hundreds waited outside for their private meetings. I had been told that I would have only a few moments with him, so I prepared a long letter detailing the negative effects of my parents' divorce on me, how I had become a cynic, and how my life at school consisted of teasing the girls and playing practical jokes on the teachers, while my life at home consisted mostly of fighting with my siblings and watching television.

I was moved by the Rebbe's slow reading of my letter, occasionally marking passages with a short yellow pencil. When he finished, he looked up at me and I saw in his piercing blue eyes a sea of infinite kindness. He said to me: "You are too young to be a cynic, especially since you will grow to be a source of *naches,* inspiration, joy, and pride to your family, your school, and the entire Jewish people. I bless you today to grow to be a light unto all people." He then asked me to write to him and to inform him of the progress I was making in achieving these goals, and he said that he would write to me too, a promise he kept. When I emerged from his office, I felt filled with hope for the first time in my life. That very night I decided to leave my Jewish day school and enter a rabbinical seminary.

In some religions the purpose of life is to perfect oneself and become more Godly, a noble objective to be achieved through spiritual pursuits such as faith, prayer, charity, and abstinence. For Judaism the purpose of life is the healing of the world. Man is invited as a junior partner in creation to assist God in purging the world of evil, indifference, and injustice and imbuing it with compassion and loving-kindness. The Jewish dream of creating a world with no war or conflict held immense appeal to a young child whose heart had been broken by the dissolution of his parents' marriage.

The Jewish mission is not to teach the world how to make money, but rather what to do with money once it is made. Our purpose is not to teach the world how to develop atomic energy, but rather to what use such energy should be put. The Jews have always served as the lamp lighting the way for humanity to find God. Our purpose is to show direction, thus ensuring that all the goals of mankind remain pointing firmly heavenward. The Jewish people are like an arrow, a vector, always reminding humans to lift their eyes toward the infinite expanse of the cosmos and see reality for what it really is, that there is an invisible God behind all human events, and that man can find Him if he but lifts the curtain of nature, which conceals the God of history.

This book seeks to demonstrate the modern relevance of the world's oldest monotheistic faith to men and women of all ethnicities, nationalities, and persuasions. It was not written, nor was it intended, primarily for a Jewish audience. The L'Chaim Society, the educational outreach organization I founded at Oxford University in 1988, has been one of the few Jewish organizations in the world with a high proportion of non-Jewish members. Every Friday when I served as Rabbi at Oxford, of the hundred or so students who joined us for the weekly Sabbath meal, more than a third were non-Jews. They came not to convert to Judaism—only a handful of students converted in the eleven years I served as Rabbi there—but rather to grasp a spiritual framework that is all about the celebration of life, that glories in human warmth, and that teaches that God is loving, comforting, and approachable.

It is my great hope that in these pages, no matter how close or far Judaism feels to you, you too will experience some of its life, dynamism, vibrancy, and soul-piercing depth.

Shmuley Boteach
Englewood, New Jersey

Introduction

The Jewish Millennium

THIS BOOK IS WRITTEN IN THE BELIEF that the next thousand years will be a Jewish millennium. For the first time in its long and trying history, the world's oldest monotheistic faith is going mainstream, breaking free of its insular shell. First, there are the celebrities. Madonna, Michael Jackson, Roseanne Barr, and many others have Judaism and its mystical component, Kabbalah, and have spoken of the inspiration it has provided them. Non-Jewish and Jewish celebrities are going to synagogue to find spirituality, and miracle of miracles, they are enjoying it. Then, there are the pundits. Rabbis and Jewish thinkers are regularly sought by the mainstream media for their opinions on all kinds of issues. The Judaism-based teachings and morality of Rabbi Harold Kushner, Dennis Prager, and Dr. Laura Schlessinger have attracted millions of followers.

In the future, the core components of our religion may serve as a locus of spirituality for men and women of all faiths. In the same way that millions of Westerners have adopted individual components of Buddhist and Hindu spirituality, meditating or practicing yoga, non-Jews may find fulfillment through Jewish practices such as honoring the Sabbath as a day of rest and contemplation and imposing a period of sexual separation in marriage so as to enhance passion.

1

The Dualist Society

For the past two thousand years, Christian thought in the West has been dominated by dualism. According to Christianity, God and the world, our souls and our bodies, our minds and our hearts, even heaven and earth, are in conflict. Humans have been conditioned to believe that they must choose between lust and love, altruism and mammon, ambition and piety, and spirituality and materialism. Christianity fashioned a world in which celibate monks were cheered for sequestering themselves in monasteries and vows of poverty guaranteed entry into the kingdom of heaven. Spirituality required that the needs of the flesh be sacrificed to the ascetic pleasures of the soul. And for the past millennium, this philosophy flourished.

But all that has changed. This is a generation that insists on having it all. Modern men and women today reject dualism, refusing to choose between the spiritual and the material worlds. We seek material prosperity coupled with spiritual growth. Young professionals work themselves to the bone so that they can shop, vacation, and indulge in a materialistic orgy of cars and technogadgets. But on their vacations, while they bronze their bodies in skimpy bikinis on Mediterranean beaches, they read books like *The Road Less Traveled* and *Care of the Soul*. After a grueling sixty hours in the office, they volunteer at soup kitchens on weekends to find personal fulfillment. They are redefining success to include not only financial rewards but also the attainment of spiritual goals.

This is what makes Judaism an ideal spiritual model for "Generation X," the "X" representing the confluence of the dual spiritual and material modalities. The quintessential posture of the Jewish Bible is monism. There is one God and He is everywhere. It's all holy. You don't have to choose! Both heaven and earth emanate from the same source. It is all of God. In Jewish spirituality the objective is not to relinquish the earth and go to heaven, but to create heaven *on* earth. Hence, Judaism is the only religion that from its inception has celebrated sex rather than castigating it.

An Age of Noise

In this epoch of cell phones, beepers, E-mail, and fax machines, humans are subjected to work and noise seven days a week, twenty-four hours a day. We are rarely afforded a moment of solitude. I predict that more and more people, Jews and non-Jews, will begin to embrace the particularly *Jewish* observance of the Sabbath as a way to quiet the clamor and to regain a sense of balance and peace. Get ready to see non-Jewish families setting aside one day a week in which they don't answer the telephone, rent videos, or surf the net. Modern-day amusements are as incarcerating as they are liberating, and we all need a weekly break. Every Saturday will be designated as an uninterrupted family day, during which cell phones and Palm Pilots are switched off. The millennium eve is the ultimate example of how people's natural desire for peace and quiet has already asserted itself. On the night of what should have been the biggest party for a thousand years, 60 percent of Americans chose to experience the millennium at home with their families, rejecting the hoopla for something "more simple and meaningful." Sounds a lot like a Jewish Shabbos (Sabbath) to me. And why not? Millennium eve was a Friday night.

An Age of Scandal

Hardly a day passes without someone who had previously been a hero being exposed for questionable or unpardonable behavior. People are afraid to run for office because of what the press might dig up. People yearn to contribute to society but are told that because they are flawed, they have nothing to give. Here, again, Judaism teaches that world redemption—making the world a better place—must always precede personal salvation—becoming a perfect person. Even imperfect people can contribute vastly to the world's perfection. Bill Clinton's having survived the Monica Lewinsky affair was an example of the triumph of Jewish values over Christian ones. Most of the Christian clergy were calling for his head. After all, in Christianity, faith and personal salvation supersede action and world redemption, and flawed people cannot contribute to making the world flawless. Hence the great emphasis on doctrines like papal "infallability." But the message the American people gave was this: *If he's doing a good job for the country, then he should be allowed to stay and get on with it, whatever his shortcomings.* Oscar Schindler was a man known for womanizing, drinking, other scandalous behavior, and for joining the Nazi party. His personal life was an embarrassment. However, he was responsible for saving the lives of more than twelve hundred Jews. The Jewish message that people should be judged by their contribution to society rather than the content of their character is gaining ground. It is the perfect spiritual message for today's generation of imperfect people who still have a social conscience.

An Age of Loneliness

Loss of intimacy is a primary characteristic of the modern world. There are more broken relationships than ever before. In the United States 63 percent of all marriages end in divorce. People work hard and neglect their spouses and children, developing better relationships with their laptops than with their loved ones. The Jewish emphasis on family, community, respect for parents, and regularly celebrating festivals together is a wholesome remedy. We see more and more nations aping the Jewish model of community. Witness the fact that the Dalai Lama consulted a group of Jewish spiritual leaders about how to preserve the integrity of his spiritual community in the absence of a national homeland, an encounter immortalized in *The Jew in the Lotus,* by Rodger Kamenetz. More and more, people long for the kind of emotional closeness and intimate support that can only be found in family. The Jews have survived as a nation because they have first survived as a family.

Rediscovering the Little Things

Kabbalah teaches us how to sanctify the seemingly insignificant moments of life, helping us overcome the monotony of routine existence. Jewish mysticism is about making the ordinary extraordinary and the natural miraculous.

This is especially crucial to modern society, where our lives are lived in anticipation of "the big moment." We've become addicted to artificial excitement.

The result, of course, is rapid burnout. What has been lost is a down-to-earth appreciation for the simple joys of reading the great classics, playing with our children, humming inspiring melodies, taking long strolls, and enjoying everyday conversation with friends. Instead, we sit at home and watch videos and DVDs, devices that transport us into a world of fantasy and adventure. People have forgotten how to be engaged by life itself.

The mystical side of Judaism reminds us that there are spiritual sparks scattered throughout the world, from the majestic mountain peaks to the slums of the city. The Infinite is everywhere. Every time and every place can have great significance as long as we choose to impregnate the moment with meaning. Once when a colleague apologized to Albert Einstein for keeping him waiting on a bridge, Einstein said, "You didn't keep me waiting. . . . I was standing here and working." Kabbalah conditions us to discover the intensity and electricity of simple undertakings like prayer, friendship, and love. This explains why Kabbalah has become so popular especially among celebrities who are struggling to adjust to a healthier life pace. The Kabbalah teaches them how to find the peaks within the valleys so that they can wean themselves from addictive, artificial highs without giving up the excitement of life.

Sex and Relationships

Judaism's highly insightful teachings on how to best sustain sexual passion in relationships and engender greater intimacy may be our best-kept secret. Twelve respected publishers turned down my manuscript for *Kosher Sex,* telling me that a book by a Rabbi on sex would be laughed out of the bookstores. Once published, the book became an international best-seller. Many non-Jewish couples who have read the book have begun to follow the Jewish practice of introducing erotic obstacles in marriage by, among other things, instituting a period of sexual separation in their marriages. Likewise, they warmed to the biblical message of rediscovering sex as the highest form of knowledge and the tool by which husband and wife become one flesh.

The idea of the world's adopting core Jewish spiritual institutions is of course not new. Even in the ancient world, societies began adopting the Jewish Sabbath. And this was done despite great resistance from leading ancient thinkers. The Roman philosopher Seneca, for example, castigated the Jews as lazy for resting one day a week. In the coming decades we will begin to see the *modern* world following suit and adopting core Jewish spiritual practices. I predict that more and more non-Jewish men and women will want to study Judaism and will use it to further their spiritual growth and ethical development. This will happen, not because Judaism is a better religion than the world's other great faiths, but because it is more suited to our times.

A Jewish wave is coming. For eleven years in Oxford I witnessed it swelling. It will make a great splash in all the world's cities. Scores of non-Jews will surf its crest. My hope is that this book will serve as a beachhead where all can land safely.

PART ONE

Elements of Judaism

1

Foundations of Faith

Judaism as the Cornerstone of Western Civilization

*I will insist that the Hebrews have done more to civilize man
than any other nation.*

**—LETTER FROM JOHN ADAMS TO
THOMAS JEFFERSON**

*Being a Jew is like walking in the wind or swimming: you are
touched at all points and conscious everywhere.*
—LIONEL TRILLING, *Partisan Review*, 1985

WHILE LIVING IN BRITAIN FOR ELEVEN YEARS, I noticed that the
Jews and the English have something in common. They are both
phenomenal inventors but poor entrepreneurs, terrific with ideas
but hapless with business. Both nations formulate bold new concepts, but fail abysmally at bringing them to market. During my
time in Britain, I read countless articles lamenting the fact that
British inventors repeatedly come up with remarkable innovations—
they invented the world's first computer, for example—only to see
their ideas developed and marketed in the United States, where ven-
ture capital is more readily available. Take that problem, multiply it

a thousandfold, and you have the history of the Jews. The Jews are responsible for most of Western civilization's cherished moral and social institutions, all of which today go by different names and are attributed to other religions and peoples.

Imagine for a moment that Thomas Edison—who had a stellar record not only of inventing terrific products but also of obtaining the patents and marketing them—had all his inventions stolen or developed by someone else who took full credit for their discovery. Then imagine that one day, long after Edison had died, his grandchildren were asked by his son to help him to organize a tribute to their grandfather, the great inventor, the genius. "What genius?" they asked. They had no idea that their grandfather was responsible for the lights in the room, the phonograph howling in the background, indeed, most of the electrical accessories without which they would find life intolerable. They might still participate in organizing the tribute, but only after their father cajoled and coerced them, with a large dose of guilt thrown in.

This is a useful analogy for appreciating and commiserating with the plight of modern Jewish parents, who must similarly badger their children to perpetuate a tradition that, to them, consists of nothing more than empty, arcane, and antiquated ritual. A generation of Jews is estranged from their heritage. In thinking of golden civilizations and of high points in history, the average secular Jew will conjure up images of pontificating Greek philosophers, Roman legions shimmering in the dazzling sun, and the artistic wonders of the Renaissance masters. Tell him that in terms of world history the Jews have outshone all these civilizations, and he will break into fits of giggles. The Jews, he thinks to himself—aren't they the ones who were defeated by the Romans, slaughtered by the crusaders, expelled by the Spaniards, disemboweled by Chmielnicki in the Ukraine, massacred by the Russians and the Poles, and cremated by the Nazis? Every Jewish child studies in school about how each nation in the past *lived*, and about how the Jews *died*.

In the modern vernacular we would say that Jews have bad PR, a strange testament to a nation whose biblical calling was to serve as a "light unto the nations." Judaism today isn't even a force shaping the public debate. It has been completely superseded by Christianity and Islam. This seems highly ironic in light of the unique gifts granted to the world by the Jewish people and acknowledged by historians and leading scholars. Consider the following examples of just a few of the Jewish contributions that have been co-opted under foreign names: The Jews gave the world the idea of the one God. Today his name is *Jesus Christ* and *Allah*. The Hebrew Bible's idea that all men are created as equals in God's image today goes by the name *democracy*. The idea of a brotherhood of nations and of peace being superior to war, rooted in the Books of Isaiah and Jeremiah, today goes by the name *United Nations*. Consider also that the teaching of Leviticus 19:18, that one must love one's fellowman as oneself, today is called the *Golden Rule*, its origin attributed to the Book of Matthew and to Jesus' Sermon on the Mount. And the Jewish idea that life must be dedicated to the service of humanity and the pursuit of justice, goodness, and ethics today goes by the name *secular humanism*.

The historian Paul Johnson puts it this way:

One way of summing up 4000 years of Jewish history is to ask ourselves what would have happened to the human race if Abraham had not been a man of great sagacity, or if he had stayed in Ur and kept his higher notions to himself, and no specific Jewish people had come into being. Certainly the world without the Jews would have been a radically different place. . . . All the great conceptual discoveries of the intellect seem obvious and inescapable once they have been revealed, but it requires a special genius to formulate them for the first time. The Jews had this gift. To them we owe the idea of equality before the law, both divine and human; of the sanctity of life and the dignity of the human person; of the individual conscience and so of personal redemption; of the collective conscience and so of social responsibility; of peace as an abstract ideal and love as the foundation of justice, and many other items which constitute the basic furniture of the human mind. Without the Jews it might have been a much emptier place. (Paul Johnson, *History of the Jews*, p. 585)

It seems that only anti-Semites are honest enough to attribute to the Jews the world's recent obsession with social justice. Jew-haters acknowledge the profound influence of the Jew, although they call it a conspiracy. The Jews injected values into the world and alerted mankind to a higher moral authority that would hold us accountable for our actions, thereby robbing human beings of the unbridled pursuit of their passions, and this made the Jews the most despised nation on earth. In 1899, Houston Stewart Chamberlain published *Foundations of the Nineteenth Century*, a highly anti-Semitic work, which was extremely well received by the intellectuals of the day. (The *London Times Literary Supplement* called it "unquestionably one of the rare books that really matter.") Chamberlain wrote, "I cannot help shuddering . . . at the portentous, irremediable mistake the world made in accepting the traditions of this wretched little nation . . . as the basis of its belief." According to Dennis Prager and Joseph Telushkin in *Why the Jews?* "Chamberlain hated the Jews for their monotheism and moral values which prevented the natural human being from possessing unrestricted freedom: 'The Jew came into our gay world and spoiled everything with his ominous concept of sin, his law, and his cross.'" Indeed, this was the basic argument of Nietzsche's hatred of Christianity. In essence, he said that the Jews had played a big joke on the world in the form of the Christian. Strong German Teutonic knights had been instilled with the attributes of compassion, forbearance, humility, and prayer and had thus been made into sad mediocrities. The arch anti-Semite Richard Wagner called for a new German religion with no Jewish or Christian influence: "Emancipation from the yoke of Judaism appears to us the foremost necessity." Indeed, the Jewish promulgation of morality and Godly ethics ensured that the Jews would be the most influential and simultaneously most hated nation in the world.

Why Judaism?

Why is Judaism uniquely empowered to offer us insights into our world and ourselves? Moreover, how much relevance could Judaism possibly have to non-Jews? The answer is much more than we might assume.

Ours is a generation desperately seeking spiritual sustenance. In this atmosphere, spiritualist and New Age books top the best-seller lists, and spiritual gurus of every denomination are sought out by young Western minds as an alternative to a suffocating materialism. Yet books on mainstream religions like Judaism and Christianity can often be found only in specialty bookstores. So what do I hope to accomplish with a new book on Judaism?

I believe that the age of Judaism has arrived. In the past two millennia, Christianity and Islam have been the decisive factors shaping world history. These religions concern themselves with macrocosmic issues—political, economic, and social. Christianity and Islam have forged empires and count among their adherents mighty princes. By contrast, there have been virtually no Jewish empires or princes in all that time. Indeed, Judaism has had little to say about the big questions of national existence, such as how to run governments, create dynasties, and subjugate infidels. Rather, robbed of real temporal power ever since the destruction of the first Temple by the Babylonians in 586 B.C.E., Judaism has concerned itself with small questions: whom to marry, how to be a good son and honor one's parents, how to practice honesty in business, how to wrestle with and ultimately conquer the darker angels of one's nature, how to refrain from gossiping behind a friend's back, how to overcome feelings of jealousy and celebrate the good fortune of others, and finally how to imbue everyday life with passion and meaning. The Jews have turned their creative powers inward rather than outward and focused on perfecting themselves and the world around them. No wonder that for tens of generations, the Jews have had the most highly developed communal structures and the strongest family life. Stated simply, whereas Christianity and Islam have spent the past fifteen hundred–odd years for the most part concerned with the world at large, Judaism has been focused on the small world of man.

The world at large is better today than it ever was. To be sure, the terrorist outrages in the United States in 2001, the constant terrorism against innocent Israeli civilians in the Middle East, and the wholesale starvation of innocents in war-torn parts of Africa remind us of how vulnerable humans still are and how far we are from a lasting and just peace. Nevertheless, it is almost unthinkable that a global conflict like a third world war could break out today. Wealthy countries operate highly developed foreign-aid programs for the benefit of poorer ones, and world leaders who seek and create peace are lauded as heroes, whereas warmongers are treated as terrorists and thugs. Although we still have a long way to go, there can be little doubt that an international war is today being waged against poverty, disease, terrorism, and injustice. But while the macrocosm is improving, the microcosm—the inner world of man—is deteriorating with alarming rapidity. Divorce and infidelity rates are higher than ever. The crime wave, the curse of the Western world for several generations, today even involves children who shoot one another at school with guns. Drug and substance abuse climb, with no end in sight. Antidepressants, Prozac for example, remain the miracle drugs of a despondent and depressed generation. (One in four Americans has been treated at some point for depression.) People flock to movies and watch endless hours of television in an effort to escape the monotony and pain of their lives for a while. What can be said about a generation for whom celebrity gossip is its highest indulgence? How content can today's men and women really be when they choose to live vicariously through men who can throw a ball through a hoop, or women who wiggle their behinds on television at the MTV music awards?

What our generation requires above all is a way to master our lives in a confusing world of endless possibility and choice. We want a creed that will offer us passion and success without substantial sacrifice. Ours is a pleasure-seeking generation, where fun is as important as achievement. Judaism can provide it. While other nations were perfecting the art of war and building armies and navies, Judaism was perfecting the art of building solid families and communities and closing the generation gap to ensure that an ancient tradition could be passed from father to son and mother to daughter with minimal disruption. No other method of living has so celebrated life amid a devotion to spiritual values. Judaism offers a spiritually based philosophy that is concerned primarily with life in this world, rather than the hereafter.

Cornerstones of Civilization

Western civilization is predicated on various foundation stones, and it is the purpose of this book to demonstrate not only the roots of some of these ideas in Judaism and the Bible but, more important, how Judaism is a program of action designed to internalize these concepts within the heart of man and society. As a general introduction to some of the themes that will be found in this book, I have compiled the eighteen cardinal tenets of the modern world as I see them, and I have shown how each emanates from a different strand within the fabric of the Bible and Jewish faith.

The Belief in the Brotherhood of Mankind and the Kinship of All Living Things.   This belief is predicated on the understanding that we all emanate from a single source in God, and thus humanity is one family, responsible for each of its members. Because we are all children of the one God, there is hope that all humankind can live together in peace and harmony. This is not a concept based on dualism, or two warring powers, but a belief that one God is the master of the universe and source of all life. Evil is therefore always weaker than good, and benevolent forces will always triumph over darkness. An all-encompassing unity is at the heart of creation. There are no opposing forces at odds in the universe. This emanates from the belief in one God and one Creator.

The Belief in the Equality and Infinite Value of All Human Beings and in Their Dignity, Which Must Be Upheld and Protected by All.   Every human is special and irreplaceable. Our worth is not judged by our possessions, but by our divine, immortal soul. Human life is sacred.

This stems from the biblical statement that man was created in the image of God. ⟶ all are equal & unique

History Is Directional and Continually Evolves for the Betterment of Mankind. Every good deed, however small, is significant and cumulative and ultimately brings us closer to the perfect world, which is in our power to bring about. Action is far more significant than dogma or belief. The right thing should be done even if for the wrong reasons. **This springs from the ancient Jewish belief that history began in chaos but will culminate gradually in the messianic era. The Messiah will one day perfect the world, but in the meantime we must contribute to the world's completion. We bring light to our darkened planet by carrying out the mitzvot, the divinely prescribed religious actions that foster holiness and goodness in our world.**

Peace Is Superior to War, Forgiveness Higher Than Vengeance, and Cultivation of the Mind and Spirit More Noble Than Cultivation of the Body. **This stems from the Jewish insistence that the Sabbath, a day of rest, is holier than all the workdays of the week, as well as from the ancient messianic prophecies that promised a perfect world devoid of conflict and hostilities.**

Man Is Utterly Free—Empowered with Freedom of Choice, He Is Capable of Liberating Himself from the Cage of Human Nature. There is no fate—not in the stars, not in our genes. We are responsible for our own actions and will be rewarded for good deeds and held accountable for bad. Humans, unlike animals, are always in control of their destiny. **This idea flows from the Festival of Passover and the exodus from Egypt, which emphasizes that the Jew has been permanently and irrevocably redeemed from Egypt, the symbol of human and natural bondage.**

Law Is Ineffective Unless It Is Immutable; Morality and Ethics Must Be Anchored in an Absolute Divine Standard. There is a universal standard of conduct by which people must treat one another. Man cannot be trusted as the arbiter of his own morality. Law, the best means for communicating love, translates human potential into actuality. Any society not based on the dictates of law is unjust. There is no moral relativism at work in creation; rather, God's law represents the noblest ideals of goodness. **This crucial concept arises out of the Ten Commandments and the Festival of Shavuot, celebrating God's giving the Jews the law at Sinai.**

Man Is Not Master of the Planet, but Must Seek to Be One with the Universe, Protecting All Life and the Environment. Man is custodian of the earth, and the world is his garden, which he must nurture and protect. Sadistic treatment of animals or abuse of the environment is a grave sin, which will result in man's being driven from the earth. **This idea emanates from Adam and Eve's being placed in the Garden of Eden, as well as from the Festival of Sukkot, a seven-day period of total immersion in nature, which sensitizes man to its wonders.**

Leadership Is the Cornerstone of Human Inspiration and Social Change. Strong leadership is central to every healthy society. "Without vision," as King Solomon said, "the people will perish." **This concept emerges from the centrality of the Messiah to social change, as well as the critical role the Kohen-Priests and the Rabbis have played in Jewish history.**

Man Must Have Values by Which to Live. A healthy life is one in which priorities are set. Those things that are eternal and valuable, like family, must be placed before the ephemeral and superficial, like career and success. A day of rest every week is essential in retreating from the bustle of everyday life in order to reconsider priorities and rejuvenate the spirit. Judaism is solely responsible for teaching man that rest has a higher function than simply facilitating more work. **This is another idea that stems from the weekly Sabbath, a day that cannot be compromised for commerce or financial gain.**

The Sabbath is an uninterrupted celebration of values, wherein the important is never superseded by the urgent.

Man Is More Than the Sum Total of His Actions. Man possesses an internal soul that transcends the negative things he does. Man can always reinvent himself and turn his life around. Renewal is at the heart of retaining passion in life, and man is possessed of an infinite capacity to recreate himself. **This idea stems from the Jewish belief in repentance and the numerous biblical examples of God's heartily accepting sincere regret, most notably in the story of the prophet Jonah and the city of Nineveh. It is also the theme behind Rosh Hashanah, the Jewish New Year, as well as Yom Kippur, the Day of Atonement.**

Man Must Harbor a Hatred for War, Violence, and the Sight of Blood. **Instilling these ideas is the purpose behind the Jewish dietary laws of kashrut and strict prohibitions against eating blood.**

↳ how come all Israelis must join army?

The Family Is the Bedrock of Society and the Most Important Social Unit. **Some of the most important biblical observances, such as the eating of the paschal lamb, can be done only in the family. Similarly, the Bible always counts the Jewish people in denominations of tribe and family.**

Man Need Not Bow His Head in Submission in the Face of Seeming Divine Injustice, and Humans Must Never Accept the Suffering of Their Fellowmen in Silence. Man's highest calling is wrestling with God. We are invited to enter into a real relationship with God, involving give and take, not merely bowing and submission. **This idea, found only in Judaism, traces its origin to the name Israel (Yisrael), literally, "he who wrestles with God," as well as to the giants of Jewish history, like Abraham and Moses, who contended with God about punishing sinners.**

Men and Women Are Different but Equal.   Men and women have different ways by which to maximize their fullest, unique potentials. **This stems from Adam and Eve's having been created separately, but as complements to each other, as each other's helpmates. The Bible gives different laws for men and women, and both kinds of laws are vital to the nation.**

The World Is Enriched by Cultural and Ethnic Diversity.   Racism is evil because it denies the improvement that every people brings as it joins the family of nations. By working together, respecting one another, and being enhanced through exposure to one another's differences, we create a family of nations, or to use the biblical metaphor, a garden whose beauty is dependent on its different colors and fauna. **This critical idea, which the world has only recently begun to appreciate, is inherent in the concept of the Jews' being the nation chosen to bring together the disparate contributions of all other nations within one divine framework.**

↳ sounds a little ~~eve~~ missionary

The Most Beautiful Things in Life Are Those That, like Love, Are Invisible, Transcendent, and Cannot Be Experienced with the Five Senses.   **This follows from the belief in God, holiness, and spirituality.**

Man Must Do the Right Thing Because It Is Right, Even If That Makes Him Unpopular or Jeopardizes His Vital Interests. **This, one of humankind's hardest lessons, has been taught to the Jew by two thousand years of anti-Semitism.**

Doing the Right Thing for the Wrong Reasons Is Far More Important Than Waiting for the Proper Motivation. **This idea is based on the Jewish obsession with world redemption, which always comes before personal salvation.**

differs ~~se~~ from Christianity

A Religion That Instills Values

Now that Western society has adopted or at least pays lip service to the values I listed, the question that follows is this: Why do we still need religion? Judaism has imparted a wealth of content and meaning to the lives of the earth's inhabitants, but now that its role as a harbinger of these eternal values has been fulfilled, can it not be consigned to the dustbin of history? Isn't religion nothing more than an attempt to make people better? So let's get rid of the ritual and focus on the message.

There are two answers to the question why we still need religion. First, religion's highest purpose is not to perfect the state of humankind, but to draw people closer to God and, by extension, to one another. Second, although religion's secondary purpose is to uplift man from the level of the animal, it is not enough simply to *teach* man values. Rather, a program must be established that actually *instills* values into the human psyche so that they are translated from the abstract into the permanent. Stated somewhat differently, values, unlike knowledge, which can be taught, can only be experienced and absorbed. They are useless unless they are ingrained within the human character. We forget sometimes how easy it is for ideas and ethics to go out of fashion. Just sixty years ago, the Nazi beast trampled on all eighteen cardinal tenets, and had the Germans won the war, they might have instilled completely new ideals and built a world based on darkness. All great ideas, as well as civilization itself, corrode with time. The monumental values I have listed cannot remain like flowers cut off from their roots—they will slowly wilt and die. In promoting a moral and just planet, Judaism is not just a collection of ideas. More significantly, it is a program of action by which to bring Godly ethics and values to mankind, ensuring that they take root within the individual and each successive generation. The purpose of Judaism is to translate spiritual abstractions into a tangible reality that becomes an inseparable part of human living. Libraries of books have been written about Judaism.

This one differs in that it seeks to present the ideas behind the Jewish faith and set them in an insightful and universal philosophical context, rather than to serve merely as a how-to guide. Moreover, other books present Jewish ideas as having evolved historically, whereas this book proposes that the Jewish religion is a holistic set of inextricably linked values that together comprise a state-of-the-art system for maximizing human goodness and potential. I enjoin you to accompany me on this journey, whose terrain, though arduous, culminates in a land flowing with milk and honey, and in a world filled with justice and purpose.

2

The Triumph of Feminine over Masculine Values

Why Judaism Has Always Viewed Women as Superior, Rather than Equal, to Men

There are only two ways to live your life. One is as though nothing is a miracle. The other is as though everything is a miracle.

—ALBERT EINSTEIN

In order to be a realist you must believe in miracles.

—DAVID BEN GURION,
television interview, 1956

I felt there's a wealth in Jewish tradition, a great inheritance. I'd be a jerk not to take advantage of it.

HERMAN WOUK,
on his return to Orthodox Judaism

JUDAISM CAME INTO THE WORLD to sensitize man to the God that was all around him. Whereas other religions instructed humans to climb to the heavens, where they would find God, Judaism taught men and women simply to open their eyes and discover that they are in God's bosom. Conditioning mankind to experience the reality of God is the principal objective of the Jewish faith, but this sensitivity cannot come about until man harnesses his inner feminine energy. Women have a spiritual intuition that men lack. Only the reduction of aggression and competitiveness—which hinder man from recognizing the truth—can redeem him from his own self-centeredness and focus him fully on God. All of Judaism springs from a single core idea, revealed collectively to the Jewish nation at Sinai: the triumph of feminine-passive over masculine-aggressive values.

Judaism is not perceived as a religion that makes waves. Since Judaism has never had territorial and expansionist aspirations, the idea arose that it is evolutionary rather than revolutionary. Nothing could be further from the truth.

The introduction of Judaism into the established world order was the greatest revolution of all time and led to the greatest hatred of all time, anti-Semitism. Here was a people who proclaimed to the ruling classes that all humans were created in the image of God, that man was bound by a divine moral code and could therefore not steal or murder as he pleased. Until the giving of the Torah, or Law, at Mount Sinai, man loved only his relatives or his countrymen and kinfolk—those to whom he had blood ties or with whom he shared an identity. ("Torah" refers to all twenty-four books of the "written law" plus the "oral code" as written and compiled by the ancient Rabbis in the Mishnah and the Talmud.) Common interests preceded common values. In one stroke, the Torah commanded man to love the stranger, the orphan, and the widow and to protect their interests. Might did not make right, and not only the fittest survived. God's providence spread like a canopy over all of creation, protecting the weak and oppressed. The Almighty legislated exacting punishment for those who took advantage of the unfortunate and those who lacked a natural protector. The Torah forbade employers to exploit their employees, insisting that wages never be withheld. Likewise, the Torah mandated a comprehensive social welfare system in which every man and woman of commerce was obligated to deliver at least 10 percent of their profits to the poor.

The Torah also made marrying a woman against her will illegal and imposed extremely harsh penalties on rape.

The Bible restructured the social hierarchy as well, undermining the ruling elites who exploited the poor and making meritorious action, not noble birth or victory in battle, the sole determinant of human greatness. Indeed, Judaism established a priestly class to re-place the warrior class as the leaders of the nation. The pursuit of love and justice was enshrined as man's highest goal. The Jews proclaimed to the world that people could transform themselves from peasant to landowner, from selfish to selfless, through per-sonal effort.

Tuning In to the Divine Will

Prior to the giving of the Torah at Sinai, paganism was the order of the day. Paganism must be differentiated from idolatry. Idolatry is the worship of idols, stones, the sun, the moon, and the stars. Paganism is the worship of the forces of nature. Pagans pay homage to the earth's elements and ascribe divine qualities to wind, fire, earth, and water. But they also worship human nature and feel that it is their highest duty to indulge the natural instincts. In paganism, man can-not remain monogamous, for fear that he is missing out on the pleas-ures his genes have programmed him to pursue. In short, pagan man submits to the forces of nature without restraint. But Judaism taught man that he had to surrender himself to the rule and the immutable law of the one, true God, and that his nature could be reoriented to coincide with the divine will.

All this the Jews transmitted to a lawless world that worshiped stone. How must the prevailing caste systems and aristocratic orders, *the establishment,* have reacted to such a revolutionary message? This is the meaning behind the Talmudic proclamation that Mount Sinai was so named because hatred, *sinah,* descended from there to the Jewish nation. As Rabbi Michael Lerner points out, ruling elites have always feared the Jewish passion for social justice and thus have por-trayed the Jews as schemers and conspirators. The nature of every or-

ganism is to expel an irritant, and the Jews—with their message of
sanctity, morality, equality, and holiness—have from time immemorial served as the world's greatest pests. Judaism was always meant to
unsettle rather than *become* the establishment. Perhaps this explains
why, though Christianity and Islam converted hundreds of millions,
the Jews remained small in number, yet created a revolution in established thinking.

Judaism is a religion that simply cannot flourish amid banality. Its
revolutionary calling does not lend itself to placid and unruffled
communal life. The Jewish soul brims with fire and a passionate attempt to awaken the world to its Godly possibilities.

The First Feminine Revolution

To be sure, the injection of Jewish values into history was a revolution. But what is not always appreciated is that it was a *feminine* revolution. Indeed, all of Judaism can be defined as the long-term
introduction, and ultimate triumph, of feminine values over masculine ones. Prior to the giving of the Torah at Sinai, the world operated on masculine-aggressive principles. Dominant within society
were those who exerted cunning and brute strength. Competitiveness and ruthlessness were the hallmarks of society. Vengeance and
victory won out over forgiveness and harmony. Great men were
those who vanquished their enemy in war and forgave no slight.

In fact the great men of history have overwhelmingly been military figures like Hannibal, Julius Caesar, Genghis Khan, and
Napoleon. Duels were fought between men to defend their honor.
History is replete with stories of so-called great men who killed their
fellowmen in challenges over trifling offenses. Indeed, a man who
would not seek to settle a slight with a pistol was dismissed as cow-
ardly and feminine. No man could grow to be a ruler in the ancient
world unless he was first a conqueror. The glory of the mighty em-
perors of Rome was dependent almost entirely on expanding the
borders of the empire and brutally crushing their opponents, including women and children.

Into the world of masculine values came Abraham, who invited all strangers into his tent, and Moses, who insisted that the Hebrew must love the stranger and the oppressed. The Almighty forbade blood feuds and vengeance. Judaism taught that peace was superior to war, forgiveness the master of vengeance, introspection and study better than hostility and competition, and motherly selflessness greater than indulgent self-promotion. Judaism taught humans to cultivate their nurturing instinct at the expense of their competitive streak.

For the most part, our world today accepts the superiority of peace over war. This, however, is a recent innovation. Prior to the First World War, statesmen and royalty attired themselves in military dress because greatness was won on the battlefield. Those who averted a conflict or did not aspire to be soldiers were dismissed as cowards, not fit for public office. It was only the horrors of mass slaughter of the First and Second World Wars that alerted the world to the blessings of peace.

Today, of course, the desire to win glory on the battlefield has been largely transmuted to the desire to make money on Wall Street. I can imagine vividly the nightly scenes at our home when I was a boy. My father would arrive home late after a long day at the office, like so many other modern-day dads. My mother would quietly sit and eat dinner with him, long after the children had gone to sleep. Her message to my father was the same on almost every occasion. "You have five beautiful children, thank God. Isn't that enough? Why do you need a bigger business, more money?" And my father, who of course justified his absence by his loving desire to provide for his family, would sit silently pondering her words. I suspect that the same scene has been repeated in countless homes since the pursuit of capital supplanted the pursuit of victory in battle. Men have almost always defined their success in external terms, constantly seeking to outdo their peers, and many women have also followed suit.

According to the German philosopher G. W. F. Hegel, human beings, like animals, have natural needs and desires for objects outside themselves, such as food, drink, shelter, and above all the preservation of their own lives and bodies. Man, in contrast to animals, also desires the desire of other men—that is, he wants to be "recognized." In particular, he wants to be recognized as a human being with a certain worth or dignity, a being that is superior to the animals and that occupies a central place in the world. Thus he is willing to risk his life in a struggle with his fellowman, the single goal being to attain respect and prestige.

Only man among the animals is able to overcome his most basic instincts—including the instinct for self-preservation—for the sake of abstract principles and goals. Whereas other animals risk their lives for food and shelter, humans will risk food and shelter—indeed their very health and welfare—in order to gain prestige and recognition. The desire for recognition drives two primordial combatants to seek to make the other "recognize" his humanness by staking his life in a fight to the death. But as the two battle, the natural fear of death begins to inhibit both combatants, and the one who submits to this fear and surrenders becomes a slave to the other, more heroic, combatant, and thus the relationship of master and slave is born.

This desire for recognition, or what Hegel called "the thymotic urge," is central to all human undertakings. Each of us requires some form of external recognition in order to substantiate our worthiness and existence. Loving oneself is never enough. We all desire the appreciation and corroboration of others. We require our peers to cherish our contribution to their lives. But men and women have traditionally gone about achieving this desire in radically different ways. For men, the love of a woman and the adoration of their children, contributing humbly to one's community, and having the respect of a small circle of friends have never been enough. Men have always desired to be princes, knights, and captains of industry. Women, too, have desired to be princesses, but this usually meant finding a Prince Charming rather than having dominion over a state. Women have never indulged their competitive instincts as much as men and have placed far more emphasis on the importance of love and relationships. For women, being "somebody" was generally defined as being in a series of concentric, loving, and wholesome relationships. Significance was bestowed through "being" rather than "doing."

The Jewish mystics explain that the six days of the week represent the masculine-aggressive dimension in creation. They are the time for work, success, and development, when everything is governed by considerations of human utility. Conversely, the Sabbath day, which has always been described by the ancient Rabbis in feminine terms— the Sabbath Queen, the Sabbath Bride—is a time for rest, nurture, study, tranquility, and holiness. The six days of the week engage us, but the Sabbath mothers us. The days of the week belong to the office, but the Sabbath belongs to marriage and the family. The days of the week are about man's mastery over the elements, but the Sabbath is about man's mastery over himself. What the Jews gave the world was the idea that the Sabbath was holier and higher than the days of the week. The feminine-passive, our nurturing and mothering instinct, is superior to our predilection to domination and victory. When Isaiah and Jeremiah promised an era of eternal harmony and peace, a time when nations would beat their swords into plowshares and no father would again instruct his child in the art of war, they asserted the predominance of the feminine-passive dimension of humankind over the masculine. Indeed, women are responsible for only 3 percent of violent crime in our society, are twice as likely to attend synagogue or church, and are three times more faithful than their husbands in marriage.

Five hundred years ago, well before any assertion of women's rights, Rabbi Isaac Luria, the most outstanding Jewish Kabbalist of all time, wrote that the Messiah would not come until husbands began to obey their wives. He was referring to the need for men to undo the damage of the sin of the golden calf—when women admonished their husbands for their faithlessness in forgetting the God who had just redeemed them from Egypt. But he also meant that men would have to learn that their competitive instincts and win-lose philosophy, born of a scarcity mentality, would have to bend to the maternal, harmonious instinct of win-win, in which the earth's inhabitants support one another in an era of infinite abundance and everlasting peace. Judaism championed the nurturing, as opposed to the competitive, spirit within us.

It is clear that in many families the father feels it his primary duty to *discipline* his children, whereas the mother sees her primary duty as *cherishing and nourishing* her children. According to Judaism, though there is a need for discipline, that need is transitory, whereas the need for nurturance and love is eternal. Children who are not sufficiently disciplined may still make valuable contributions to the world around them, but those who have not been loved will have life-long and debilitating insecurities.

The Jewish people are the midwives of the world, playing the soft woman to the harsh masculine posture of the other nations. It is not a role we are ashamed of. We have never cultivated the masculine tendencies of other nations. One might even go further and suggest that the Jews are the battered wife of the Gentile nations. The Jews have forever suffered persecution and torment at the hands of their Gentile brethren but have still refused to embody their aggressive ethos. We see this posture being adopted even by the State of Israel, which, had it practiced the oppressive and tyrannical policies of most of its nondemocratic Arab neighbors, might have brutally suppressed all the Palestinian uprisings that have threatened its stability with harsh finality.

Until recently the Jews were a poor, scholarly people who spent their lives praying to their God, learning His laws, and raising children whose first love would be Godliness and ethics. To be sure, we have paid a heavy price. As people who have been nagging others to recognize God and pursue peace, we have had more than our share of slaughter and murder. Like a woman bereft of defenses, our vulnerability has been exploited by others. But now others are following our example and attempting to be more feminine and compassionate themselves. The contemporary result of the projection of this ancient Jewish light into history is that heroism and bravery are no longer defined on the battlefield. Today, heroism is found in passively conquering our inner predilection toward wickedness, and bravery is found in acts of charity and kindness to the stranger, the orphan, and the widow.

No general today is equal to a winner of the Nobel Peace Prize. In the United States a man who eschewed the military, avoided the draft, and even publicly protested against his own country's involvement in a foreign war was elected president. One of the most respected recent political figures, Nelson Mandela, would have been dismissed as a weakling just two generations ago. Rather than calling for armed insurrection and wholesale slaughter of the ruling white majority in South Africa, he advocated a policy of peaceful noncooperation and resistance. Later, when he assumed power in South Africa, he pursued a policy of reconciliation and healing with the white minority. The same is true of the esteemed twentieth-century figures, the Reverend Martin Luther King, Jr., and Mohandas (Mahatma) Gandhi. Like a fiery Old Testament prophet, King changed the world as we know it through the power of the spoken word. He had no armies or tanks when he dismantled the iron wall of segregationist oppression. And Gandhi brought the world's greatest colonial power to its knees through the peaceful spirit of nonviolent protest. That these figures could be so much more revered today than the seemingly gallant terrorists who sacrifice their lives in order to bring about political ends, such as the demonic warriors responsible for the outrages of September 11, points to the triumph of the feminine-passive values of Judaism over the masculine-aggressive values of the ancient world. Indeed, aspiring conquerors, the likes of Saddam Hussein or Osama bin Laden, are today seen as contemptuous thugs, so great has the change in established thinking become. Men who revel in their feminine energy—who are peaceful, nonconfrontational, charitable, domesticated, and loving—are respected far more than the alpha males of old who used bullying, fear, and intimidation to achieve their aims. To be sure, it has taken well over two thousand years, but the triumph of Jewish over pagan values has finally been achieved.

Judaism taught us to live for *Shabbat*, our "bride" and queen, rather than for the masculine "days of the week," in which a man is important because of the car he drives or the titles he has earned. Even in business today, the established thinking goes that corporate titans must always think "win-win" rather than "win-lose," as Stephen Covey so forcefully argued in his best-seller *The Seven Habits of Highly Effective People*. The idea of seeing one's competitor as kin and ensuring that he also benefit from a deal is a total reversal from the cutthroat commercial practices of just a generation ago, wherein putting the competition out of business was as important as winning new customers.

This embracing of feminine-passive values is also evident in the Jewish passion for study and cerebral pursuits. Jews have traditionally been known as the people of the book, and indeed, the most famous Jews of history, such as Moses and Maimonides, have nearly all been Rabbis and teachers rather than rulers and conquerors. A teacher is a facilitator, someone who shines his light upon someone else rather than reveling and basking in the spotlight himself. He is a nurturer rather than a celebrity.

The Demise of the Facilitator

Here we arrive at a paradox: The world at large—the macrocosm—has borne witness to the supremacy of Jewish feminine-passive values over the warlike and competitive masculine-aggressive values. But the world of man—the microcosm—has done just the reverse. People are making the mistake of putting career before relationships and social status before inner dignity. Today we are witnessing the discrediting of the facilitator in contemporary society. The boom in business over the past few years has been merciless and all-consuming, devouring families, marriages, and friendships. It seems that we have time for little other than the pursuit of status and riches.

In Judaism, man's highest calling is to be a lamp, a light, a source of illumination to others. Light represents the facilitator, the belief that we are created not only to be powerful ourselves, but primarily to empower others. Light exists for no purpose other than to illuminate its environs. It possesses no selfish agenda. All light is outwardly directed. To be a light is to nurture the development of another. Not just to succeed ourselves, but to encourage, applaud, and welcome the success of others. Not just to feed ourselves, but to nourish the stranger. Not just to triumph ourselves, but to mentor others so that they can achieve their dreams.

Nevertheless. the emphasis in modern-day society is on the development and promotion of self. Selfishness is inculcated into contemporary college students, who are taught that their highest calling is to give *themselves* as a gift to humanity: to be a great man or a great woman. The altruism of the sixties college radical is today the stuff of documentaries. It has no contemporary corollary. That recognition is much more important than service is instilled as a matter of course, beginning with the fundamental importance of leaving the university with the proper accreditation and degree.

Although rich nations today donate large percentages of their GNP to poorer nations in the form of loans and direct aid, "personal growth," "career prospects," and "personal fulfillment" are the catchwords of today's younger generation. I know many husbands and wives who have divorced their spouses because they felt that they were not "growing" in the relationship. The belief that perhaps we were created primarily to help one another, to dedicate our lives to the success of our fellows, is rejected today as unrealistic sentimentalism. People enter into relationships seeking to receive rather than give, and they discard those relationships that are not sufficiently fulfilling. Spouses are encouraged to leave a partner who ignores or is indifferent to their needs. "You must leave your husband," I have heard countless unhappy wives told. "You have an *obligation* to yourself." Determining whether their husbands were committed to change so as to bring them happiness was too time consuming and old-fashioned. Even parenting is often pushed off until financial stability is achieved. People have a single child and then complain endlessly that they find it impossible to cope. Families are becoming smaller, since parents have begun to see large families as starving the world and as a personal hindrance. Even when we do have children, we leave them to be raised by television and Nintendo so that our own hobbies are not disrupted.

My wife is respected among my students far more than I am, mostly for her character rather than her "achievements." Many of the female students who are her friends look up to her *despite the fact* that she dedicates her life largely to mothering. It has become common in the modern era for a woman who has chosen mothering as her life's calling to answer in embarrassment when a professional woman asks about her career. Euphemisms like "homemaker" or the downright ridiculous "domestic engineer" are used to help conceal their shame. The man or woman who has chosen to be a facilitator is rejected as a role model and subtly encouraged to make him- or herself the main beneficiary of the effort.

I see my life as an opportunity to reverse the mistakes made by my beloved father and the countless other men of his generation who, with the best of intentions, put their careers before their marriages and family. Before being accused of hypocrisy, I immediately admit that I am still far from that goal, although I have made substantial progress over the past few years, thank God. For a man, marriage is redemptive. Sharing his life with a woman, a man will learn to be more feminine. I believe firmly that women have the power to bring redemption to men. The main lesson a wife can teach her husband is to be satisfied with her love and that of their children, rather than needing the adulation of the world. Wives who push their husbands to ever-higher planes of professional achievement are doing them a profound disservice. I still take a far greater sense of pride in seeing my name on the cover of a book than in showing pictures of my children to business associates. But I know that this is not a redemptive lifestyle. It requires correction and I am dedicated to reversing the error. Who will correct errant men who sacrifice all in the name of career, if not the soft, gentle, and sensible women in their lives? Who will lead self-obsessed men to God, if not women, who possess a naturally higher spiritual sensitivity?

The purpose of the Jewish social revolution was to teach humans to be more compassionate and nurturing and that success at home with family was more important than success among business associates. But it appears as though the undeclared purpose of the modern world is to reverse this and to make women more masculine. Rather than witness the much-desired feminization of men, we are instead witnessing the masculinization of women. Of course, women can have careers. They are just as smart and capable as men and have always been so. That is patently obvious. But they should still derive their greatest sense of satisfaction from their role as friends, wives, daughters, and mothers, rather than as lawyers, doctors, or investment bankers. Isn't this what a wife would also expect from her husband? That what pleases him most in life is not that he is an executive in a large corporation, but that he has the love and admiration of his wife and children?

I believe sincerely in work as an important and integral part of self-fulfillment and satisfaction. Man was endowed with both a majestic quality, which expresses itself in achieving dominion over his environment, and an intimate quality, which expresses itself in being one with those who surround him or her. Nevertheless, our work should always be peripheral to our existence, rather than central to it. Our deepest satisfaction must come from being facilitators and enabling others to be happy. We must always put love before material success. Only then will we know the ecstatic pleasure of being freed from the confines of the ego. We must find our truest fulfillment in being parents, brothers, sisters, friends, and contributors to our community and society. The Talmud says, "The mother cow has a far greater desire to feed her calf than the calf has a desire to drink its mother's milk." Real human satisfaction is derived from giving rather than receiving, from being needed rather than from needing.

Contemporary social commentators have discussed the emasculation of today's men at the expense of aggressive women who are taking male jobs and proving that they cannot only compete with but triumph over men in the universities and professions. To be sure, for thousands of years women were deprived by men of the right to maximize their fullest potential. This crime has been corrected, but at what price? Rather than speak only of the emasculation of men, we should speak of the defeminization of women. Aggression is not a good thing in men or women. Blind ambition is equally debilitating in both. So why should women be proud that they are competing with men at the expense of their own precious feminine gifts?

There is a dangerous social upheaval at work today in which the agents of feminine values—women themselves—are fast becoming apostles of masculinity. In counseling married couples I am accused of usually taking the wife's side. This is because men seem to have a defective sexual nature. They have an extremely short sexual attention span. Their wives notice how they shift their affection and attention away from them and onto strangers, and they respond by becoming bitter and striking back. Arguments ensue. A wife must teach her husband to love a personality more than a body. To love foreplay and hugging as much as sex. And to value a relationship as something other than a means to an end. But because women today have become as professionally driven as men, they have scarce time for family and marriage. Who, then, will raise tomorrow's children? Not the mother only. She must teach her husband how to experience the awe and magic of fatherhood, so that he will also invest himself in his children. The decentralization of the home is one of society's greatest maladies, one that requires urgent attention. Being a loving spouse and parent is life's most noble profession. Nurturing a human life is far loftier than selling computers or being a movie star. It will take proud and accomplished women who celebrate their feminine gifts to overcome the masculinization of their gender.

Rose Kennedy, the matriarch of a legendary political family, was never embraced as a role model for American women. Many attribute this to the fact that she dropped her career to raise nine children and always remained in the background. Once, when asked in an interview why she dedicated her life to her husband and children rather than herself, she responded that it was simple mathematics. Had she made something of her life and career, she would only have given one great person to the world. But as a mother she was able to nurture nine personalities, most of whom made an impact on the world.

The demise of the facilitator is further evidenced by the lack of respect accorded the teaching profession. What kind of signal are we beaming out to children when they see that investment bankers own yachts and racecars, while many schoolteachers can barely afford to pay their mortgages? Of course, it wasn't always like this. Once upon a time, to be a teacher was seen as the most exalted vocation. In days gone by, being a facilitator was far superior to being the man or the woman who captured the headlines. Socrates, Plato, and Aristotle were all teachers. Their names were more famous in their day than the politicians and kings of the era. They became famous for molding great minds rather than focusing only on their personal success. But who could seriously entertain the possibility today that a professor or thinker would be more famous than the president of the United States? All of us today want to be *the* man, *the* woman, and never he or she who helps *craft* the man or the woman.

When Bill Clinton was president, he visited Oxford, his alma mater, and I invited fifteen Rhodes scholar friends for dinner after they had met privately with him. Inevitably, we asked one another if we envied him, if we too wanted to be president of the United States. Everyone else, after some prodding, answered in the affirmative. When the question finally came to me, I said, "No, in all honesty, I have no ambition, nor any desire, to be president of the United States." I told the students, "I don't say this out of humility. Rather, I am more ambitious than that. I would like to be the man to whom the president comes when he needs answers, when he seeks advice. I want to be a repository of wisdom, a beacon of light."

In the Bible, the Jews are described as being a "light unto the nations." Light is nothing more than a facilitator. It has no substance, and it cannot be captured. It lacks the strong qualities of the desk, the intricate and complex circuitry of the computer, or the beauty and splendid color of the painting on the wall. *But it makes them all possible.* Without light they may as well not exist. Light is only the facilitator, but as such it is the single most important ingredient in our world. Without the sun, the earth would be uninhabitable. Without the facilitator, existence as we know it would be impossible. When God creates heaven and earth, he therefore immediately follows them first with light.

Contempt for the Environment

Even the environment has not escaped our contempt for the facilitator. A plant does nothing but service the needs of humans. It oxygenates our planet and ensures that we can survive and breathe. But we humans require more tangible uses from our environment. So we have cut down our rainforests and made them into paper pulp and furniture. We have mown down whole orchards to make room for factories and leisure centers. The facilitator has little place in our lives, since we have immediate needs that call for immediate results. Having lost our appreciation for the facilitator, we have also lost our vision and a plan for long-term goals.

Perhaps only when we are suffocating from a lack of oxygen on a frozen, sterile planet that has been sacrificed in the name of development will we finally wake up to the importance of the facilitator. Perhaps only when an entire generation of ignorant children has been raised by uninspired teachers will we value the role of those who impart light. Perhaps only after we have so degraded the role of teachers and thinkers that prejudice is pervasive will we return to respecting the role of the facilitator and aim to play the part ourselves.

One of the most moving family moments of the Jewish week occurs when the mother and matriarch of the household gathers her daughters around her, in the presence of her husband and sons, and lights the Sabbath candles at sunset on Friday night. Just as light is being taken from the earth, the woman of the house, the chief facilitator, makes light available. She empowers her family to shine like the flickering flames, bringing healing and warmth throughout their coming week. The weekly Sabbath lights symbolize how we all must emulate the fire and flame of a candle, illuminating our surroundings and helping others to fully develop their potential. The Sabbath candles remind us that the highest good we can live for is to help our fellowman, even at personal expense and sacrifice.

Asked once how someone might rescue himself from a painful personal predicament, Rabbi Israel Baal Shem Tov, founder of the

Hassidic movement, replied: "When you have a problem which seeks resolution, find someone who has the same problem. Pray for him and help him first. And God will then shower upon you abundant blessing and you will thrash your way out of the darkness and into the light."

3

Creating Heaven on Earth

Yes, I am a Jew, and when the ancestors of the right honourable gentleman were brutal savages in an unknown island, mine were priests in the temple of Solomon.

—BENJAMIN DISRAELI,
in reply to a taunt by Daniel O'Connell

WELL BEFORE KARL MARX DISMISSED RELIGION as the opiate of the masses, writers had attacked religious individuals as weaklings, in need of a crutch. This also happened recently, when Governor Jesse Ventura, in an interview in *Playboy* magazine, dismissed all religious people as being weak. "Organized religion is a sham and a crutch for weak-minded people, who need strength in numbers." Thinkers of all ages have proposed the idea that God is an invention of humanity, the response to our feeling helpless in a dark and empty universe. As H. L. Mencken wrote: "God is the immemorial refuge of the incompetent, the helpless, the miserable. They find not only sanctuary in His arms, but also a kind of superiority, soothing to their macerated egos: He will set them above their betters." Similarly, Francis Picabia wrote: "Men have always need of god! A god to defend them against other men." Modern-day man is proud to have rid himself of the superstition of the ancients, and science appears able, at least in theory, to explain virtually all cosmic phenomena

41

without resort to supernatural beliefs. Increasingly, religion has no real place in the contemporary world.

There is some truth to these criticisms. Religion *is* a source of strength to the helpless, life to those verging on death, hope to those in despair, and inspiration to the disillusioned. The saying goes that there are no atheists in the foxholes. Even confirmed nonbelievers often cry out to God in the face of insuperable tragedy. I admit that religion is a crutch. Experiencing insecurity is part of being human. Some gain strength by placing themselves at the center of an ever-expanding circle of possessions. Others need to dominate their peers. Still others try to fill their existential void by sleeping with as many members of the opposite sex as possible. I therefore see nothing wrong in relying on God to give our lives meaning—surely a better choice than those others. In moments of despair, man comes to terms with his own vulnerability, and herein lies the door to religion through which many of the faithful enter.

Having acknowledged that religion is a crutch, I must stress that this is but an infinitesimal part of what it is. Indeed, it is tragic that religion today is rarely more than the final refuge of the hopeless in moments of catastrophe. The higher objective of religion focuses far more on the potential greatness of man than on his obvious weakness. Ultimately, religion unlocks the vast store of sanctity and purpose that would otherwise remain trapped within us. Religious lives become suffused with meaning, not squandered on vain, temporal pursuits. Rather than simply catering to human constraints, *real religion begins where human limitations end.* Religion affords us the opportunity to enter into a meaningful relationship with God. Judaism in particular seeks to lift up man from the ranks of the animal, raising him higher than the angels.

Of course, every world religion is distinguished from every other by a unique theology and by the details of its observance. Judaism, however, is radically different, distinguished not simply in dogma but, fundamentally, in its *orientation.*

Those Who Aspire to Heaven

Man seeks above all else to enjoy a relationship with God, and the first purpose of religion is to provide it. As humans come up against obstacles that cannot be surmounted, when they encounter the inevitability of death, they naturally reach up to the heavens in search of refuge and redemption. Like a child holding onto the corners of his mother's skirt, every human being seeks to be attached to his or her Source in the heavens. But in seeking to experience a loving relationship with his Creator, man immediately encounters a barrier of steel. God is "up there" in the heavens. He is aloof and infinitely removed from human contact. Whereas man is vulnerable, God is invincible. Whereas man can be irrational, God is the supreme embodiment of objective intelligence. Whereas man is unkind, God is infinitely giving. And whereas man is mortal, God is eternal. God is everything that man is not, making the Deity and man infinitely incompatible. How then can they enjoy a relationship? How may God be apprehended? It is this question that serves as the starting point for all religions.

There are two principal ways for man to bridge the chasm separating him from his Creator. Man can attempt to ascend to the heavens or to bring the Almighty down into this world. And it is precisely this issue that distinguishes Judaism from other world religions. Whereas other religions teach the individual to shed his physicality and ascend to the heavens, Judaism strives to reveal God's glorious presence in the midst of our shared physical world. Whereas other religions beckon man to leave the earth behind and ascend to the heavens, Judaism enjoins man to create heaven on earth.

In the "upward-looking" religions, man must renounce his place on earth and seek to rise up to the heavens. Only by forsaking the pleasures of the physical realm can he become spiritual. On this model, religion serves as a *ladder*: If you do this and don't do that, you will climb to a higher level and grow closer to the Deity.

All religions except Judaism share this characteristic: They shun the physical in favor of the spiritual. Virtually everything man desires and embodies, from his limited intelligence to his corporeal flesh, is alien to God. Man sleeps, eats, lusts, has sex, pursues gold, and dies and becomes fodder for worms. God does none of these things: "He who watches over Israel will neither slumber nor sleep" (Ps. 121:4). How then can man expect to come close to God when he is so desperately deficient? The only answer is that he must divest himself of his peculiar human limitations before embracing God. In fact, most of the religious journey in non-Jewish religion involves teaching man to unload these human impediments so that he can enter the heavens and find eternal bliss. Hare Krishnas achieve enlightenment by becoming wandering mendicants, renouncing all material possessions. Buddhists seek nirvana through the total extinction of self, the annihilation of all human worries and ambitions. Islam teaches that the highest fulfillment of religion lies in holy war and dying as a martyr for the spread of one's faith. Christianity's holy men and women have traditionally committed themselves to poverty, chastity, and silence. What most religions have in common is contempt for the physical in general and sex in particular. *Asceticism of varying degrees is the common thread.*

The most poignant example of religion's antiworldliness is the general religious attitude toward death. Were religion about man serving God in life, one would expect great doctrinal disdain for death. Instead, death is seen as a beneficent release from the cage of an un-Godly body and a corrupt world. Death brings redemption and elevation. The death cult has a history that can be traced from the Pharaohs of Egypt to Christianity of today. Churches are surrounded by cemeteries, and relics of saints serve as the highest spiritual articles within the great cathedrals. Indeed, for Christians it was specifically the suffering and death of Christ while in bodily form that brought forth human salvation.

As Rabbi Samson Raphael Hirsch puts it, the essence of Christianity is the feeling of absolute dependence on a Higher Power. Christianity aims at showing man his impotence, frailty, his death, and decay. He is shown the bestial forces that overwhelm him, and he is allowed to wish for the still higher power that, through faith, should save him from their fetters. Christianity teaches man that dark passion and evil lurk in his own breast, so that he becomes frightened of himself and seeks salvation at the altar of Christ. For this reason Christians often build their houses of worship over the tombs of the dead, celebrate the holy mysteries at night, and pray fervently for relief from the power of the evil in the world and in their own hearts. Christianity ties man to the Divine by passiveness, by the fear of human existence.

Judaism is radically different. It is a religion of this world, a religion of life. It absolutely rejects both the belief that God occupies the heavens and shuns the earth and the counterpart disdain for physical existence. On the contrary, Isaiah declares, "Holy, holy, holy is the Lord of Hosts; *the whole earth* is full of his glory" (Isa. 6:3). It is in *this* world that God is to be found, and it is in this world that man must live a Godly life. Holiness must pervade his every action, for no realm of existence is outside God's dominion. *Judaism declares that the rejection of the physical world is essentially a rejection of God's omnipresence.* The great medieval Jewish philosopher Rabbi Judah Halevi wrote in his magnum opus, the *Kuzari:* "The servant of God does not withdraw himself from secular contact lest he be a burden to the world and the world to him; he does not hate life, which is one of God's bounties granted to him. . . . On the contrary, he loves this world and wishes for a long life."

The objective of man from a Jewish perspective is to draw close to God, not by ascending to the heavens, but by causing God to dwell here on earth. Far from rejecting physical existence, Judaism views all of creation as having a potential for holiness. There is a Godly way to eat and drink, a Godly way to think and speak, and a Godly way to have sex. The Ten Commandments, given by God on tablets of stone, illustrate the majestic scope of God's demands and man's mission. They soar from the most basic "I am the Lord your God" to embrace the whole gamut of human existence. Even thoughts are included: "Thou shalt not covet." This was the work that was inaugurated by Abraham. Before Abraham, God was known only in the heavens. Abraham made Him sovereign over the earth. Rabbinical legend tells of a heavenly dispute in which the angels asked God why He had forsaken them in favor of Abraham. The Almighty responded, "You angels made Me Master over the heavens, where I have always been King. But Abraham made Me Master over the earth, where previously I was unknown."

If all that exists in the physical world has potential for holiness, then the charge of man is to reveal that latent holiness through his actions. Every action in accordance with God's law serves to sanctify the world, to make it a place fit for God's presence. The essence of the divine revelation at Mount Sinai was that God came down to the human realm, revealing Himself for all to see: "And the Lord *descended* upon Mount Sinai" (Exod. 19:20). This exemplified to the Jewish nation what was to be its mission throughout history. Judaism brings God down into our lives. *Judaism is not about reaching for the heavens, but about consecrating the earth*. A most powerful demonstration of Judaism's embracing of the physical world is the circumcision of the male sexual organ, a sign of God's covenant with the Jew. Circumcision is an expression of moral freedom, an affirmation of life. It represents the capacity of man to use *all* his powers, even his sensual inclinations, for an inspired and ethical life, consecrated in the service of God. The human libido can proclaim the glory of God no less than the winged seraphs of heaven.

By charging men and women to submit of their free will to the law of God, the law of life, Judaism makes them conscious of both the possibility and the power of free choice. It shows them the One, only, free, Almighty God, Who in His omnipotence created the world and man for His service. Night and day serve Him, even death serves Him, and so does life. It is He who created passion in man's breast so that man, with independent power, might master it and harness it in the service of God. Judaism shows man the One Who molded him in light and freedom as a spark of His own free almighty essence. With this spark God elevated man above all that lies bound in blind necessity and invited him into His immediate proximity. Pleasure, life, power, freedom, and happiness are for Judaism the heralds that lead to God. Judaism builds its sanctuaries on the pinnacles of life. Death and decomposition remain far from the halls of its temple. What Judaism demands in the service of God is not merely the prayers and litanies of those in desperate straits but the complete and joyful, free and happy devotion of man in His rule over the world. The quintessential Jewish question is not how we may respond to tragedy, but rather what we do with our success. The fundamental difference between Judaism and Christianity is expressed by Samson Raphael Hirsch in *Horeb: A Philosophy of Jewish Laws and Observances*: "Judaism allows man to find God where man *finds* himself; whereas Christianity allows man to find God where man *loses* himself." From the Christian ascetic stance of rejection of the physical world, it is but a short step to the embracing of an isolated monastic lifestyle and even the flagellation of the flesh. Jesus' disdain for material comforts and financial prosperity is summed up in the Gospels' oft-quoted statement, "It is more difficult for the rich man to enter the kingdom of heaven than it is for a camel to pass through the eye of a needle" (Matt. 19:24).

The Task to Unmask

If, as Judaism asserts, God is to be found as much on earth as He is in the heavens, how is it that so many of us fail to notice Him? The truth, of course, is that nature conceals Him. (The Hebrew word for nature is *tevah,* which also means sunken and submerged.) God is submerged behind the mask of nature, and it is the task of man to reveal Him. This is perhaps the central message of the Book of Esther, the celebrated story of how a wicked minister's designs, in ancient Persia, to exterminate the Jewish people is thwarted by the beautiful and secretly Jewish queen who is elevated to the throne after a beauty contest.

The name Esther comes from the Hebrew for "hidden," and the apparent, though illusory, disappearance of God from His world is a pivotal theme of the book. Esther is unique among the books of the Hebrew Bible in that it contains no explicit mention of God. To be sure, His crucial contribution to the tale is not in doubt; He is clearly playing a major supporting role, yet His name fails to appear in the cast of characters—He has no lines! Of course, there is an explanation for this glaring omission. The events described in the Book of Esther occur in a world that is in many ways similar to our world today. Unlike the rest of the Hebrew Bible, where God is overtly performing miracles and wonders, in Esther's era He seemed to have disappeared. The Jews had been thoroughly conquered, their Holy Temple destroyed, and their people scattered in exile. Prophets no longer received prophecy. Worse of all, the Persian Empire had issued a decree to annihilate the Jews. It certainly appeared that God had deserted His people, if not the entire world. At this moment a miracle saved the Jews, but for the first time, it was a miracle that could be explained naturally. It would be possible to read Esther and fail to notice God's involvement in the story. This, perhaps above all, is the book's message for today. *God is the hidden source of every leaf and every drop of dew. It is up to us to unmask nature and uncover the Godliness intrinsic to our world. Although denial is always a possibility, enlightenment and faith is an inevitability. We need only open our eyes.*

It follows that Judaism embraces, rather than dismisses, every human facet and every created being. Man must never disdain his world. He should pursue love, happiness, pleasures, even riches, but with one central caveat: It must be done in accordance with the divine will. Sexual desire is not evil. Far from it. When practiced between two committed and loving adults who have been consecrated in marriage, it is the holiest of human undertakings. The pursuit of wealth need be neither selfish nor evil, provided that a man or woman gives a substantial proportion of their income to the needy, always fills their home with guests, and constantly attributes their success to God's beneficence.

Man has a right, indeed an obligation, to partake of the bounty of the earth. But that bounty must never exclude God. This is the foundation of the Jewish institution of blessings. Before eating, say, an apple, a Jew declares, "Blessed are You Lord our God, King of the Universe, Who created the fruit of the tree." By so doing, he or she brings holiness into what might otherwise be a base, animalistic pursuit. He or she recognizes God's bounty and, simultaneously, the gift that is physical existence. The key question in material acquisition is not how much a person partakes of the world, but the extent to which one makes God one's partner. This idea is similar in concept to the act of making love. Above all, love is powerful when it is experienced. No pronouncement of love can ever equal a hug. To feel love is to capture its essence, whereas to see or hear of it captures merely its periphery. Man is meant to experience God with all his senses, rather than just apprehend him with the abstraction of faith.

Those Who Claim a Place on Earth

Judaism has often been accused by Christianity of being weighed down by legalism. Christians are portrayed as being able to take flight with their heaven-centered faith, whereas Jews remain tied down with law and ritual. But Judaism's earthward orientation, far from serving as a stumbling block to spiritual exultation, is instead its greatest blessing. It guarantees that the believer need never compartmentalize his religious and nonreligious personae. Judaism is firmly grounded in reality and can therefore accommodate all of man's earthly ambitions. The man who plows with the ox is the same man who sits with a prayer book in synagogue. He need not assume the artificial face of piety to discharge his religious duties. Riches become a curse only when they isolate man in his own sphere, when he owns a home into which none are invited for fear that they may sully the carpets. God does not wish to be thought of only in the synagogue. What kind of relationship is that? A woman wants her lover to think of her even as he sits in the boardroom, not just the bedroom. When a Jew enters a house of worship, he need not leave his human crust outside.

Judaism is best described as a celebration of life, no aspect of which is intrinsically un-Godly. And though Judaism condemns animalistic indulgence, the Talmud declares that in the world-to-come God will hold man accountable for refusing to partake of any pleasures that God has permitted, thinking that he would be more Godly as a result. Asceticism has a place only in a religion that imagines Satan behind every dollar bill and every sexual urge. But a religion that sees sparks of divine light hidden in every heart and behind every tree teaches its adherents to bring this light to the fore. God wishes to be discovered within His world, and man is charged with this task. Celibacy and excessive pietism have no place within the Jewish pantheon. Indeed, the ancient Rabbis declared that fasting on the holy days, such as the Sabbath, is a sin for which one must do repentance. "But let the righteous be joyful; let them exult before God; let them be jubilant with joy" (Ps. 68:3). Jewish festivals are replete with food, wine, song, and celebration.

What ultimately separates Christianity from Judaism is not the belief in Christ or sainthood. Rather, it is that the Christian believes in heaven, whereas the Jew believes in earth. The Christian accepts the fall of man, but the Jew affirms the divine image imprinted on every human. Christianity advocates lofty faith, and Judaism celebrates hard action. And whereas the Christian speaks of love, the Jew says that there can be no love without justice and thus preserves the law.

The idea that bringing God into the world is the focal point of the religion generates the following central tenets of Judaism:

Revelation and Prophecy. Judaism is about God's coming down to man and revealing how He may be approached and served rather than man's merely theorizing about what would make the Deity happy. Judaism is not a religion of the philosopher but of the romantic, not of the rationalist but of the revelationist. The central moment in the Jewish religion was the revelation of God at the foot of Mount Sinai to the collective House of Israel just weeks after the Israelites had emerged from the crucible of Egyptian slavery. Other world religions, most notably Christianity, place their emphasis on dogmatic theology, whereby man exercises his mind to its uttermost limits in an effort to understand God's mysteries. They emphasize the *comprehension* of God within the eye of the mind. Judaism, however, stresses the *apprehension* of the deity through Godly works. Ju-

daism is experiential, as opposed to philosophical. It is a religion of
action wherein God is captured through a Godly deed.

The Use of Physical Objects in Religious Worship.   Judaism has been
much maligned by other religious thinkers—for example, Saint Paul
in his epistles—as being burdened and overrun by a concern for the
minutiae of life, rather than focusing on serving God through faith.
"For if a person could achieve salvation through good works [the
law], then Christ would have died in vain" (Gal. 2:21). Similarly, "we
conclude that a man is put right with God only through faith and
not by doing what the law commands" (Rom. 3:28). But for Judaism,
good deeds, mitzvot, are far more important than faith. The Jew
worships God with an array of physical objects. The use of these objects in religious ritual and the vast scope of Jewish law derive from
Judaism's obsession with consecrating the earth. The Jew is charged
with bringing the very dust of creation into the camp of holiness. Judaism is not concerned with creating little sanctuaries of Godliness,
but rather with uplifting all the earth to a higher spiritual plane.
Therefore, a Jew must dispel the notion that ascribes holiness to the
synagogue and the church, but not to the marketplace or the bedroom. This kind of spiritual compartmentalization is wholly foreign
to Judaism. From a Jewish perspective, the street is as holy as the
basilica—each provides an opportunity to create a sepulchre of sanctity. Thus, there are as many laws regarding behavior in the street as
for behavior in the synagogue; and as many laws regulating lovemaking in the bedroom as for ethics in the boardroom.

   The operative mode of thought in Judaism is that the absence of
God from our physical world is nothing but an illusion. An inscrip-
tion found on the wall of a cellar in Cologne, Germany, where Jews
hid from the Nazis, read: "I believe in the sun even when it is not
shining. I believe in love even when not feeling it. I believe in God
even when He is silent." God hides behind the veneer of nature. Miracles are not a sudden intervention of God in the laws of nature.
Rather, these laws are upheld by God at every instant. The only
thing distinguishing nature from miracle is the degree of regularity.

When women conceive without problems, we call that nature. But when a woman is infertile for many years and suddenly becomes pregnant, we call it a miracle. Man's objective is to make the invisible God a visible and potent force throughout society. It may appear that God resides in the holy man more than the peasant. But both are born with a Godly soul and with inherent holy potential. The goal is to translate that potential into the actual, so that the Almighty is manifest in every atom of His creation.

Action as Opposed to Meditation. In other religions, notably Hinduism and Buddhism, the emphasis is on personal enlightenment. A world of cerebral thought, the inner world of man, is seen as superior to the external reality with its corruption and darkness. Man is bidden to withdraw into a world in which he escapes the gore of everyday life by appealing to his higher senses and faculties, ultimately achieving negation of self and nirvana. Christianity, with its emphasis on the primacy of faith and its tradition of monastic withdrawal, is similar. In Judaism, however, it is not the purpose of man to be defeated by, or to escape, the darkness of the world. Rather, he must seek to enlighten the world around him. By bringing God into our world and promoting love and justice, we bring supernal light, a Godly freshness that brightens the world and cures it of the putrid air of selfishness.

World Redemption Precedes Personal Salvation. In the religions that disdain physical existence there is no real emphasis on the need for man to establish love and justice in this world. Rather, the emphasis is on personal salvation. In some religions, man betters the world primarily so that he will not be corrupted by an unholy environment. But the objective is inner, as opposed to outer, perfection. By practicing acts of kindness, man merits a place in the eternal world. Religion is thus viewed as essentially an *individual* and personal endeavor. In Judaism, however, the ultimate purpose of existence is to redeem the *collective* world. The pursuit of love and justice are ends in themselves, irrespective of their effect on man.

Making the world a better place is the highest religious calling. Therefore, even if man gives charity for the wrong reasons—to see his name up in lights or to receive a knighthood—he is still praiseworthy, since the condition of the world precedes the state of his soul. Every action that brings goodness to the world is good in an unqualified sense, even when impelled by imperfect motivation.

Central to Judaism is the belief in the coming of the Messiah, a time in which God's light will shine openly in the world. The Jewish apocalyptic vision is of an eternal era of peace and brotherhood *on this earth,* rather than in the heavens. When a Jew speaks of the world-to-come, he or she means this world the way it will be when it is perfected. But he or she is still talking about the physical earth. The Jew is supposed to establish God as a tangible reality in the physical world, thereby reenacting the easy harmony that once existed between heaven and earth. The Jew rejects mind/matter, body/soul, and heaven/earth dualism in favor of an all-encompassing monism. God's light envelops the whole of creation. As the sun lights up the earth, God illuminates the cosmos.

Emphasis on the Sublimity of the Everyday. Judaism celebrates the everyday aspects of life, rather than the great miracles of the past, and the faith of the simple man in the street above the martyrdom of saints. It is, after all, the little hello and goodbye kisses between husband and wife, rather than the once-a-year anniversary celebrations, that represent the meaningful part of their relationship. The Jew delivers over to God not only his overtly spiritual aspects—his faith, his charity, his goodness—but even those things that have no overt religious content, like his business affairs, his sex life, his professional aspirations, and his material wealth. Judaism seeks to impregnate the minutiae of life with meaning rather than having man lust only after fireworks displays. Religious men and women are expected to deliver over to God all of themselves and not just the grander aspects of their being. If you love someone, you love *all* of them. Our relationship with God encompasses what others would dismiss as mundane.

Law.   In Christianity the purpose of the Gospels is to convey to man the core teachings of Jesus, the son of God, and how he lived. In Judaism, the purpose of the Scripture is to teach us, not so much about God—there is precious little in the Torah about God's being—but rather about ourselves and how we might live Godly lives. *Whereas the Christian Bible is a book about God incarnate in a body, the Jewish Bible is a book about man and a history of how he struggled in his developing relationship with God.* Thus, law, or precise rules of how we must live and behave, are central to the Jewish religion. Saint Paul attacked the law as an impediment to righteousness: "Therefore no one will be declared righteous in his sight by observing the law; rather, through the law we become conscious of sin. But now a righteousness from God, apart from law, has been made known, to which the Law and the Prophets testify" (Rom. 3:20–21). But to the Jews, divine law constitutes the channels of communication—the most highly tuned frequency—by which man can apprehend God. If we are to establish a relationship with God and make Him a part of our world, then we must accommodate His will. In Judaism, the laws of the Torah are a revelation of the divine will, the observance of which establishes a loving relationship between Creator and creature.

The Sabbath.   When Adam and Eve sinned in the Garden of Eden, the special light of truth that had radiated throughout the world in the original seven days of creation became hidden. Suddenly, the world was shrouded in darkness. In only one time and one place did God's light remain burning brightly: The time was the Sabbath day, the place was the Holy Land of Israel. Since time and space are the very matrix of material existence, it is the objective of the Jew to further elevate both these components to holiness. God Himself began this process by making one day and one place holy. The objective of the Jew is to continue this process by making more times and more places holy, until all the earth once again shines with spiritual light. The week is structured in a way that even if the Jew remains completely idle, every seven days he is overtaken by the spirit of the Sabbath, which beckons him to make the other weekdays holy as well.

Thus, the Jewish parent who plays with his or her children during the week cordons off this special and holy moment even on a regular weekday so that nothing can intrude, in much the same way that we refrain from answering the phone on the Sabbath. The Jew extrapolates beyond the confines of the holy Sabbath day and imports its sanctity to every weekday endeavor, so that God is his partner in all ways and in all things.

4

The Bible and the Patriarchs

The Bible—that great medicine chest of humanity.
—**HEINRICH HEINE,** *Ludwig Boerne*

The Jews . . . trudged around with it through the middle ages as with a portable Fatherland.
—**HEINE,** *Confessions*

HAVING EXPLAINED THE CENTRALITY OF ACTION TO JUDAISM, as well as its feminine nature, I address the question, Why religion at all? Increasingly for many men and women, there is no compelling answer to this question. To be sure, Jews still light the Chanukah Menorah and munch matzah on Passover as a matter of culture and tradition. But should the religious component be preserved? Why would a society that can explain a solar eclipse as something other than God's venting his anger still need religion? If it is embraced primarily in moments of crisis, of what use is religion today, especially to people in the West, who do not face poverty or persecution?

The truth is that today's society, for all its financial and material comforts, does not seem any happier than previous generations, whose lives were marked by hunger and disease. Contemporary life may be described as the incessant pursuit of meaningless distractions. Happiness comes in the form of an adventure movie or a sexual conquest. We read trashy magazines and watch shallow

television talk shows, and regurgitate celebrity gossip, all in an effort
to forget our pressures and burdens. But what are we running from?

Searching for an
Existential Cure to Boredom

I would argue that the greatest evil stalking the earth and sucking out
the quality of our lives is *pervasive boredom.* In a world where labor-saving machines and high-paying jobs leave us with more free time than
we need, we are confounded by what to do with it. Instead of a blessing, our free time has become a curse for us. Here, then, is the greatest
argument for religion in the modern age. The purpose of religion is to
challenge man to rid pain from the world, increase love, discover wisdom, and come to know his Creator. Religion is the clarion call to
man, beckoning him to devote his energies to a higher purpose.

Despite the dramatic rise in urban crime, I do not believe that a
wave of evil has pervaded our planet. Rather, in our incessant search
for excitement and a cure to our boredom, we have sunk to the depths
of depravity. We will try almost anything to bring some passion into
our lives. When the very soul of Britain was rocked a decade ago with
the gruesome murder of Jamie Bulger by two ten-year-old boys who
kidnapped and tortured him, leaving him to be mutilated on railroad
tracks, a wave of clerics spoke of the hidden evil in our midst ready to
rear its ugly head at any time. But this is nonsense! Does anyone really
believe that ten-year-old boys are evil? Was it the devil who grabbed
hold of the hands of the teenage students at Columbine High School
in Colorado who opened fire on their teachers and classmates? Or
rather was it the search for excitement, revenge, a quick thrill, and an
outlet for their anger? Teenagers today will watch the most inane TV
shows to escape their boredom. And since the only example of excitement they have is watching Bruce Willis pump lead into bad guys, did
this not become their model of an intense emotional rush? Children
today are bored in school and bored at home. And as the Talmud says,
when one has nothing to do, one ends up doing what one ought *not*
to do. What is the teenage drug craze other than an attempt to exper-

iment with that which is forbidden? Had someone offered these children a ride on the Space Shuttle the night before they carried out their murders, would they have rejected the offer in favor of killing children instead? Had we somehow engaged their higher imagination, found a healthier outlet to their anger and frustration, would they still have resorted to violence?

A recent study showed that 90 percent of husbands who are unfaithful to their wives claim to love them. They cheat merely out of desperation for something new and exciting and in search of an end to the drudgery of their married life and a sexual routine that is passionless and predictable. Similarly, the history of mankind is a history of wars and battles. Do people really enjoy dying and murdering? Or is the explanation rather that they will do anything for a quick thrill? Philosopher Robert Nozick writes that people do not give boredom the credit it is due for animating human action. War, according to Nozick, is one of the great boredom solvers in the world. Ask men who have fought in wars how they look back on their experience. Most of them hold it to have been in many ways the best time of their lives, unless they were severely wounded. Camaraderie such as they never knew. Meaning, excitement, purpose, and the most profound emotional high. It all came together in moments of heated, armed conflict.

It was in His own image that God created man. Just as God is a Creator, so too is His human shadow. Possessed of limitless energies, man must be preoccupied with good if he is not to find a greater emotional rush in evil. And religion's high purpose is to afford man a holy and redeeming channel to direct his talent and gifts.

Arnold Toynbee, in his monumental, twelve-volume opus, *A Study of History*, draws the conclusion that what led to the decline of civilizations is that once they reached the apogee of their success, once they no longer had to struggle to survive or set up an infrastructure, once they had no more enemies to fight, they began to corrode from the inside. Civilizations must respond creatively to new challenges, and once a society is intoxicated with prosperity, it no longer has the impetus to so respond. Creativity and vision are lost. Listlessness and laziness set in. Edward Gibbon charts the same deterioration in his classic *Decline and Fall of the Roman Empire.* No civilization has successfully made the transformation from survival to success. It should come as no surprise that the United States, the richest country in the world, is the one with the worst drug problems and depression. It is the country that consumes the most television and that, sad to say, is purveying an increasingly shallow culture to the rest of the world.

There are those who believe that prayer becomes important when one discovers that one's child has leukemia. Many believe that the ultimate purpose of religion is to teach man how to deal with adversity, to help him struggle with the vicissitudes of life and uplift him in his moments of despair. It is beliefs such as these that have led atheists to attack religion as the opiate of the masses, as we explored earlier. Man, they argue, turns to religion to overcome his feelings of cosmic loneliness and abandonment. Unable to confront the meaninglessness of existence, man invents myths that soothe his anxiety. The purpose of religion, however, as we have seen, is not to help man deal with his own helplessness, but rather to teach him what to do with his moments of triumph and with the abundant leisure that follows success. Religion's noble calling is to give man something to live for when he no longer needs to struggle just to survive.

In Judaism, we do not work six days and rest on the seventh in order to work harder in the coming six days. On the contrary. We work six days in order to have food, clothing, and security so that the Sabbath can be a meaningful day of study, reflection, fraternity, and introspection, unencumbered by financial concerns. On the Sabbath we are afforded an opportunity to read, argue, debate, study, think, meditate, pray, ponder, and ultimately stand in awe in the presence of what we have found. No man who struggles every day just to feed his family will ever have the time to concern himself with the infinite essence of God, the great questions of existence. (It is no coincidence that the overwhelming majority of great philosophers and thinkers were men and women of means.)

Living for a Higher Purpose

That modern-day man is utterly lost without work and something to strive for is best demonstrated by the obsessive nature of today's career-oriented society. Professional success today is a fixation that leaves almost no time for contemplation and enjoying the transcendent side of life. God, family, friends, the pursuit of knowledge, and acts of goodness are all subordinated to the overriding need for a good job and public recognition. A recent study showed that 40 percent of today's businessmen could not cite a single hobby they had. And look at what has happened to the Christian Sabbath. Sundays, once a time set aside for church and family, are more likely now to be spent strolling through a shopping mall.

There are only two things in this world that are truly interesting: God and man. Only these two have infinite depth. Only these two have personality. We tire of everything else quickly. We cannot watch even the most sensational film more than a few times, but we can have endless hours of conversation with the same person. Because that one person is infinitely creative. On days like the Sabbath when we dedicate ourselves to cultivating human friendship and human company and enhancing our relationship with God, we cultivate that most important of all personality traits: *depth*. Religion is the still, small voice that whispers in the ear of the man obsessed with the golf course that he was created for higher things. Religion is the thunder of conscience that pierces a woman's heart when she goes on a shopping spree after turning away the hungry man with just a few coins. Religion is the soothing rain that quenches the fire of a man's or woman's passion as he or she is drawn into an illicit relationship that will compromise their marital vows.

Unlike Oswald Spengler in his *Decline of the West,* Toynbee did not regard the death of civilization as inescapable. Rather, given sufficient impetus and direction, civilizations can continue to respond creatively to successive challenges. Unlike Karl Marx, Toynbee saw history as shaped by spiritual, not economic, forces. We must begin to cultivate the life of the spirit if we are not to be haunted by the ghost of Spengler's predictions. We can do this by rediscovering the pleasures of prayer, a lust for learning, a passion for people, and delight in the divine countenance.

The Inspiration of the Bible

When I was a young student in rabbinical seminary in Jerusalem, we would go every Sabbath day down the road to listen to an elderly Hassidic Jew, with flowing white beard, who would regale us with stories of the tremendous self-sacrifice necessary for him to establish pockets of Jewish education in the former Soviet Union. The man came to be known to the Russian authorities as *Subbota*—Sabbath in Russian—because he refused to work on the Sabbath. He was tortured and beaten every week, but in twenty years of incarceration, he never once desecrated the Sabbath. He told us these stories while sitting in a wheelchair, because the beatings had destroyed his legs. And he taught us more about the Sabbath than anything we could have read.

Herein lies the Jewish passion for holy books in general, and the Bible in particular. The Jews are the people of the book. Hundreds of thousands of great tomes dot the Jewish scholarship landscape, written by legendary sages such as Saadyah Gaon, Rashi, Maimonides, and Rabbi Yehuda Lowe. But the central book of Judaism is, of course, the Bible. From a Jewish child's earliest years, his or her education focuses on the great events, personalities, and laws of the Bible. But what is this greatest best-seller of all time? Is it Jewish history? A compendium of law as to how humanity should live? A chronicle of God's interaction with man?

The Bible is all these things, but it is much more. It is designed to be a book of living inspiration. The main difference distinguishing the Christian New Testament from the Jewish Hebrew Bible is this: The New Testament is a book about *God* (as he incarnated himself on earth), whereas the Hebrew Bible is a chronicle of *man*, from his earliest efforts to know the invisible God. The Hebrew Bible provides the inspiration that influences men and women of faith to emulate the lives of the great heroes of Jewish history.

The ultimate purpose of religion is to impart inspiration—to give man not just the vision of a higher purpose, but the wherewithal to make it a reality; not just to *be* inspired, but to *live* an inspired life. Life's most important ingredient is inspiration, without which man is almost indistinguishable from the inanimate rock upon which he treads. Real inspiration comes, not from being exposed to great ideas, but rather from being exposed to great *personalities*. Ask any successful individual what was the source of his or her success, and he or she will cite a high school teacher, college professor, mother, father, cleric, or friend who served as role model and/or inspiration.

The most important books of the Torah are the Five Books of Moses, and among these the greatest sources of inspiration undoubtedly are Genesis and Exodus. Here we read not only of great men and women at the dawn of history, but also of men and women just like you and me who rose to unparalleled heights of holiness by responding to a divine calling that entailed monumental sacrifice. We learn of Abraham, who is asked to leave behind everything he cherishes—including his family and father's household—to find a higher destiny; Jacob, who wrestles with an angel of destruction and triumphs; Joseph, who overcomes feelings of vengeance to embrace the brothers who flirted with fratricide; and Moses, who gives up the luxurious life of an Egyptian prince to redeem an enslaved nation. These figures teach us goodness on a monumental scale.

The Bible is not a history book. There is no need for any of us to know that Abraham once walked the dusty plains of ancient Mesopotamia. Rather, reading about Abraham is a challenge to *be* like Abraham, to walk in his ways, to emulate his truth. Although he lived over three millennia ago, in the Bible, Abraham is a living, breathing creature who imparts to us words of living inspiration. The Talmud says that the patriarchs did not die, since their children continue their legacy. Every time a Jew invites a guest home for the Sabbath—in the spirit of Abraham—he perpetuates his legacy and breathes new life into his immortal ancestor.

Teaching by Example and by Prescription

God established two separate covenants between Himself and the Jewish people: a Sinaitic covenant, formulated at Mount Sinai, and a patriarchal covenant, made with Abraham, Isaac, and Jacob well before they had offspring. The Sinaitic covenant was established with the Jews for all eternity, and the Jews collectively committed themselves to adhering to all of God's commandments when they uttered the immortal words, "We will do and we will listen." And God in turn adopted the Jewish people as His chosen nation.

The patriarchal covenant, however, does not seem to have imposed any specific commitments except circumcision. So why was it necessary? The answer is simple: It imparts teachings to the Jewish people by example rather than by prescription. Whereas the Sinaitic covenant tells the Jew what to do and how to act as a member of the covenantal community, the patriarchal covenant addressees the "I" awareness of the Jew, teaching him how to *experience* his Jewishness. It sensitizes him in specifically Jewish ways. It expresses attitudes, ideals, and sentiments that still speak to us. It guides our consciousness, for we are duty bound not only to act like Jews, but also to *feel* like Jews. In a word, it is the backdrop to the Sinaitic covenant, the latter being the behavioral fulfillment of truths, values, and Jewish self-awareness established by the former.

Abraham, the idol smasher, is hospitable to the stranger. In emulation of his open home, every Jewish couple marries under a wedding canopy, symbolizing a home with no doors. In the name of divine justice, Abraham intercedes even for the wicked people of Sodom and Gomorrah. Ever since then, Jews have been at the forefront of fighting for social equality and justice. Sarah's wisdom regarding Ishmael draws divine approval, and ever since then Jewish men have been conditioned to allow their wives to make the most important decisions regarding positive and negative influences within the home. And Abraham, of course, with his unparalleled readiness to sacrifice his son Isaac on an altar to God, sets the stage for future Jewish willingness to lay down their lives for their Creator throughout time. In studying and constantly hearing about the lives of our patriarchs and matriarchs, we absorb their values into our collective consciousness, until we are completely and positively influenced by their lofty example. The ancient Rabbis said, "Every person should ask himself, 'When shall my deeds be like those of Abraham, Isaac, and Jacob?'"

The lives of our patriarchs and matriarchs portray the total historical experience of our people. The Rabbis also say, "God gave Abraham a sign that whatever happened to him would occur to his descendants." The lives of the patriarchs still nourish our consciousness as Jews, even as the Sinaitic covenant guides the format of our lives.

Being in constant touch with the Bible is therefore a prerequisite of the total Jewish experience. Man is not meant to respond to God only as a disembodied voice. Rather, he is designed to acknowledge the God that lurks within, that is an integral part of his very being. What better way to hear that inner calling than to witness men and women whose entire beings were transformed by, and became, the living personification of that call.

Life in the Valley and in the Mountain

The Jew must read in the Bible the story of the man Moses, whom God took up to a mountain for forty days and forty nights, teaching him His law and offering him a taste of Paradise. Later, whenever God gives Moses commandments concerning the building of God's home on earth—the tabernacle—He tells him to build a house "according to the plan which I showed you on the mountain." All of us live two different, often contradictory, lives. There is the life we lead in the valley and the life we live on the mountain. We are mostly in the valley, uninspired, harassed by the minutiae of life that continu-

ally annoy us and keep us from seeing the big picture. Most of us
lead the life of a firefighter, battling life's emergencies—that in turn
circumscribes our vision. Then there are moments—however fleeting—of clarity, when we are raised to the mountain. A wind of inspiration comes over us and we are lifted to the highest spiritual
peaks. Contention and jealousy are drained from our heart, and we
experience the fraternity of the human family, a vision of what we
all can rise to be. In the same way that religion seeks to impart inspiration, it seeks to inspire man to discover these sacred moments,
which leave a lasting impression.

After we come down from the mountain, we must return to earth,
but we can still conduct our lives according to how we viewed things
at those lofty heights. The Bible is that mountain. According to tradition, before Moses died, he divided the Bible into fifty-three sections and ordained that one section be read every week. Every seven
days, when a new portion of the Torah is read, the Jew is exposed to
the giants of history, men and women who were mountains of
virtue, and is inspired to follow their lead.

5

Losing Faith

Patience with others is love. Patience with self is Hope. Patience with God is Faith.

—ADEL BESTAVROS

You can do very little with Faith, but you can do nothing without it.

—SAMUEL BUTLER, *Notebooks*

THE BIBLICAL NARRATIVE OF ADAM AND EVE'S SIN in the Garden of Eden is central to both Judaism and Christianity. But there is an essential difference. To the Christian, it is a story of the fall of man. Adam and Eve were given but one commandment, which they promptly transgressed. As a result, they incurred spiritual damnation, and mankind fell from its exhalted spiritual station. Only the subsequent death of the son of God on the cross could redeem mankind and bring about human salvation.

For the Jew, however, the consequences of Adam's sin pertained more to the world that surrounded man than to man himself. The sin in Eden caused the world, rather than Adam and Eve, to change. What was once a world filled with light became submerged in darkness.

For a moment, let us reflect on the world inhabited by Adam and Eve from the ancient Kabbalistic perspective. Adam and Eve lived in

Eden, a world that was perfect. Where is this Eden? On some lofty mountaintop? In a heavenly abode currently hidden by a cloud? The Jewish sages explain that the world inhabited by Adam and Eve is actually the same world where we all dwell this very minute. But the world that Adam and Eve knew was radically different from our own because it was perfect. How was it different, and what made it better than the earth that we inhabit now?

The explanation given in Jewish mystical sources is simply that the world of Adam and Eve was bathed in light. According to most biblical commentaries, well before heaven and earth were created, while the cosmos was still *"tohu vavohu"*—a morass of chaos and void—the first thing God created was light: "And the Lord said, 'Let there be light.'" The most important thing in life is light. Light is the source of our inspiration. It is what brings us the most joy. It is the symbol of our hope.

The world into which Adam and Eve were immersed at the outset of creation was perfect because it was filled with light. It was a world in which truth always triumphed and where the Godly origin of the world, and the guiding hand of God behind every human success, were immediately evident amid the cloak of nature. Theirs was a world of clarity and lucidity, where man was able to instantly discern between good and evil, where the light of God shone through the world unhindered. The world was visibly sustained by God and could not be detached from Him. Everywhere one looked, one found His presence. The divine signature was on every created object.

But when Adam and Even sinned, when they plucked the fruit from the forbidden tree, they removed light from the world. By acting against God's will, they brought darkness into the universe and detached the world from its source. Their sin masked the truth of existence, and man would no longer have transparency in his world. Decisions about right and wrong would no longer be straightforward. Man could even deny God's presence and ascribe his achievements to his own efforts.

In the Christian tradition, it was *Adam* who fell as a result of his disobedience to God. His soul was damned, his future was dark. In the Jewish tradition, however, what fell was not *Adam*, but his environment. The *earth* became dark. We can infer from the fact that the Almighty points to two kinds of trees, a good tree and a bad tree, that there was already evil in the Garden of Eden. God instructs Adam to partake only of the good tree. So how was the world of Eden different if even in the garden there was evil? The answer is that the evil was *clearly identifiable*. There could be no mistaking it. God said to Adam and Eve, you may eat from this tree, but not from that one. There was a patent and overt distinction. If man chose to do evil in the Garden of Eden, he knew exactly what he was getting himself into.

Chaos

There was a time when you could look at the world and see God, the undeniable source, behind the facade of nature. Our world, through its magnificence and majesty, was a testimony to God's glory and splendor. A man would look at the Himalayas and immediately perceive the infinite power of Almighty God who created them. A woman would look at a sunset and her first reaction would not be, "My, what awesome natural beauty," but rather, "How wondrous are Your works, Oh Lord!" (Ps. 92:6). But once the light was taken out of our world, it became possible for the world to deceive. Suddenly, you would look upon creation and claim that perhaps it had created itself. A man could be successful in business and could lie to himself and his circle of friends and proclaim what Moses warned us against: "My own strength and the labor of my hands has brought me all this prosperity" (Deut. 8:17).

The sin of Adam was to bring chaos into the world. Adam took all the good that God had given him—the love, the blessings—and used them to commit evil, to act in contradiction to the divine will. Adam's mixing of good and evil resulted in an inextricable mixture of good and evil, light and darkness, which continues to this very day. And in this lies our world's imperfection. The pain of life is that there is no clarity, no illumination. We go into relationships hoping for the best, but also prepared for the worst. A man can invest his money and never be certain that he will not lose every last penny. Worse still, one cannot have the blessing of children without simultaneously incurring the trials and tribulations of raising them. Every rose has thorns; every couple about to be married should expect to argue. There is no love without grief. It is specifically by tapping into natural human competitiveness, a desire to outperform our fellowman, that we are able to generate enough income to build hospitals and orphanages, and it is specifically the scientist who yearns to win a Nobel Prize who will one day find a cure for AIDS.

A boyhood classmate became one of my closest friends because his parents argued much as my own. One day at the age of fifteen, he was tragically killed in a car accident. His parents found comfort in each other, and their marital bickering ended. That something so wondrous can result from something so ugly is part of the curse of Adam. Similarly, I read of a man who won the lottery, only to watch his eldest son die of a drug overdose one year later, a result of having too much cash in his pocket. Good fortune leading to tragedy also results from the chaos and the mixture of good and evil that prevails in our world.

The greatest source of pain in life is the doubt and insecurity of not being sure of the way forward. Husbands and wives could more easily solve their marital dilemmas if only they knew for certain that the person they are married to is preordained and is the best partner for them. In the absence of such certainty, they don't try hard enough to make their marriages work, since they ascribe an arbitrary quality to their relationship. As divorce is always an option, they think to themselves that they may have made a mistake. Had they not decided to have a roast beef sandwich that day and bumped into their spouse, they would have been spared all this aggravation. Because clarity in any given subject is hard to come by, we search endlessly for the proper guidance to make our lives work, rarely achieving our objective satisfactorily. One of the hardest things in life is decision making, and there are times when we actually feel persecuted by the decisions, especially the big ones, that we have to make. In a world shrouded in darkness, we often find ourselves wholly confounded by even the simplest choices. There can be little doubt that the secret to a successful and meaningful life is to make the right decisions. But without a source of illumination, how can we know what they are?

Without the overt Godly light that once permeated our universe, God has become an enigma apprehended through belief rather than conviction, since spirituality cannot be experienced with the five senses. You can't taste God's existence like dinner; you can't smell it like the scent of the sea. Rather, you have to accept it on faith. But the ultimate purpose of creation is for us to rediscover God as a tangible reality, rather than a mere abstraction. No man, woman, or child who roams the earth should ever have to maintain faith in God. The prophet promised that the time would come when we would once again be able to "see God" as a living presence, rather than having to repose faith in His existence. We are not meant to have to believe. Rather, we should be able to see, with our very eyes, God's presence on earth and all of His blessings. *Therefore, we might say that Judaism's purpose is to make us lose our faith.*

Here we begin to understand that Judaism insists on the use of material objects in divine worship in order to demonstrate the innate holiness possessed by these objects. By using cow parchment to write a Torah scroll, we again establish a link between God and the world. The use of wool for the fulfillment of the commandment of *tzitzit*, the fringes attached to the Jewish prayer shawl, reestablishes the divine signature that the wool once possessed in the Garden of Eden. Making a blessing over food and thanking God for all that we eat reestablishes the divine imprint that was once visible on all that the earth and trees produced. If we could not use physical objects in religious ritual, it would be an admission that there is no God within them. We would be thickening the veil of creation rather than puncturing it and allowing the Godly light to be manifest.

The Torah as a Way to Illuminate the Darkness

Once man lost his way and brought chaos into the world, he needed guidance and instruction. The Torah brought light into the darkened planet, thereby undoing the effects of the sin of Adam. The Torah tells us that we may be drawn to a pleasurable and fulfilling diversion on the Sabbath, like going to a football stadium, but it is just part of the subterfuge and darkness. Far better to shut out the noise of the outside world and enjoy family and friendship. The Torah teaches us that though the prospect of cheating to make a bit more money seems appetizing, ultimately that decision would just pull us into the darkness. We look at a McDonald's cheeseburger and see something edible and perhaps delectable. The Torah tells us, however, that from its vantage point, the mixing of milk and meat will lead to spiritual corrosion. We cannot see it because the world obscures the God Who created the world and Who forms the basic fiber of its existence. The Torah then becomes like a huge searchlight highlighting and exposing the true nature of things.

But accepting the Torah's instruction, against our own sensory perception, requires one inescapable ingredient—*belief.* Since you cannot see all these things that the Torah claims to be true, you have to put faith in its teachings. In Christianity the acquisition of faith represents the apogee of religious attainment, but in Judaism the purpose is to lose one's faith. The light of the truth should illuminate our eyes and become self-evident. As the prophet proclaims: "The day will come when your eyes shall see your Master" (Isa. 30:20). At the giving of the Torah at Sinai, the Jews did not believe in God. They saw Him. They heard Him. They tasted Him. They smelled Him. They experienced Him. God for them at that moment was as much a living reality and an existent Being as the mountain itself. Similarly, at the splitting of the Red Sea, the greatest miracle recorded in the Bible, Moses sang with the Jewish people and pointed with his hand: "This is my God and I will glorify Him!" (Exod. 15:2).

There was a time when men of inspired religious vision knew for certain that God existed. The only thing they questioned was whether *they* existed. In the presence of God they felt so insignificant that they really questioned whether their being wasn't just some illusion. Today we have come full circle. All of us are certain that we exist. But we question daily whether God exists.

The light of the world will only be fully restored in the messianic epoch, when creation will be restored to its luminescence and "the covering of the sun will be removed and the Lord will shine forth in all His glory" (Isa. 60:20). Then, none of us will need to believe, because we will see the living God of Israel in all His majesty. "On that day God will be Sovereign King over the entire earth" (Zech. 14:9). And finally, the ancient prophecy of Isaiah will be fulfilled. "For the earth shall be filled with the knowledge of God like the waters of the sea cover the ocean-floor" (Isa. 11:9).

Until that glorious day arrives, it is our duty, our mission, our highest calling to spread the light of goodness, the light of Torah, the light of compassion and good deeds, illuminating our hearts and minds and enriching the lives of our fellowman. "For the commandment is a flame, and the Torah is its light" (Prov. 6:23).

6

God

The Lord was not in the wind . . . not in the earthquake . . . not in the fire. And after the fire, a still small voice.

—1 KINGS 19:11

My religion consists of a humble admiration of the illimitable superior spirit who reveals Himself in the slight details we are able to perceive with our frail and feeble mind.

—ALBERT EINSTEIN

A STUDENT OF THE GREAT RABBI ZUSYA OF ANIPOLI came to the Hassidic master and asked him why God allowed atheism to flourish. Worse, why the Almighty created a world that lent credibility to atheistic claims. "You must know, my child," answered Rabbi Zusya, "that atheism and agnosticism are two of the most important doctrines in the world. Imagine if people were absolutely sure that God existed. They would see a hungry man in the street, but would not feed him. They would say, 'Don't worry, God will provide. He will not allow the man to go hungry.' Then they would witness the orphan going naked, but they would not clothe him. Again, they would say, 'Don't worry, there is a God. And He would never allow an orphan to go unfed.' But since we all sometimes question the existence of God, when we see another human being in need, we run

75

to help, because we may be the only ones to assist him. God lives through us."

Often the most potent and frequently used terms in any language are also the most elusive and mysterious. We speak and hear the word *God* countless times in our lives, but who and what is God? And what relevance does He have for modern-day men and women who have largely forgotten Him? As Rabbi Joseph Soloveitchik wrote in a haunting passage in *The Lonely Man of Faith*, "Who is He who trails me steadily, uninvited and unwanted, like an everlasting shadow, and vanishes into the recesses of transcendence the very instant I turn around to confront this numinous, awesome, and mysterious 'He'?"

The Jewish religion is predicated on the concept that man was created to serve the one, true God. To do so effectively, in addition to accepting the decrees of heaven unconditionally, man must make the effort to understand and apprehend the God he is serving. This is the twofold purpose of Judaism: to make God known and to teach man how he may draw closer to God by fulfilling the divine will and becoming holy.

What Is God?

An article in *Time* magazine in 1997 cited the remarkable statistic that 90 percent of all Americans believed in God. But on closer examination it was discovered that people's conception of God differed widely from the God who is introduced to us in the Bible. Simply stated, the biblical conception of God is this:

1. God is one and completely unified. He has no partners and is not composed of any parts. He does not begin anywhere, and he doesn't end anywhere either.

2. God is the source of *all* existence. He is Creator of heaven and earth, all cosmic forces, and all forces of nature. He is the source of light and darkness, goodness, and what appears to us as evil. "I form light and create darkness...I am the Lord who does all these things." (Isa. 45:7) There is no existence outside of Him. Everything that

exists is contingent upon Him for its being. Rabbi Shneur Zalman of Liadi, founder of Habad Hassidism, takes this a dramatic step further by saying that there is nothing real in all existence other than God. Everything exists within God and the goal of man is to annihilate his sense of self and separateness from God. God is the one true existence, with the rest of us being fully dependent on Him.

3. God is the supreme regulator of the earth, and the controller and director of history. Nothing happens outside His providence. As such, he is not only a detached Creator but an active governor, not just an initiator but an involved regulator.

Inherent in this Jewish conception of God is the complete rejection of idolatry and paganism, dualism and deism. (The latter is the doctrine that maintains that God, having created the world, withdrew from it completely.)

Ancient man knew enough of his own limitations to recognize and pay homage to lofty powers in the universe, which he deemed responsible for the ordering of life. Uncorrupted by the shallow distractions of modernity, he seemed to have had a natural intuition for the transcendental. He invented the idea of many different gods to fit the variety of phenomena that he witnessed. There was a god of lighting, a god of the oceans, a god for men, and a separate god for women.

Israel's idea of God, however, expounded in numerous biblical passages, painted an awe-inspiring spiritual portrait, forever putting paganism on the defensive. There is one God, it proclaimed, and He is the only true, completely independent existence (Deut. 6:4; Isa. 45:21, 46:9), above and beyond the confines of time and space. He has no body, nor can He be represented in any physical form. Good and evil do not represent different and contending kingdoms. Both emanate from the one, true God, which is why theodicy—the reconciliation of the good God and the existence of evil—has always been a problem for Judaism. We do not excuse evil as emanating from a source outside God. We don't conveniently blame all bad things on the devil. There is no Zoroastrian cosmic strife between antagonistic forces. By the same token, humankind constitutes a single family, all nations emanating from the same source in the God-head. Adam is the human father of all men. At the end of days, the human family will be reunited in an era of eternal brotherhood (Isa. 2:2–4).

That the most powerful forces in life are those that are invisible should not surprise the modern reader, for isn't the same feature true of love? And for that matter, is it not also true of the deeply in-grained psychological forces that have such great sway over our be-havior? Modern science acknowledges the same with the quantum and atomic theory. God cannot be seen, but his potency can be felt.

God's words to the Jewish people in uttering the first of the Ten Commandments—"I am the Lord your God who has taken you out from Egypt"—constituted an extraordinary demand. Until that time, all humanity worshiped only the tangible items grasped by the senses. Here the Almighty was asking the Jews to put the subtle and the abstract before the material and the concrete. Imagine speaking to a young man of twenty years, all raging hormones, who is dating a beautiful young woman. Speak to him about how love is much more special than sex, and he will simply not understand. He is not yet old enough, experienced enough, to appreciate the sublimity of love. Indeed, if you were to suggest that he refrain from sex until he is in love, he would think you had fallen off the moon. Sex provides immediate gratification. The delights of love are far more subtle and require a lengthy sensitization process in order to be appreciated.

With this we can get an inkling of understanding into how radical God's command was to the Jewish people to forsake the worship of the sun and the moon—which provide instant, tangible comfort and benefits—and devote all their energies to the intangible, invisible God. But this also allowed the Jews to develop an appreciation and love for subtlety and gentleness, which took other nations far longer to acquire. Maturity is perhaps best defined as an appreciation for de-layed gratification, the ability to forsake short-term, ephemeral goals for longer-term, more subtle goals, like doing homework and pursu-ing an education rather than just watching television. God de-manded this maturity of the Jews at the birth of their nationhood.

Furthermore, God, by insisting that He has no body or gender, was sensitizing the Jews to His omnipresence. He was to be found not only at the summit of mountaintops or accompanying the warrior into armed battle, but also in every drop of dew and in the innocence of a child. God was everywhere that man searched. Although in early books of the Bible there are memorable instances of divine manifestation—the ten plagues at Egypt, the revelation at Sinai, the exalted prophecy of Moses—with the passage of time, God recedes more and more into the background.

The Jewish order of the Hebrew Bible is different from the Christian one. In the Jewish order, the Five Books of Moses are followed by the Prophets, and then by the Writings and the Apocrypha. The Christian order places the Prophets last. In the Jewish order, God reveals Himself strongly in the Five Books of Moses, no longer shows Himself but at least speaks to the prophets, and ends up only as a source of inspiration for the later Books of Psalms, Esther, Proverbs, and Song of Songs. The Almighty's gradual withdrawal behind the facade of nature was meant to show the Jews that God was not only at Sinai. Nor was He only engaged in conversation with the wise and the pious. Rather, "there is no place devoid of His presence" (*Bamidbar Rabbah* 12:4).

A New God

This Jewish conception of God contrasted sharply with the Greek mythological gods, who had parents and children, ate and drank, seduced and fornicated, and had uncontrollable desires and passions. Judaism categorically rejected the absurdity of these imaginary and fanciful gods. Whereas ancient man could not overcome the hurdle of creating gods in his own image, the Bible declared unambiguously that it is man who is created in God's image.

Idolatry, though it lingered for centuries, was also doomed to extinction by this new conception of God as a disembodied, invisible Force. Images depicting the deity would gradually be abandoned. The Bible itself ordained that sculpture like the cherubim should be set up atop the ark in the Holy of Holies, but they represented the throne, not the Deity (cf. Ps. 68:5[4]); its occupant no human eye could behold and no mind could conceive. In the celebrated words of Joseph Albo, a medieval Jewish philosopher, "If I knew Him, I would be Him." The Jewish God transcends all description.

The invisibleness of God has radical implications for every aspect of life. The gratification of the senses has become a cherished goal. Our world prefers sex to love, money to inner peace, and greed to selflessness. We are a generation alienated, not only from God and spirituality, but also from our deepest selves.

Once in trying to patch together a marriage I told the husband that he must be more tender to his wife and not berate her so much. "But what should I do," he asked me, "when the things she is doing are just wrong? Should I ignore her faults, just for the sake of my marriage? Wrong is wrong!" His immediate desire was to right wrongs, but more fundamental was his desire to have a loving companion, however imperfect. This is a subtle quality, not immediately tangible to the senses. It may thus be overlooked in favor of the coarser distinction of who is "right."

Our belief in this conception of God conditions us to the idea that everything we touch, hear, smell, taste, and see is designed to awaken us to spirituality and holiness, rather than to serve as an obstacle on our spiritual journey. A man who comes home and finds a hot meal waiting for him would be a fool, not to mention a highly unromantic husband, if he sees before him merely a plate of food. What is really before him is a profound statement of love from his wife. If he sees only the food, he will compliment his wife and read the newspaper. If, however, he sees the affection that produced the meal, he will reciprocate her love by hugging or sincerely complimenting her, and she will feel cherished. The key lies in seeing the subtle within the obvious.

This was the greatness of Abraham. At the dawn of civilization, everyone experienced the brightness of the sun, the soft colors of the rainbow, and the cool shade of a tree and worshipped them for their utility. Abraham saw these things as a window onto the Divine. He looked beyond material existence and saw a master intelligence bringing unity to creation. In so doing, he fostered a people who would value peace over war, learning over conquest, charity over greed, and marriage over ephemeral, commitment-free pleasures. The Jewish nation was born to champion the subtle and feminine qualities of the spirit and dignity over the hard-edged masculine values of brute strength and honor.

This is why Judaism passionately insists that God is utterly mysterious and undefined. When God appeared to Elijah the prophet, Scripture records that first "there was a great wind, so strong that it was splitting mountains and breaking rocks in pieces before the Lord, but the Lord was not in the wind; and after the wind an earthquake, but the Lord was not in the earthquake; and after the earthquake a fire, but the Lord was not in the fire; and after the fire a still small voice."

The contrast with the Christian God could not be greater. Jesus is very well defined. He has a name, he is male (in Judaism, God is neither male nor female), and there is a record of his life and actions while on earth. In Judaism, the hidden God possesses no body and transcends all emotions. God is the *source* of all life and every living creature. God is as close to the snail as He is to the human, equally the creator of the star cluster spanning millions of light years and of the gnat, barely spanning millimeters.

Unity

The most essential Jewish idea about God is His absolute and indivisible unity, and thousands of Jews throughout history have been martyred with the classic formula of faith on their lips, Shema Yisrael: "Hear O Israel, the Lord is our God, the Lord is One." The great Jewish thinker and law-codifier Maimonides writes: "God is one; He is not two, but one. The oneness of any of the single things existent in the universe is unlike His Unity. He is not one as a species, since this includes numerous individuals; nor one as a body, since this is divisible into parts and sections, but a Unity which is unique in the world" (*Mishneh Torah,* Laws of the Cardinal Principles of the Torah, Chap. 1).

The universe has no competing powers that oppose God's sovereignty, nor has God created the universe and abandoned its running
to the laws of nature. All history accords with His will. "The cosmos
is the work of God, and all nature declares His glory" (Ps. 19:2). "All
things belong to Him, and He is the Lord of all" (1 Chron.
29:11–12). Judaism is a profoundly holistic philosophy of existence
and life. Man, like the world around him, can integrate all his diverse impulses into one effective system. He need not feel torn asun-
der, for example, by the conflicting impulses of intellect and
emotion. In the same way that the world at large is not diffuse, neither is the soul of man. The universe, in all its measureless diversity,
remains a homogeneous whole.

The pagan notion of demonic forces that wage war against the
deities is, therefore, wholly alien and repugnant to biblical theology. Even Satan is no more than the heavenly prosecutor, serving
the divine purpose. The classic Jewish mystical text, the *Zohar*, sees
Satan as a divine agent, whose mission is to exercise every charm in
the seduction of man, thereby providing him with choice. In understanding the role of Satan, the *Zohar* gives the analogy of a prostitute who is sent by the king to test the moral stamina of his son,
the crown prince. Even while employing all her attractive guile in
an effort to seduce the prince, the harlot hopes that he will not succumb. His fate, however, is entirely dependent on his exercising his
own judgment.

What was also revolutionary about the Jewish idea of a single,
unified, indivisible God was its correlation for unity within creation. Man has always debated whether there is a clear and all-em-
bracing unity to existence. Does everything reduce to one essential
point, connecting all organic and inorganic matter, every idea, phenomenon, and human being? Or is everything detached, separate,
unrelated, and ultimately contradictory? Is the world constructed of
the pieces of a puzzle ultimately yielding a single portrait, or are the
parts incongruent? In his seminal work, *The Hedgehog and the Fox*,
the late Isaiah Berlin, whom I had the unique privilege of befriend-
ing at Oxford. quotes the Greek poet and fabulist Archilochus, who

said: "The fox knows many things, but the hedgehog knows one big thing." Berlin writes:

> There exists a great chasm between those, on one side, who relate everything to a single central vision, one system, less or more coherent and articulate, in terms of which they understand, think and feel—a single, universal, organizing principle in terms of which all that they are and say has significance—and, on the other side, those who pursue many ends, often unrelated and even contradictory, connected, if at all, only in some de facto way, for some psychological or physiological cause, related to no moral or aesthetic principle.

This conflict can be traced to earliest man, in the discrepancy between paganism and monotheism. Prior to rise of the first Jew, Abraham, paganism dominated the earth. Man accounted for the huge variety around him by postulating the existence of many gods, each responsible for a separate force and phenomenon within nature. Into this pagan world rose the monotheistic knight, Abraham, who professed the existence of a God that none could see, Creator of all the cosmos, and ultimate regulator of world history. Abraham put forward the idea that all existence emanated from a single, unified source, whose energy and presence pervaded all of creation. According to the Talmud, he did so by a process of logical deduction and elimination. At first, witnessing the brightness and brilliance of the sun, and how its warmth is vital to all forms of life, Abraham prostrated himself before its rays and worshiped it as the supreme deity. But in the evening, the moon, which seemed much less impressive by comparison, launched a rebellion, assisted by the heavenly host of the stars, and defeated the sun, and the earth was shrouded in darkness. Abraham then worshiped the moon as the conqueror of the sun.

But in the morning, when the sun rallied its forces and reestablished its preeminence in the skies, Abraham rejected both as canceling each other out, and he turned to the other forces of nature in his search for the ultimate deity. He began to worship the air around him. It encompassed all of creation and surely must be the great divinity he hoped to discover. But he then pondered man's superiority to the air, since man, while being porous and having many bodily cavities, was still able to contain air and breath, thus proving he was its master. But having seen the lowliness of man and the repeated errors he could commit, Abraham was not about to worship himself or any other man. It was then that the great truth dawned upon him. The deity was an all-encompassing Being, who transcended and called into being the existence of nature, but also made up its fabric and served as its underlying, invisible essence. Abraham began to understand that all of nature was a veil that masked the presence of the deity, and that man must learn to apprehend the hidden Creator. God was everywhere, all around Abraham, and the young boy came to know and worship the one, true God, source of all life and existence.

Free Will

The unity of God finds its corollary in a radical social philosophy of peace and integration. The ultimate fraternity of man, amid endless internecine warfare, is not just a possibility but an inevitability, since we all stem from, and are encompassed by, the divine unity. Jews and Arabs may fight each other for centuries to come, but ultimately they will lay down their swords and beat them into plowshares because of an underlying harmony in their individual identities. Both emanate from the same celestial source, and both are made of the same cosmic stuff.

We must certainly ask how to explain the conflict and contradiction within our lives and our world if all mankind and nature stem from a single source. The answer is to be found in God's greatest gift to creation: free will.

Divine unity within the cosmos is so complete that the only being that can rebel against God is, ironically, the one who was created in His image. Animals are ruled by instinct and nature; they cannot transcend their biological programming. Ten thousand years from now, lions will still be preying on zebras and beavers will still be building dams. Both are utterly predictable. Only humans were empowered by the Creator with an ability to define their natures and act in defiance of the divine will. *And it is precisely our free will that gives meaning to creation.* Free will makes possible right and wrong, good and evil, meaning and nothingness. Free will gives significance to our actions and, ultimately, permits us to draw close to, or reject, our father in heaven. In this light, we may understand the following ancient rabbinic explanation of the creation story.

The Rabbis noted that after each of the first five days of creation the Bible records, "And God saw . . . and it was good." On the sixth day, the day of Adam's creation, the wording changes subtly: "And God saw . . . and it was *very* good." What was being crowned with that extra word? The Rabbis answered that it was man's "evil inclination," the desire to be bad, to rebel against God, the drive for base physicality, meaninglessness, and a world devoid of God's presence. But how could the "evil inclination," the source of all sorrow, be "very good"? The answer, of course, is that it is only the desire to move away from God that makes meaningful our choice to cleave to Him. It is the opportunity to choose the wrong path that makes us free beings, as opposed to robots. Without a drive for evil, none of us could ever be good.

As we have seen, Hegel sees the starting point and explanation for human social interaction as the primordial struggle for prestige, a battle for dominion in which winner becomes master, loser becomes slave. Other philosophers, including Locke, Hobbes, and Rousseau, pioneer the concept of an "original position" to explain and justify particular social structures. Some conceive man as being fundamentally noble and free, others take him to be, in essence, brutal and animalistic; one side views man primarily as an individual, the other side as essentially one part of a greater whole. Judaism too has an "original position." It is the story of Adam's creation. At its most fundamental level, the story of human existence is not about power or prestige; it is about a human being, endowed with free will, responding to the word of God. The story of Adam is the story of human existence par excellence. We, like Adam, stand before our creator, *choosing* our response to the divine command. This is the true meaning of "the image of God." We, like God, are free.

The story of Adam and Eve contains another crucial message—that man is capable of reorienting his nature and becoming a Godly being while fully immersed in the affairs of the earth. The Garden of Eden teaches us that the ideal state of man is on earth and that heaven on earth is a possibility. That pristine state has been lost, but the dream of its restoration motivates our every action as Jews. Man is capable of restoring that exalted spirituality by hating sin and practicing acts of loving-kindness. There is no need to ascend to the heavens. Rather, man can reconstruct a perfect world by following the divine blueprint. Having been created in the image of God, man, like his Creator, is entirely free.

The Rabbis point out that both the lower animals and the higher angels have the same Hebrew name, *chayot*. Stretched within this vertical continuum of existence is man, halfway between angel and beast. By exercising his freedom of choice, man can either rise to the level of the angels or descend to the level of the beast. Man's freedom to resist or obey the will of God is a restriction of the Deity's power that is totally unknown in the physical universe. This restriction is an act of divine self-limitation, know in the Kabbalah as *tzimtzum,* contraction or condensation. In His love for man, God has, so to speak, set aside an area of freedom in which man can elect to do right or wrong (Deut. 5:26, 30:17). In the language of the ancient Rabbis: "Everything is in the power of Heaven except the reverence of Heaven" (Talmud Bavli, *Berachot* 33b).

Man must live up to the responsibility of reflecting the divine image by dedicating himself to acts of love and justice throughout his life. The Bible compels man above all else to emulate the deity by embodying traits of love and justice in all that he pursues: "He loves righteousness and justice; the earth is full of the steadfast love of the Lord" (Ps. 33:5). A similar note is sounded in Hosea: "I will betroth you with righteousness and with justice, with steadfast love, and with mercy. I will betroth you with faithfulness; and you shall be mindful of the Lord" (2:21–22 [19–20]).

Transcendence and Immanence

Judaism was also radical in insisting that God is paradoxically both transcendent, beyond space and time, and immanent, involved in human affairs and responsive to human prayers. The Bible insists that these contradictory qualities inhere in a single, unified being. In so doing, it provides the most profound understanding of God ever postulated.

The Bible uses many epithets for God. He is King, Judge, Father, Shepherd, Mentor, Healer, and Redeemer—to mention a few of His aspects in His relationship to man. Different biblical teachers conceived God's character from different historical angles. Amos was conscious of God's justice. Hosea underscored His love and made forgiveness and compassion the coefficient, as it were, of divinity: "I will not execute My fierce anger . . . for I am God and not man" (11:9). Elsewhere, in biblical and rabbinic literature, the names used to describe God include Shaddai (Almighty), Ha-Kadosh Barukh Hu (Holy One, Blessed Be He), Ribono Shel Olam (Master of the Universe), Ha-Makom (The Place), Ha-Rahman (The Merciful), Shekhinah (Divine Presence), En Sof (The Infinite), Gevurah (The Mighty), Tsur Yisrael (Rock of Israel), Shomer Yisrael (Guardian of Israel), and Melekh Malkhe Hamelakhim (Supreme King of Kings).

The common denominator of all these names and descriptions is that they convey either the idea of God's awesome might (e.g., King of Kings), that which the Kabbalists would describe as the masculine energy of the Godhead, or God's nurturing and mothering instincts (e.g., The Merciful), conceived by the Kabbalists as the feminine energy within the Godhead. The masculine aspect of God is the immanent God of history, demonstrating peculiarly male-aggressive characteristics. This is the aspect of God that is like a disciplinarian father, rewarding and scolding mankind in accordance with its actions. Represented in the Kabbala by a line because of this divine energy's tendency to descend from above to below in a direct column (masculine physiology), it is the God who comes down into the world to interact with human affairs. It is the God who uses a stick to educate man to turn from his foibles and embrace sanctified living. It is the stern God of justice.

But there is also the feminine God of creation, represented by an all-encompassing circle (feminine physiology), who hovers above creation like a protecting angel, nurturing man through the endless struggle of life, always patient even in the face of human corruption and darkness, awaiting man's repentance and embracing of the light. Like a mother who loves her children whether they are deserving or not, this God is prepared to forgive man even in his moments of extreme ugliness. This is the infinite side of God, capable of giving birth to universes and endowing all creation equally with life, regardless of merit. The feminine God is the God of compassion. Placed together, the linear and the circular light represent God in all His perfection. A line and a circle together form the number ten (10), representing fullness and completion. Indeed, the Kabbalists maintain that God manifests Himself through ten channels, or *sefirot,* which represent the full panoply of celestial attributes.

To understand these two seemingly conflicting aspects of the deity, we must delve deeper into the nature of the Divine One. There are two main currents in world philosophy about God. One underscores God's otherness, His transcendence, having nothing in common with the world and serving merely as its ultimate, yet detached, source. The other underscores God's immanence, or accessibility, God's closeness to man and His empathy with the human condition. The latter, represented in Western philosophy mainly by Spinoza, maintains that God is identical with the world and nature—the pantheistic view that nature is sacred and holy. Spinoza and later pantheists denied the existence of a transcendent God outside nature, and it was for this heretical view that Spinoza was the subject of the last great excommunication within the Jewish faith, carried out by the Jewish court of Amsterdam in the year 1656.

The former view, represented in Western philosophy mainly by Descartes, sees the world as the creation of a God so powerful and aloof that by necessity He is removed from it, having set the mechanism of creation in motion. This view of God is the one most common among today's watered-down believers, who affirm that God is indeed the Creator but claim He no longer regulates world events, since to do so would be beneath His infinite glory and dignity. When most people speak of Mother Nature, this is exactly what they mean, a God who is cloaked and veiled by nature, indifferent to human activity, unresponsive to the pain of human tragedy. Explaining God as a passive being unmoved by historical events is a way that many theologians have dealt with the greatest challenge to faith, the problem of suffering. Rabbi Harold Kushner's best-seller, *When Bad Things Happen to Good People,* describes God as being subject to the laws of nature. Thus, though He indeed commiserates with our suffering and offers us comfort in moments of woe, there is little He can do to save the righteous man from a hurricane or a volcano. Even God is subject to nature's laws. This vision seems to have brought comfort to millions of readers.

Close inspection reveals that both conceptions of God—as either wholly transcendent or wholly immanent—are deficient. The immanent God of history seems inherently weak and unimpressive. Why pray to a God if He is nothing more than a caring big brother, incapable of altering human events? And if God is synonymous with nature, then we are alone in an impersonal universe, abandoned to the elements. Religion becomes an absurdity. The God that is only historical is also too unpredictable and volatile to be of any use to humanity. He gets angry at people when they do evil. He punishes the wicked and rewards the righteous. But since He reacts to different human events and epochs, does that mean He ages as well? Can we really love a God who gets angry and loses His temper? The Cartesian transcendent view of God is similarly fraught with difficulty. Can a stoical God, who is calm and silent in the face of human misery and famine, endear Himself to vulnerable humans who look to Him for comfort and salvation?

Judaism offered the world a revolutionary view of God that was transcendent and immanent simultaneously. God encompasses the world from without and animates it from within. He is the Creator, an impersonal God who fills and regulates the infinite expanse of space, as well as a personal God, attentive to human needs and mindful of human cries. He reaches out to man in his travail—comforting the bereaved, healing the sick, and establishing a covenant of mutual love with man in which the earth is never forsaken. God is both the substance and the fabric of the universe, its body and its soul, its matter and its spirit. He can indeed alter suffering, but even when He appears silent, He is quietly present in the cataclysm, comforting those who ache. He is both King and Comforter, Master and Redeemer, Father and Friend, Disciplinarian and Lover. Only God can contain within His infinite being these diametric opposites. God is the playwright, who calls forth the characters into being, as well as the director, who oversees every aspect of the production. He is the owner of the team, but also its quarterback. He is sovereign, reigning supreme, but also prime minister, involved in every aspect of government.

The ancient Jewish mystics explained it this way: The Almighty contracts His infinite presence in what is known as *tzimtzum*. This contraction yields a *makum panui,* or empty space. This space is not empty in a literal sense, since God is omnipresent; rather, it is like a condensation in which God's essence is present but concealed, affording man the illusion of freedom. The world is brought into existence within this "empty space," thereby hiding the immediacy of God's presence and allowing man the opportunity for freedom of choice. Man feels God in the synagogue, but not in the corridors of Congress, and can exercise his human capacity to choose his own destiny, thereby demonstrating kinship with His infinite source. Only a being who is capable of acting in contradiction to God's law is ultimately deserving of God's love. But the purpose, of course, is to choose good and reject evil: "I call heaven and earth to witness against you today that I have set before you life and death, blessings and curses. Choose life so that you and your descendants may live" (Deut. 30:19).

Without God, What Do Humans Have in Common?

For those of us growing up in the Judeo-Christian ethic of Abraham's making, the existence of a single, indivisible God seems a natural, intuitive, and altogether logical supposition. Paganism and polytheism seem vestiges of man's tribal past. But in truth, noting the multifarious nature of created existence, paganism is a far more natural conclusion. Why should we not assume that men and women have separate gods? How could earth and the oceans have the same ruler, when they are so different?

In light of this consideration, we can begin to see how radical Abraham's discovery was and the revolution it represented. Today's world is becoming increasingly fragmented. It makes perfect sense that once society has lost its belief in the all-encompassing unity of God, it should begin to believe in the disparate nature and disconnectedness of all creation. After all, aren't men "from Mars" and women "from Venus," with little intrinsic unity or ability to get along? Divorce is careening out of control, and young people find no compelling reason to marry. There seems to be no real peace ahead for the Jews and Arabs in the Middle East, and many other regional conflicts are spiraling out of control, rife with divisive nationalist sentiment. In a world that is witnessing the clash of civilizations, the demise of religion, and the demise of the belief in the one God who is the source of all life and Father to all humanity, the belief in a family of nations seems a futile fantasy rather than an achievable dream.

Descriptions of God

The Talmud relates the following story:

> An emperor said to Rabbi Joshua ben Hananiah: "I want to see your God, Rabbi Joshua." "You cannot see Him, Caesar." "Nevertheless, I want to see Him." So Rabbi Joshua had the emperor stand facing the sun during the summer solstice and said to him, "Look directly into

the sun, Caesar." "I cannot." Rabbi Joshua then said, "If you say of the sun, which is only one of the servants standing before the Holy One Blessed be He, I cannot look directly at it, how much less can you look at the presence of the Divine Presence." (*Hullin* 60a)

Judaism accepts the idea that there can be no positive description of God. We cannot say what God *is,* only what He *is not.* His Being completely transcends human apprehension. But whereas we cannot give a blind man a positive description of color, we can tell him that it is not something he can feel or taste. The same is true of the deity. We can say that God is infinite, or not finite. He has no limitations. By stripping away many of the adjectives that we use to describe empirical phenomena, we can, through negative association, come to know something of His essence. Many of the great Jewish sages even maintained that we could not say that God is compassionate, wise, forgiving, and the like, since this too involves positive description and is an arrogant claim on the part of mortal man to know the unknowable. Rather, all we can say is that God is not unkind, not unwise, and not unforgiving, and so on. The Kabbalists add that even the negative descriptions we give about God are said about His *sefirot,* or emanations, rather than about His essence.

Ten *sefirot,* or mystical spheres, were offered by the Kabbalists as a solution to the problem of how the infinite God interacts with His finite creation and becomes intelligible to man, without being affected by such finite reduction. If He is infinite, then He must exist above time. Thus, for God, there cannot be a time before and after creation. Similarly, man below seems to see very different manifestations of God, even to the point of contradiction. In Egypt, God manifested strict justice toward the wicked Egyptians, destroying their lives and property through ten plagues. At the splitting of the Red Sea, He showed Himself to be a warrior who effortlessly decimated Pharaoh's legions, and simultaneously as a caring Father who rescued the forlorn Israelites who were plunged in the Red Sea. At Sinai He was a lawgiver, and in our time, He manifests Himself passively and indirectly in the processes of nature. What, then, is God, and why is He so inconsistent?

To this the Kabbalists answered that God has no description whatsoever. He is beyond all positive, and even negative, descriptions. He is utterly infinite and removed from all earthly portraiture. But His infinite essence clothes itself within ten spheres, or channels of revelation, through which He interacts with His world. The relationship between God's essence, referred to by the Kabbalists as the En Sof (literally, "there is no end"), and the ten *sefirot* is analogous to clear water being placed into ten glasses, each of different color. Red would represent God's anger, blue his compassion, green His splendor, and so on. Viewed from the outside, the water will invariably appear red, blue, green, or yellow, depending on the color of glass into which it is placed. In reality, however, the water has not changed color at all and only appears this way to the outside observer.

The same is true of God's relation to the universe and humans. His infinite essence transcends all classification. But in the process of interacting with the finite world, God clothes Himself in the ten spheres, or emotions. To the inhabitants of the lower worlds like ourselves, that makes it appear as if He has assumed some definition.

Father and King

In Judaism, unlike Christianity, the Deity has no earthly manifestation, and no man could ever proclaim himself to be God. To do so would be the ultimate act of heresy. It would also significantly alienate some segment of society, for if God is a man, the women are less Godly than men, and alienate blacks if God is white, and so on. The ancient Rabbis were at pains to emphasize that the various anthropomorphic descriptions of the Creator in the Bible—the face of God, His outstretched hand, His back—were nothing more than allegorical language designed to make the Creator accessible to the human mind. The mature religious thinker must divest the Deity of such conceptions, since God is infinitely removed from anything remotely human. Even words like Father and King are used only to convey God's tenderness, never any sense of physical materialization.

Whereas in Christianity, God is conceived only as Father, in Judaism, He is both Father and King. Likewise, in the Bible, humanity is described as being both children and servants of the Lord. Each captures an element that the other is lacking. Love and fear constitute the two motivating forces in every area of human life. Love is where one serves God out of a desire to draw closer to Him, whereas fear is where one engages in religious worship because of the consequences of neglecting one's spiritual obligations. In the first scenario, the motivation is to establish and advance a relationship, *to draw near to someone for whom we care.* In the latter, the motivation is to refrain from severing an already existing relationship, *to remain fastened to someone powerful and on whom we are dependent.* The son will always love his father more than the servant will love his master. But precisely because there is no fear, the son may act insolently toward his father and may even rebel, as in the case of Absalom, who rebelled against his father, King David, and tried to overthrow his rule and replace him as king of Israel, only to die in battle, at the hands of Yoav, David's general. Such a possibility, however, is entirely remote from the servant-king relationship, which demands total loyalty and absolute submission.

So which is God's primary attribute, love or justice? Father or King? God's justice and mercy are both affirmed in His proclamation to Moses at Sinai before the giving of the Ten Commandments: "The Lord, the Lord, a God compassionate and gracious, slow to anger, abounding in kindness and faithfulness, extending kindness to the thousandth generation, forgiving iniquity, transgression, and sin; yet He does not remit all punishment, but visits the iniquity of the fathers upon children and children's children, upon the third and fourth generations" (Exod. 34:6–7). Love and compassion dictate that the sinner can always be forgiven and must be allowed to return from his errant ways. But justice and truth dictate that for every sinful action there is a negative consequence that cannot be avoided.

God's mercy is revealed in the fact that he redeemed the people of Israel from slavery in Egypt to make them His people and enact a covenant with them: "When Israel was a child, I loved him, out of Egypt I called my son" (Hos. 11:1). His justice is revealed in the fact that He holds the Israelites accountable if they sin and do not uphold their side of the covenant: "You only have I known of all the families of the earth; therefore I will punish you all your iniquities" (Amos 3:2).

But these attributes are obviously incompatible. Which, then, is superior? The ancient Rabbis declared that God originally sought to create the world with strict justice. After all, justice is the guardian of truth. But He then saw that the earth could not endure. People are imperfect and humanity is frail. He therefore mixed into the world's foundation a healthy measure of love and compassion. In describing the need to balance the two, the ancient Rabbis compared God to a king who, in order to prevent a fragile goblet from shattering, must mix hot and cold water when filling it. Thus the world exists because of the admixture of the attributes of mercy and justice *(middat ha-rahamim* and *middat ha-din)*. Behind this parable lies a complex development of biblical ideas in which the two divine appellations, the Tetragrammaton (YHWH) and Elokim, were understood to refer to the two main manifestations of God's providence: the first, the attribute of mercy; the second, that of justice. God's justice is often tempered by His mercy: "My heart recoils within me, My compassion grows warm and tender. I will not execute My fierce anger, I will not again destroy Ephraim; for I am God and not man" (Hos. 11:8–9).

Is God's truth or His mercy His main attribute? Is He primarily slow to anger or quick to visit retribution on the wicked? The Bible recognizes that without justice love itself becomes a form of injustice; but justice in itself is not enough. It can only serve as a foundation. The superstructure—the bridge between God and man—is grace. Love, therefore, is the most supreme attribute of God. This idea finds expression in various areas of Jewish law in which the interests of peace most often supersede those of law and justice. In fact, a Jewish court's first mandate in settling a legal dispute is to try to persuade both parties to accept an out-of-court compromise—to establish peace—rather than enforce the strict requirements of the law. Similarly, most Jewish prayers are geared toward appealing to God's attribute of kindness rather than strict justice. We supplicate God to be mindful of His love for us, even when we may not be deserving. We wish to relate to the Almighty as a child to a father, rather than as a servant to His king.

"My Ways Are Not Your Ways"

Often man is blind to God's loving-kindness, since God's actions are frequently unintelligible to humans: "For my thoughts are not your thoughts, nor are your ways my ways, says the Lord" (Isa. 55:8). Nevertheless, God does not expect man to remain silent in the face of seeming divine injustice, and the tradition of challenging God in the face of apparent divine indifference to human tragedy goes back to Judaism's earliest days.

In the well-known biblical tragedy of Job, God reproaches Job's friends, who took the position of defending God against Jacob's complaints, and Job is rewarded despite his searing indictment of God's actions. The God-man relationship flowers in an evolutionary process of education: Man is gradually weaned from his own inhumanity, from atrocities like human sacrifice (Gen. 22:2–14), from bestial conduct, and from wronging his fellowman. The goal again is love: "You shall love your neighbor as yourself" (Lev. 19:18). It is a corollary of the love of God: "I am the Lord" (Lev. 19:18). Reward and retribution play a role in the divine educational procedures, but their functions are limited—they are not ultimates. The eternal fires of Hell are never used as a deterrent, though punishment of the wicked after death is obscurely mentioned (Isa. 66:24; Dan. 12:2), nor is Paradise used as an inducement. Judaism is based on the idea that man must choose God for love of God and because He is the truth, and for no ulterior motive. Every other inducement is a subtle form of idolatry and self-serving goals.

Indeed, the love of God for humanity is the central motif of rabbinical Judaism. The nearness of God is the predominant theme of the Talmud and Midrash. God mourns because of the evil decrees He has been compelled to pronounce upon Israel; because of their current ways, He goes into exile with His children; He studies Torah and gives His view on halakhic topics, and is overjoyed if the scholars triumph over Him in Halakhah, as indeed happens in several Talmudic narratives.

So far we have examined the Jewish *definition* of God. Fundamentally, however, God is met in a direct existential encounter, which is true revelation. Judah Halevi argued in his medieval masterpiece, the *Kuzari,* that God is apprehended existentially far more than he is comprehended rationally. Experiencing God is superior to merely believing in Him. Ultimately, Judaism emphasizes that God is found experientially, through the great historical events of revelation, rather than merely in the minds of the philosophers. In his anguished consciousness, man encounters God, who is the Creator of the world, and above all, man discovers his own dependency on God. This meeting reveals God as an all-powerful and loving Father. His love for man results in commandments that bind every individual for whom the divine-human encounter is a reality. The commandments are the essential will of God revealed to man, whereby he can execute God's will and thereby draw near to Him.

Entering a Relationship with God

We may pay God token homage in keeping with the practice of our receding religious faith, but how many today really *believe* in God as both Creator and Regulator of history? Do we recognize that it is in God's power to make our lives successful, far more than any exertion of our own effort? Who today prays to God as if the offering of that prayer will make or break his or her career? How many husbands and wives whose marriage are rocky cry out from the depths of their despair for God to save their union? In short, how many of us today relate to God, not just as some spiritual abstraction, but rather as Parent, Master, and tender Friend accompanying us through all of life's vicissitudes? The prophet Micah expressed it succinctly: "He has told you, O mortal, what is good; and what does the Lord require of you but to do justice, and to love kindness, *and to walk humbly with your God?*" (6:8). No wonder religion has died so horrible a death in the modern age. God is a stranger.

The great novelist Franz Kafka penned his father a letter, but the elder Kafka died before having had the chance to read it:

> It would have been thinkable that we might both have found each other in Judaism or that we might have begun from there in harmony. But what sort of Judaism was it that I got from you? . . . It was impossible to make a child, over-acutely observant from sheer nervousness, understand that the few flimsy gestures you performed in the name of Judaism, and with an indifference in keeping with their flimsiness, could have any higher meaning. For you they had meaning as little souvenirs of earlier times, and that is why you wanted to pass them on to me. But since they no longer had any intrinsic value, even for you, you could do this only through persuasion or threat.

These lines could be written by almost any child growing up in a Jewish or Christian home for whom religion has become a burden, a dead carcass to bear, rather than a fountain of living waters.

Central to every religion is the idea of faith, that there is a spiritual reality not immediately detectable by the human senses, but nonetheless as real as the material world. Religion ultimately is about the reality of God and man's journey to discover Him and make Him part of man's daily life. The world's religions have various ways of portraying the faith experience. In Judaism, it is conceived as being in a relationship with God, both on a national and personal level. Judaism is not about simply submitting before God, but rather about joining God as a partner in the unfolding drama of creation, giving succor to the needy, love to the forlorn, and food to the hungry. Biblical references abound of God as the bridegroom of the nation of Israel and the Jews as his chosen bride. This imagery reaches a dramatic and powerful apex in the incomparable love poem, Song of Songs, according to tradition written by King Solomon, which the ancient Rabbis interpreted as allegorical of the love between God and the Jewish people. "You are beautiful as Tirzah, my love, comely as Jerusalem, terrible as an army with banners" (Song 6:4). "Many waters cannot quench love, neither can floods drown it" (Song 8:7).

Man requires a relationship with God, his heavenly source, and religion seeks to establish and maintain that relationship. This is reflected in the beautiful words of the medieval Jewish poet, Rabbi Judah Halevi: "When far from Thee, I die, while yet in life; but if I cling to Thee, I live, though I should die" *(Kuzari).*

The principal distinguishing characteristic of Judaism, however, is its emphasis on action as the cornerstone of the divine-human connection. Faith and love of God cannot subsist naked and alone; they must be clothed in deeds, expressed in righteous behavior. In marriage, love and motivation mean little if not reflected in romantic gesture. A husband and wife must always express and demonstrate their love. Feeling it in their hearts is insufficient. A father excusing himself by telling his son that he loves him but cannot show it does not make up for the deficiency of emotion.

The same is true of religion. In Judaism it is insufficient to have faith. Rather, the Talmud declares that the righteous *live* with their faith, and establishes this principle as the all-encompassing rule of Judaism: "It was Habakkuk who came and based [all the Torah] on one [principle], as it is said, But the righteous shall live by his faith" *(Makkot* 24a). To be sure, Judaism has always utilized and appealed to rational deductive proofs for the existence of God in an attempt to establish an intellectual concept of faith and religious certitude. Indeed, a certain proximity to Him can be established with philosophical insight and knowledge. But intellectual speculation within Judaism is never a replacement for the religious relationship itself, which is communion with God, and which is higher than knowledge. Maimonides compared man's obligation to love God with the intense, all-consuming love that a lovesick man feels for a woman. The God who transcends human intellect and philosophy is reached by love alone. The greatest expression of that love is the man or woman of faith who lives in accordance with the divine will.

The basis of every relationship between two parties is the need to accommodate each other's needs. Each partner is possessed of an intrinsic will that is the deepest definition of his or her being. Our inner will transcends even our thoughts. The very act of entering into a relationship is an undeclared, yet tacit, acceptance of the simple fact that no desire of one's beloved is trivial or irrelevant. Rather, if our beloved is dear to us, we will always seek to make that person happy, and this primarily involves accommodating the beloved's innermost will. If a woman tells her husband that she loves flowers, then he cannot buy her a box of chocolates instead with the excuse that it's the thought that counts. Thus, the man or woman of faith who dismisses observance of the Jewish dietary restrictions because they do not lend themselves to his or her rational apprehension is no different than a husband who refuses to buy his wife flowers because he cannot understand why she should crave something that has no shelf life. Even his offer to buy her a ruby or emerald in its stead is still a rejection of her intrinsic womanhood. If she would only think like a man, if she would only crave those trinkets whose value does not diminish with time, then he would accommodate her. Such a man is incapable of being in a relationship, because he expects everyone to be just like him. Similarly, the man or woman of faith does not try to create God in his or her own image—accepting as binding only those religious practices he or she feels ennoble human life—but rather accepts that God too has an intrinsic will that must be accommodated, irrespective of its immediate appreciation on the part of the human mind.

The idea of the God-man relationship mirroring that of husband and wife finds its strongest expression in Kabbalistic writings. According to Kabbalah, God, as mysterious as this may seem, has needs, much in the way that man has needs. God informs the Jewish people that He requires them to accommodate His will, like refraining from desecrating the Sabbath, His holy day. The Creator reveals to man that justice for Him is as great a passion as success is for humans. So if you wish God to grant you success, you must always act justly. God and man discover each other in accommodating the other's innermost desires. For a marriage to be successful, it is necessary for husband and wife not only to celebrate birthdays and anniversaries but also to greet each other lovingly every day. Likewise, man must proffer gratitude to His Creator every waking hour and aspire to know God in all his ways.

Hence the first Jewish step in knowing God is an unconditional acceptance of His expressed will, though we may not understand it. Real love in Jewish thought goes beyond attempting to make sense of each other; it involves an inner experience that translates externally into a desire to cater to the wishes of one's beloved. This idea may seem unintelligible to today's men and women, who prize communication above accommodation. But those whose marriages last understand there can be nothing more romantic, and no better way to make someone feel cherished, than to respect, anticipate, and respond to the other person's needs and desires. This is not to say that action without love is sufficient, but rather that according to both the spirit of the law and the law itself, the details of how God must be worshiped and the minutiae of the spiritual life are essential in serving God.

To be sure, the idea of action in conformity with the divine will as superior to pure faith is one that few can appreciate in our modern, technologically advanced society. The man of faith who loves and serves God today may be seen as an anachronism, unable to let go of his superstitions. Modern man worships his own reason, and for some, technology has replaced the God of the Bible. To be sure, many millions still attend synagogue and church. But this seems far more to do with cultural and aesthetic motivations than with pietistic and religious identity. What has been lost in the world today is the idea of God as the rock of our salvation. We define security today as a steady job and money invested in stocks and bonds. True believers who put God before material success, who would rather talk about God than football, are today dismissed as crazed fundamentalists. God, no longer a comforting friend, has become a distant abstraction, called upon only in the most extreme cases of illness or emergency. God's relegation to the nether reaches of society results primarily from, first, arrogance on the part of modern-day technological man, who is blinded by his own ingenuity and devices. He considers himself sophisticated and invulnerable and has no deep-seated need for God. And, second, it stems from the failure of institutionalized religion to impart a true faith experience.

God Is an End and Never a Means

A spiritual renaissance seems to be gripping large segments of Western civilization. In place of the lapsed Catholics of yesterday, there are today born-again Christians and "born-again" (or returned) Jews. But many are not really running to the light so much as running from the darkness. There are people in contemporary society so enmeshed in materialism and the pursuit of their agenda that they return to God as a reaction against their own suffocating selfishness. Indeed, to many, God is He who provides meaning, fulfillment, and salvation, somewhat like yoga, a refreshing spiritual escape from the all-consuming immersion in materialism. But this is not the Jewish God. Judaism is a religion that is profoundly deiocentric, or God-centered. Every human action should be impelled by a love and fear of God and should be undertaken for the express purpose of fulfilling His will and drawing closer to Him. The ancient Rabbis declared, "Know Him in all thy ways." Judaism's main point about God is that in any discussion concerning the deity, God must always be perceived as the end, and never the means.

No woman would be impressed with a man who proposes marriage declaring that he believes that the experience of marriage will mature him and better him as a human being. A woman wants to know that a man wants to marry her for one reason alone: because he loves her. Man must approach God with the same level of selflessness and desire. God is the fulcrum of existence, around which all aspirations and attainments must revolve. Serious discussions of divine reward or the afterlife have little place in Judaism, and most of the discussion in the Talmud about where the soul goes after death is surrounded by misty and contradictory speculation on the part of the Rabbis. There is good reason for this. The Rabbis never wanted anyone to serve God on the basis of one day being rewarded. They taught: "Do not be like servants who serve their master for the sake of receiving a reward, but rather be like servants who serve their master without the intent of receiving a reward; and let the fear of Heaven be upon you" (*Ethics of the Fathers,* Chap. 1). Judaism has not used portraits of demonic suffering in Hell, or even luscious pleasures in heaven, to attract adherents or inspire its faithful. There are no beautiful virgins who will pleasure the Jewish believer, as there are in the Muslim afterlife.

Rather, the Jew serves God out of a disinterested love of truth alone. There is no guarantee that loving and serving God will lead to any higher reward or ennoblement of character. Indeed, Jews have suffered torture, inquisitions, crusades, gassing, and the fires of the crematorium. Inhuman pain and diabolical suffering have never succeeded in prying the Jew away from his Father in heaven, and judging from past history, they never will.

7

Idolatry

As a house implies a builder, a dress a weaver, a door a carpenter, so the world proclaims God its Creator.

—RABBI AKIBA, *Midrash Temura*

If God created us in His image, we have certainly returned the compliment.

—VOLTAIRE

MONOTHEISM, THE IDEA OF THE ONE GOD, while revolutionary in its time, is today commonplace, even self-evident. The Jewish revolution, it would seem, having had fantastic success in the dissemination of the knowledge of the one God directly, through its own devices, and indirectly, through Christianity and Islam, is now at its end. But idolatry is far from being a discarded relic of a primitive past. Indeed, the continuing financial prosperity of modern man is helping him build the greatest idol of all, namely, himself!

Maimonides explains that the ancients were originally monotheists and that the worship of the one, true God preceded paganism. Indeed, the generations following Adam worshiped God and paid homage to His unity. Paganism originated when ancient man made the mistake of believing that part of loving God was admiring and paying homage to the magnificent celestial bodies that He had set in the heavens. Men looked up to the radiant sun and the mystical glow of the moon's crescent and thought to themselves, "How great God must be if He can create things as special as this. Indeed, it is probably the will of the Creator that we write poems and sing songs to glorify the sun and the moon. It is surely His will that we praise the extraordinary works of His creation." Although this began with the best of intentions, after a few generations the people began to forget about God in favor of the things He created, since He was invisible and these radiant bodies were far more tangible. Maimonides says that their offense is analogous to a man who walks by a beautiful building and offers praise to the hammer and chisel, rather than to the architect who designed the building. God began as an abstraction, rapidly became a myth, and was finally relegated to the nooks and crannies of the human subconscious. It took the courage of the great patriarch Abraham to draw back the curtains of creation, thereby exposing the true nature of the world—the Creator who hid behind it—reintroducing the earth's inhabitants to their source and Creator.

Modern Idolatry

Today's confidence that we have graduated from idolatry is based on the erroneous notion that idolatry entails prostrating oneself before stone, a mountain range, or a golden calf. Thus it would appear that the Bible, with its incessant attempts to pull man away from idolatry, in this matter has no contemporary relevance. But the real definition of idolatry is simply living for something other than God, or in the analogy of Maimonides, worshipping the hammer and chisel for the work of the architect. Idolatry means not only worshipping idols but also elevating something human or material to the status of a sacred object. The rejection of a transcendent spiritual realm is idolatry. The God of Israel is an all-consuming fire, tolerating nothing beside itself. A passion for materialism snuffs out the Godly fire in our hearts. Belief that there are forces such as stars and constellations that control our destiny, such as in hard-core astrology, is certainly idolatry, as is any belief in a predetermined fate. Man is governed not by fate, but by the morality of his actions. Idolatry can mean fearing another person more than we fear God. It includes elevating a political cause over the exercise of morality and respect for human rights: For example, it is idolatrous to believe that the Land of Israel is holy for any reason other than God's proximity to it. The Bible declares explicitly that the holiness of the land of Israel, to which the Jews are so irrevocably attached, is entirely due to the fact that this is "a land which the Lord, your God, cares for; the eyes of the Lord your God are upon it, from the beginning of the year to the end of the year" (Duet. 11: 12). It possesses no intrinsic holiness. Indeed, nationalism—the love of the state—has often served as a substitute for man's love of God. All idolatry arises from the hubris of creating God in our own image rather than recognizing that it is we who are created in the image of God.

We become idolatrous whenever we allow our lives to move away from a Godly and goodly purpose. God is meant to be the focus of our existence, around which all else revolves. The sum total of our thoughts, actions, and speech—the money we make and the relationships we create—should lead us to a more sublime, higher purpose, making us more spiritual and sensitive human beings. Idolatry is the act of replacing that focus with something else, whether it be the pursuit of money, sex, art, education, celebrity, or even religion.

In this light, we can appreciate why idolatry is the most serious sin in the Bible. If a person has character flaws—a bad temper or an inability to be charitable—we can say that he or she is basically a good person but an element of his or her personality needs refinement. Idolatry, however, means that one's entire life is fundamentally misdirected. It is not like a man who occasionally yells at his wife, but rather like one who has fallen in love with another woman, who thus has abrogated the marital covenant. When one practices idolatry, or lives entirely for money or power, one is traveling on the wrong road completely.

An individual may sacrifice to his man-made god, pray to it, and worship it with all his heart and soul. But if it is a false god, then he is not merely committing an error, he has dedicated his life to something utterly pointless. In the modern age, many of us make the mistake of living for materialistic pursuits—cars that break down, homes that slowly deteriorate, sexual relationships that leave us feeling empty, academic degrees that, if not employed to a higher cause, lead to arrogance and vanity. The belief in God is the focal point of Judaism and of human living, because if there is no God, then man can live only for himself. This is why Maimonides says that all the commandments are designed to wean us away from idolatry. Life is far too precious a commodity to squander.

The Deification of Celebrity

It would behoove modern day man to remember that the Biblical instruction which remains the most relevant of all are still the first two of the Ten Commandments: *I am the Lord Your God; you shall have no other gods before me.* God alone should be the epicenter of our lives, the heart of our existence, the soul of our actions. We must brook no substitutes.

If we were to make an honest assessment and engage in sincere introspection, we would have to admit that all of us who indulge in and partake of the popular culture have become closet idolaters. And in no area is this more true than in the ardent obsession and fanatical fixation with the lives of celebrities. Celebrity gossip has become the new language of social dialogue. Our hero worship of those with face and name recognition has gone from a past-time to a devotion; from a form of recreation to a noxious form of veneration.

Our modern idols have moved from the stone-carved totems of the ancient world to the perfectly sculpted bodies of movie stars and rock idols. Rather than pray to the heavenly stars, we bow before our movie stars. Rather than talk of the beauty of God's creation, we talk of George Lucas's film creations. Rather than talk about how we can connect with God, we talk about who Julia Roberts is connecting with. And rather than contemplate the mysteries of the Universe, we seek to uncover the enigma of Marlon Brando.

That so many people today are more interested in talking about Russell Crowe's latest flame than light a candle to illuminate the cosmic darkness that can expose the Creator is beyond debate. The supplantation of God with the deities of the silver screen is a trend that has grown mightily over these last decades. That MTV and Access Hollywood has supplanted Ecclesisastes and Proverbs is perhaps to be expected. This is, after all, a secular age. But what I find truly shocking is that most people have a greater interest in their favorite celebrities' lives than even their own. As a culture, we have chosen to live vicariously through our celebrity idols, placing far more interest in their shenanigans than in our own personal development. A wife would rather read what Jennifer Lopez wore at her latest concert than learn what kind of day her husband had at the office. Teenagers would rather ponder 'N Sync's new album than their own academic record. Husbands drool with delight at the strippers on the Howard Stern show but would never strip themselves of their defenses and be completely emotionally open with their wives. Celebrity culture is all-consuming and has become a dangerous and destructive obsession. Go to the home pages of any of the leading web sites like AOL and MSN, and the first thing you'll see posted, well before the latest violence between warring parties in the Middle East, are the warring record labels out to sign Whitney Houston. Our deities today are women who can wriggle their behinds at the MTV Music awards and men who can throw a ball through a hoop.

Since my earliest days in Rabbinical seminary, I have harbored a dream that one day Jewish spirituality would go mainstream, that a religion that has indirectly influenced the world's most important ideas and institutions would finally earn a popular voice. Once I became Rabbi at Oxford and hosted famous men and women as speakers to our students, I mistakenly convinced myself that celebrities and the microphone they had to the world offered a foolproof means by which to advance a Godly message. All it took was get the celebrities on board and the rest of humanity would follow. After all, if you can't beat 'em join 'em. If the world was obsessed with celebrity, then why not utilize a man or woman's prominence and popularity to highlight a noble cause. Kobe Bryant and Britney Spears are the ones whom the youth follow, not the rabbis, priests, or social philosophers. So what harm could be done by floating these ideas through the mouthpieces of superstars who found them engaging.

I have since learned that you cannot promote God through individuals who in the popular imagination have come to supplant God. I have come sadly to realize that I was engaging in the promotion of idolatry, amidst the best intentions. For when using a celebrity to talk of values, the message will always be less important than the personality. A man or a woman who spends their lives cultivating the spotlight finds it difficult to deflect that light onto anything of lasting value. They need every last speck, or they feel plunged into darkness. The light of the idea will be absorbed and lost in the aura of the star. If the purpose of knowing God is to be weaned off false idols, then God cannot be taught by those who have allowed, and perhaps even encouraged, their own deification.

Throughout my life, I had always prided myself on being above celebrity gossip. While those around me read *Us Weekly* and *People*, I attempted to focus on far more serious periodicals. I tried to study the Bible, read history and biographies, write essays on relationships, and generally keep my TV watching, movie-going, and magazine reading to a minimum. But I learned that for all my supposed aloofness, I could become just as obsessed with celebrity idolatry as anyone else and unwittingly undermine the two first commandments.

When Michael Jackson and I started *Heal the Kids*, the intention was to reprioritize children in the lives of their parents, healing them of infectious insecurity and imparting to them a sense of value. We both agreed that parents' neglect of their children was causing anger and anxiety in the young generation, a development that if not corrected could undermine civilization as we know it. With every passing day there was another child pulling a gun at school and pumping lead into teenagers and teachers. The crisis had to be addressed. But what I never expected was that the interviews I did about the organization in attempting to jointly promote this wholesome message would nearly all revolve around what Michael's Neverland Valley ranch looked like, what brand of clothing he purchases for his children, and whether or not I had ever seen him moonwalk. But neither did I shy away from those questions, believing that in time they would lead to more substantive inquiries. I mistakenly believed that the obsession with a personality would gradually yield to a curiosity for the message. But after a while, it is the personality that becomes the message, and you are just dragged along for the ride.

I am reminded of what Elie Wiesel, long a true hero of mine, once told me, in a discussion of the popular culture. "Shmuley," he said, "you don't want to believe in an 'us' and 'them' mentality. You want to believe that God's message can be channeled through any medium. But I fear that you will discover that the culture will first change you before you change it."

The Jews were brought into the world as witnesses to God's presence, and our highest mission must be to return God to the center of human life rather than being supplanted by the human personality. We do this by being advocates and exemplars of Godly living, responsible members of a spiritual community, loving spouses and parents, and devoted servants of the public good. The more attention we draw to ourselves, the more we subvert the reason for our being. Similarly, we dare not allow ourselves to live vicariously through our favorite celebrities in place of leading a purposeful and authentic existence.

This does not mean that all hero worship need necessarily lead to idolatry. Indeed, I have all my life longed to look up to, and be inspired by, great men and women. But I now understand that a true hero is the man or woman who makes God into the hero; someone who has subordinated his or her ego to a higher ideal, who has placed God and humanity at their core and who seek to highlight a spiritual message rather than just boost their ratings. It is fine to follow obsessively in the footsteps of the Lubavitcher Rebbe, the Pope, Billy Graham, Nelson Mandela, and Martin Luther King, Jr. Indeed, Hasidic Jews have pictures of the Rebbe up in their homes because his saintly life is a catalyst to emulate his own saintliness. The lives of these people are not arrows pointing to themselves, but vectors pointing to the heavens and to their fellow man. The same is even true of impressive sports icons like Kurt Warner of the St. Louis Rams who immediately declared, upon winning the MVP Award of the 2000 Super Bowl, that his achievement is entirely due to the glory of God. I have watched many times how, upon the completion of any game, he joins his teammates in a huddle prayer before running to indulge the media's questions. Indeed, his first reaction after winning the Super Bowl was to bow his head in prayer.

I do not seek to judge any celebrity who has allowed the public to get carried away with a fascination for the minutiae of their lives. But neither do I seek to propagate a love of the Creator through men and women who have not yet learned the lesson that God is the source of their glory, and that they only bask in the spotlight because God is the creator of light. Neither can I condone modern men and women allowing their human potential to remain so tragically underdeveloped as they indulge in discussions of whether their favorite actress will win the Oscar, rather than focusing on their need to achieve victories in the real game of life.

During interviews I conduct about relationships or religion, I am often asked about my association with Michael Jackson. I simply respond, "He is a decent man and a normal human being." In other words, he is not God. We dare never make any man or woman into an idol. According to Jewish tradition, this is the reason that God hid Moses' burial place, whose location remains a secret until this very day. It was to ward off the possible deification of Moses and the establishment of his sepulcher as a shrine. To be sure, Moses wrought great wonders in Egypt. But he was merely a conduit of God's awesome might.

Like many celebrities, Michael has devoted time and resources to promoting noble causes and deserves the credit for doing so. But it is the causes that must receive the attention. We dare not deify any man. In seeking to rectify the strong gravitational pull that a superstar can exert over one's life, I chose to decline Michael's kind invitation to his 30th Anniversary concert in New York the day before September 11. While I had always dreamed of seeing him live on stage—and he can truly thrill like no other—I wanted to know if I still had the power to resist the magnetic attraction of a favorite celebrity, if the fireworks display of the Madison Square Gardens posed a greater thrill for me than the thunder and lighting of Mt. Sinai.

I once enjoyed and sought out the limelight, and sometimes still do. But having had significant exposure to the celebrity culture and discovered that all false gods, including myself, are hollow representations of the real article, I now wish to dance to a more heavenly tune and have my heart beat to a more eternal rhythm.

Religion as an End in Itself

A realization first hit me in my twenty-second year when I began to assume the full responsibilities of a communal and university Rabbi at Oxford. Like so many of my colleagues, I lectured my students on the importance of never desecrating the Sabbath with mundane activities or anything relating to work, marrying within the faith, and celebrating the festivals, *because it was incumbent upon them to be good Jews.* I spoke of the beauty of Jewish life and Jewish tradition and how we could not allow ourselves to be the generation that severed the link with the faith of our ancestors. But an alarm should have gone off. Was I beginning to speak of religion as if it were an end in itself, as if the preservation of tradition and an adherence to Jewish law were the ultimate purpose of the Jew, instead of religion being the means by which man created a loving relationship with God?

The *akeida,* the binding of Isaac, presents one of the great paradoxes of the Bible. What *was* God's intention in commanding Abraham to murder his own son? Rabbi Menachem Schneerson, the Lubavitcher Rebbe, offers the illuminating insight that Isaac was more than just a person. He represented *Judaism.* The monotheistic faith that Abraham had fathered would continue only through Isaac. Ishmael had already gone off the path and become a pagan idolater. If Isaac died, Judaism would die with him. In essence, the test God presented to Abraham was to choose between his God and his religion. God gives you a command that pits His will against the essential tenets of your faith. Which would Abraham put first: his relationship with God or his religious rituals?

Would Abraham show that he was religiously inclined because he loved doctrine, theology, and ritual or because he loved God? Would Abraham destroy the faith he fathered if God commanded him to do so? Abraham passed the test, and both he and his son survived to establish God, for all ages to come, as Master of the Universe and centerpiece of religious devotion.

There are those who promote religion as an end in itself—a means by which man can be moral, rituals that lead to greater family cohesion, a method for curing man of his material lusts. In so doing, they are guilty of making religion, even monotheism, into an idol, a foreign god. For example, when people are killed in the name of religion, man forsakes God's commandment not to murder in favor of his own fervor for his faith and a hatred for the infidel. To most of us it is inconceivable that religion can be at odds with God.

Religious Fundamentalism

But what happens when the commandments themselves become idolatrous? No longer menaced by communism, the world is now threatened by religious fundamentalism. Far from being merely an abuse of religious goals, fundamentalism supplants God with religion itself. Religious fundamentalism is the contemporary world's most dangerous idol. We witnessed this most horribly in 2001 in the tragedy of the World Trade Center in New York and the Pentagon in Washington, D.C.

None of the major religions is immune from fundamentalism. Indeed, with every passing day, even some segments of Judaism are seen becoming more extreme, not to mention the truly evil incidents of Islamic suicide bombers or Christian extremists who assassinate abortion doctors. In Judaism, centrist Orthodoxy has largely ceased to exist, and very religious Jews are becoming more judgmental of those who adhere to lesser standards of observance. In condemning those who are less religious, they deify themselves and forget God, Who is the only judge.

The religious man is one whose heart is open to all his fellow beings. As the ancient Rabbis proclaimed: "Who is wise? He who learns from everyone."

There can be no question that religion can be the source of abundant goodness, spiritual light, and human love. But society today is in great danger of creating an idol of organized religion. The deification of religion constitutes the main reason for religious fundamentalism, wherein people are prepared to put the practice of their faith ahead of their relationship with God. Contrary to popular belief, fundamentalists are not God intoxicated. Rather, they are almost totally bereft of God, having replaced Him with the worship of ritual. In reality, they are intoxicated themselves. They have no relationship with God. For Osama bin Laden, God is not the Allah of the Koran. Instead, God is the projection of all Osama's bitter hatreds and prejudices. He creates God in *his* own image. If Osama hates America, then God hates America. And if Osama desires the slaughter of innocents, then be sure that God desires it too. Religious fundamentalists have far more in common with nationalists than with God worshipers. The religious fundamentalist is as distant from God as the world's staunchest atheist. Those who love and worship God are happy for people to embrace Him in any way they can. Their main priority is that God become central to people's lives. But religious fundamentalists actually get riled, to the point of violence, when people embrace God in a way of which they don't approve. They are not interested in promoting God, but rather in promoting their religion. We should stop calling terror organizations like Al Queda and the Hamas, religious extremists. Rather, we should refer to them for what they are: worshipers of their own petty prejudice.

What religious fundamentalists exhibit most is arrogance. They display neither compassion nor humility, the only gauge by which to determine whether an individual has achieved a proximity with God. As one comes closer to God, one experiences one's own insignificance in the face of divine perfection. Conceit and proximity to God are directly incompatible. The arrogant man, the know-it-all, for whom life is a destination rather than a journey, is too full of his own sense of importance to allow God to permeate his life. He is a full cup into which no spirituality can be poured. As Rabbi Israel Baal Shem Tov said, "There is no room for God in a person who is full of himself."

Modern-day Jewish Orthodoxy must be extremely careful lest they risk deifying the Halakhah, Jewish law, as a foreign God. We are witnessing a generation of Orthodox Jews who are not being weaned on God worship, but rather are being encouraged to be religiously observant. But there is no commandment in the Torah to observe ritual. Rather, there is a commandment to become Godly by observing ritual. God never commanded us to be *good* Jews, but *God-fearing* Jews. The individual who observes Jewish law because he wants to be religious is analogous to a man who is far more interested in being a good husband, in the generic sense, than in pleasing his particular wife. He devours every how-to book on becoming the perfect spouse, thereby glorying in the art of being a model husband, rather than focusing on making his wife happy. He does not focus on pleasing his wife, for she is a mere afterthought. He has not even begun to connect with her. Rather, this man is in a relationship with himself.

To be great scholars or be respected for their learning is not a reason for Jews to study the Torah. Rather, they must do so because they want to know what pleases their Master in Heaven. Intermarriage is wrong, not because it endangers the continuity of our people, but rather because it distances the individual from God, Who commanded the preservation of the Jewish faith community. Observing the Sabbath is mandatory, not for us to be good religious Jews, but rather because, since the Sabbath is God's day, desecrating it removes us from the divine countenance.

We are even seeing how Jewish law is being used to prevent Jews from coming closer to their Father in heaven. If we always followed the criterion that the purpose of Halakhah, Jewish law, is to establish a bond between God and man, then we would not make tragic mistakes that allow the Halakhah to become a fence isolating wayward

Jews from the Creator. A case in point: How could an Orthodox congregation possibly prevent a Reform Jew, or a Jew who drives on the Sabbath, from being called up to the Torah as was the case with many British Orthodox congregations when I lived there. Shouldn't the Halakhah facilitate greater observance on the part of all Jews so that they can recite a blessing on God's eternal law and be brought into God's tent? Does it make any sense to publicly castigate Jews who drive on the Sabbath or even to scream "Shabbes" at them—carried out in some religious neighborhoods in Israel—when all it will achieve is to push them further away from God? To be sure, homosexuality is forbidden by the Bible. But why aren't homosexuals lovingly encouraged to keep the rest of the commandments? Why are they ostracized from the community and from their God? And why are Jews who have married outside our faith not encouraged to participate in other areas of Jewish life to the best of their ability?

Reforming Judaism—changing or discarding ancient Jewish law—is not the answer, for it betrays an ignorance of the purpose of the law, mistakenly presuming that man may determine which laws, or threads of attachments, are more important to God than others. It is a denial of God as a living Presence whose intrinsic will is as relevant today as in the days of Abraham. Discarding tenets of Jewish law that have seemingly lost their modern relevance is analogous to a college student refusing to carry out an assignment from his or her professor on the grounds that the lecturer did not explain why the assignment was important.

By rejecting the supremacy of Jewish law as the consummate vehicle by which man comes close to God, and embracing a more palatable, comfortable, and rational Judaism, Reform Judaism, notwithstanding the nobility of its intentions, is guilty of rejecting God's right to be more than human—in fact, to be God, and thus not always accessible to temporal intelligence. Judaism is a deiocentric religion, not anthropocentric. God, not man, is at its center. And we dare not manufacture a God of convenience. It is arrogance on our part to believe that we can come close to God by virtue of our own devices or purity of motivation. Even a thoroughly decent man will not necessarily engender the love of a woman unless he shows her that he takes her needs seriously. The same is true of an ethical person who wants to be in a relationship with God.

The key to Jewish and universal religious rejuvenation is not to compromise the integrity of religious law, but rather to emphasize that the purpose of the law is to bring people closer to God. By fulfilling the divine will, we please the Creator and He lovingly embraces us in His bosom.

Judgmentalism

All too many of the religious individuals with whom I am in contact have, over time, become increasingly judgmental. Often, an increase in their judgment and condescension is commensurate with an increase in their observance. In fact, judging, rather than loving, one's fellow man seems to have become the central calling of many people's entire faith. It is ironic that one of the first steps that some Jews who return to their roots and to Jewish tradition take is to judge the lifestyles and values of those who are less observant than they. The Christian Right spends much of its time condemning the loose mores and lifestyles of the general population and especially of television and film. We even witnessed the truly lamentable spectacle of two leading Christian clergymen saying that September 11 happened because God had removed his protection from an increasingly sinful nation. I am not one to defend what I, too, see as an increasingly base popular culture. But the implication that American sin was the cause of September 11 is an abomination, and clerics making the assertion should be silenced. Moreover, I object to the belief that being judgmental or critical is the first calling of religion. Becoming born-again or more religously observant should be about embracing God rather than rejecting materialism. It should involve enhancing the light rather than condemning the darkness. The purpose of religion, from a Jewish perspective, is not to focus on the world *the way it is* and condemn it. Rather, it is to posit a realistic and positive vision of *the way the world ought to be* and to inspire the earth's inhabitants to realize that vision, or at the very least to take a few small steps in the right direction. The truly spiritual person finds it difficult to be dismissive of any person, place, or thing, because he perceives God to lie wherever his eyes roam.

Why do I contend that judgmentalism is the very antithesis of the religious experience? Why am I so vehemently opposed to religious censure? Because the whole purpose of religion is to provide a means by which the individual can experience God. Logically the closer one draws to God, the more awed one becomes with God's perfection and infinite expanse, and hence the more humble one becomes. Simply stated, the more we focus on God, the less we focus on ourselves. I accuse religious extremists of the error of taking *themselves* far too seriously. They have no humility. The first product of a true proximity with God should be abnegation of self. The religious extremist who is prepared to harm, maim, or murder in the name of God takes himself so seriously that he claims to know God's true wishes despite His express, written commandments. God says, "Thou shalt not murder." But the extremist modifies this to allow murder of the infidel, someone who professes a different faith.

Balance and Imbalance

If religion should humble us, how is it that it creates arrogant people? How could the perpetrators of the September 11 attack claim to be devout and pious Muslims? Why are there so many judges and juries in the camps of the believers? Why is there malice rather than mercy, cruelty rather than compassion, loathing rather than love, and rejection rather than recognition? Maimonides believed that good and evil are not two sides of a single coin. Instead, good is the perfectly balanced medium surrounded on both sides by extremes of evil. This fascinating concept suggests that goodness is found in balance, in maintaining an equilibrium between two extremes. And all forms of extremism are evil. Every individual who wishes to lead a healthy and balanced life must find the golden mean between assertion and denial of self. For a marriage to succeed, a husband and wife must know when they have a legitimate right to make demands and emphasize a need, and when they must bend and allow room for the other to grow. A parent must find the balance between strict discipline and hypercriticism on the one hand, and shirking responsibility through ignoring the child's mistakes and flaws on the other.

So too with religion. The successfully spiritual individual is he or she who strikes a balance between affirmation and abnegation of self. Certainly, God wants us to subordinate our ego and will to His. He wants us to put what is important to Him well before that which is important to us. He wants us to lead a life in accordance with religious teachings and moral guidelines, irrespective of our appreciation or understanding of their merit. However, the Almighty does not want automatons or robots who worship Him. Having endowed man with the most precious of all gifts, the freedom to choose to be what he desires, the Almighty wishes for man to choose what is right. The Almighty wishes for us to seek to understand His law amidst a general posture of obedience. Subjugation of self means making God's will central to one's being. Affirmation of self means retaining the right to choose and pursuing one's own agenda.

Judaism has a built-in mechanism to assist man in achieving a balance between being a self-asserting individual on the one hand, and an obedient servant of God on the other. This is one of the principal reasons I revere the Jewish faith. It is composed of two important cornerstones of Judaism, the fulfillment of mitzvahs (mitzvot, or divine commandments) *and* the study of Torah. Observing the mitzvahs entails a supreme subordination of the human will to God's will. A believer might want to go skiing on the Sabbath, but he must rest. He might prefer, when he travels, to be able to have a hot meal at any restaurant, but if it is not kosher, he cannot. Although he may not understand or appreciate any of these divine strictures, he must still bow his head in submission and live within God's rules. This is the side of Judaism that demands obedience.

Nevertheless, God commanded that man study the Torah and apprehend the divine will to the best of his ability so that he might develop a deep appreciation for God's law. The Almighty willed not only that humans subordinate themselves but also that they elevate themselves by becoming bound with body, mind, and spirit with the Divine Presence. Man asserts his own unique gifts in comprehending God's laws, rather than just submitting to that which is greater than himself.

This is also the reason Judaism *insists* that every man or woman of faith strive to incorporate within themselves the dual, and seemingly antithetical, virtues of love and fear of God. Fear of God is represented by the man of faith who cowers in the face of God, who stands in awe and humility, abnegating his person to the all-encompassing majesty of the Divine Presence. Love of God is represented by the man of faith who feels himself to be in a relationship with God, who feels that God needs him as much as he needs God. These two antithetical emotions are described in Jewish mystical thought as being "like the two wings of a bird without which the bird cannot fly." The laws of propulsion dictate that there must be opposing forces pushing from opposite sides in order for the bird to achieve flight.

The same is true for the religious believer. One cannot develop spiritually and raise oneself above the mundaneity of life unless one focuses on the will of God and on one's responsibility to be sensitive to God's will and to make oneself secondary to it, yet never compromises one's humanity in the process. Religion is about the paradox of being present and absent simultaneously. God does not desire that in the course of fulfilling His will we cease to feel the beautiful human traits of compassion, joy, mercy, tolerance, fraternity, gratitude, and empathy. By doing mitzvahs and fearing God, we become spiritual. By studying Torah and loving God, we become human. We elevate and enhance, rather than repress and suppress, our natural human condition.

The religious extremist fails on both counts. He has no humility because he begins to see himself as being inseparable from God. He talks himself into believing that whatever he feels or does is the will of God. To be sure, in his warped mind he sees himself as an obedient servant who is subordinated to God's will. But the disdain he feels for God's children betrays his arrogance. Yigal Amir decided that Yitzhak Rabin was a traitor who deserved death. Instead of thinking to himself, "Who am I? Even if I think this, I am not God, and my opinion is of no real significance," he decided that becoming judge and executioner would meet with favor in the God's eyes. Osama bin Laden decided that he alone understood God's true will, even though that understanding directly contradicted everything that God revealed through His prophets. Here we have the most dangerous facet of religious extremism. When the believer can no longer distinguish between himself and God and believes that because he is religious, he is closer to God than those who are not like him, virtually any form of cruelty rests in his power. *He has granted himself the divine license to create and destroy life.*

The religious fanatic fails in the development of a human self as well, since he suppresses his natural love and empathy for his fellow man in his belief that God would have wished him to do so. He dismisses his humanity in the corrupt belief that it hinders him from carrying out a divine imperative. God does not want him to love the heretic, but to destroy him. Here we come to the second most dangerous facet of religious extremism. A human being becomes a dangerous religious fanatic whenever he concludes that his humanity is incompatible with his religion, that his empathic feelings are an impediment to his faith. God does not want us to suppress our humanity, but rather to cultivate our goodness and holiness by channeling our actions to works of public and private utility. The fanatic abhors this notion. Hatred is his God. Murder is his ritual.

What the religious fanatic and the complete atheist, like Lenin or Stalin, have in common, and the reason that their barbarism is potentially limitless, is that neither answers to a higher moral authority. The atheist does not believe in God, only in human constructs. He himself, or a collective humanity, becomes the ultimate arbiter of his morality. With this in mind, one shudders to think what would have happened had Hitler won the war and imposed a Nazi ethic on the world. Likewise, the religious fundamentalist, in that he cannot distinguish between himself and God and thereby equates his own whims and decisions with those of the Creator, has no higher moral authority and is thus capable of any inhuman atrocity. In the same way that Hitler and Stalin made themselves into gods, the fundamentalist uses his powers of delusion to persuade himself that everything he thinks or does comes directly from God. Thus he can do no evil.

Bringing God Back

When I began my rabbinical studies at the age of fourteen, I quickly found myself lost amid the myriad details of a truly vast religion. I went in despair to the head of my Yeshiva, an elderly and learned sage, and asked him to sum up the whole of Judaism for me in a single axiom. He held my shoulders lovingly as if I were his only son and said, "The essence of Judaism is this: Take God very seriously, and never ever take yourself seriously."

God must be restored to Judaism, and every other religion, as its raison d'être. The true test of the authenticity of any system of faith is the degree to which God is at its epicenter. As a warm, engaging, loving, and benevolent Creator, He will serve as the foremost incentive for less observant secular Jews to reembrace their faith. And a God who is resolutely returned to all elements of Orthodox Judaism will breed a new humility, thereby destroying the destructive effects of judgmentalism and opening the doors of Jewish spirituality to all who wish to drink of its life-giving waters.

8

Prayer

Finding the Hidden Within the Apparent

If thou shouldst never see my face again,
Pray for my soul. More things are wrought by prayer
Than this world dreams of.

—ALFRED LORD TENNYSON,
"The Passing of Arthur"

Pray: To ask the laws of the universe to be annulled on behalf
of a single petitioner confessedly unworthy.

—AMBROSE BIERCE,
The Devil's Dictionary

Prayer is not asking. It is a longing of the soul. It is daily ad-
mission of one's weakness. . . . It is better in prayer to have a
heart without words than words without a heart.

—MOHANDAS K. GANDHI

AS A YOUNG BOY, I OFTEN WITNESSED MY PARENTS ARGUING.
Their discord left them in their own world of pain, and I remember
feeling lonely. But it was also at this age, not yet eight, that I started
concentrating on the words of my daily prayers. They comforted me

and shielded me from loneliness. In prayer I was sensitized to the omnipresence of God; He is always with me. "He heals the broken-hearted, and binds up their wounds" (Ps. 147:3). I felt that God would never abandon me and I would never be alone.

Now, many years later, I am a Rabbi with a family of my own. Sadly, prayer is not the same companion it once was. Consumed with myriad responsibilities, I, like so many other religious people, go about my daily prayers in a manner designed to discharge my obligation. Rather than enjoying the journey, I rush to the finish line.

Imagine a man who is impoverished and forlorn, inhabiting a small shack on the edge of town. Because of his weakness, he is regularly harassed by passing army troops who ransack his meager food supplies and steal his cattle. They have no fear of being brought to justice because the man from whom they steal has no protector to whom he can turn. Then one day they watch as the old man slowly clambers up the steep hill to the king's castle, is admitted to the royal throne room, and cries out to the king to end his suffering at the hands of the royal soldiers.

This story illustrates precisely what prayer is all about. There can be no greater distinction for man than to know that God listens when he cries out. That the Supreme Creator of heaven and earth suspends all His affairs and listens to the distressed wail of His human children when they are in pain gives humankind incomparable dignity. Human beings attain significance because they can commune with the Divine. In *Who Is Man?* Abraham Joshua Heschel, one of twentieth-century American Jewry's most eminent thinkers, writes, "Dark for me is the world for all its bright cities and shiny stars, if not for the knowledge that God listens to me when I cry." Prayer is like a bright ray of sun that penetrates a dark and gloomy day. Indeed, if not for the knowledge that we expose the wounds of our hearts to the One above, who could tolerate being immersed in a world of such misery? The ear of God lifts us from the realm of forlorn paupers to the majestic heights of princehood. Like a parent who cannot turn away when her child breaks into tears, each of us is God's beloved child, and He listens intently to our voice.

But our generation has little understanding of, and even less appreciation for, the emotional prayer. One of the reasons that accounts for this loss is that we have lost an admiration for the power of words. In Judaism, words are of surpassing importance. The Bible relates how God created the world with words rather than action: "He *said*, 'Let there be light, and there was light.'" This same truth is reflected in everyday life. We use words to create other people. Give someone a compliment, offer him a kind word when he is feeling low, and watch him come to life. A man who works at a sewing machine churning out hundreds of garments per month feels ignored and unimportant until his boss comes by one day and tells him what an excellent job he is doing. Similarly, one abusive and angry word can make us feel nonexistent and existentially threatened. Indeed, words are the channels of creative consciousness. Without words our thoughts would remain locked in our minds like a wellspring covered by arid earth.

Why do words have such power? Because they are the fountain of the soul and the stream of human consciousness. Words, the very fiber of revelation, convey our spirit. They are the pipeline through which all sentiment must pass. Words represent a transcendent human capacity to rise above our own sphere and touch another human life. The words I use in conversation are a reflection and an effusion of my innermost essence. But they not only reflect the condition of my own soul; they also have the capacity to shape another soul. Words of prayer are the very bricks from which is built the bridge connecting God and man.

Prayer Transforms God into a Living Reality

The ancient Rabbis identified several core ideas underlying the concept of prayer:

Prayer Causes Man to Acknowledge His Dependency on God. Far from serving only as a link joining the finite and the infinite, prayer is *the* supreme act of faith because it makes God a living reality. Where

and to whom we turn in instances of great peril is an indication of
our most deeply held beliefs. In moments of crisis, when man, rather
than calling out for human assistance, raises his eyes and lips heavenward and entreats his Creator for salvation, he acknowledges that
God is the Master of the world and that nothing can happen—for
better or for worse—without His authority. Nobel Prize–winning author Isaac Bashevis Singer said, "Whenever I am in trouble, I pray.
And since I'm always in trouble, I pray a lot." Relying on God rather
than mere human intervention and calling out to Him in prayer is
the oldest tradition within Judaism. It was the hallmark of the patriarchs, who, according to the ancient Sages, instituted the three daily
prayers of morning, afternoon, and evening.

In its purest sense, Judaism is an affirmation of the personal God
of history and a refutation of the indifferent God of the deists.
Prayer is an acknowledgment that God alone can provide comfort
and redemption. A friend whose marriage was crumbling told me
that he had done everything to keep it together, from going to marriage counselors to taking his wife away on a safari, all to no avail.
"Nothing has worked," he told me, "and I am now ready to give
up." "Have you tried praying?" I asked him. "If you could open
your heart to God in prayer, you may also prove capable of opening
your heart to your wife's love and needs." It seems that we pray
only after we have exhausted every other route. When humans call
out to God to provide sustenance for themselves and their families,
they translate God from an irrelevant abstraction to a living and
tangible force with a direct impact on the world. Prayer is greater
than faith because faith causes man only to think or feel; prayer
forces him to act.

By praying we effectively proclaim, *Let there be more God in this
world.* Let us cause all the earth to recognize His name. Let His glory
illuminate the dark corners of the earth and the dingy alleys of the
mind. There is nothing so inspiring, so moving, and so ultimately
liberating as watching a man or woman approach the holy ark of the
synagogue, long after the other congregants have left, and implore
God for mercy, as tears moisten his or her cheeks.

In everyday religious living, God is not felt so much as trusted. To be sure, the person of faith believes in God and tries to live by His dictates. But He is still relegated to the realm of the distant and obscure. In prayer God becomes intimate and close. He becomes necessary. Like a lover pining for the touch of his beloved, man yearns for the warmth of God.

Prayer Is the Guarantor of Humility, the Prerequisite for a Relationship with God. One of life's great conundrums is reconciling greatness with humility. On the one hand, Judaism spurs humans to action, bidding them to tame nature and erect a glorious edifice fit for the King of kings. On the other hand, we humans are not to grow arrogant from our achievements. Whereas the ancient Rabbis counseled moderation in our emotions, when it came to humility, they encouraged man to go to an extreme: "Be very, very humble, for the ultimate hope of man is to become food for the worms." Indeed, the greatest Jew of all time was also the most humble: "And the man Moses was the most humble man that was on the face of the earth" (Num. 12:3). How could a man who spoke with God face-to-face have possibly been humble?

If I were a teacher of nuclear physics in a high school, I could feel that I knew more than most people about my subject. I could feel arrogant because I was knowledgeable in such a difficult field. But if I were invited to work together with Albert Einstein in his laboratory, I would immediately discover that everything I *thought* I knew was meaningless compared to Einstein's grasp of the subject. I would come to terms with my own inadequacies and stand humbled in the face of true greatness. This is what happened with Moses, but infinitely more so. Because Moses had stood closer than any other to God, he was also the most humble man who ever lived. The result of such close proximity with God was the complete abnegation of self. Having enjoyed the constant and lifelong presence of God, Moses felt himself to be insignificant and unworthy.

Humility is the essence of religion because it is the only way to measure our closeness to God. The closer we become, the more spiritual and humble we feel, which is why holiness is always accompanied by humility. We could never imagine an arrogant saint. In the face of eternal life, we come to know our own mortality. In the face of infinite light, we come to experience our own darkness. In the face of omniscience, we come to understand our own ignorance. And in the face of boundless compassion, we come to feel our own selfishness.

If humility is the prerequisite for Godliness, then prayer is its guarantor. Man, in being forced to acknowledge his dependence on God, becomes aware of his own limitations. By supplicating God, rather than relying on his own devices, man goes to the opposite end of his ego.

Praying from a Book Versus Free-Style Prayer.   On one level, prayer is about asking God for our daily needs; on a higher level, prayer is a reminder to man of what is important in life. If we had a child who was sick, in the hospital, would we pray to God for a larger, more luxurious car or wall-to-wall carpeting? The history of humankind is one of mistaken priorities and muddled values. Part of prayer's supreme purpose is to recalibrate our desires. Prayer takes us away from the strict confines of thinking of everything in terms of pure self-interest. When we do take a journey far away to the opposite end of our ego, we are suddenly empowered to see life from the vantage point of the Divine. When we listen to the words of the prayers and open our hearts to their power, we focus on life's meaning and purpose. When a man prays daily for the health of his children, he is reminded of how much more important they are than spending more time at the office.

We must rethink our entire approach to prayer. Rather than seeing it merely as an opportunity to come before God and request our daily bread, prayer conditions us to renew our commitment to God, family, and friends—because what else does a man pray for than his family's health, his community's well-being, and peace on earth? Prayer is like a chorus of bells going off in the mind, alerting us to the human mission and obliterating our false illusions: "My God, guard my tongue from evil and my lips from speaking deceitfully. Let my soul be silent to those who curse me . . . open my heart to Your Torah; and let my soul eagerly pursue Your commandments" (concluding prayer of the Amida, the daily silent prayer service).

In this light, prayer takes place not only when we open our mouths to God in supplication. It is like a daily heavenly lecture in which God exhorts us never to get distracted from life's most important purpose. Jewish prayer is recited in Hebrew; the text comes from the Siddur, the Jewish prayer book, which includes Psalms and an order of blessings arranged by the men of the Great Assembly more than two thousand years ago. Many have complained that the rigidity of a set prayer book is stultifying and impedes individual concentration. They object to having to pray in a foreign language rather than their mother tongue, and they protest at having a fixed text composed of words that were consecrated and written thousands of years ago. My students tell me that they would rather take a banjo out into the fields and "sing a new song to the Lord" that is both personal and spontaneous. They feel stultified and uninspired in having to pray from a prepared text.

Their objections miss a crucial point. *The great secret of Jewish prayer is that it is not about talking, but listening; not about beseeching, but imbibing.* We awaken in the morning and pray to God, not so much to praise Him as to listen to the beautiful words that remind us of His omnipresence and that it is to Him that all terms of endearment should be offered.

The words of the prayer book are like a chisel that slowly carves away our stony edges and fashions us into divine beings. These words tenderize our hearts so that we may serve the one, true God. Jewish prayer is an art where man remains silent and allows the ancient prayers to ignite his soul and fashion his heart. Reading the Jewish prayers, then, is like walking though an art gallery and being inspired by timeless masterpieces. We derive inspiration from great paintings, which bring out the natural color and vibrancy of our soul. Prayer calls upon us to hearken to the eternal voice from Sinai demanding that we always place the Almighty in a position of preeminence: "I am the Lord your God. You shall have no other Gods before Me."

This is not to say that there are not moments when we have to offer our own personal prayer. On the contrary. Judaism recognizes two principal forms of prayer, the empathetic and the inspirational. Empathetic prayer is designed to create a spiritual emotion and ambiance—this is what I have been discussing. It is carried out even when a person may not be in the mood to pray. He or she awakens in the morning, anxious to get on with his or her many daily responsibilities. He or she is harried by the overwhelming burden of living, holding a job, and supporting a family. But he or she is religious, so he dons his tefillin (leather boxes containing biblical passages on parchment) and begins to pray. She covers her eyes and recites the Shema. Slowly, by concentrating on the meaning of the words, each begins to empathize with their power. They awaken within him or her a desire to draw near to God and worship Him sincerely. The person no longer feels so anxious to go out and make money. Experiencing the splendor of God, becoming worthy of the Divine Presence, and showing compassion to humanity become as important goals to him or her in the coming day as earning the respect of peers and moving up the corporate ladder. "Bestow peace, goodness and blessing, life graciousness, kindness and mercy, upon us and upon all Your people Israel . . . for by the light of Your countenance You give us . . . righteousness, blessing, mercy, life, and peace." What began as words in the daily Amida prayer ends up becoming our deepest longing and our greatest desire. In prayer we are taught what to wish for.

There is also inspirational prayer, which is far more spontaneous. It occurs when man is moved to offer thanks to God for the wonders of creation. One sees a beautiful sunset and is suddenly moved to praise God, who makes such beauty possible. One witnesses a relative recovering from illness and is moved to offer thanks to the Fountainhead of all life, the Healer of all illness. Surely, we all have experienced moments in which the splendor of creation so overtakes us that we feel the need to offer homage and praise to "He who spoke and brought the world into being."

As a sixteen-year-old rabbinical student, I found myself pulled toward a scene on the streets of Jerusalem one evening when a large crowd of people had gathered around a young girl who had been hit by a taxi. She was bleeding profusely and looked lifeless. I watched in horror as the paramedics tried to revive her, but there were no vital signs. Suddenly, she moved her hand and opened her eyes. I can still recall my feeling of elation. I felt that God was good and I had to thank Him. I ran through the darkened Jerusalem night singing and dancing the words of Psalm 92: "It is good to give thanks to the Lord, to sing praises to your name, O Most High; to declare your steadfast love in the morning, and your faithfulness by night" (Ps. 92:2–3). Rarely have I danced so joyously and so spontaneously, and rarely have I experienced so innate a desire to offer gratitude to God.

Although inspirational prayer is important, the rule should be prayer as empathy, where man comes to be educated by the process of prayer. In empathetic prayer, man opens his heart to God, thus making himself into a receptacle for the Divine. Rather than our trying to tell God how much our heart swells over with love and thanksgiving, we are giving God Himself the opportunity to tell us what He is in His essence and how He can be discovered. Inspirational prayer allows us to discover God in certain places and at certain moments. Empathetic prayer teaches us to uncover the hidden God in all places and at all moments.

Prayer As Hope. Hebrew prayer is also the vehicle of hope. For two thousand years, the Jewish prayer book has been the embodiment of Jewish hopes for the return to our homeland and our reconstitution as an independent people, free from pogrom and persecution, living openly once again as the chosen and beloved of God. In prayer, a tormented and beleaguered people could look up to the Almighty and see their future with optimism. Prayer is a statement of man's refusal to be reconciled to the mistakes of his past or to the fate of his future. It is man at his most defiant. When we pray, even the most outlandish wishes enter the realm of possibility. We pray for the redemption of mankind in general, and of the Jewish nation in particular. We pray for the ingathering of Jewish exiles and even for the resurrection of the dead. And since the former, however improbable for two thousand years of exile, has now come to pass, why not believe in the latter? If the Jewish nation could be resurrected from the dead, why not the individual? In a paraphrase of the famous and oft-quoted statement of Theodor Herzl concerning Zionism, "If you will it, it is no dream," the Jewish outlook on the future might be rendered thus: "If you *pray* for it, it is no dream." Prayer gives us the hope that we are capable of translating our goals into realities. The divine ear is never deaf to our cry, and we understand how God will never forsake us. He will always be at our side as we seek to make the things we pray for into things we live for.

Perhaps the ultimate purpose of Jewish prayer is to serve as the pivotal bulwark against callous indifference. The man who does not pray is the man who has given up hope. He reads of the terrible suffering of his human brethren on the opposite side of the globe and then turns the page of the newspaper to another story. But the man who prays cannot simply turn the page. In reading of the suffering of another human being, he can at the very least offer a prayer on that person's behalf. He can raise his eyes heavenward and ask the Almighty to have mercy on all aspects of His creation. In so doing, he shows that he is not indifferent to the evil of this world. And chances are that he will also choose to send money, volunteer, or offer other assistance. But not to pray is to surrender unconditionally to the capricious nature of random events. By praying, we dare to hope.

What Is Prayer?

It is important to distinguish between prayer and superstition. The ancient beliefs of pagan, pre-Judaic humanity were largely governed by superstitions resulting from a sense of fear. Man turned to the gods of his invention, not out of love, but as an acknowledgment of helplessness in the face of the elements. At the other end of the spectrum, modern-day man has largely ceased praying, because he feels himself to be self-sufficient. Somewhere in between is a perfect religious medium in which man comes to God, not only to ward off earthquakes and volcanoes, but also to find sublimity and redemption. Whereas ancient man primarily prayed to avert disaster, the sincere man of faith prays to raise himself from the mundaneness of earthly existence and to bring true and eternal meaning to his otherwise shallow, materialistic pursuits.

Modern-day man may be prepared to call out to God for salvation, but only in the face of insuperable adversity. If his son is ill, he will first call out to the best doctors. Only when they have given up hope will he pick up the vocation of his ancestors and cry out to God, the way Moses did when he prayed for the recovery of his sister, Miriam. By so doing, man reduces prayer to nothing more than superstitious sentimentalism, a mantra to ward off demons. He forgets that Moses was in constant communication with God. Moses did not turn to the Almighty only when distressed.

This arrogance has repercussions well beyond the religious sphere, and it is not merely the invisible God who is rejected by mankind's newly found self-reliance. Marriages today dissolve because people are afraid of becoming too dependent. We *love* today, but we don't *need* to the same degree as yesterday. Prayer is a tacit acknowledgment that God needs to be needed. The ancient Rabbis stated that there is nothing that makes God happier than to receive the heartfelt supplications of people in need. And we are all in need, constantly. God wants us to feel that without Him we are lost. In referring to the Deity, King Solomon said, "How much better is your love than wine, and the fragrance of your oils than any spice!" (Song 1:2–3). Indeed, numerous verses in the Prophets refer to the sweet savory offering that God finds in the sacrifices in the Temple, which today are supplanted by the daily morning, afternoon, and evening prayer services. Like two lovers who steal time during their working day to meet alone, the man of faith runs to meet his Creator thrice daily, offering love and praise.

Prayer is not only an act of communication between God and man. Rather, it is a time for man to open his heart to Godly consciousness, so that man can become the object of God's thoughts. Like a man who loves a woman and who will do anything to get her attention, and looks for moments in which she can be reminded of his existence, prayer is man's attempt to become the center of God's attention. In prayer man aspires to create a dialogue with God so that he can be the subject of God's affections.

The Siddur Sensitizes Man to the Everyday Blessings of Life. The Jewish prayers are designed not only to communicate the glory of God, but also to sensitize man to the presence of God in every aspect of his life. Man is a curious creature, one who seems capable of appreciating his blessings only when they are taken from him. He tends to value everything in retrospect, finding guilt and regret in not having taken advantage of his faculties while they were still in bloom. What a radical difference it can make, therefore, for man to be reminded daily of the infinite blessings that surround him in life. The message: Appreciate what you have while you have it! Prayer therefore instills appreciation while safeguarding against insatiability. Man is a creature that focuses far more on what he lacks than on what he possesses. Discontent is his natural state. A great Rabbi once said that in material things a man should always feel satisfied, whereas in matters of the spirit, he should always be hungry. Unfortunately, the reverse is usually true. People always seem to want more money, but rarely more learning or a more refined character. Prayer provides a remedy to this situation by sensitizing man to the miracles that surround him and to the God who accompanies him at every turn. Jewish prayers are primarily concerned with finding God in everyday life.

In finding God in all aspects of creation, man comes to identify his own spiritual character. Prayer is a supreme act of self-awareness in which man comes to know not only the transcendent, external deity but also the inner Godliness that constitutes his deepest self. Prayer is a mirror to our Godly soul and the window by which man comes to fathom the magic and mystery—the hidden layer of Godliness—that pervades the universe. Immediately upon awakening, the Jew offers a prayer to God for restoring his soul after the death-like experience of sleep. The next blessings enumerate the wonderful gifts that are restored to us daily and to which man becomes desensitized through overfamiliarity. Among others, we thank God for giving us sight, clothing our nakedness, granting us the dignity of walking with erect posture after the natural curvature of sleep, and renewing our strength so that we can face another day.

The Jewish prayers continue with the rhythmic words of Psalms, which have a dual purpose: alerting us to the presence of God in the everyday and extolling His greatness. "You open Your hand, and satisfy the need of every living thing" (Ps. 145:16). "The Lord watches over the strangers; he upholds the orphan and the widow, but the way of the wicked he brings to ruin" (Ps. 146:9). "He covers the heavens with clouds, prepares rain for the earth, makes grass grow on the hills. He gives to the animals their food, and to the young ravens when they cry" (Ps. 147:8–9).

The Jewish prayer service then continues with the quintessential statement of Jewish faith: the proclamation of the absolute unity of God in the Shema, "Hear O Israel, the Lord [is] our God, the Lord is One." Thereafter, the service reaches its peak of intensity with the Amida, recited standing and at a volume audible only to oneself and to the Creator. The Amida serves as the anchor of every Jewish prayer service. Having discovered God in the awe and splendor of empirical existence, the worshipers are ready to enter before the King. In his throne room, we stand before Him as humble servants and request our most basic needs, while offering praise to His majesty.

According to tradition, the Amida prayer was instituted by a woman, Hannah, the mother of the prophet Samuel. Having been barren for many years, she came to the Holy Temple in Jerusalem and prayed for a child silently, something that had never been done before.

> Hannah was praying silently; only her lips moved, but her voice was not heard; therefore Eli, the High Priest, thought she was drunk. So Eli said to her, "How long will you make a drunken spectacle of yourself? Put away your wine." Eli ordered her out of the Temple. But she responded, "No, my lord, I am a woman deeply troubled; I have drunk neither wine nor strong drink, but I have been pouring out my soul before the Lord." (1 Sam. 1:13–15)

This silent form of prayer was ultimately adopted by the Jews and instituted by the Rabbis as the common form of Jewish prayer—to pray out of a spirit of meditative contrition and sadness.

Prayer As a Response to Mortality and the Existential Crisis. Today, most people resort to prayer only in moments of crisis, which most of us define purely in external terms. Ancient man was moved to pray to his gods upon witnessing a solar eclipse, the eruption of a volcano, the jolt of an earthquake, or the failure of his crops. Today we turn to God during extreme financial hardship or debilitating illness. Substantiating the need to cry out to God in moments of external threat, the ancient Rabbis even point out the biblical obligation for the Jewish community to assemble and pray in moments of significant peril, such as the invasion of a foreign enemy or the spread of a deadly plague.

This attitude blinds us to the ultimate truth that life itself involves unending inner crisis. The man of faith, as a sensitive and feeling individual, prays on a daily basis because he understands that real distress is not external, but internal. To live is to be in constant conflict, even when all appears to be going well. Life itself is filled with loneliness, foreboding, anxiety. Every day human beings are forced to question themselves and their direction in life. Nor does distress come upon man sporadically. It is experienced daily. Human existence is itself a *tzarah*, a crisis, every day bringing cause for insecurity and stress. Sometimes man contemplates his existence and recognizes that he is trapped on an island in a vast, impersonal universe, that his life and all his achievements are transient and that he amounts to no more than a drop of cosmic dust that will vanish with the wind. At such moments he shudders at his own helplessness. When he realizes that no one, even his most cherished relatives, can ever fathom his individual pain, and that death will ultimately render his existence meaningless, his life becomes a crisis. The man of deep sensitivity understands that all of life is but a faint glimmer, a fading ray, in the face of eternal darkness.

When men and women delve deeply into the tenuous nature of human relationships, the capriciousness of human existence, the unpredictability and fragility of human life, when we stare into the vast and infinite abyss of space and look back on our own insignificance, we begin to experience the intense and personal pain that existentialists call *vertigo*. The feeling was beautifully expressed by King Solomon in Ecclesiastes: "For the fate of men and the fate of the beast—they have one and the same fate: as one dies, so dies the other, and they all have the same spirit. Man has no superiority over beast, for all is vanity. All go to the same place; all originate from dust and return to dust" (3:19–20).

In these moments of vulnerability, man finds refuge in his source, the only Being in the cosmos who can understand his pain and who will never reject him. Prayer, then, is not a religious rite, but a psychological need. It is the cure to existential loneliness. Without prayer, life becomes a game of endless distractions that keep us from staring into the abyss. Only in the infinitely compassionate bosom of God can man be anything but alone. To pray, then, is to address the human crisis. To call out to God from the depths of our heart is to address the pain that festers at the core of our personality. "The sum of the matter, when all has been considered: fear God and keep His commandments, for that is the whole of Man" (Eccles. 12:14).

Prayer As a Response to the Human Need to Be Understood.   There is a second way in which prayer relieves human loneliness. Every human being goes through three levels of loneliness. The first is simply "aloneness," a feeling of isolation, which can be remedied simply by superficial social interactions, by being around other people. All of us, especially those who live alone, feel the occasional need to go to a public place and hear the normal everyday banter of our fellow humans. It's this simple drive that makes something like a shopping mall so infinitely attractive.

The second level is what we may call "loneliness" itself, a feeling of lacking, not of love, but *appreciation*. Man is the only being who is aware of his aloneness. Even when he is in the midst of a big crowd, he may still feel alone. Often, the very existence of the crowd itself—the fact that a person becomes just a small atom in a huge society—becomes the source of man's aloneness. The reason for this is that all of us want to feel special. The greatest human need is actually to become needed. Each of us wants to be wanted, needs to be needed, desires to be desired. We want to feel that we have a unique contribution to make to the world. This type of loneliness results not from lacking someone who loves us, but rather from not having someone who *needs* our love. It is rooted deeply in the soul and is remedied by entering into a loving relationship with a person who tells us that he or she *needs* us, is dependent on us, that the sun wouldn't seem to shine tomorrow if we were not around. Since all human beings are deficient, we rely on one another for mutual enrichment. Finding no one to value our unique gift is the virtual equivalent of death, and more than a few people have taken their lives after feeling abandoned by their loved ones and the world. We all seek to share our lives with a man or woman who, if we didn't wake up tomorrow morning, would be fundamentally broken. We all wish to be the sun to a darkened planet, one that requires our light.

But there is a third level of loneliness, orders of magnitude more heart-wrenching than the previous two. Contained deep within our hearts and souls is the desire to be *understood*. The deepest loneliness is the fear that we will never be fully known, that there is no one who can truly fathom our depths or fully grasp our pain, that no one will ever join us in our deepest spaces. True loneliness is having an ache that no one can heal, an aspect of ourselves that no one can comprehend. And here is the greatest paradox of human existence. What makes me special is that there is no one else like me. But what guarantees my individuality also assures my isolation and loneliness. If I am me, then no one else can ever fully understand me. Here lies the reason so many choose to become conformists. All they are looking for is companionship, and they believe that in order really to bond with somebody else, they must first relinquish their uniqueness. Before entering into a relationship you must first forfeit part of yourself so that you and your partner may find common ground. Every relationship, then, involves a compromise of one's personality and character. Although it may serve a higher purpose, it is a significant concession nonetheless.

In this recognition lies perhaps the loftiest purpose for prayer. Man cries out to God as the only Being in the universe who can truly understand man *without* his having to compromise himself. Even the most loving marriage or the most trusted friend can never completely alleviate human loneliness. Your spouse can love you, and your friend can comfort you. But they can never fully understand you, hence the separate relationship with God. Since God is the architect of man and the provider of his soul, He can comfort us in our loneliness without our conceding our individuality. Upon recognizing his isolation, man needs someone to talk to and confide in, and he calls out to the Almighty. Prayer is an acknowledgment that only God can enter the innermost recesses of our hearts, only He can fully grasp our pain and comfort us from loneliness.

Despite the fundamentally solitary nature of prayer, Judaism insists that prayer is best conducted within a quorum of at least ten individuals. This is curious. Is it not much better to pray on one's own, when one can bring forth the deepest emotions from one's heart? Is not prayer the natural effusion of supplication and praise from the individual to His Creator? Is this not a private act? Why pray in a synagogue being watched by others?

Some people believe that the principal goal of man is personal salvation. To them man's first concern must always be to climb the mountain of righteousness for himself, to ensure that his every act and thought is just and pure. Judaism rejects this view. From the vantage point of Judaism, it is not personal salvation but *world redemption* that is man's first responsibility. Therefore, when man comes before God to express his deepest desires, when he calls forth his most private thoughts, he must do so in the company of the community. For although his words remain private, his prayers must not be only for himself.

Separation of the Sexes in Prayer

In most world religions, prayer, especially the institutionalized variety, is a moment of profound joy and security. One sits together with one's spouse and children in the place of worship and sings inspirational hymns that overwhelm the senses and satiate the spirit. Not so in Judaism. In the synagogue, men and women, husbands and wives, sit separately during the prayer services because prayer is not about feeling security and hope but about loneliness, dread, despair, and helplessness. "From the depths I called to you, Lord"—the Psalmist reminds us that real prayer takes place when we cry out to God, not from the broad spaces, but from the abyss. Man prays to God upon experiencing his own sense of vulnerability.

Prayer is not a time for a man to feel that his family is his greatest blessing. Nor is prayer inspired when feeling surrounded by the consoling presence of one's family. Rather, it is a time for men and women to feel completely dependent on God and understand that even their spouse, who is their foremost happiness, comes as a gift from God, humankind's ultimate and constant companion. In prayer we approach God as individuals, not as a collective or as a family. The Psalmist proclaims: "I will sing to the Lord with my soul; I will chant praises to my God with my entire being. Do not place your trust in munificent benefactors, in mortal man, for he does not have the ability to bring deliverance. When his spirit departs, he returns to his earth; on that very day, his plans come to naught. Fortunate is he whose help is the God of Jacob, whose hope rests upon the Lord his God" (Ps. 146:1–5). The separation in prayer conveys the idea that amid the beautiful relationships that surround us, our love for and attachment to God must always come first. Prayer is a time to experience awe rather than comfort, trepidation rather than ease.

In Orthodox Judaism men and women sit separately when praying, and there is a visible divider between them. Judaism, as a pragmatic religion, understands that a visible man or woman may win out against the invisible God. Prayer requires intense concentration, and minimizing distraction is therefore a primary consideration. Yet, in this age of liberalism and egalitarianism, many profess a profound sense of discomfort upon witnessing the separation of the sexes in Jewish houses of prayer.

I could increase the number of people who participate in our prayer services tenfold if I simply got rid of the *mechitza,* the partition separating men and women. But then I would not attract those people to whom prayer is most important and who have the greatest need to pray—the men and, especially, the women who have not yet been fortunate enough to find a full-time partner in life or to start a family. It is to their needs that a Jewish community, and hence a synagogue, must cater.

The synagogue, then, is not a place where someone who is single should be made to feel uncomfortable. Whereas at the synagogue family picnic, singles might be made to feel out of place, within the closed doors of the House of Prayer their Creator embraces them and makes each feel special and not in any way deficient for not having (yet) found a spouse.

Once in Oxford I hosted a Jewish Nobel laureate and his wife at our home for the Sabbath. His wife was extremely friendly, but she made it clear that she would not be attending our prayer services. "When we married, my husband was Orthodox and we prayed at a Shul with a divider. I got tired of sitting alone behind the curtain," she told me. Ever since then they had been praying at a Conservative synagogue where couples sat together. "I will not attend your synagogue and be a party to discrimination against women," she told me. "But what about people like my mother?" I responded. "After her divorce, my mother raised five children completely on her own. The one party whom she could turn to and pour out her troubled heart was God, every Sabbath at the synagogue. Should she walk into the synagogue and immediately feel inadequate or deficient? Should she be reminded of her unpartnered state every time she came to synagogue? Should she have to look around and see all the blissfully happily married women, and be made to feel like a pariah with no place? And what of the men and women who cannot remedy the problem of sitting alone, because they are widowed, divorced, or just plain single?" I asked her. "Shall they be reminded of their loneliness every time they enter the synagogue?" To this she had scarcely a response. "I never thought of that," she admitted.

The Home, Not the Synagogue, the Focal Point of Religious Life

For the first thousand years of their existence, the Jews did not have synagogues. They had the Tabernacle in the wilderness under Moses, followed by one grand Temple in Jerusalem, where they made their pilgrimages, prayed, and offered their sacrifices. The need for synagogues came about with the destruction of the Temples and the concomitant need to establish individual houses of prayer. Throughout Jewish history the *home* has always been the focus of Jewish life. Judaism operates through a series of concentric circles, and the family is at the center. This is why all the Jewish festivals occur around the family table; guests are invited; there is eating and singing and a celebration of life. The synagogue must be seen as the exception, rather than the rule, of Jewish living.

The Jewish people today constitute a nation in crisis. Although millions continue the tradition and a great many are today returning to the fold, the majority are still assimilating. There are fewer than fourteen million Jews in the world today—and a nation with numbers that small cannot sustain the current level of 50 percent assimilation and have a viable future. A critical number of Jews is necessary to sustain basic Jewish communal functions and institutions. Today we run the risk of falling below that threshold. For the Jewish community to thrive, flourish, and prosper, we need Jewish day schools and rabbinical colleges, synagogues and Jewish community centers, a strong State of Israel and an equally strong diaspora. The only thing that can guarantee that a Jew emerges into the outside world with his Jewishness intact is the identity that is instilled within him in the home. Only the home has the capacity to internalize Jewishness, influencing the way we dress in the morning and make love in the evening.

What has led to the abandonment of Jewish tradition on the part of millions of Jews? To be sure, there are many factors, among which are the effects of emancipation and the end of persecution, the tragedy of the Holocaust, and the transplantation of Jews from traditional Europe to free America. But a salient factor, in my opinion, is the replacement of the home for the synagogue in Jewish life. The synagogue has its important place as the center of Jewish *prayer*. But it was never designed to be the center of Jewish *life*. Rabbis are guilty of perpetuating this mistake, however unwittingly. For thousands of years, the Jewish custom has been to get married outdoors, under the canopy of the heavens, beneath the moon and the stars. The symbolism behind this was that the couple should propagate like the stars and that the couple should learn that even in the darkest moments, there are points of light representing their love that will rescue them from despair.

But because of the mass abandonment of Jewish tradition, many rabbis feel they can remedy the situation by monopolizing Jewish life and concentrating it in the synagogue. A rabbi should be conditioning his congregants to find God everywhere—in their businesses through honest conduct, in their marriages through tenderness and faithfulness, and in their homes by having kosher kitchens and mezuzot (small parchment scrolls with verses from Deuteronomy) on their doorposts. Instead, the rabbi teaches the congregation that in order to experience anything holy or spiritual, they must come to the synagogue. So marriages for instance, now take place within the synagogue, rather than in their proper outdoor location. This compartmentalization of Jewish living and the dividing line that it sets up between holy and profane snuffs out Jewish commitment because it makes Judaism into a conscious undertaking instead of a total way of life. It is the equivalent of conditioning a man to see his marriage as taking place only in his home but not once he steps out the front door.

That the synagogue has become the focal point of Jewish life is a tragedy for the Jewish nation because no synagogue can equal the warmth and friendliness of the home. The centrality of the synagogue has succeeded in alienating many young people who have not been raised with tradition. They enter the synagogue and are immediately led into a prayer service in a language they don't understand. I have watched countless students with no knowledge of Hebrew arrive in our synagogue service, hold the prayer book upside down, and pray not for life or health, but for the imminent end of the service. In contrast, if they come to a family's Friday night meal, they can eat, drink, and laugh in a language they understand. Many of Orthodox Judaism's returnees were initially inspired by witnessing the home life of a religious family.

There is another reason why the home must retain its centrality in Jewish life. One of the strongest alienating factors in modern-day religion is its compartmentalization. The man or woman of faith must move from the religious realm to the secular and back again. If God is in the synagogue, but not at home, people who enjoy tradition feel like yo-yos. At home they can dress and speak as they please. When they go to synagogue, they have to dress up and be on their best behavior. They feel unjustly pulled between heaven and earth. People feel that they have to be serious in church or synagogue, and their discomfort is obvious. A non-Jewish student sitting in my office told me that he liked coming to the L'Chaim Society but that he was beginning to feel alienated from his church. I did not feel that this was a positive development, and I asked him why he felt that way. Whenever I have been approached by non-Jewish students who felt distant from their church upbringing, I have always tried to bolster their Christian faith. He replied that when he goes into the church, he stops being who he is and dons "my artificial, religious self. It feels like a charade."

People want to approach their relationship with God holistically. They want God to accompany them in every aspect of their lives, and they need to feel spiritual when they work and when they love, not just when they pray. This is why the home must be the first place where everyone discovers God. We must find God when we eat, when we sleep, and when we socialize with friends. Here God becomes synthesized with our everyday living, instead of being a companion who accompanies us weekly in a house of worship. What is needed today is the discovery of God as a friend and a loving father, rather than as a stern patriarch.

In contemporary times, the rabbis must lead the way by demonstrating that their roles do not revolve around the synagogue. Rather than the rabbi appearing to his congregants every week as an aloof figure in a clerical robe, he should demonstrate that the most important functions he undertakes are outside the synagogue. He should be a teacher who offers many classes from the intimacy of his own home. He should be a pastor who visits people to discuss everyday issues of life in their homes. He should organize outings for the community children and show them how to roller-skate and climb mountains while wearing yarmulkes and keeping their Jewish identities intact. We live today in a pleasure-seeking generation that wants holiness, but without compromising its fun.

The synagogue will forever remain a serious place of prayer. This is proper, and we should not seek to change it (although we should always try to make it livelier). But we should be moving the focus of Jewish life away from the synagogue to the more relaxed and natural environment of the home, away from Rabbis and Cantors and more toward the parents and grandparents.

PART TWO

The Jewish Faith

9

The Sabbath

The Sabbath has been instituted as an opportunity for fellowship with God, and for glad, not austere, service of him.

—JUDAH HALEVI, *Kuzari*

An artist cannot be continuously wielding his brush. He must stop at times in his painting to freshen his vision of the object, the meaning of which he wishes to express on his canvas. Living is also an art. . . . The Sabbath represents those moments when we pause in our brushwork to renew our vision of the object.

—MORDECAI KAPLAN,
The Meaning of God

More than Israel has kept the Sabbath, the Sabbath has kept Israel.

—AHAD HA'AM,
Al Parashat Derachim (At the Crossroads)

A FORMER OXFORD STUDENT WHO NOW WORKS at a bank in London told me that his workaholic boss hassles him whenever he leaves work early on Friday in deference to the Jewish Sabbath. "That's because you challenge him," I said. "Whenever you leave

151

early, you remind him that there are things in life more important than making money. He then must ask himself why he is still at work rather than at home with his family."

The Bible provides two explanations for the mitzvah of Shabbat (the Sabbath):

> Remember the Sabbath day to sanctify it. Six days shall you labour and accomplish all your work; but the seventh day is Sabbath to the Lord; you shall not do any work . . . *for in six days the Lord made heaven and earth, the sea, and all that is in them, and he rested on the seventh day.* Therefore, the Lord blessed the Sabbath day and sanctified it. (Exod. 20:8–11)
>
> Safeguard the Sabbath day and sanctify it, as the Lord, your God has commanded you. Six days shall you labour and accomplish all your work; but the seventh day is Sabbath to the Lord; you shall not do any work. . . . *And you shall remember that you were a slave in the land of Egypt, and the Lord, your God, has taken you out from there with a strong hand and an outstretched arm;* therefore the Lord, your God, has commanded you to observe the Sabbath day. (Deut. 5:12–15)

The Sabbath is a paradox, celebrating both *God's* activity and *human* freedom. We subjugate ourselves to God's mastery and, simultaneously, rejoice in the mastery we have over ourselves. It celebrates both our freedom to rest, as well as our servitude to God. So what is it then? Is the Sabbath about God or about man? Is it about our dependence or our *in*dependence?

The Sabbath includes all these aspects. It is the day on which we release ourselves from the mindless slavery of materialism. By subordinating our lives to God's purpose, we liberate ourselves from the crushing obsession with property and status. The Sabbath does not distinguish between master and servant, boss and employee. It is a sanctuary in time, an island of serenity from which the noise and distraction of life are excluded. Above all, it is the day on which we welcome God and human love into our lives.

Life today is busier than ever before. Labor-saving devices, rather than relieving us of drudgery, spur us on to more activity. This is the age of the entrepreneur. The starting gates of wealth and success are wide open, and millions are racing to the finish line. I have grown accustomed to having to wait three or four months to meet friends for a simple dinner, so congested are their schedules. Most people today suffer from sleep deprivation, as they fight to cram more and more into their hectic days.

Social commentators could read much into the modern obsession with squeezing the most out of life and the lust for professional success. Some would call it capitalism gone mad. Others would see a valueless society in which money and material acquisition have supplanted family and the pursuit of enlightenment. Others might even speak of a subconscious death wish on the part of young professionals who are pushing themselves too hard. The Jewish diagnosis would be that this is the age-old misguided scenario of the earth's inhabitants sacrificing time in the acquisition of area, expending precious moments in the conquest of space, squandering their lives to gain possessions. One of the principal objectives of Judaism, however, is to teach people to value time far more than space, indeed, to dedicate space toward the acquisition of time. Judaism believes that the purpose of money is the purchase of special, unforgettable moments, rather than the reverse.

Sanctuaries of the Spirit

Judaism divides the empirical world into three fundamental components: time, space, and mankind, who acts upon time and space. The purpose of religion is the consecration of all three through man, using time and space in the service of the Creator. The man of faith seeks to make time and space holy by creating sanctuaries of the spirit, geographic areas as well as special moments of refuge and sanctity in which God is experienced as a living presence. But whereas most world religions put the bulk of their emphasis on space, Judaism's emphasis is on time. Any traveler through Christian Europe will see the great monuments to space that the believers of old built for their Lord. Wondrous cathedrals of unmatched splendor rise toward the heavens.

To be sure, there are some beautiful synagogues and there were, of course, the great Temples in Jerusalem, the first destroyed by the Babylonians, the second by the Romans. Indeed, Israel itself, a space consecrated by God as a holy land, is central to the Jewish religion. But for the majority of Jewish history, the Jews have not been on their land and have not had a Temple. Rather, the Jewish religion thrives on cathedrals in *time* rather than cathedrals of space. The very first act of consecration recorded in the Bible is when God hallowed the Sabbath day. In fact, the first time the word *holy* is used in the Bible is in connection with the Sabbath day: "So God blessed the seventh day and made it holy, because on it God rested from all the work that he had done in creation" (Gen. 2:3). Similarly, the first commandment (mitzvah) given to the Jewish people upon their emergence from Egypt was the sanctification of the new moon and new lunar month. They were to witness the monthly rebirth of the moon and consecrate the time as *Rosh Chodesh*, the first day of the new Jewish month.

Taking this idea further, in other religions space consecrates time. A geographic location is first chosen for a cathedral or shrine, and only later do actions undertaken within it, such as prayer or acts of confession, become sacred. In Judaism, the reverse is true. Special moments and supernatural events that have come to pass in a certain place lend that location its solemnity and sanctity. In other words, time sanctifies space. Mount Moriah, the domain where the Temple was built in Jerusalem, was sacred because, according to tradition, it was there that God took clay from the earth, fashioned it into the guise of a man, breathed life into it, and called that being Adam. On the same site, many centuries later, Abraham was commanded to bring his son Isaac as a sacrifice to God and ended up substituting a ram in his place. The site (space) became holy because of the great moments (time) that transpired there. The place where a couple enjoyed their first kiss will always be special to them. So too, the places where God and the Jewish people consecrated their everlasting bond are sacred.

Lost Appreciation of Time

We have lost an appreciation for the sublimity of time. Modern man, with his computers, satellites, and rockets, is permanently engaged in pushing back the frontiers of space. People spend their lives working and expending nearly every waking effort to acquire money and possessions. Property comes before precious moments. Times for family and friends are regularly sacrificed in favor of attending business meetings and writing reports. Human relationships suffer greatly. With the scarce amount of time that husbands and wives, parents and children, have for each other, is it any wonder that divorce is at its highest rate ever, and that many children are acutely insecure?

Judaism conceives of life in a fundamentally different way. Man is meant to expend space in the acquisition of time. Parents work so that they can afford to fly home their offspring in college for holidays. Material gain is to be used in the acquisition of special moments. "Remember the days of old, consider the years long past" (Deut. 32:7). Man is conditioned by the Bible to embrace time as life's most precious gift. The Sabbath is designed around the idea that man should work six days so that he can enjoy a tranquil and uninterrupted period of intimate, divine communion. The Sabbath is a day of relationships, prayer, and enlightenment. Moreover, each of the festivals that punctuate the Jewish year represents time set aside for reflection. The Jew works throughout the months in order to save up money and celebrate these sacred moments with family, friends, and community. In Temple times, the Jew was obligated to make three pilgrimages each year in order to share these special moments with the Almighty Himself in His chosen home. Jewish life is about capturing the moment and living for glorious times, not about conquering vast tracts of land or seizing glorious works of art. With the notable exception of King David, Jewish history has no famous conquerors. Conquering space has never been a Jewish pastime. But utilizing time well is a crucial tenet of Judaism. Our famous men are great Sages who were celebrated for using their time wisely, devoting it to the service of God and humanity, and acquiring knowledge and wisdom. Similarly, the Bible records that Abraham "was elderly, filled with days" (Gen. 24:1). Most people's lives are measured in years. But Abraham's was measured in days, since he impregnated every moment with meaning and purpose. He never squandered a *day*.

To go to a holy place, one must undertake a long and arduous journey, leaving behind family and home. But to enter into a holy time, man need only remain passive, in his natural surroundings, until the sacred moment overtakes him. Like a boat rising in the high tide, man is naturally uplifted and transported by the magic of the spiritual moment. While one is in a holy place, one is *enveloped* by a holy time. The Jewish year is like a spiral in which man continually comes back to the same periods of sanctity, each of which evokes a different season of the spirit and calls forth memories of an earlier period in the development of the Jewish nation.

The lesson for each of us in our daily lives is to remember the preciousness of the moment. The time we parents have with our children when they are young and adorable is fleeting. We must put people before property and relationships before riches. We must carve out meaningful moments before, after, and even during work to read, think, love, and learn. The ancient Rabbis warned, "The more property one acquires, the more worry one acquires." Our prosperity must be used as a *means* rather than an end. Money should be used to buy time, to acquire sacred moments with family and friends. A wealthy man once said to me that the only real blessing of wealth is the freedom it buys its holder. Only when wealth is used to release us from worry and allow us to pursue noble goals can it be construed as a blessing. Otherwise, wealth is nothing more than a gilded cage.

My Son Is the Sabbath

God made many wondrous things during the seven days of creation, but none so precious as the Sabbath. Of all the precious moments that dot the Jewish temporal landscape, none is as rich as the Seventh Day. Of far greater significance than the duration of creation is the fact that it was crowned by the Sabbath (Gen. 2:1–3), bringing rest and refreshment to the toiling world. The concept of a day of rest, sanctified by the divine example, is one of the greatest spiritual and social contributions to civilization made by the religion of Israel.

The creative pause, devoted to spiritual renewal and family, was utterly unknown in the ancient world. In fact, the Jews suffered ridicule on account of their day of rest from some of Rome's most prolific literary figures, including Seneca, Juvenal, and Tacitus. The seven-day cycle by which humanity today reckons time and regulates its affairs has its origin solely in the Hebrew Bible. All attempts at changing this pattern and moving the day of rest into a different time frame—including the establishment of a ten-day week during the French Revolution—have met with failure.

The holy Sabbath is the goal of the week. Yet, our business-oriented world treats rest as enabling further exertion of labor. It makes sense that workers will be more productive if they are given time to refresh and renew their energies. Many make the mistake of believing that the Sabbath was given by God to man to reinvigorate himself so that he might be more productive in the coming six days. Leon Trotsky said that he would preserve the Sabbath, even in the atheistic culture of the Soviet Union, because all workers needed time off. This rationale stems from the idea that man's noblest goal is physical toil rather than moments of spiritual reflection. But the fact that the Sabbath is the holiest day of the week—by far transcending the six days of work—lays waste to this misconception.

Indeed, in Judaism the six days of work are all a preparation for the one glorious day of rest. Echoing this point, the celebrated medieval Jewish pietist and sage Rabbi Judah He-Hasid said: "One who goes to sleep on the Sabbath should not say, 'Let us sleep so that we can do our work when the Sabbath is over,' but rather let him say, 'Let us rest, for today is the Sabbath'" *(Sefer Hasidim)*. When man works hard to store up some treasure, it affords him a meaningful day of relaxation in which, unencumbered by material concerns, he can focus on the purpose of his creation, the direction of his life.

Placing the Important Before the Urgent

Never before has life been so busy. Our lives are governed by constant emergencies in which everything seems urgent and pressing. Never before have men and women been so harried. The ring of mobile phones drills a hole through our ears, dozens of E-mails that must be answered pile up, and faxes and snail mail stream through our in-trays. Just when we thought we could relax, we have to travel thousands of miles for a business meeting. The greatest casualty of this lifestyle is that the urgent is always placed before the important. Modern-day man is no fool. Ours is the most literate, educated, and informed generation of all time. We know all too well the difference between right and wrong, ephemeral and eternal, urgent and important. So why have our lives lost their equilibrium? *The answer is that although we know what is important, we have no time for it. The important is always superseded by the urgent.*

Sociologists point out that children today seem to be less well behaved than in earlier generations. Girls and boys are involved in sexual relationships at younger and younger ages. Young people are shooting one another. The misbehavior and wrongdoing result from a lack of guidance by parents and the children's desire to be noticed. We have no time for our children, pacifying them with television and toys rather than showering them with attention and love. I once overheard a conversation between a mother in her thirties and her mother. The younger woman complained that it was so hard to raise children these days. Her mother responded, "In my day it was much harder. We had no television. We actually had to spend time with our children." Lacking adult care, our children have no healthy direction for their abundant energies. Children compensate for a lack of parental love with hurtful behavior, their appeal for affection and attention.

We all recognize that time spent with children is important. You sit down to play with your children or to read them a story. But suddenly, the phone rings. And though your children are more *important* than the phone call, the call is *urgent*. If you don't run to pick it up right now, you will miss it. When you return to continue the story you were reading, you notice that it is seven o'clock, and there is a very important item on the evening news that you just cannot miss. Later, when you return for the third time to resume your time with your children, you look at your watch and remember that the gym will be open only for another half hour, and you once again run to accommodate the urgent and in the process compromise the important.

And so we continue, blindly trampling on the most precious things in our lives. Later, when we retire in our old age, our deepest regret will be that although there is nothing urgent, we cannot pursue the important, because the opportunity has passed. We wonder why our children don't visit us more in our retirement, and we remember that—like a bank account that is almost empty through lack of deposits—we never built strong relationships with them when they were young. Furthermore, having devoted little or no time to study and the pursuit of knowledge, we have not developed a craving for learning, so reading books and gaining insight is not sufficiently stimulating. Neither does religion engage us, since our lives were devoted to shopping and television. And as we have no relationship with God, we don't find His presence comforting. Having grown up in Miami Beach, one of America's largest retirement communities, I can attest to the fact that many of our elderly while away their retirement years playing cards and sitting idly in deck chairs in the sun. The Lubavitcher Rebbe once said that retirement should be about putting on "new tires," rededicating our lives to all that is important once we finally have the time to pursue it. The problem is that by the time we arrive at this special stage, it is often too late: We have largely forgotten what *is* important. As in the famous Harry Chapin song, "Cat's in the Cradle," our children have no time for us, just as we had no time for them.

On the Sabbath nothing is urgent. It is for this reason that God gave man the Sabbath, a period in which man is freed from the tyranny of the urgent. The Sabbath is not about learning a sense of priorities, the relative values of urgent and important. Rather, the beauty of the Sabbath is that on that day *there simply is nothing urgent*. We are elevated to a higher plane of living.

A family sits down at the Sabbath table to partake of the Sabbath meal. The father makes the blessing over wine, which is then shared by the entire family. They then wash their hands for the eating of the challah, the special braided Sabbath bread, and indulge in the peace and pleasure of a meal together. Suddenly, the phone rings. But this time, nobody rushes to pick it up. It is forbidden. No electricity can be used on the Sabbath. The time for the evening news arrives. But nobody runs to turn on the television. The world can wait. The family is impervious to events outside the home, for the only reality is the warmth, love, and kinship they share around the table with one another and their guests. Conversation does not concern the latest film or which football team will make the playoffs. Rather, the children read aloud what they have learned at school of the weekly Bible portion, and the family speaks of God as a close and reliable friend. By so doing, the family members treat one another as being as holy as the Sabbath.

Most modern people have never been immersed in an environment where intrusion by stereo music, television, telephone, or any other electronic device is prohibited. The Talmud explains that at the completion of the six days the world was missing one pivotal ingredient, namely, peace. "When the Sabbath came, peace came with it." The modern world is full of noise—advertising, consumerism, ambition, plus the constant blare of television. The serenity of the Sabbath—an island of calm in the turbulent seas of commercialization—offers an environment of tranquility and quiet.

On the Sabbath, man comes to know the sacred. By indulging in an uncorrupted period lasting twenty-five hours, he learns to extrapolate beyond this once-a-week haven and incorporate sanctity into other periods of his week. He learns to create a daily Sabbath consisting of a few hours at a time.

My old dentist is an Orthodox Jew and a close friend. Although a consummate professional, on one occasion, he put a filling in my tooth that dissolved the next day. I could not eat on that side of my mouth and called him at home, telling his daughter that it was urgent. She returned to the phone saying that her father was preoccupied. "Tell him it's an emergency," I said. "My filling has fallen out." She again returned to the phone. "My Daddy said that he is celebrating his mother's eighty-second birthday, and you will just have to call him in the morning at the office." The Bible says that honoring one's parents is a sacred duty. Here was a man who treated his mother as the Sabbath. My tooth would have to wait.

When Moses first encounters the Almighty in the wilderness, he sees a burning bush. He approaches the bush to investigate the wondrous sight. The Bible says that at that point the Lord spoke to him from the bush, and the first thing He commanded Moses was to remove his shoes, "for the ground which you now stand on is holy" (Exod. 3:5). *Judaism is about teaching man to find the hallowed ground upon which no foot can trample.* Judaism sensitizes us to the moments of sanctity that pervade our lives. And the Sabbath is the single greatest lesson in discovering that sanctity. We must establish time spent with parents, spouse, siblings, and children as hallowed ground upon which no commercial or recreational pursuit may trespass.

Imagine if we could each make just make two hours every day into a personal Sabbath. A mother sits to play with her children on a Wednesday evening. The phone rings, but she refuses to answer it. Her children are the Sabbath. A man talks to his wife when he returns home from work. Rather than have his wife wait as he sends one last fax from home, he understands that the time he spends working on his marriage is sacred time upon which there can be no intrusion. Suddenly, he has made room in life for the important. He has liberated himself from the confining strictures of the urgent. Indeed it is my fervent belief that the answer to Sigmund Freud's famous question, "What is it that women want?" is precisely this. A woman wants her man to make her into the Sabbath. She wants him to prioritize her over all that is urgent. She wants to be the centerpiece of his life. Women marry in order to feel supremely important to the man who pledges himself to their happiness.

God's Day

One of the recurring themes of the Bible is the prohibition against working on the Sabbath (Exod. 20:10). Many make the mistake of thinking that as long as they don't go to their jobs on Saturday, they are not desecrating the Sabbath. But the Sabbath is meant to be a passive day. The frenetic activity to which people are accustomed during the week prevents them from appreciating and indulging in—indeed, enjoying—the passive side of their natures. Obsessed as we are with doing, we have lost the capacity to simply be. The passive state makes us anxious and uncomfortable. Indeed, in everyday conversation, we don't even know how to listen. Instead, we bob our heads to show that we are listening. Likewise, we feel uncomfortable when people give us compliments, because we don't know how to receive. The passive state is massively disconcerting. Furthermore, even religiously inclined people today reject the classical interpretation of work. They feel that by pursuing leisurely pursuits, they are not desecrating the law or spirit of the Sabbath.

In a public debate that I participated in, a leading Reform Rabbi said that it was ludicrous that in the modern age we should continue to ban things like lighting a fire or driving on the Sabbath. He argued that the Sabbath was a day of rest, and therefore anything that a person found restful, such as gardening or going to a musical concert, would be consonant with the spirit of the day. He promoted the idea that lighting a fire on the Sabbath was once prohibited because of the labor involved in rubbing stones and sticks together to generate a spark. Shallow perceptions such as these derive from the highly misguided idea that the purpose of the Sabbath day is simply to reenergize ourselves for another grueling week at work.

The Sabbath is not a day of rest from work. Rather, it is a day of rest from our own physical *creativity*. The entire theme of the Sabbath day is that God created heaven and the earth in six days. On the seventh day He rested and commanded man henceforth to do the same. On the Sabbath we rest from *the kind of work that God undertook in the original six days,* namely *creative* labor.

The Sabbath is designed for man to remember that God is the Creator. Man is engaged in a constant battle against nature. By exercising his intelligence, skills, and hard work, he seeks to bring nature to heel, subjugating it to his dominion. Throughout the week man erects buildings from logs and stone and raises capital for new businesses. Indeed, our ability today to control disease and prevent floods bears witness to the considerable progress we have made in our attempt to become masters of nature. But in this effort, one great fear looms over us: the possibility, even probability, that we will forget that we too are *creatures*, as well as *creators*, and that God is the ultimate master. Man has been endowed by God with an enormous capacity for creativity. But man can easily begin to deify himself.

In other words, in the same way that man is distinguished by his intelligence, labor, and art, so too these attributes can lead him to take himself too seriously and make an idol of himself. Think of a tycoon whose only interest in life is his next business acquisition. Think of a father who is never home with his children, but always at the office. Think of a woman for whom shopping is the week's greatest thrill, or a woman who delays marriage and commitment well into her forties, busy as she is climbing the corporate ladder. Too much work makes man a monolith and uproots the vitality from his soul. We are all grateful for the enormous technological advances of the past century, but perhaps we are beginning to create *too* much. Like Dr. Frankenstein, we may have crossed a line that can lead only to catastrophe. Polls showing that the vast majority of people opposed the cloning of human beings demonstrate our alertness to the possibility of compromising our uniqueness through unrestrained innovation. The heated ethical debates on stem cell research illustrate the same point.

The creative side of man is being deified. Indeed, art itself has become an idol. Not long ago, art focused on religious subjects. I do not believe that this subject matter is intrinsically better than any other, but it does show that mankind once felt the obligation to devote creative energy to praising the Creator and His handiwork. But many people believe that works of art transcend laws of morality, as if they are outside God's domain. I have participated in several radio debates about censorship—even self-censorship—in art. The secular experts invariably expressed horror at the very idea of censoring human creativity. In 1993, when terrorists exploded a car bomb outside the Uffizi Gallery in Florence, the newspapers first gave a detailed report on which masterpieces had been damaged. Only later did they mention that people had died in the blast as well. Art should ennoble and enhance human life, but never supplant it. Such idolization of human craftsmanship is precisely what the Sabbath is designed to combat.

By refraining from creative labor for one day a week and dedicating that day to God, we acknowledge God's mastery over the earth and our dependency upon Him for life and sustenance. By refraining from *creating*, man learns his true place as part of, rather than master of, *creation*. Therefore, even recreational activities like gardening or playing music, in which man takes elements of God's created universe and brings improvement to them through exercising his higher creative talents, are prohibited. As a general rule, the labors prohibited on the Sabbath can be defined as follows: any activity of a constructive nature that makes some significant change in our material environment. Significance is determined in relation to usefulness for human purposes. Thus, some of the more common prohibitions for the Sabbath include: plowing, sowing, reaping, baking, bleaching, dyeing, tying a knot, tearing, trapping or hunting, building, demolishing, kindling a fire, writing, erasing, sewing, grinding, cooking, and putting the finishing touch to a newly man-ufactured article. There are, in addition, thousands of tributary forms of work that are prohibited within the thirty-nine main cate-gories. Thus, turning on any form of electrical appliance is prohib-ited because it completes, or builds, a circuit, allowing the free flow of electrons; thus it constitutes both building and putting the final touches on a manufactured article.

In addition, carrying from a private to a public domain is prohib-ited. Observant Jews, therefore, do not walk into the street on the Sabbath with anything in their pockets. Why? Unlike the other for-bidden actions, this does not involve man's mastery over creation, since there is no material change in the concerned object. Rather, in the same way that ceasing from any kind of creative labor acknowl-edges God as the source of our power over nature, so desisting from carrying acknowledges God's sovereignty over all affairs of society. Carrying from place to place signifies commerce and the exchange of ideas and goods between people in society. Carrying, or transfer-ring material objects from one domain to another, is characteristic of work by which humans pursue their purposes in business and else-where. It is an a priori expression of ownership and domination and is thus prohibited on the Sabbath, a day on which the earth and all its host are consecrated to a more exalted proprietor. A community that ceases carrying on the Sabbath acknowledges God as the source of its structure and puts the seal of divine approval on all its ambi-tious communal programs and aspirations.

For six days of every week, man uses the raw materials that the Almighty created and enhances them by changing their form and position. Man cuts down trees and builds a house, cooks raw vegeta-bles and makes them edible, and experiments with medicines and finds cures for disease. In so doing, man is living up to the highest human calling, which is to imitate God Himself. Just as the Almighty is a creator, so too man is a creator. Man is welcomed, even obligated, to join the Almighty as a junior partner in creation. But one day a week, the world is elevated to a higher state of perfection. On that day, man must know his limitations. He retreats from his role as creator and exercises no jurisdiction over creation. He finds peace in becoming one with nature and the universe. The Sabbath day was given for man to acknowledge his role as a component, rather than as master, of creation.

The Sabbath is also the great equalizing factor in society. The Bible commands that on the Sabbath day the bondsman and the maidservant must rest, just as their master rests. Imagine how revolutionary a teaching this was in ancient times, when slaves were seen as nothing more than the animated tools of their masters. By recurring weekly, the Sabbath reminds us that man, having been created in the divine image, possesses an intrinsic and infinite worth that cannot be measured in commercial terms.

Leisure: Its Use and Abuse

Modern-day men and women have forgotten the value of peace and rest. Many seem confounded by their moments of leisure, feeling lost when they have nothing to do. They end up squandering their free time on insubstantial pursuits like watching television, sunbathing, reading celebrity trash magazines, and obsessively discussing their local sports teams.

I believe that the greatest disease in modern society is not drugs, violence, or crime, but boredom. Indeed, the former result from the latter. In earlier times, leisure was reserved only for the aristocracy, who had servants to deal with their mundane matters. The average man spent most of his life struggling to feed his family and survive.

Historians like Arnold Toynbee have written of the relation between the fate of a civilization and the way its members use or abuse their leisure. In ancient Rome the day's work was usually done by noon or shortly thereafter, with the rest of the time spent in pleasure and amusement. More than half the days of the year were holidays. Wealthy and with many servants, many citizens of the Roman Empire distracted themselves in watching gladiatorial combat, engaging in political intrigue, and participating in orgies. By the time of the barbarian invasions of the late third and early fourth century, there

were scarcely any Romans commanding or fighting in their own legions. Nearly all leading Roman commanders were mercenaries from
the far-flung empire. Corrupt internally, the empire was overrun by
people with a far greater hunger for success. Rome, like so many
other great civilizations that preceded and followed it, was never defeated, but rather decayed from within.

The notion that a man or a society's true character is revealed in the
disposition of leisure time is anticipated in the Talmud. In an oft-
quoted statement, the Talmud declares that a man's character can be
tested in three ways: *be'kiso, be'koso, u've'kaaso,* "by his pocket" (Is he
a miser or generous?), "by his cup" (What does he say and do when al-
cohol has removed his social inhibitions?), "and by his temper" (Is he
the master of his emotions in the face of provocation?) (*Eruvin* 65b).
But according to some, there is a fourth index of character: *af be'sa-
hako,* "by his play" (How does he use his leisure? or What activities
does he choose to engage in when life does not compel him to act?).
Boredom—conceding failure when challenged by leisure—leads to the
erosion of meaning in life.

One man who understood this exceptionally well was Victor
Frankl, the wise Holocaust survivor who founded the therapeutic
school of Logotherapy. In *Man's Search for Meaning,* Frankl wrote:

[There is a] kind of depression which afflicts people who become
aware of the lack of content in their lives when the rush of the busy
week is over and the void within themselves becomes manifest. Not a
few cases of suicide can be traced back to this existential vacuum. Such
widespread phenomena as alcoholism and juvenile delinquency are
not understandable unless we recognize the existential vacuum underlying them. This is also true of the crises of pensioners and ageing people. . . . Moreover, there are various masks and guises under which the
existential vacuum appears. Sometimes the frustrated will to meaning
is vicariously compensated for by a will to power, including the most
primitive form of the will to power, the will to money. In other cases,
the place of frustrated will to meaning is taken by the will to pleasure.
That is why existential frustration often eventuates in sexual compen-

sation. We can observe, in such cases, that the sexual libido becomes rampant in the existential vacuum.

The ancient Rabbis acknowledged this existential vacuum and declared it to be the reason God gave man commandments after the flood in which the earth's evil inhabitants perished. Boredom had led them to sin in the first place, so the Almighty decided that it would be better for man to preoccupy himself with life-affirming and holy responsibilities.

Rabbi Norman Lamm points out that the word *sehok*, or play, is frequently used in rabbinic literature as a euphemism for the three cardinal crimes: unchastity, idolatry, and even murder. To the ancient Rabbis, *sehok* represented the misuse of leisure. Indeed, the Sages anticipated the modern discovery that boredom may lead to mental breakdown and offered legislation that would protect all people from a forced idleness that could rob them of their human faculties.

In one poignant example, the Talmudic Sages ruled that the enforced idleness of a housewife, either because of an abundance of servants or because her husband prevented her from working, was intolerable and unacceptable. Rabbi Eliezer maintained that even if she had a hundred maids, she ought to do some work in the household, "for idleness leads to *zimah,* unchastity." The Rabbis said that if the husband took a religious vow to abstain from benefiting from his wife's work, he must divorce her and pay her dowry and settlement. The reason: Idleness leads to boredom and eventually to feeblemindedness, even lunacy. Summing up the negative consequences of inactivity, the Rabbis declared, "When there is nothing to do, you do what you ought not do." How many teenagers who are wasting away on drugs would be popping "Es" if they had been passionately absorbed in their studies or works of communal enhancement? Here, the debate as to whether there is too much violence on television is beside the point. What is important is the very fact that these adolescents have so much spare time to watch television in the first place. This leads to a desire to get drunk or go "wilding," or do something else that brings a pleasurable respite to the incessant boredom.

Perfecting the Inner World of the Spirit

The Bible does not require that man be idle on the Sabbath—indeed, the Torah sees nonactivity as harmful. Instead, the Bible seeks the inversion of his creative talents, where the focus is not on perfection of the external world of the senses but perfection of the internal world of the spirit. As Rabbi Norman Lamm suggests, the difference between the prohibited labor and the recommended repose lies not in the *fact* of creativity, but rather in the *object* of one's creative powers: oneself or one's environment, the inner world or the outer world. One day of the week, man focuses on internal perfection as the goal of his creative capacity. On the Sabbath, man looks at himself as the agent of change that God has selected to act as master over the planet, to scrutinize his inner heart as to its sincerity and holiness, and to refresh and replenish his spiritual powers so that he is not only productive but also holy, not only useful, but also spiritual.

Stated in other words, whereas through work we attempt to master creation by using our creative talents, through leisure we attempt to master *ourselves*, a far greater challenge. Throughout the week we attempt to master the world around us. On the Sabbath we attempt to conquer the world inside us and elevate our nature to a holier plane.

Rest That Leads to Self-Discovery

Based on this new understanding of rest, Rabbi Lamm identifies two different concepts of leisure. The first is where a man ceases his usual labors, and this respite from his weekly routine and daily activity allows him to rediscover himself by emerging from the workweek. Overwhelmed by a set pattern of work, man begins to identify himself principally by the functions he performs in society or family, and his human dignity is threatened. I have seen young students suffering from this work-induced malady of a loss of one's identity as a unique human being. When I asked students what they intended *to be* upon graduating from Oxford, they usually told me investment bankers, lawyers, or doctors. I pointed out to them that they had told me what they are planning *to do,* but not what they intended *to be.* Modern men and women have lost a sense of their uniqueness and define themselves almost entirely by their productive output. They have exchanged the personal for the functional, the spiritual for the practical. Therefore, the Sabbath comes to their rescue. By disengaging, by ceasing work, man is permitted true self-expression and can discover who he is and what makes him special. Rest, therefore, is the use of leisure to restore one's individuality in all its integrity. Leisure affords men and women the opportunity to resolve their "identity crisis."

Rest That Leads to Self-Transformation

A deeper dimension to rest—which necessitates prayer, contemplation, study, and every other tool of spiritual enrichment—can lead to *self-transformation.* In this higher form of rest man not only fulfills himself but goes outside of himself. This is not about merely discovering one's identity, but rather creating a new and better identity. This is the inner and deeper meaning, as well as the highest fulfillment of, the Sabbath. The day of rest is ultimately a day of re-creation, not relaxation. The highest form of re-creation is inner transformation.

When Alexander the Great asked Diogenes whether he could do anything for him, the famed philosopher replied, "Just stand out of my light." Indeed, many schools of meditation promote a discipline of nothingness, in which man's highest inner fulfillment is attained in a moment of complete passivity and quietism, in which the dizzying noise of the outside world is simply shut out.

The Jewish way of resting on the Sabbath is devoting the day to prayer and Torah study. Intellectual development alone has never been enough for the Jew; it must be informed with moral purpose. Whereas the ancient Greeks regarded the use of leisure for contemplation as a central element in their culture—the Greek word for leisure, *schole,* is the origin of our word *school*—the Jew always used his free time to enhance his relationship with God and ascend spiritual heights in the study of the Torah. Jewish tradition has it that it was Moses himself who instituted that a weekly portion of the fifty-three sections of the Bible be read in the synagogue, a custom that continues until this day.

Every seven days, a Jew is meant to be immersed into a twenty-five-hour period in which he cannot switch on lights, turn on the television set, go for a drive, call his friends, go the movies, or buy a beer. Only by ceasing to *do* can he begin to *be.* The Sabbath is a time for man to be animated by the subtler, more lofty aspects of life. Men and women are afforded an opportunity of coming face to face with the great heroes of the Bible—Abraham, Sarah, Joseph, Moses, David, and Deborah—through the weekly reading of the Torah and the Prophets. Jews are compelled to enjoy reading and learning, and meditating on the higher questions of existence and life. Without this weekly practice, life can become, as it has for many, nothing more than the endless pursuit of meaningless distractions.

10

Gender in Judaism

Anyone who knows anything of history knows that great social changes are impossible without feminine upheaval. Social progress can be measured exactly by the social position of the fair sex, the ugly ones included.

—KARL MARX

True love always makes a man better, no matter what woman inspires it.

—ALEXANDRE DUMAS, *Camille*

And verily, a woman need know but one man well, in order to understand all men; whereas a man may know all women and understand not one of them.

—HELEN ROWLAND

OF THE MAJOR SOCIAL CHANGES IN THE WORLD over the past one hundred years, perhaps the most significant concerns the role of women in society. Modern woman has emerged as man's equal in nearly every sphere, but the general perception is that religion has lagged behind this shift. In the eleven years in which I served as Rabbi at Oxford University, few issues fired as many arguments as that of Judaism and gender. Students were disillusioned by what they perceived to be discrimination against women. Many female students avoided Orthodox Jewish services because they didn't want to be segregated from the men during prayers. They cited many other examples of Judaism's discriminatory policy against women, including the prescription of different laws for men and women and the traditional prohibition against women becoming Rabbis or leading Jewish religious worship in the synagogue. Men are obligated to keep all the commandments of the Torah, whereas women are absolved from any commandment that is time dependent, such as wearing a prayer shawl, reciting the three daily prayers, and lighting the Chanukah Menorah. Examples of commandments that are incumbent on both men and women are eating kosher food and the obligation to give charity. These apply at all times of the day and year. But commandments such as the recitation of the evening prayer *maariv*, is something women are relieved from since it is tied to a particular time.

In an age in which success outside the home is the overall delimiter of achievement, Judaism, with its traditionally more private, homebound, nurturing role for women, appears chauvinistic and prejudicial. "Why are we hidden behind the *mechitza* [the partition in the synagogue]?" many young students asked me, as they noisily left our prayer services, never to return. "Why can't I get up in front of the congregation and have an *aliyah* [call to the Torah, reserved exclusively for men in Orthodox synagogues]?" "Why must women dress modestly and remain locked behind layers of clothing?" This spills over into more comprehensive complaints. Why the general Jewish attitude of separating the sexes? Why does Judaism insist on so many safeguards in friendships between the sexes, such as the rule that men and women cannot be together in a locked private room unless they are married? Why can't women dress like men, wearing slacks, jeans, and tank tops? And conversely, why does the Bible specifically prohibit a man's wearing clothing that is for a woman: "A woman shall not wear a man's apparel, nor shall a man put on a woman's garment; for whoever does such things is abhorrent to the Lord your God"? (Deut. 22:5).

To be sure, women have made great progress in Judaism. Just one hundred and fifty years ago women found it very difficult to formally study anything but the most basic Jewish texts, and there certainly were no female academies of Jewish study prior to the 1917 founding of the first Bais Yaakov women's seminary by Sarah Shneerer in Cracow, Poland. With the proliferation of women's seminaries, it is today common for Jewish women to study the same curriculum as men, mastering all the great Jewish texts and their myriad commentaries. Even Talmud, once a taboo subject of study for women, is now offered at many Jewish women's seminaries, and in virtually every community there are wives who are far more knowledgeable than their husbands in all matters of Jewish thought and law. One thing that has not changed and may never change in Orthodox Jewish circles, however, is a woman's more private ceremonial role and her exclusion from public rabbinical ritual duties. Areas such as these pose a great problem for educated and ambitious women who are accustomed to full equality in the workplace and society. Indeed, the need to dismantle the differences between the sexes is a prevailing assumption of contemporary society. It is an assumption I should like to challenge.

The subdivision of all life into male and female is a matter of fact, but have any of us ever paused to ask why? Why are there women at all? Why men? The Creator could have made the world with only one gender reproducing asexually. The ancient Jewish mystics explained that the differences between men and women are far from meaningless and arbitrary. According to the Kabbalah, there is no equality of the sexes. Rather, women stem from a much higher spiritual source than men, which is shown in their earlier maturation, more refined characters, more spiritual dispositions, greater inclination toward fidelity and commitment in relationships, and general reluctance to engage in physical violence. Men stem from God's finite and limited light, women from His infinite light. Men, represented by a line (reflecting the male anatomy), are time bound and find their spiritual source in the immanent God of history. Women, in contrast, represented by a circle (the female anatomy), flow out from their higher source in the transcendent God of creation. They are above time.

The different roles for men and women in Judaism appear to some to elevate the male role at the expense of women, but Judaism has always maintained that the feminine transcends the masculine. From a Jewish historical perspective, the imperative of man is to move away from a masculine-aggressive posture—a love for war, honor, and vengeance—and toward the feminine-passive virtues of love, compassion, empathy, and understanding. The messianic era will be a "feminine" period in which the infinite light of God will shine unhindered by the currently obstructing "male" concealments in nature.

The Need for Special Gender Roles

There is no denying that Judaism's attitude toward women with respect to the performance of public religious ritual is consistent with the Psalmist's lyrics: "the glory of the King's daughter is her *inward* beauty" (Ps. 45:14). Thus, in terms of *religious ritual roles,* women's is more private than men's. Women are not deterred by Judaism from pursuing any profession. On the contrary, Judaism insists that every individual maximize his or her fullest human potential, both professionally and personally.

I will argue that two noble intentions stand historically behind the different roles of men and women in Judaism. The first is for women to retain their mystery, the second, for them to show the way for men to realize a higher spirituality.

Dismissing Judaism as misogynistic grossly misses its perspective and does not account for the innumerable rabbinical statements that place women before men. The Talmud declares that a woman is a man's greatest blessing and that a man without a wife lives without joy, blessing, and good. A man should love his wife as himself and respect her more than himself (*Yevamot* 62b). When Rabbi Joseph heard his mother's footsteps, he would say, "Let me arise before the approach of the Shekhinah" (*Kiddushin* 31b). The Rabbis declared that Israel was redeemed from Egypt by virtue of its righteous women (*Sotah* 11b). They further declared that a man must be careful never to slight his wife when speaking to her, because women are prone to tears and sensitive to wrong (*Bava Metzia* 59a), and that women have greater faith and deeper spirituality than men (*Sifri Numbers* 133). Women also have greater powers of discernment than men (*Niddah* 45b) and are especially tender-hearted (*Megillah* 14b).

Few today doubt that women are just as capable as men, and that they can be doctors and lawyers, Nobel laureates and heads of state, corporate chairs, and business consultants—or full-time mothers and wives, whatever suits their fancy. Judaism, however, identified intrinsic goodness and special qualities in the female character and was concerned that women who take upon themselves any male role be careful not to squander their precious feminine gifts. Even while doing a "man's" job, they should never compromise their inner femininity. There are practical reasons for this. The first is that the masculinity of men and the femininity of women is what sustains the polar attraction between the sexes. Since married life and the family are the hallmarks of Jewish communal living, the Bible took extraordinary steps to ensure the continued attraction between the sexes and thereby the viability of long-term male-female relationships.

What draws a man to a woman is not the fact that she is the same as him, but rather that she is his *opposite*. Indeed, erotic attraction is dependent on the need to overcome the obstacle of gender. We call the process of overcoming that obstacle *seduction*. Men and women differ in far more than their anatomy. A woman possesses an essential femininity that is manifest intellectually, emotionally, and especially spiritually. Traditionally, young boys play with other boys, and young girls with other girls. But in our teens, this begins to change and we feel drawn to the opposite sex, not because of what we have in common but because of what we *lack* in common. Maintaining these differences is essential in sustaining this gravitation of opposites.

The Talmud remarks that in the region most determining their gender differences, their genitalia, men's are on the outside, whereas women's are obscured from view. This highlights the delicate mystery that is fundamental to a woman's nature. The total submission of a woman to a man would not only be improper, it would invite boredom. A relationship must serve as an endless journey of discovery. Curiosity and the constant desire to explore the other gender is essential to attraction. The female body and the female nature point to a "feminine mystique" in which a woman becomes ultimately unknowable to a man, thereby guaranteeing the male's eternal pursuit of the female. Judaism therefore always kept women in a slightly more screened-off state so that they would not suffer overexposure and compromise their mystery.

Modest dress is a good example. A woman who dresses modestly elicits great passion from her husband simply by undressing. The rule is simple: If a man does not wish to undress a woman in his mind first, he will not wish to undress her with his hands. Modest dress, a form of concealment, inspires lust and desire, in short, eroticism. Erotic obstacles are essential to the maintenance of seduction and passion. Men need this adventure of mystery, and it affords them a constant safari of the body, ensuring that they do not grow listless. They have limited attention spans, especially sexual attention spans. Very few women need their husbands to dress up in lingerie for them, but men often require these artificial inducements to heighten attraction.

The ancient Rabbis adopted the idea of a greater capacity for focus in women, as well as a more fully developed spiritual intuition. That is why, they argued, men must wear the *talit katan* (mini prayer shawl) to remind them at all times of God's commandments, as well as the tefillin (phylacteries used during morning services), which places God's words upon the mind and heart. Women do not need external reminders. God's words are actually *written* on their hearts and embedded in their souls. Women are far more conscious of God as an internal experience, one which is one with their being.

Masculine and Feminine Energy

I could draw upon historical Talmudic and rabbinic sources to respond individually to each of the objections to the role accorded women within Judaism. For example, to some women's dislike of the segregation of the sexes in synagogue, I could respond that its purpose is to ensure that each person approach God as an individual rather than as a collective. But what is needed is a holistic approach, which I offer here. We have to peel away the revealed layers of law and tradition in order to understand Judaism's philosophy of masculine and feminine energies.

It will be apparent to any student of the Bible that there are two distinct aspects to God, two divine energies. First there is God the Creator, distinguished by transcendence, emanating an infinite light that encompasses and fills the world, remote and removed from the coarse world of man. This aspect of God does not get involved with the minutiae of human life or the events of history. For the small things, there is the God of history, distinguished by immanence. This God listens to our cry and is involved in every facet of human behavior, punishing the wicked and rewarding the righteous. The infinite side of God, otherwise known as the God of Creation, is always described in feminine terms; the immanent God of history is masculine by comparison. The infinite God of creation, represented by a circle, is the spiritual source of women. The disciplinary God of history, represented by a line, is the spiritual source of men. Indeed, the symbols mirror the physical characteristics of men and women, as mentioned earlier.

Since women emanate from God's infinity, only they can call forth life from nothingness. The masculine form is more disciplinary and aggressive, the feminine nurturing and subtle. For a human being to lead a fulfilling life, he or she must encompass both forms, the power of speech and the power of silence, the power of strength and the power of compassion, the power of giving and the power of receiving. Although individual men and women encompass both of these dimensions, they primarily embody one. A man's principal role is to use his more aggressive tendencies to *refine* material existence, whereas a woman's is to use her subtle femininity to *reveal* the inner Godliness and holiness pervading all of existence. Traditionally, a father's role is to discipline his children and teach them to curb their passions, and a mother's is to teach her children to develop their inner capacity for life and love. Men build civilizations; women build communities. Men seek to distinguish themselves; women seek never to betray themselves. Men battle darkness, while women foster light.

When God created Adam and Eve and placed them in the Garden of Eden, He commanded them to "work the garden and protect it." There are those who must *work* the garden—till the soil, plant the seeds, remove the weeds, and harvest the produce. And there are those whose primary task is to protect the garden. Their job is not to bring new holiness or Godliness into the world—the planting is being done by someone else—but rather to nurture those aspects of the world that are already holy. In the rearing of a child both aspects are vital. There is the need to mold a child's character by instilling values and imparting knowledge. There must be an authoritarian figure, usually a man, who disciplines the child when he or she does wrong and rewards him or her when he or she does right. But endless discipline will ruin a child and undermine his or her self-confidence. A child is not a piece of marble than can be sculpted and resculpted. There must be a recognition that there is a beauty to the child. There must be someone who doesn't seek to mold so much as reveal, one who doesn't seek to chisel so much as inspire. This requires a nurturing figure, usually a woman, who shows the child unconditional love. A mother is someone who sees only her child's goodness. Because he is innocent and precious, she seeks to protect him from nefarious influences and from danger. True to these stereotypical roles, my father was the one who always saw to it that my siblings and I were disciplined and trained; my mother always protected us and told him that we needed room to grow. Both were right. And both parental roles are necessary.

As in parenting, there are two ways of looking at the world. The masculine way is to see the need to till the soil and harvest the wheat, to view all the world's imperfections and focus on making the world better. The world is inhabited with evil spirits and the man is the dragon slayer. Therefore, the Torah gives men mitzvot to do, each entailing a physical object that a man can elevate to a higher state of perfection. The feminine way of looking at the world entails seeing not the demons, but the angels, not the world's darkness, but its inherent light. The woman protects an already holy world from corruption. Hence, the Jewish religion has given women mitzvot, such as the observance of the kashrut laws, which safeguards the family from eating anything that will be injurious to their spiritual makeup.

Women's perhaps best-known mitzvah is lighting Sabbath candles every Friday evening. She is symbolically making the statement that the house is beautiful already; what it needs is to be illuminated so that its beauty is seen. A wife teaches her husband to remove the dark glasses of cynicism, giving him radiance and hope. A woman finds goodness in her husband even when others sees only his shortcomings.

Ultimately the feminine path is superior to the masculine path. But the world is not ready for the feminine path. To offer an analogy, everyone should be able to leave our homes without locking the front door. Today, that would be an invitation to theft. The full power of feminine energy will not be realized until the male energy has finished its work. When the impulse to always conquer and possess has been neutralized, we will then all be able to live together in harmony, unencumbered by contention and competition. There will come a time when there will be an authentic feminine revolution, when mankind will be more about "being" than "having." One day the messianic era will dawn, when the world's Godly reality will be overtly manifest. We will all live in a feminine-passive rather than a masculine-aggressive world. The peacemakers will be the heroes, and the warmongers will be condemned as criminals. This is not to say that the masculine energy serves no divine purpose. Indeed, we need it to build and to refine, to struggle and to triumph. But even so, the masculine energy is meant ultimately to expend itself once the evil of the world has been eradicated and should then slowly transmute itself into the beauty and splendor of the feminine. Indeed, this is the general rule of all life. In our younger years we are more ambitious and restless. In our mature years we are more thoughtful and introspective. In our youth we are cantankerous. In our golden years we are comforting.

The idea of a woman reflecting the female component in the God-head is a central idea of the Kabbalah. The woman is the Shekhinah, the Divine Presence, commanding increased respect. The *Zohar*, the key work of Jewish mysticism, in a famous passage says:

> It is incumbent on a man to be ever "male and female" [married] in order that his faith may be firm, and that the Shekhinah may never depart from him. What, then, you will say, of a man who goes on a journey and, being absent from his wife, is no longer "male and female"? His remedy is to pray to God before he starts his journey, while he is still "male and female," in order to draw to himself the presence of his Maker. When he has offered his prayer and thanksgiving and the Shekhinah rests on him, then he can depart, for through his union with the Shekhinah he has become "male and female" in the country as he was "male and female" in the town. . . . When he does return home again, it is his duty to give his wife pleasure, because it was she who acquired for him his heavenly partner. (*Zohar*, Genesis, 49b–50a)

In this beautiful passage the *Zohar* affirms the need for the masculine to be forever tempered by the feminine; the need for husbands to be completed by their wives.

In the same vein, Rabbi Isaac Luria, the greatest mystic of all time, used to kiss the hands of his mother on the eve of the Sabbath, the feminine component of the week. In his circle the custom arose of reciting a passage from Proverbs on the Sabbath in praise of the Shekhinah. Eventually the origin of the custom was forgotten and was adopted by Jewish men far removed from Kabbalism who recited the passage in honor of their wives. To this day, one of the most moving events of the Jewish Sabbath ritual is when a husband looks at his wife and recites to her the tribute to a wife of excellence, the Aishet Chayil passage, according to tradition, by King Solomon.

A capable wife who can find? She is far more precious than jewels. The heart of her husband trusts in her, and he will have no lack of gain. She opens her hand to the poor, and reaches out her hands to the needy. Strength and dignity are her clothing, and she laughs at the time to come. She opens her mouth with wisdom, and the teaching of kindness is on her tongue. Her children rise up and call her happy; her husband too, and he praises her: "Many women have done excellently, but you surpass them all." Charm is deceitful, and beauty is vain, but a woman who fears the Lord is to be praised. (Prov. 31:10–11, 20, 25–26, 28–30)

The mystical insights found in the *Zohar* account for the differing functions of each sex within the Jewish faith. The *Zohar* first explains the public and more active role accorded to men: their leading of prayers, functioning as Rabbis, obligation to attend synagogue regularly. Since a man does not immediately see God's light illuminating the world, he must immerse himself in an environment where even he experiences the presence of God. Divine ritual becomes an alarm clock, ringing at all hours, alerting him to wake up and smell the coffee. Women, however, can find God even at home. They are much more capable of discovering the hidden within the apparent. We must not misconstrue woman's more private role within Judaism as secondary. Those who have spiritual fulfillment do not need to shout it from the pulpits of the synagogues any more than those who are truly in love need to demonstrate it in public places. Subtle dignity and quiet spirituality are far more formidable than anything overtly aggressive or physical. True religious piety and holiness do not holler. They speak in a strong and steady voice, resonating from within.

Removing Conflict from Human Situations

There is another consideration in the Torah's absolving women from time-bound commandments such as the donning of tefillin and wearing *tzitzit,* both of which are done during the day. It is not to exclude women from a spiritual regimen, but rather to recognize that women, hailing from the infinite, are not bound by time the way that men are. Their spirituality transcends the confines of spatio-temporal existence; thus they are obligated only in those commandments that apply at all places and at all times, like the requirement to eat kosher food. Men, representing the masculine-aggressive, do not feel holiness in time, and are not naturally in harmony with the all-surrounding presence of God. They therefore require time-bound commandments, which sensitize them to the presence of God both in time and space.

In the narrative of the giving of the Torah at Mount Sinai, we read: "Then Moses went up to God; the Lord called to him from the mountain, saying, 'Thus you shall say to the house of Jacob, and tell the Israelites: . . . if you obey my voice and keep my covenant, you shall be my treasured possession out of all the peoples. Indeed, the whole earth is mine'" (Exod. 19:3–5). The ancient Rabbis explain that "the house of Jacob" refers to the women, and "the Israelites," to the men. Thus, God commanded the study of the Torah and the observance of the commandments to the women before He commanded it to the men. It is to the Jewish community's eternal regret that historically women have not been afforded ample opportunity to claim this inheritance. The Torah, the living embodiment of God's true essence and His infinite wisdom, must be made accessible to all Jewish men and women. One of the world Jewish community's foremost goals must be to redress this imbalance. I am heartened by the extraordinary growth of Jewish female prayer and study groups, which should be encouraged to flourish.

A few years ago, a young woman wrote to me that it was tragic that the potent feminine energy was not being used to bring healing to a broken planet. I couldn't agree more. It is the women of the world who will cure us of the insecurity of masculine aggression. Surely this should be the ultimate goal of the feminist revolution: to topple the walls separating spirit from matter and soul from body, to bring true harmony finally between masculine and feminine energies. Men think within dualistic structures that are always at odds, but women approach life more holistically and harmoniously. Men perceive a rupture in existence. They see evil and rush to vanquish it. Women take a higher view and perceive the possibility of union within all that is. Our world is being increasingly ruled by fragmentation and isolation. The feminine energy is one of repair and sharing. Women today, with their higher and more immediate powers of spiritual insight, can teach the world the relevance of religion to contemporary living and help mankind discover our underlying spiritual potential. Women cannot accomplish this if they use men as their spiritual role model, especially in the Kabbalah's insistence on the innate spiritual superiority of women to men.

A more feminine approach to human relationships would also breed greater understanding between men and women and heal many relationships. The ancient Rabbis said that the altar of God weeps for every marriage that dissolves. If men and women cannot live together in mutual respect and harmony, then we might accuse the Almighty, from whom they both emanate, of not being unified, of not being One. But for this special and unique feminine energy to help revitalize the world's faith, men and women must realize their respective, equal roles and strive to complement each other in the struggle to improve life. Now is the time for women to radiate the healing warmth of their nurturing energy and bring heat to an increasingly cold and dark landscape.

11

Suffering

Reward, Punishment, and the
Problem of Suffering

God is involved in man's destiny—good or bad. To thank him for Jerusalem and not question him for Treblinka is hypocrisy.

—ELIE WIESEL,
Prayer and Modern Man

Suffering is by no means a privilege, a sign of nobility, a reminder of God. Suffering is a fierce, bestial thing, commonplace, uncalled for, natural as air.

—CESARE PAVESE,
The Burning Brand: Diaries 1935–1950

Suffering does not ennoble. It destroys.

—DOROTHY ALLISON, *Skin*

If suffering brought wisdom, the dentist's office would be full of luminous ideas.

—MASON COOLEY, *City Aphorisms*

I read the book of Job last night—I don't think God comes out well in it.

—VIRGINIA WOOLF

EVERY NATION POSSESSES CHARACTERISTICS for which they are well known: the Italians, artistry; the French, pageantry; the British, political institutions. Perhaps the saddest commentary about the nation of Israel is that suffering nearly always tops its list. The Jews are known universally as a people who have experienced unspeakable horrors and misery throughout their long history. Indeed, exile, expulsion, and state-sponsored terror have been endemic to Jewish history, and thus a comprehensive response to the problem of suffering is mandatory in any discussion of the Jewish faith.

That discussion becomes all the more poignant in light of the contrary biblical prophecies. The divine promises made to Abraham, Isaac, and Jacob entail a bountiful future for their offspring. There were repeated assurances, part of the covenant God forged with all three patriarchs, of the Jews becoming "great like the stars," "a multitude like the sands of the seas," "in you shall be blessed all the nations of the world," and so on. Yet, the Jews remain a tiny nation and have scarcely, if ever, constituted more than one-third of 1 percent of the total world population. Having lost more than a third of their number in the twentieth century in the Holocaust, today there are fewer than fourteen million. At times the world Jewish population has verged on total extinction, owing to repeated programs of mass murder. What happened to God's promises of prosperity to the Jewish people? Their persecution throughout history seems to constitute a blatant contradiction of the good things God said would be their lot.

Suffering comes in two forms, external and internal. External suffering occurs when things in life go wrong, such as losing a job or being abandoned by a spouse, or more serious issues such as the loss of a child or a world war. External suffering can often be escaped. Amid the horrors of the Spanish expulsion and Inquisition, many Jews were able to immigrate to benevolent countries, for example, the Netherlands. During the Nazi terror, many Jews were able to escape to the United States, Australia, and South Africa.

Internal suffering, however, is utterly inescapable, and we are all subject to it by virtue of being human. Internal, or existential, suffering is brought about by our very existence as mortals. When we contemplate the vulnerability of human life and the ephemerality of all human actions, our dependency on others and our need for material sustenance, our being trapped alone in an indifferent universe and dark cosmos, the meaninglessness that can accompany life and the inescapability of death, we develop a profound sense of despair. It seems that one of the ingredients that most unites people the world over is that we are all in pain in varying degrees; each of us has our measure of heartaches. Joy and happiness seem elusive; always taunting us from an unreachable promised land beyond. Much of the joy people do experience in everyday life is brought about simply by distraction: going to movies, watching television, buying clothes, pursuing the opposite sex. But the pain of life is always present, just beneath the veneer, and is bound to surface at some point. Therefore, the less we think about life's meaninglessness and how we squander our lives on vain pursuits, the happier we seem to be.

The Demise of Faith

The fact that religion has survived all these years is nearly miraculous. Prior to the 1860s, organized religion enjoyed a social and cultural supremacy in the Western world that is unknown in our time. Of course, even then there were heretics, atheists, and agnostics. But they were a minority. Those who lived outside religious norms were classified as radicals and often were outcasts. In general, the early atheist writers and thinkers were aggressive atheists, since they spent most of their time on the defensive.

Today, the situation has come full circle, with religion having been increasingly marginalized. Several causes are responsible for the modern demise of religion, but it is my first purpose to show how the unspeakable horrors of the twentieth century served as a nail in religion's coffin.

The Essentials of Faith and
Their Essential Disintegration

Judaism is a religion of 613 commandments, along with thousands of tributary laws. Because of the size and complexity of the law, many giants of Jewish thought have sought to codify the fundamental articles of Jewish faith. Maimonides is famous for having summarized the essence of Judaism in thirteen cardinal tenets, and Rabbi Joseph Albo encapsulated it further into three major principles. But however one condenses the essentials of Jewish faith, the following principles are always included, for upon them there can be no compromise for traditional Judaism:

1. There exists an eternal, omnipotent God, Creator of heaven and earth and all forms of life contained therein. These did not arise spontaneously, but were called into being by a special act of creation.

2. This Creator directly communicated His will to humans through His Torah, which serves as His incontrovertible and revealed testimony to mankind.

3. Humans are the jewel of creation, endowed with special purpose and intelligence, serving both as a privilege and a grave responsibility. Man has the freedom of choice to be good or evil, to accommodate the wishes of the Supreme Being, Who created him in His image, or to ignore the will of his Creator and lead a life devoid of moral sensitivity.

4. God is good and just. He rewards the righteous and punishes the wicked. Because of man's special responsibility and freedom to act in accordance with his own will, and because he has been entrusted by God as custodian over the earth, man is held accountable for his actions. If he acts out of kindness and generosity, he will be rewarded with a good life; if his actions are evil, he will be punished. Despite the apparent prosperity of the wicked and the suffering of the righteous in our present world, this state of affairs will be corrected at the end of days, when goodness will abound.

Strife, jealousy, and contention will be removed from our world, to be replaced with love, truth, sincerity, and friendship. "In his [the Messiah's] days the righteous will flourish; prosperity will abound till the moon is no more . . . and his enemies will lick the dust" (Ps. 72:7–9).

We have witnessed how each of these sacred principles, one by one, has been subtly eroded. First, Darwinian evolution explained the diversity of life on earth through genetic mutation and natural selection, rather than a purposeful Creator. Although Darwin never actually refuted the existence of God, his claims severely undermined belief in a Creator, who no longer seemed necessary.

Furthermore, Darwin challenged the belief that man is unique within creation. From an evolutionary viewpoint, man descended from primates and is biologically similar to his cousins, the big apes. The only area in which man is distinguished from the animal is the quantitative edge of his intelligence. Man is not in any way *qualitatively* superior to the animals, and his life, therefore, is endowed with no greater purpose than theirs.

Sigmund Freud further diminished our self-esteem by asserting that man is far less a master in his own mental household than he once supposed. Whereas Judaism had always emphasized the absolute belief in man's freedom of choice, Freud argued for the existence of autonomous regions of the mind that could not be subjected to man's conscious control. The id would always remain primal and uncivilized, thriving on, and serving as the impetus for, man's most ignoble instincts. Resistance was futile. The more man sought to suppress it, the more his unruly unconscious would manifest itself in the form of neurosis and psychosis. By postulating a base, animalistic impulse at the very heart of man, Freud too emphasized the kinship between man and the animals. Modern-day determinist psychology has taken this argument further by advancing theories that view human behavior as the confluence of genetic disposition and environmental influences. Man has only the illusion of choice. He is conditioned from earliest youth by society and the people around him.

The next nail in the coffin came from criticism of the claims of divine authorship of the Bible. By maintaining that the Bible is a complex set of books that should not all be treated identically, and by pointing out the apparent contradictions coming to light as a result of archaeological investigation, Bible critics dealt a powerful blow to belief in divine revelation at the foot of Sinai. Although knowledge of these claims is not as widespread as that of evolution or psychoanalysis, their existence has cast grave doubt in academic communities. From my experience at Oxford University, the claims of biblical critics posed a formidable challenge to faith to many of my students, and we debated the claims of Biblical critics constantly.

But nothing undermined the case for religion as much as the wholesale slaughter of the twentieth century. Those unprecedented wars and genocides killed more than 100 million people, estimates historian Paul Johnson in modern times. This staggering number reveals the inhumanity in our midst and may lead us to believe that we are alone in the universe. What can be said about a benevolent God who allowed Hitler, Stalin, Mao, and Pol Pot to flourish, all in a fifty-year time span? If God exists and is standing by as a disinterested witness or, indeed, if He is powerless to stop it, then why pray?

When I first had the privilege of hosting Elie Wiesel to lecture to Oxford's students in March 1990, he was asked by a student whether he still believed in God after the Holocaust. He responded, "Of course I believe in God after the Holocaust, and my belief in Him has not wavered even a bit. But because I believe in Him, I am very angry at Him."

The existence of suffering is the greatest challenge to faith because it undermines its central premise: that God exists and loves His creatures, and that every time a human being aches or grieves, he can entreat his Creator to take notice and expect Him to come to his aid. A child who has been abandoned by his father at an early age does not care if the parent still lives elsewhere on the planet. God's silence in the face of suffering of innocents is a far greater indictment than His potential non-existence. Of what use is a Creator who, having called man into existence, subsequently decides to abandon him to fate and the elements? Simply stated, if God is not good, then He is not worthy of worship.

Mainstream Responses to Suffering

In the fifth chapter of Exodus, Moses offers a complaint to God. It is the first record in the Bible of a claim of a divine miscarriage of justice. Moses had been sent by the Almighty to demand the Jewish people's release from Pharaoh. Not only did Pharaoh refuse to free them, but he gave orders that the burden of the Jews was to be intensified—straw was to be withheld from their building of bricks, yet they would be required to fulfill the same quota per day. "And Moses returned unto the Lord and he said, 'Lord, why have you dealt ill with this people? Why is it that you have sent me? For since I came to Pharaoh to speak in your name, he has dealt ill with this people; neither have you delivered at all Your people'" (Exod. 5:22–23).

Immanuel Kant pointed out that if it is arrogant to defend God, it is even more arrogant to assail Him. Yet the Jew in particular, and the religious man of reason in general, has always grappled with cosmic questions. This is in part what distinguishes the reasonable person from the fundamentalist. The latter, by intense uncritical devotion, is rendered an automaton, untroubled by reason. The lesson from this challenge by Moses is that man must seek to understand seeming divine injustice. How has Judaism traditionally approached the problem? There are five major responses, as grouped together by David Birnbaum in his book *God and Evil*.

1. Finite Man Cannot Comprehend Infinite God's Ways.   The universe is somehow better with apparent evil in it. God's ways are inscrutable. He has His ultimate purposes, known to Him. Man must have faith in God's justice. God's ways will be made understandable to us in the next world.

2. Man Is Punished for His Sins and Failings.   The iniquities of the fathers are visited upon the sons ("vertical responsibility"). Man is punished in this world to increase his reward in the next world. There is no suffering without sin. All men are imperfect and sin in some way. Suffering occurs because of evil deeds or neglect of religious observance.

3. Hester Panim: *Hiding of the Divine Face.*   There are moments when God temporarily abandons the world, suspends His active surveillance. This concept is almost never applied in a general defense of God's goodness in the face of evil, but rather as a response to a particular catastrophe, like the Holocaust.

4. Good People Suffer Along with the Wicked.   According to the Talmud, "When permission is given to the angel of destruction, he makes no difference between righteous and wicked." The righteous suffer because they are held to a much higher standard. A righteous person's suffering is atonement for all people. The righteous will get their reward in the world-to-come. Righteous men or women suffer or die an early death because they are "gathered in" prior to the appearance of great evil.

5. Freedom of Man.   There are self-willed constraints on God's intervention to protect man's freedom. Suffering is an indispensable spur to human aspiration and achievement. Suffering pushes man over the brink to rise up against oppression, to demand freedom. Suffering provides the flip side of reward and goodness. Without one there cannot be the other.

The reconciliation of the good God and the people who suffer is known in philosophy as theodicy, and the fact that all these different theodocies appear in Jewish thought is a testimony to their individual inadequacy. Clearly, each of these five has a gaping hole that offers the sufferer little consolation.

Notice that the five major categories of traditional responses have a common denominator. They all implicate man in his suffering—either because of his sinfulness and ignorance or because suffering is beneficial and redemptive—and exonerate God. What these responses have in common are varying degrees of letting God off the hook, while damning man for his iniquitous nature, ignorance, and lowliness. Is this an authentic Jewish response to suffering, based on the sources in the Bible, or a later Jewish attempt to honor God at all costs, once suffering became the norm for the Jewish people in their long and tragic history?

I suggest that the latter is true, which is why I will now attempt an authentic Jewish response to suffering, based on the early examples of the Jewish patriarchs and prophets. What we will discover is that when our biblical forebears were confronted with suffering, they always *implicated God and exonerated man.* Indeed, the approach of exonerating God at human expense is highly inadequate and unsatisfactory. Righteous and decent people who suffer cannot accept the idea that their deeds have been so terrible that they warrant such tragedy. After all, is there anyone who really believes that the Jews of Europe could have been so sinful that they merited being turned into soap and lampshades, incinerated into dust and ash? The Torah is not a history book, but rather a book of instruction. When it recounts for all eternity the interaction and dialogues between the Almighty and Abraham and Moses, it is recounting these stories for posterity so that we might emulate their response.

Jewish Responses to Suffering

Clearly a people who have faced two thousand years of persecution will have evolved a highly developed concept of theodicy. Yet, the Jewish response to suffering remains at once defiant and strongly biblical. Beginning with Abraham and his defiant posture before God at Sodom and Gomorrah, and continuing on through Moses and his entreaties on behalf of the Jewish people, the giants of Jewish history have categorically refused to bow their heads and simply accept apparent divine injustice. The Jewish response to suffering is to struggle with God, to wrestle with the divine. Since man is in a relationship with God, he has the right to make certain demands that are necessary for the health of the God-man relationship.

Judaism begins with the premise that man needs health, happiness, and financial sustenance in order to serve God. Those who lie in hospital beds or have lost a child harbor too broken a spirit to offer meaningful service to their Creator. Judaism does not seek a *response* to suffering, so much as its *alleviation*. The biblical patriarchs and matriarchs never sought an explanation from God as to why people suffer. Rather, they demanded of the Creator that He cease visiting any pain on humanity, whatever His higher purposes might be. Therefore, through torture, inquisitions, pogroms, crusades, massacres, and the Holocaust, the Jewish spirit has never broken and the Jewish flame has never been extinguished. Through every plague that God has visited on the earth's inhabitants, the threefold Jewish response has been (1) to beseech and demand from God a cessation of the plague; (2) to devote their energies, through medicine and technology, to finding a cure; and (3) to pray for the speedy arrival of the Messiah, who would bring redemption to mankind and an end to the earth's imperfections.

Central to the Jewish response to suffering is a staunch rejection of the belief in its redemptive power. According to Judaism there are no ennobling qualities in pain. It irritates me to hear people speak of how much they have learned from hardship and suffering—as if similar lessons could not have been acquired through less painful means. Indeed, I argue that those Jews who see in suffering a redemptive quality may still be practicing the Jewish religion, but have ceased thinking as Jews. *The belief in the redemptive quality of suffering is a profoundly Christian concept.* In Christianity, the suffering servant, the crucified Christ, brings atonement for the sins of mankind through his own sacrifice and torment. The message: Without suffering there can be no redemption. According to Christianity, if Jesus had not suffered and died on the cross, mankind would still be damned. Suffering is therefore extolled in the New Testament: "And not only that, but we also boast in our sufferings, knowing that suffering produces endurance, and endurance produces character, and character produces hope" (Rom. 5:3–4). "If we are being afflicted, it is for your consolation and salvation; if we are being consoled, it is for your consolation, which you experience when you patiently endure the same sufferings that we are also suffering" (2 Cor. 1:6). Indeed, Paul even made suffering an obligation, encouraging the fledging Christians to "share in suffering like a good soldier of Christ Jesus" (2 Tim. 2:3).

In Judaism, however, suffering is anything but redemptive. It leads to a tortured spirit and a pessimistic outlook on life. It scars our psyches and brings about a cynical consciousness, devoid of hope. Suffering causes us to dig out the insincerity in the hearts of our fellows and to be envious of other people's happiness. If individuals do become better people as a result of their suffering, it is *despite* the fact that they suffered, not because of it. Ennoblement of character comes through *triumph* over suffering, rather than its endurance.

Several years ago I was privileged to meet former Beirut hostage Brian Keenan. He was in great pain and yet he maintained a warm and beautiful smile and wrote something extremely witty in his dedication to my copy of his book, the account of his ordeal as a hostage. After speaking with him for some time, I came to the realization that the special qualities he possessed—his love for his fellowman, his warmth, earthiness, and optimistic view of life—had been present prior to his ordeal. He did not gain them because he suffered, but rather his greatness lay in the fact that he retained these beautiful traits *in spite of* the fact that he had suffered. Speak to any Holocaust survivor, even the most celebrated, such as Elie Wiesel or Simon Wiesenthal, and ask them what they gathered from their suffering, aside from loneliness, heartbreak, and misery. To be sure, they also learned the value of life and the sublime quality of human companionship. But these lessons could easily have been learned through life-affirming experiences that do not leave permanent scars on the psyche.

I believe that my parents' divorce drove me to a deeper understanding of life and a greater embrace of religion. Yet, I know people who have led completely privileged lives and have deeper philosophies of life and are even more devoted to their religion than I. And they have the advantage of not being bitter, cynical, or pessimistic the way I can sometimes be because of the pain of my early childhood. The college students I know who were raised in homes in which their parents gave them huge amounts of love and attention are the most healthy, balanced, and loving of all. They are usually also the best students. Those who were neglected or demeaned by their parents can also be positive and loving, but a Herculean effort was first needed to undo the scarring inflicted upon them by their parents' treatment. Whatever good we as individuals, or the world in general, receive from suffering can be brought about in a painless, joyful manner.

Whereas the word *Islam* means "submission to God," and Christianity advocates the obedient leap-of-faith, the word *Yisrael* (Israel) means "he who wrestles with God." When a Jew protests to God, it is not a challenge to divine providence, because we are not challenging God's authority or asserting that He has visited his cruelty or injustice upon humanity. Neither are we maintaining that God's plans have gone askew. Rather what we are saying is this: We believe that somehow this must be to our benefit, and that You are a good and Just Creator. But You are also all-powerful, and would it not therefore be possible for You to bring about this desired end by less painful means? We are asking God to change the means He employs to achieve His always just and noble ends. As for those who argue that suffering humbles the heart and ennobles the spirit, would they pray to the Almighty that He visit even greater suffering on mankind to induce further ethical merit?

Shadowlands

A child misbehaves, breaking everything in sight. His parent is obviously cross and warns him to behave. Yet, even while offering a reprimand, the parent fully understands that it is natural, even desirable, for a child sometimes to run amok. If the child sat still all day long, or if at five he showed the quiet and mature restraint of a thirty-year-old, his parent would drag him to a psychiatrist. So, the role of a child is to misbehave, and the job of the parent is to correct the child and maintain discipline. Each party carries out his role legitimately, although the roles are in conflict.

Likewise, as human beings, it is not our role to concern ourselves with God's affairs or to justify His actions by saying that the suffering of other people carries an internal, albeit latent, good. "The secret things belong to the Lord our God, but the things revealed belong to us and to our children forever, that we may follow all the words of this law" (Deut. 29:29). Why God brings suffering upon mankind, especially on the righteous, is something that transcends human comprehension. Moreover, it is none of our business. God must pursue His plan. But human beings are charged with the eternal pursuit of love and justice, *even if it means sparring with the Creator.* These are two legitimate roles that may often conflict. The moral imperative beholden upon us when we witness the suffering of another individual is to cause it to cease, not to attempt to understand it ourselves or explain it to others. And if it is something over which we have no control, such as an incurable illness or a powerful aggressor such as the Nazis, our obligation is to shake the foundations of the heavens against this seeming miscarriage of justice.

The question to pose in such a case is not, "Please, God, explain to us why bad things happen and how it fits into Your overall plan for creation," but rather: "Master of the Universe, how could You allow this to happen? Was is not You who taught us in Your magnificent Torah that life is sacred and must be preserved at all costs? Where is that life now? Was is not You who promised that the good deserve goodness and not pain? Where is your promise now? By everything that is sacred to You, I demand that this cease." Far from being an affront to divine authority, these words are part of the human mandate. Remaining passive in the face of human suffering is a sin against both man and the Creator.

British author C. S. Lewis, in the biographical movie *Shadowlands,* embraces a position of Christian acquiescence as the proper response to suffering. The classic dualist approach maintains that suffering is necessary to distinguish between pain and happiness. Lewis's dying wife (Joy Davidson, who is in fact Jewish) tells him that the happiness that they experience together now, the fact that she is alive and they are married, is directly dependent on the impending tragedy of her death. He accepts this position as long as she is alive, but as soon as she dies, the once submissive Lewis becomes angry with the religious platitudes offered by his friend, the doctor of divinity at Magdalen College. He shouts and orders the minister to be silent, swinging his cudgel at the thought that God could somehow desire anyone's death, especially a good person who has caused no one harm.

I sympathize entirely with this response, not because Lewis was pained and was thus incapable of submission to the will of God at that moment, but rather because his wife, like every decent human being, deserved a long and happy life and was promised one by the Almighty Creator. How could this cleric be so sanctimonious and arrogant as to dismiss the death of someone else's beloved in the belief that it carried with it a cosmic reason? The Garden of Eden, the perfect world that God created, had no suffering, thereby demonstrating that perfection is tied to a decided lack of suffering. Let us cease the thought that suffering is beneficent. To eternally challenge suffering is the only legitimate theological response.

Contrasting Views of Adam's Sin

The sin of justifying human suffering is especially heinous for a Rabbi because it betrays a fundamental ignorance of Jewish theology. Judaism sees death, illness, and suffering as aberrations in creation that were brought about through the sin of Adam in Eden. When God created the first man and woman, he placed them in His garden and told them that they were permitted to eat from all the trees of the Garden, with the exception of one: the tree of knowledge of good and evil. "And the Lord God commanded the man saying,

Of every tree of the garden you may eat; But of the tree of the knowledge of good and evil, you shall not eat from it; *for on the day* that
you eat from it you shall surely die" (Gen. 2:16–17). The verse is puzzling. Adam and Eve did indeed eat from the tree of knowledge, yet
they did not die on that day. In fact, Adam lived on for more than
nine hundred years! How to account for this discrepancy? Judaism
and Christianity deal with this difficulty in startlingly different
ways.

According to traditional Christianity, the meaning of God's warn-
ing that sin would bring immediate death was that Adam and Eve
would die a *spiritual* death. Thus, as soon as man committed the
"original" sin, his soul died and he was damned. Christianity traditionally recognizes a body-soul dualism whereby people are viewed,
not as integrated beings, but as possessors of an eternal soul and an
ephemeral body, which is the vessel designed to accommodate the
needs of the immortal soul. Only the soul can be restored in heaven
through an affirmation of belief in Christ. According to the Jewish
interpretation, the meaning of the verse was that on the day Adam
defied God's command and ate of the tree of knowledge, he would
be *condemned* to death; he would lose his immortality. As God's direct handiwork, whom He had created in His direct image, man was
never meant to experience death. Like his Father in heaven, man
was meant to live eternally. As long as Adam remained attached to
the infinite source of life, he was eternal like his Creator. By sinning
against God, Adam and Eve severed themselves from the infinite
source of life and immediately they began to decay and die. Through
his transgression, Adam brought death and destruction into the
world. He might live many more years, but one day he would succumb to death, just as every apple when detached from a tree suc-
cumbs to decay.

The implications of this rabbinical exegesis on this crucial passage
of Genesis are profound. There was never meant to be a place for
death in our world. Neither was there ever any plan for life to include suffering or pain. The Garden of Eden, previously this earth,
was perfect. By detaching himself from God and worshipping his

own sensual lusts, man became vulnerable and has been suffering for it ever since.

This rabbinic teaching also declares that suffering has no meaning. As it was never part of the original plan, it has no purpose. It was an aberration, a mistake to be corrected, a crooked line that can still be made straight. No human was ever predestined to suffer or die. Neither will any form of misery be present in the perfect messianic age that has been promised for three millennia by the Almighty through His prophets and Sages. Only now, in this interim period between life in Eden and life in the perfect world-to-come, are we ravaged by cancer, AIDS, car crashes, hatred, and genocide.

To hasten the arrival of the promised world of the future, man must today drown the world's imperfections in endless deeds of loving-kindness. The Jew finds comfort in the immortal words of the Psalmist, "I will not die but I shall live, and proclaim the works of the Lord" (Ps. 118:17). We will wrestle with the heavens and draw our swords against the angel of death. And notwithstanding how many unfortunate casualties we take in the interim, in the words of Winston Churchill, "we shall never surrender." We shall employ every means—medical research, philanthropy, comforting words, and an infinite number of prayers—until the time that God recognizes our deep disenchantment with the world and finally reinvolves Himself visibly with history, removing from our midst those tragedies that are still beyond our ability to prevent. Neither will we accept that those who have already perished shall never rise again. We firmly assert our conviction that we will be rejoined with them in an era of peace and joy. "Multitudes who sleep in the dust of the earth will awake" (Dan. 12:2). "But your dead will live; their bodies will rise. You who dwell in the dust, wake up and shout for joy. Your dew is like the dew of the morning; the earth will give birth to her dead" (Isa. 26:19).

Man's mission was never to make peace with suffering and death, but to abolish them from the face of the earth for all eternity by joining God as a junior partner in creation. By studying medicine and offering aid to people in need, we live up to our highest calling of having been created in the divine image. *The atheist doctor who struggles to cure AIDS is infinitely more in tune with the Jewish response to suffering than the minister of religion who tells his flock that suffering is part of the divine plan.* The sinning businessman who may have never stepped into a synagogue but makes a loan to a colleague to save him from bankruptcy is more in tune with the Jewish response to suffering than the Rabbi who seeks to give a rationalization for why children die of leukemia. Rabbis who try to give meaning to the Holocaust and explain it as punishment for Jewish sin have at best missed the whole point of humanity's mission on this earth. Our role as humans is not to give meaning to aberrations, but to heal them with Godly light. Human beings are commanded by God to occupy themselves with life, never with death. Our energy must be dedicated, not to explaining hurt and pain, but to combating them and to healing wounds.

Clerical "Comfort" and Defiance

Could the God who instructed us to move mountains and shake the earth's foundations in the face of injustice suddenly require us to remain silent in the face our compatriots' pain? Does He not want us to plead and argue on His behalf? Would He prefer that we remain dumb like the lamb, even in the face of another's slaughter? Rationalizing suffering serves only to dissuade us from our true mission. The Jew is a catalyst of history who always raises his head to hope against hope. A true minister of religion teaches his flock to be defiant when unconquerable illness overtakes a parishioner. Never bow your heads in subjugation and never capitulate. Always fight for life, always beg for mercy, and never condemn your fellowmen.

As long as we can explain why people can be gassed or die of miserable illness, the pain associated with these losses will be mitigated. That is not meant to happen. Our obligation is to shake the foundations of the heavenly throne and entreat the Almighty for peace and long life. We will *not* understand why parents are bereaved of their children. We refuse to explain away the extermination of innocents. In this respect, we must use our pain, not to look for reasons, but to demand the messianic era. We must turn our pain to something life affirming and good. We must not question why innocent Israeli soldiers die in battle at the age of eighteen in defense of their permanently endangered homeland. Rather, we must arm ourselves, but at the same time search meaningfully for peace, but with reliable partners whose main wish is peace, not extracting concessions. We do not seek to understand why these things happen, but to prevent them from happening again.

I became convinced at an early age that notwithstanding the imperfections of life, we could all be happy or at least go down fighting. The real enemies were cynicism and complacency, which had to be battled to the death. Despite having witnessed endless quarrels in one's parents' home, one could still lead a storybook existence with one's spouse in the future. The attitude prevalent in society is for people to attribute their condition or shortcomings to their environment, parents, job, or upbringing. But Judaism, rejecting the idea of fate, teaches that man creates his own destiny.

It came as a total surprise to me when I began to meet people who disagreed with me violently. They felt that my position of wrestling with the divine, fighting against fate, was naive at best, grave heresy at worst. I was particularly astounded to hear this position advocated most vehemently in many Jewish religious quarters. Virtually every lecture I have delivered to audiences on the subject of suffering meets with the following response: Secular Jews and non-Jews find my words refreshing, redeeming, and inspiring. I do not say this to sound arrogant, rather, to point out the degree to which less observant Jews and non-Jews embrace this defiant message. They feel that this interpretation of suffering affords them the opportunity to voice their grievances to an otherwise benevolent Creator who is prepared to listen and soothe, rather than to rebuke and tell them that their own actions precipitated the pain they now experience. But the greater the level of religious observance, the greater the level of discomfort with my views on this subject. Hence, I stress that my ideas are not idiosyncratic; they are in accordance with biblical and traditional Jewish example and thought. It is an ancient staple of Judaism to challenge God, especially in the area of human suffering. This was how Abraham acted upon hearing that Sodom and Gomorrah would be destroyed because of the inhabitants' iniquity, and this is why Moses protested time and again when the Almighty threatened to devour the Jewish nation for its sins, in their long trek across the wilderness of Sinai.

I delivered my first major lecture on the subject of suffering to fifty Jewish employees and vice presidents at the world headquarters of a bank in the early 1990s. The more religious participants were aghast. "How can you challenge God?" they asked me. "Who are you to question His justice? Are you implying that God is unjust? Shame on you. And you call yourself a Rabbi. When people suffer, it is in atonement for their sins. God gives us only what we deserve." The next lecture I gave provoked even stronger reactions. I was invited to address an audience of three hundred, one-third of whom were devoutly Orthodox. When I finished the talk, the first questioner began by stating that this was the most comforting lecture he had ever heard on the subject of suffering. But subsequent questioners rose to heap scorn and ridicule on everything I had said. It was not long before people were openly calling me a heretic and describing my talk as "blasphemous," "sacrilegious," "profane," and "deeply offensive to the sensitivities of all religious people."

It didn't end there. First, the sound engineer who had promised me a copy of the tape told my secretary that he was going to burn the tape because of its heretical content. Then, I received a phone call from Lubavitch headquarters telling me that a terrible uproar had exploded and that it could be deeply damaging to my reputation. They wanted me to respond to three letters that had appeared in the Manchester *Jewish Telegraph*. The first began as follows: "If the Lubavitch wishes to retain its credibility amongst Orthodox Jews, it will have to do something about Rabbi Shmulie [sic] Boteach who spoke in Manchester last month." After quoting several of my remarks out of context, the letter ended, "The most serious threat to Judaism this century has been the false misinterpretation of our religion by the Reformers. . . . It is an extremely dangerous precedent which must not go unchallenged."

Another letter contained the following allegations:

> Far from being inspired or impressed, there was a strong feeling of confusion and consternation at the disregard for authentic Jewish values which he expressed. . . . Rabbi Elchonon Wasserman, the leader of Torah Jewry during the holocaust—who was killed by the Nazis—stated that the reason for the horror was that "people did not believe in Hell anymore, so God brought Hell into world to prove it. . . . The holocaust was a divine punishment." Are we then to regard Rabbi Boteach as the greatest of his generation and Rabbi Wasserman as having made a mistake? As a doctor I am flattered by his remarks that the medical profession are doing more for Judaism than rabbis whose *shiurim* [lectures] we attend. However, it is obviously ludicrous to make such a suggestion.

The last letter was the most condemnatory of all:

> In the well-known *Guard Your Tongue,* . . . it states: "If a speaker has made remarks which constitute heresy, you are actually obliged to deride and ridicule him. The prohibition against *lashon hara* [slander] does not apply to such a person." I heard Rabbi Boteach's lecture . . . and he explained that according to his beliefs there is no reason for suffering. . . . The views Rabbi Boteach is presenting are opposite to those of the Torah and people must not be brainwashed by him.

The underlying premise behind each of the letters is a determination to defend God at all costs and simultaneously to indict man for his own misery. Unfortunately, sometimes people think they are defending God when really they are just covering up their own insecurity; they are not willing to accept ideas that might threaten their cozy beliefs.

Aside from their apparent fundamentalist orientation, those who argue that challenging God is sacrilegious and heretical betray an ignorance of holy writ. Let them learn how the outstanding figures of the Bible reacted to injustice and suffering. As we have seen, they objected to God and interceded on the suffering party's behalf. Never once did they capitulate and bow their heads in pious obedience. When God came to Abraham and informed him that He would crush Sodom and Gomorrah, cities that Abraham himself knew were deserving of punishment for their unparalleled iniquity, did Abraham bow his head and accept divine judgment? In one of the most dramatic moments recorded in the Bible, Abraham shook his fist at the heavens and demanded, "You are the Judge of the whole earth. Shall You not practice justice?" (Gen. 18:25). That the most righteous man on the earth could defend the most wicked and entreat God for clemency is a remarkable example that we should all take to heart. If you are a biological or spiritual descendant of Abraham, then you cannot stand idly by and watch your neighbor suffer. That would be a betrayal of everything Abraham stood for.

Moses, as we saw earlier, did not ask God to explain what good the Jews received from their enslavement. He simply demanded, in the strongest possible terms, that the Almighty bring the harrowing servitude of the Jews to a close.

For me, the most inspiring story of the entire Bible is that of Moses in the wake of the Jewish sin of the golden calf. The Bible records that Moses, after smashing the two tablets of the law into a thousand pieces, again ascended Mount Sinai for forty days and forty nights in an effort to mollify the Almighty and reverse His decision to destroy the Jewish nation. Indeed, the Bible uses the words *vayechal Moshe,* Moses was pleading so hard with God to forgive the Jews that he became physically ill. He was coughing up blood, but he would not relent. When God still did not forgive the Jews, Moses offered a statement that must easily pass as the greatest expression of chutzpah, or effrontery, toward the Creator anywhere in the Bible. "Now, if you will forgive the people," he said, "then good, but if you will not forgive their sin . . . blot me out, I pray you, from the Torah which you have written" (Exod. 32:32).

Where in the history of apocalyptic literature does a human demand that the Master of the Universe remove his name from a divine
work whose revelation is entirely dependent upon him alone—without Moses there is no Torah—so that he will not be associated with
the terrible deed of having failed to save his people? Where in ancient literature are we given another example of a mortal man threatening to cut himself off from all association with the deity if He does
not show compassion? Can one imagine the boldness and effrontery
of challenging God to purge one's name from the Holy Books if God
doesn't change His mind and forgive? I am moved every year when I
hear this passage read in the Torah. I find it the most beautiful defense of human life ever recorded. Once again, Moses establishes the
criteria for being a great Israelite. One must love all God's creatures
with an infinite love and even risk divine disfavor and destruction in
an effort to alleviate human misery.

It is not proper to battle with God over human suffering merely
because Abraham and Moses, among others, were its practitioners.
Rather, more than anything else, God wants all his children to be
close, to look out for one another. Like any parent, God loves His
children more than He loves Himself. Peace among humanity is the
ultimate corroboration of divine unity. Therefore, it was *the Almighty
Himself* who demanded that we never exonerate Him and implicate
man in the face of human suffering. The ancient Rabbis point out
that God even prodded Moses to defend the Jews when He sought to
destroy them over the golden calf. The biblical verse reads, "And
now [Moses] leave me so that I can devour [the Jewish people] immediately" (Exod. 32:10). Moses had not yet even begun to speak,
yet the Almighty commands him not to interfere—thus hinting to
Moses to indeed open his mouth and defend the Jews and not to accept the terrible fate that He had decreed for them.

God's occupation is to steer the world in the manner that He sees
fit. But our role as humans is never to examine or try to understand
God's reasoning, but rather to promote those values that He conveyed as being supreme, namely, life, compassion, goodness, and
hope. What God was saying to the great lawgiver was this: Moses, I

have just told you that I plan to annihilate the Israelite nation. Are you just going to sit there? Have I endowed you with life so that you can be passive when the lives of others are threatened? Indeed, the ancient Rabbis contrast Abraham, who defended the inhabitants of Sodom, with Noah, who is informed by God of the destruction of all mankind yet offers no protest. This, they maintain, is the reason that Abraham rather than Noah fathered the chosen people.

Here we can appreciate the centrality of messianism to Judaism. Messianism represents a stubborn Jewish refusal to accept the world the way it is, but to insist that it revert to its state of perfection. The Jew refuses to embrace the ills of the world with submissiveness. Throughout history, Jews of all persuasions, from the most pious to the most secular, have passionately attempted to improve the world and the lot of mankind. Jews are the progenitors of many of the worlds "isms"—such as secular humanism and communism—because they are always searching for Utopia. Jews will not make peace with suffering. They constantly seek to return to their promised land, and when that is not possible, then to build a new promised land. Thrice daily the Jew recites, at the end of each of the prayer services, the ancient dream of "perfecting the world under God's dominion."

Defeat of Death and Resurrection of the Dead

We religious Jews follow the examples of Abraham and Moses by challenging fate and pursuing our mission to advance the cause of love and justice. How could we account for human progress and achievement without the belief that mankind, against all the evidence, can make the world a better place and leave it in better condition for the next generation? Man is a dreamer, and his dreams result from an inexplicable conviction that he is indeed capable of making the impossible probable. When President John F. Kennedy spoke in 1961 of landing a man on the moon before the end of the decade, he was laughed at; but a team of dedicated scientists and researchers translated that dream into reality.

For the Jew, the desire to translate dreams into reality even includes the dream of triumphing over death and being reunited with one's loved ones. Maimonides lists as one of the thirteen cardinal tenets of the Jewish faith the belief that one day the righteous dead will rise from the earth and live, breathe, and speak once again (a claim that with human cloning and the duplication of DNA no longer seems so outlandish). As the bearer of a two-thousand-year-old belief in the coming of a perfect messianic age, the Jew knows at the core of his being that suffering must and will be defeated. He refuses to accord death any latitude. His focus is always on life. He cries out to God to keep his promise to abolish death from the earth and to restore those who have already died to life. It was God who promised that "death shall be defeated." Therefore we should dedicate our lives to abolishing all forms of affliction.

> On this mountain He will destroy the shroud that enfolds all peoples, the sheet that covers all nations; He will swallow up death forever. The Sovereign Lord will wipe away the tears from all faces; He will remove the disgrace of His people from all the earth. The Lord has spoken. In that day they will say, "Surely this is our God; we trusted in Him, and He saved us. This is the Lord, we trusted in Him; let us rejoice and be glad in His salvation." (Isa. 25:7–9)

This theme of challenging the Divine and of death as an aberration in creation is further reflected in the writings of the leading Hassidic thinker, Rabbi Adin Steinsaltz. In his collection of essays, *The Strife of the Spirit*, he offers a concise philosophical overview of death:

> The Jewish approach to death is that it is a problem to be solved by and for the living. . . . The basic attitude of Judaism to death, which, it is said, was ushered in with Adam's expulsion from the Garden of Eden, is that it is not a natural, inevitable phenomenon. Death is life diseased, distorted, perverted, diverted from the flow of holiness, which is identified with life. So side by side with a stoic submission to

death, there is a stubborn battle against it on the physical and cosmic level. The world's worst defect is seen to be death, whose representative is Satan. The remedy is faith in the resurrection. Ultimately, "death and evil"—and the one is tantamount to the other—are dismissed as ephemeral. They are not part of the true essence of the world, and, as the late Rabbi Abraham Kook emphasized in his writings, men should not accept the premise that death will always emerge the victor. . . . In the combat of life against death, of being against non-being, Judaism manifests disbelief in the persistence of death, and maintains that it is a temporary obstacle that can and will be overcome. Our sages, prophesying a world in which there will be no more death, wrote: "We are getting closer and closer to a world in which we shall be able to vanquish death, in which we shall be above and beyond death."

Death is the absence of life, just as evil is the absence of goodness. Death and evil are abysses that must be filled with light and holiness. Never should we succumb to fate in silent acquiescence. We must act like the human body's immune system. Whenever it senses even the tiniest germ, it declares war on the alien presence threatening the health of the body. It is not the purpose of the body's immune system to understand why the body suffers and why it has been affected by illness. When a person begins to feel ill, it is not the mind that is kicked into action, looking for reasons why a perfectly good person should suffer. Rather, it is the body's immune system that spontaneously jumps into the fray, ridding the body of the harmful bacillus. The germ has no meaning and requires no explanation. It simply must be eradicated.

The same applies to suffering. When someone is in pain, when there is a holocaust, we don't need fifty Rabbis and Priests springing into action, pulling out their word processors, and writing books explaining how God is good despite what we are witnessing. Rather, we need millions of people springing into action saving lives, alleviating anguish, and demanding from God better times. Let us dedicate our existence wholeheartedly toward being caring human beings, and let our goal be the eradication of every form of pain from the earth. At the very least, let us ensure that *we* never serve as the cause of pain to any person. Let us ensure that the only tears that our actions cause in the lives of our fellow humans are tears of joy. We must dedicate time, resources, and money to charitable endeavors. We must give comfort to our fellowman, counsel husbands and wives whose marriages are faltering, devote ourselves to medical and scientific research that prolongs life, and pray for all those suffering from illness and disease. We must institute better safety procedures to protect humans from misfortune. And we must do everything possible to create peace between nations that are at war. In the words of the Mishnah, we must "be like the students of Aaron. We must love peace and pursue peace" (*Ethics of the Fathers*, Chap. 1).

For those things that are beyond our immediate control—diseases that cannot be cured, wars that cannot be stopped, accidents that cannot be prevented—we must cry out to our Creator and demand that He put an end to these tragedies and grant us all what we deserve: prosperous, joyous, and happy lives. Lives that are filled with both spiritual and physical blessing. In this respect I maintain that it was specifically the less Orthodox, and in many cases the completely nonobservant, Jews—the pioneering Zionists who built the State of Israel—who had the correct response to the unspeakable tragedy of the Holocaust. Whereas more traditional Jews grappled with how to explain the suffering of the Holocaust within a traditional framework, many less observant Zionists rejected any theological justification or self-blame, and set themselves to work even harder toward the creation of a Jewish state. The response to death is life. The response to the destruction of the Jewish nations in Europe is the rebuilding of the Jewish homeland in Israel. Although those Zionists were not religious, they understood almost intuitively that the only authentic Jewish response to suffering was not to attempt to understand it, but to wage war against it. The Jewish flame of hope that animated these pioneers was so potent that not even the crematoria of Auschwitz could exterminate it. I applaud their efforts, and we are all deeply indebted to all of those brave and heroic Israeli soldiers who have defended our people so gallantly from annihilation over the past half-century. Religious Jews owe secular Jews a great debt of gratitude, and this gratitude alone should spur a religious effort to reach out to secular Israelis in the Jewish state and create peace between the bitterly divided factions.

Beyond the Wall

A powerful literary work on suffering is Elie Wiesel's *The Town Beyond the Wall*. The challenge to the Divine is perhaps best contained in the character of Varady, a former scholar who has become a mysterious recluse, who emerges after many years to preach a sermon to the town:

> He emphasised the strength of man, who could bring the Messiah to obedience. He claimed that liberation from Time would be accomplished at the signal of man, and not of his Creator . . . "each of you, the men and women who hear me, have God in his power, for each of you is capable of achieving a thing of which God is incapable! . . . [Man] will conquer heaven, earth, sickness, and death if he will only raze the walls that imprison the Will! And I who speak to you announce my decision to deny death, to repel it, to ridicule it! He who stands before you will never die!"

According to the Sages, Michael, the Guardian Angel of Israel, performs the role of a high priest in heaven and every day offers a sacrifice consisting of the souls of the righteous. In Wiesel's story, it is Michael who protests the sacrifice of the innocents that it is his tragic role to behold. Conventionally, we think of God and man as being vastly unequal in their dialogue, God being omnipotent and the human protester merely His creature, a pawn to be moved at will. But in Wiesel's *The Town Beyond the Wall*, we find a significant inversion of this relationship. The Orthodox Jewish thinker Norman

Lamm describes it as "a keen awareness not only of man's power but also of his self-consciousness as an autonomous agent. It is not rational or even mystical explanations that Wiesel is seeking but rather human approaches and, even more, a confrontation with the God who permits suffering" (Lamm, *Faith and Doubt*, p. 320).

The dynamism in our relationship with God because of the existence of suffering is extended to our relationships with others. Pedro, one of Wiesel's main characters in *The Town Beyond the Wall*, says, "The dialogue—or . . . duel . . . between man and his God doesn't end in nothingness. Man may not have the last word, but he has the last cry. That moment marks the birth of art . . . and friendship is an art" (p. 103). The meaning of suffering is discovered only when we cry out and protest to God, and the most effective way of dealing with suffering is to extend ourselves to other humans in friendship.

Putting the Human Before the Creator

I believe that the primary purpose of man is to love God and to serve the needs of his fellow humans under God's instruction. God is all-powerful, but man is not. God is not in need of our defense. But humans are. I believe, as Rabbi Israel Baal Shem Tov passionately affirmed, that love for God is shown mainly through one's devotion to one's fellowman. What God principally desires of us is not to defend Him, but to care for and love our fellowman. Indeed, the laws that regulate man's treatment of his fellowman account for a substantial portion of the Torah. Rabbi Akiva, one of the greatest Jewish sages, affirmed that the divine imperative to "love your neighbor as yourself," found in Leviticus 19:18, is "an all-encompassing principle of the Torah." Similarly, the great sage Hillel, when asked to sum up the entire Torah into one maxim, told a potential convert, as recorded in the Talmud: "That which you hate, never do unto others. This is the entire Torah, the rest being but commentary. Now, go and study" (*Shabbat* 30a).

My wife and I are blessed with seven young children. To be sure, there are many things a child can do to anger a parent, but one of the most troubling is when the children display selfishness and factionalism against their siblings. If one of my children breaks something in the house, I may not be amused. But I am far angrier if he or she blames it on a sibling. In the same vein, what the Almighty desires most from humanity is unity. We are his children, and He wishes to see us come together as brothers and sisters, the same wish that any parent would have. Parents love their children more than they love themselves, and they wish to see their offspring being loving to one another. The fastest way to a parent's heart is through kindness to their children. The same is true of God. Caring for the needy and raising up the downtrodden endears us to our heavenly Father.

Once while on vacation, we took the children for ice cream. My second oldest daughter pulled her sister's hair, and I told her that I would not be taking her inside the store unless she apologized. She obstinately refused. "Then you'll stay in the car," I told her, whereupon her older sister, the innocent victim, began to cry that her younger sister didn't mean it and that she would not go into the ice cream store without her. It was one of my proudest moments as a father.

If one could briefly summarize the vast contribution made to Jewish life and thought by the Baal Shem Tov and Hassidism over the past three hundred years, it would be that Hassidism taught man that in his effort to achieve proximity with God, he must learn to put his fellowman first, at times even before God, certainly in those areas where God does not require man's defense.

By challenging God whenever innocents suffer, we do not degrade God but glorify Him to the highest heavens. We demonstrate that His teachings in the Torah about love, compassion, and togetherness have had an impact upon us. Time and again the Lord bids us to defend the cause of the oppressed, to show special sensitivity to widows and orphans. Does this only apply to giving them something to eat? Does it not also apply to defending them from divine indictment? Should we tell the widows and orphans who survived the Holocaust that their husbands and fathers died because of their sins?

Maimonides, in his celebrated *Epistle on Martyrdom,* sharply rebukes a contemporary twelfth-century Rabbi's condemnation of Jews who were living in Spain during the Islamic Almohad persecutions, many of whom pondered converting to Islam rather than facing death by the sword. Maimonides goes to great lengths to show that God Himself had rebuffed and even punished those who had voiced condemnations of the people of Israel. Maimonides notes that Moses, Elijah, Isaiah, and even the ministering angels of heaven were severely chastised by the Almighty when they came to Him reporting that the Jews were sinful and had broken God's covenant, even though the empirical evidence supported their claims. So great was God's anger at Isaiah, for example, after having said, "I sit here in the midst of a nation who have defiled and profaned their lips [with prayers to idols]," that the Almighty sent a seraph of heaven with a pan of coals to put them into the mouth of the prophet (Isa. 6:5–7).

But if Isaiah's allegations were true, why was he punished? And if Moses was correct in accusing the Jews of "abandoning the path of God, assimilating into Egyptian culture, and forsaking the covenant of Abraham through neglecting to circumcise their children," why was he rebuked by the Almighty for his accurate report? The reason is that even if their reports were accurate, it was not their function as prophets to indict the Jewish nation, but to *correct* the nation. Their mandate as humans was to defend man, not to incriminate him. Only God is the Judge of the earth. The purpose of a human being is always to defend and protect his fellow human, never to denounce him. We are bidden to serve as angels of mercy rather than prosecutors. Man will always be held accountable for entering into realms that are outside his jurisdiction. God gives life and takes life; humans protect life and defend life.

Until the time that we, together with our Creator, abolish every form of pain from the earth, we must band together and comfort one another. Never should we witness a living creature's pain and remain silent.

12

Little Messiahs

From this belief in the Messiah who is to come, from the certainty which they have of conquering with him, from the power of esteeming all present things of small importance in view of such a future, springs the indestructible nature of the Jews.

—JOHANN KARL ROSENKRANTZ,
Philosophy of Education

When Messiah comes, war will end, God's blessing will be on all men, and none will risk his life for money.

—MAIMONIDES,
commentary to Mishnah, *Sanhedrin*

A MAN BRINGS SOME MATERIAL TO A TAILOR and asks him to make a pair of trousers. When he comes back a week later, they are not ready. Two weeks later, they still aren't ready. Finally, after six weeks, the trousers are ready. The man tries them on. They are beautiful and fit perfectly. Nonetheless, when it comes time to pay, he can't resist a jibe at the tailor.

"You know," he says, "it took God only six days to make the world. But it took you six weeks to make just one pair of trousers."

"Ah!" the tailor says. "But look at this pair of trousers, and look at the world."

217

It is true, the world is deeply flawed. Even the greatest optimist cannot help but notice the prevalence of injustice and suffering. Throughout every age men and women have commented on the disparity between the perfection of God and the imperfection of the world. We seem to have become obsessed with improving and perfecting society, somehow believing, with the weight of history stacked against us, that it is still possible. Why have we not reconciled ourselves to the fact that this world will always have its share of war, famine, tragedy, and tyranny?

The twentieth century was the bloodiest of all, yet we persist in hoping for an era of peace and brotherhood. What gives us the faith to hope for a cure for AIDS, cancer, and other lethal diseases? What makes us think we can somehow rid our streets of drugs and crime? Certainly, no one has succeeded in ridding the world of its ills in the past, yet we speak as if it is not just a remote possibility but something within our reach.

The engine for all human advance and the sustainer of all human dreams is the Jewish idea of Messiah. Messianism has served as the fountain of human hope for over three millennia. Messianic expectations and the promises of Utopia have already permeated society as well as the way we—both religious and secular—think of ourselves and our future. In order to fully understand messianism and its impact on civilization, it is important that we first explore the twin ideas of messianism in Judaism that speak of a messianic era, on the one hand, and a messianic individual, on the other.

The Messianic Era

The prophets of the Bible foretold of how the world will look at the end of days. The image involves the vindication of Jewish singularity and chosenness, the ingathering of the dispersed remnants of the Jewish people in the Holy Land, the reestablishment of the Temple, the universal acknowledgment of ethical monotheism, and the realization of world peace. These beliefs sustained the Jewish people for countless centuries in periods of trial.

Maimonides listed the belief in the coming of the Messiah as the penultimate of his thirteen articles of Jewish faith and the culmination of the first eleven. Although the coming of the Messiah is portrayed in Jewish thought as a future event, it informs and influences all of Judaism, both past and present. Messianism is responsible for the vast progress experienced by all those countries who live under the Judeo-Christian tradition. Messianism states that the world begins at a fixed point—creation—and improves until it reaches a glorious climax to the historical order in the form of a perfect world. This Utopia, in which war, disease, hatred, and death will be banished from the earth, is a joint partnership between the Almighty and man: "Until a spirit from on high is poured upon us, and the wilderness becomes a fruitful field, and the fruitful field is deemed a forest. Then justice will dwell in the wilderness, and righteousness abide in the fruitful field. The effect of righteousness will be peace, and the result of righteousness, quietness and trust forever" (Isa. 32:15–17). The idea that man can improve the earth is known as linear history.

Just as a basic difference between Judaism and Christianity is the belief in Jesus, so too a basic difference between Judaism and the religions of the East is Judaism's rejection of cyclical history. Those who believe in cyclical history maintain that the earth and all existence are doomed to an endless cycle of creation, destruction, and reincarnation. One cannot travel through India and the Far East and see the decimated hovels in which people live without feeling that to some extent, indigenous religious convictions have contributed to the lack of social-welfare development in the Third World. If the universe is cyclical and all that is built is destined to be destroyed, then human effort ought to be directed at perfecting the life of the spirit rather than the ephemeral life of the body. Conversely, the underlying Western Judeo-Christian mindset is the belief that history is linear, that is, it begins with the still underdeveloped building blocks of creation and culminates in a messianic epoch. Human effort to perfect the world is thus not wasted. Rather, every human undertaking in each generation is cumulative until a critical mass is reached and the Lord redeems the world of its last imperfections, which lie outside human capability. Whereas cyclical history leads to spiritual enlightenment, linear history leads to building hospitals and schools and paving streets.

> And it shall come to pass in the end of days that the mountain of God's house shall be set over all other mountains and lifted high above the hills, and all nations shall come streaming to it. And many people shall come and say: Come let us go to the house of the God of Jacob and he [the Messiah] will teach us God's ways and we will walk in His paths. For out of Zion shall go forth the Torah and God's word from Jerusalem. And he [the Messiah] will judge between nations and decide between peoples. And they shall beat their swords into plow-shares and their spears into pruning hooks. Nation shall not lift up sword against nation, neither shall they learn war anymore. (Isa. 2:2–4)

Although the Messiah will influence and teach all mankind, his main mission will be to bring the hearts of the earth's inhabitants back to God. As society moves toward perfection and the world becomes increasingly Godly, humans, with their copious free time brought about by technological advance and lack of war, will begin to explore the transcendental, "for all the earth shall be full of the knowledge of God, as the waters cover the ocean floor" (Isa. 11:9). The Messiah will teach us all to find the underlying humanity that unites us all, the Godly spark that animates man. People will begin to devote as much time to the development of their souls as their bodies. More and more people will achieve the mystical union of prophecy.

Although man will still have free will in the messianic age, he will have every inducement to do good and follow God's teachings. It will be as if the power of evil were totally annihilated. As man approaches this lofty level, he will also become worthy of a divine providence that is not limited by the laws of nature. What is now manifestly miraculous will ultimately become part of the nature of things. This change, together with man's newly gained powers to bring forth the best that nature has to offer, will bring man to his ultimate destiny, namely, living in a perfect world in which he is empowered to spend all his time coming to know the infinite Creator and thereby reaching the highest perfection attainable by mortals.

There is no ultimate judgment in Judaism. The messianic arrival is not a day of reckoning. Neither will all the world's inhabitants die and go to heaven. The ultimate holy existence from a Jewish perspective is not a disembodied spirit. We prefer earth to heaven. Rather, the dead will be resurrected and people will live in a perfect world. There man will be free to pursue the ultimate good—worship of God—and will strive for truth and goodness, unencumbered by pain, disease, hardship, material constraints, or unbridled lust.

The Implications of Directional History

Aside from the concept of God Himself, there is no more influential or exciting idea that Judaism has bequeathed mankind than that of the Messiah. That the Jews did not lose hope in the future, despite being so often persecuted, is entirely due to their messianic orientation. The concept of a righteous figure who will one day inspire mankind to redeem itself and abandon all hatred and war has no parallel in any other culture or religion that existed prior to Judaism. Above all, the concept of a directional or linear history with salvation as its ultimate destination allowed the Jews to consider even the greatest tragedies as just anomalies or upsets along the road. As long as Judaism affirmed its faith in the messianic era, it could never succumb to feelings of failure.

This idea contrasted sharply with the cyclical view of history that dominated the ancient world. Babylon offered a stagnating worldview in which history recounted man's vacillation between two opposing forces. Even the ancient Greeks wrote of the power of fate and that all hope was futile, since man could not overcome predetermined destiny. The essence of the great Greek tragedies is the gallant hero or heroine who is doomed to oblivion because he cannot overcome the power of fate. The Jews advocated instead a doctrine of free will and progress. Man was not condemned to endless cycles of repetition. Rather, positive human action was cumulative and led to a more highly developed and just society. Notwithstanding all evidence to the contrary, the story of man was one of progression and refinement.

Far more than simply a comfort and reassurance through the darkest periods of Jewish history, the prophets' vision has served as the inspiration for Jewish hopes, prayers, and actions. Indeed, Judaism may be said to be an attempt for man to perfect the world, referred to as *tikkun olam,* and to make God its sovereign, the culmination of which will take place when the final touches are added by God Himself. This aspect of messianism, its spur to action, has rubbed off on all nations that have absorbed the Jewish understanding of history.

Indeed, what inspired the nations of the world to come together in San Francisco in April 1945 to form the United Nations? The nations that convened there were still in the midst of fighting the worst war the world had ever seen, replete with genocide and the slaughter of millions of noncombatants. What made the nations that sent delegates believe that they could establish global cooperation and an end to hostilities and war? Did they not realize that international warfare was the inevitable consequence of the struggle for the survival of the fittest in a world of limited resources? Any student of history can tell you that war is endemic to mankind. Yet, these nations assembled to create global peace, ignoring all lessons of history.

On the Wall of Peace in the Plaza of Nations at UN Headquarters in New York, there is a single verse from Isaiah etched in stone: "Swords shall be beaten into ploughshares, . . . Nation shall not lift up sword against nation, neither shall they learn war anymore"

(Isa. 2:4). The leaders of the United Nations were guided by the messianic prophecies of the future. All has been foretold. Two and a half thousand years ago holy men who communicated with the Creator promised that if man, as a junior partner, joined together with God, the world could be cleansed of its ills and a global fraternity created. The earth's inhabitants could cooperate to rid the world of suffering rather than remain at odds and perpetuate a legacy of pain. Messianism is the inextinguishable candle of hope flickering within the most palpable darkness. It is the eternal ray of sunlight that Judaism has bequeathed the world.

What messianism affords is *a sense of hope*. Rather than feeling overwhelmed by the chaos of everyday life, if we believe that we are daily growing closer to a more pleasant future, we will feel that tomorrow will be better than today. Without the certainty of hope at the core of our existence, we could never maintain an enthusiasm for life. Rather, we would mope around in a state of defeat, without the optimism for improvement.

Why Hasn't the Messiah Arrived?

Many would dismiss the question of why the Messiah has not yet arrived as hopelessly naive. The Jews have been awaiting their Messiah for three thousand years. Worse, countless numbers of Jews have died for their rejection of Jesus as Messiah, and many Jews placed their faith in false candidates. How long will the Jews continue to hold up against false hope?

Long ago in the Jewish shtetls of Eastern Europe, there lived a man who could not support his family but refused to be a ward of the community. Fearing that his children would starve, the elders of the community created a post for him in which even he could not fail. They appointed him Chief Messiah Watcher. With great dignity and pride, he took up his post at the gates of the city awaiting the promised redeemer. Day in and day out he sat there, waiting to herald to his Jewish brethren the imminent moment of redemption.

One day his brother came to visit him and asked, "What are you doing sitting like a baboon at the gates of the city, doing absolutely nothing?"

"Nothing?" the Messiah Watcher asked indignantly. "You say I'm doing nothing? I'll have you know that I have been given the most important task in the community. I am the official Messiah Watcher."

"You imbecile." His brother shook his head. "Don't you realize that they are just making fun of you!"

"Well, I guess you're right," he said with resignation. "But at least it's a steady job."

The Messiah has not arrived yet, but that does not discredit the entire idea of messianism. After all, the idea is responsible for the survival of the orthodox Jewish people and their considerable accomplishments, even amid persecution. Even while we Jews are awaiting the Messiah's arrival, we must be thankful for the endless gifts that messianism has already bestowed upon the Jewish people. The twentieth-century Orthodox Jewish thinker Rabbi Joseph Soloveitchik writes, "The Patriarchic Covenant introduced a new concept into history. While universal (non-Jewish) history is governed by causality, by what preceded, covenantal (Jewish) history is shaped by destiny, by a goal set in the future" (*Man of Faith in the Modern World*, p. 70). Most historians are guided by the principle that causality dictates events. Jewish history is different. It emanates from a divine promise about the future. Jewish history is pulled, as if by a magnet, toward a glorious destiny, not pushed by antecedent causes.

This covenantal understanding, and only this, accounts for the Jewish obsession with perfecting the world. The imminent promise of a world filled with light has nagged at us throughout history and has been the source of our hope for the future. How else can we explain why the people who have suffered the most are so optimistic and dedicate so much of their creative talents toward making a better world and preaching a vision of its possibility?

The Jewish passion for messianism has influenced and brought into existence many movements that serve as secular messianic Utopias. Judaism had an impact even on those Jewish visionaries who did not lead Jewish lives. The goal of communism—the product of a secular Jew named Karl Marx—envisaged a perfect world order in which all the earth's inhabitants were provided with their needs and none were exploited by greedy capitalists. No one would ever go hungry. All men and women would share equally in the nation's blessings. Contention and jealousy would be removed from the world and peace established throughout the earth. The messianic undertones of this vision, however unrealistic in its communist implementation, are self-evident.

The Indomitable Jewish Spirit

After three thousand years of messianic idealism, the Jew emerged from the Holocaust, not broken in spirit, but energized by a dream about the future that the flames of the crematoria could not destroy. Armed with a belief in the coming of the Messiah, the Jew never despairs. A Jew feels in his bones that destiny, not causality, is the mechanism behind history. He will one day end up in the Promised Land, even if he now walks through the valley of the shadow of death. The promises of the future are responsible for the past; the prophecies of old will one day materialize in the reality of the present.

There is an awareness in the hearts of the Jews that Israel is the Promised Land. The promise is a destiny to be fulfilled. Even secular Zionists, who frowned upon religious terminology and motivations, often spoke with messianic overtones of the Jewish destiny to return to Zion.

The return of the Jews to their homeland in 1948 and the reestablishment of an independent Jewish state after two thousand years of exile defy historical precedent. That the Jews achieved this astonishing feat just three years after the Holocaust is nothing short of miraculous. The only possible explanation is that having nurtured a dream of their eventual return to their homeland, the Jews developed a longing for their land that transcended any effort to keep them away.

The Messiah Himself

I shall turn now to the personality of the Messiah. The Utopia I have been describing at the end of days requires leadership. Essential to the messianic age is the Messiah himself, a human leader who will spur humanity to finish the job of sanctifying the earth. An orchestra without a conductor will make noise, not music.

Ever since the prophet Moses led the Hebrews from slavery in Egypt to the borders of the land of Israel, leadership has been central to the Jewish nation. Many great men and women have left their mark on the Jewish people. Indeed, there is a feeling among those who are conversant with the classic Jewish texts—the Torah, the Prophets, and the Talmud—that these giants of Jewish history are in a sense alive even today. The Jews remain profoundly influenced not just by the teachings of Moses, but by his personality, charisma, humility, and integrity—all of which are timeless.

Why are leaders so important to the Jewish people? Can't social currents, as opposed to individuals, lead? It would seem more desirable for society to give rise to righteousness of its own accord, without the external stimulus of men and women in positions of power. Leadership poses drawbacks. It lends itself to tyranny and can induce a sense of dependence among the populace. Moses himself complained of this development to the Almighty: "Did I conceive this whole people? Did I give birth to them, that you should say to me, 'Carry them in your bosom, as a nurse carries a sucking child,' to the land that you promised on oath to their ancestors?" (Num. 11:12). Yet, Moses himself prayed to God that the Jewish people never be bereft of leadership. "Let the Lord, the God of the spirits of all flesh, appoint someone over the congregation, who shall go out before them and come in before them, who shall lead them out and bring them in, so that the congregation of the Lord may not be like sheep without a shepherd" (Num. 27:16–17).

The Personification of an Ideology

The reason leadership is central to Judaism is that someone must serve as the living embodiment of Godly teachings. A leader translates principles into practice, an idea into reality. A leader closes the gap that normally exists between ideology, on the one hand, and practical living, on the other. One of the great problems with ideals is that often they simply do not work. We hear the glorious stories of Abraham, who defended even the wicked habits of the people of Sodom and Gomorrah when God sought to destroy them. We read in the Bible that Moses was the most humble man who walked the earth. We read of Jewish masters throughout history, like Don Isaac Abravanel, who chose to share the exile of his Jewish brethren in Portugal rather than lead a comfortable life in Spain as finance minister to Ferdinand and Isabella. These stories inspire us, but they also pose a problem: Who is to say that these stories have not been embellished as they were told to successive generations? Even if they are completely true, how can a man or woman who lived centuries ago speak to a new generation whose challenges are totally different from their own? Of what practical value is a knowledge of the life of Abraham if his example is outside an ordinary person's reach?

When a man or woman of your era lives up to these lofty ideals, you can no longer dismiss great virtue as being outside your personal reach. *The primary purpose of every leader is to take away the excuse from each of us who wants to renounce a virtuous life.* As the embodiment of an ideology, a leader challenges us to lead an exemplary existence. The Talmud relates that when a poor man dies, his soul appears before the angels, who ask him whether he dedicated his life to God's Torah and commandments. The poor man answers, "Me, I couldn't. I was too poor. I had to struggle just to feed my family. There wasn't time for anything else." The angels then ask him, "Were you poorer than the great sage Hillel? Hillel was so poor that he had to climb in the snow to the rooftop of the study hall where Shemaya and Avtalyon were teaching, because he did not possess even the few dinar (coins) it took to gain entry." To the rich man who complains that he had too many responsibilities to find any time for worthwhile pursuits like Torah study, the angels say, "Were you richer than the great Rabbi Eliezer ben Hyracanus, who owned a fleet of hundreds of vessels, and yet still found the time to become one of the great scholars of his generation?" Personal example makes it impossible for us to maintain that the mountain's summit was too high for anybody to climb it.

The Bible goes out of its way to demonstrate the human qualities of its great heroes. Unlike the New Testament, which insists upon the divinity of Christ, the people presented in the Jewish Scripture are human and fallible. Adam and Eve were misled by the serpent and sinned shortly after they were placed in Eden. Noah became drunk as soon as he emerged from the ark. Abraham erred in the rearing of Ishmael, and Isaac was misguided in cherishing Esau above Jacob. The Bible further relates that Jacob made the mistake of favoring his son Joseph over his other children. Even the great prophet Moses was punished for the sin of hitting the rock to give forth water, rather than talking to it, as God had commanded. David was led by lust to cavort with Bathsheba, and God punished him by allowing the first child of that union to die.

If heroes with these faults are capable of leading highly virtuous lives, then we are challenged to do the same. The problem, however, is that we tend to dismiss these great men and women as saintly figures who are totally removed from earthly reality. To be sure, the world much admires saints, but rarely do people choose to emulate them. Raising individuals to the pedestal of sainthood is the perfect way to render them ineffective in shaping the lives of their followers and admirers. Of course, Abraham was able to defy the entire pagan world and teach the earth's inhabitants about God. After all, he was a saint! But me? I'm just an ordinary person. Therefore, by depicting all its heroes for what they were—ordinary people who led extraordinary lives—the Bible allows us to feel that we too can emulate their example.

In *The Day America Told the Truth*, a survey of American attitudes of the past few decades, thousands of Americans interviewed agreed that there was "a general decline in moral and ethical standards." The majority attributed this decline to a dearth of leadership. Americans felt there was no longer anyone to look up to. We have lost our heroes. Gone from the landscape are the charismatic political leaders of just a generation ago—the Churchills, Roosevelts, de Gaulles, and Kennedys. Even the surge in inspiration after the events of September 11 and the concomitant establishment of real-life heroes seem to have been fleeting, as the shallow celebrities of the popular culture reassert their place in our pantheon of unworthy heroes. The arrival of a noble, pious, and charismatic leader would be welcomed by a world that has ceased to be inspired. For lack of something better to do, people have fallen back on the old reliable pursuit of money and pleasure.

We no longer even believe in the power of one man to change the world, and hence we do not attempt it ourselves. We are far more focused on the futility of our efforts than on their promise. The Jewish Messiah will not be a divine figure or the son of a deity. Nor will he be a mystical angel who is immune to temptation. Rather, he will simply be someone who distinguishes himself by an ability to bring out the good in vast numbers of people. Imagine for a moment a superlative political genius who, using the vast communication networks now at our disposal, spreads his message to the entire world and changes the very fabric of our society. Now imagine that he is a true tzaddik—a righteous individual, whose righteousness is recognized by Jew and non-Jew alike. It may once have seemed impossible for a holy man to assume a role in world leadership, but the world is becoming more accustomed to accepting leaders of all races, religions, and ethnic groups. Think of the vast respect accorded to men like Pope John Paul II and the Dalai Lama. Indeed, today there are numerous religious leaders whose opinions are sought by political leaders on all issues. It is not far-fetched to picture a great man, or Rabbi, in such a role.

The Redeemer and the Comforter

Some believe that awaiting a leader to spur us on to these efforts is misguided. Rather than an identifiable historical figure, the collective efforts of humanity all represent the Messiah. (This argument is not unlike the Jewish Reconstructionist conception of God, which maintains that the deity is synonymous with human inspiration to better the world and find transcendence; God as an identifiable or transcendent being does not exist.)

Such notions display ignorance of Jewish messianism. Judaism never conceived of a Jesus-like figure who would come along and redeem mankind of its iniquity irrespective of its actions. Rather, the Messiah will be a leader who will inspire people to redeem themselves.

This idea is best expressed in the Jewish tradition that the name of the Messiah will be Menachem, which means "comforter." Thus we learn that the Messiah will bring redemption by way of comfort.

There are two ways of helping people. The first is to pull them out of trouble. This may save them but creates a lasting dependency. A far better method is to impart to the individual a capacity for self-redemption. This will set off a chain reaction of empowerment, in which one person will inspire another to bring about redemption through his own devices.

Moses and the Messiah

The first appointed leader of the Jewish people was Moses. The last will be the Messiah. The name of Moses means to "draw," to "cull," or to "extract." Moses the leader drew forth of himself and of his unparalleled stature to give to the Jewish people, who were spiritually bereft. Although Moses was a spiritual colossus, the Jews were spiritually in their infancy. Like a wet nurse, Moses took of his own milk and nourished the Jewish people. He drew forth water from his own inexhaustible spring and irrigated a parched nation. It was his own spiritual greatness that made the Jewish people worthy. Time and again, the Almighty agreed to spare the rebellious nation of Israel for

Moses' sake alone. Moses was a redeemer who acknowledged the impoverishment and need of his people and gave freely of himself to those who were beneath him.

Moses drew the Torah down from the heavens and gave it as a gift to the Jewish people. Having been slaves in Egypt who had almost completely assimilated into Egyptian idolatry, they were not intellectually, emotionally, or spiritually prepared for such intimate divine communion.

So began an unequal relationship between Moses and the Jewish people in which the nation was dependent on the righteousness and merit of the great lawgiver throughout the forty years of wandering through the desert. Moses was acknowledged as the greatest of the Jews, but his greatness made everyone around him feel dependent. The Jews needed Moses in the wilderness. He would take care of them. Everything from their food to their clothes rained down on them miraculously. Moses' leadership was in effect the leadership of the elite. He was like the great "philosopher king" so strongly endorsed by Plato centuries later.

In contemporary terms, Moses resembles a philanthropist who comes to the destitute and downtrodden not to impart hope for *what the people can produce,* but with promises of *what he can contribute.* Moses is like a First World government patronizingly approaching the Third World with foreign aid. The act is selfless and humanitarian, but it also may be considered condescending, from strong to weak, from the haves to the have-nots. Because of this dependent model of leadership, Moses was able to take the Jews out of Egypt, but he could not bring them into the Promised Land. The Jews would have to create an independent commonwealth. They would have to fight their enemies and displace nations that were already in the land. A permanent dependency on Moses was not conducive to these goals. Therefore, the leadership had to be passed on to Joshua, a man of far less stature than Moses. But in fact, that was exactly what the new situation called for.

Once while I was in France, I chanced upon a set of handicapped skiing championships. There was a young girl competing in a ski wheelchair. She was practicing with her mother on a small slope. She fell over and could not get up. On the third attempt to rise, she burst into tears and called for her mother to lift her up. Her mother refused. "But I can't move my feet," she shrieked, sobbing. "But you can move your arms. Pick yourself up," her mother responded. A few moments later she was going down the slopes in her race.

This is the role of the comforter: to remind us of our own potential; to be a catalyst for us to achieve it; to remind us that even in the face of great adversity, the human spirit cannot be crushed. The comforter neither focuses on what we lack nor promises to compensate for our faults. Rather, the comforter is the *facilitator*. He or she is there to remind us that we possess everything that the comforter possesses. The comforter serves in the role of catalyst rather than provider. The ultimate role of the comforter is to make him- or herself unnecessary. The comforter trains us to focus on our *capabilities* rather than our *predicament*. Whereas the redeemer focuses on the actual, the comforter focuses on the potential.

Moses saw a slave nation that needed his salvation, but the Messiah sees a capable nation that already possesses the ability to change the world. The Messiah will not act magisterially and undertake people's responsibilities for them. Rather, he will stimulate action and transformation. He will orchestrate human effort into a coherent whole that will create the conditions necessary to usher in the redemption. In a word, rather than making followers, the Messiah is a leader who will inspire others to become leaders as well.

The Moses-style redeemer has a limited role. After the redeemer has lifted people out of a helpless and passive state, they need a messianic redeemer who will enable them to fulfill their destiny through the catalyst of his person and their own efforts. Moses lifted the Israelites from the depths of despair. He nursed them and nurtured them to maturity, but not to independence. This is why they reverted to pagan idolatry just after his demise. Moses was foretold of this development by the Almighty Himself: "The Lord said to Moses, 'Soon you will lie down with your ancestors. Then this people will begin to prostitute themselves to the foreign gods in their midst, the gods of the land into which they are going; they will forsake me, breaking my covenant that I have made with them'" (Deut. 31:16).

But once they had established themselves in the Land of Israel and had built the Temple, the people of Israel needed to be in a partnership with God, yet responsible for their own destiny. It was as if Israel was in its dependent childhood under Moses and had gained adult stature and responsibility once in the Promised Land. The essential relationship of God to Israel in the land was that of *Comforter*, for God sought to encourage and guide Israel to fulfill its destiny, which had been sealed with Moses at Sinai. God said to the people that the success or failure of the Temple and the Jewish kingdom depended on them. If they led exemplary spiritual lives, all would be well. If not, disaster would ensue. Everything rested in their hands.

As yet the Jewish nation is still awaiting the fulfillment of its spiritual destiny, and the holy Temple awaits restoration. We are still scattered throughout the world and are still suffering the trauma of the Holocaust. The concept of the Menachem-Messiah beckoning in the distance reminds us all that we can rise out of the ashes. Not just a symbol of the ability of Jews to attain redemption whatever the circumstances, the Messiah represents the ability of all of us to find our fullness, destiny, and redemption. Into a world that has become disillusioned about the future and is concerned with self-preservation and prosperity will come a comforting redeemer who will renew human belief in the possibility of creating a majestic world built on the twin foundations of love and justice.

Now, more than ever, the Jewish people are in need of a comforter. The Holocaust was the first Jewish tragedy that led to the abandonment of God and Judaism. God was seen as a father who had deserted his children to the ugliest of fates, and there was a mass exodus away from the faith. If a man loses a son, the Rabbi comes to the place of mourning, sits next to him, and tells him how fortunate he is to have another son. This is the essence of comforting the bereaved. One attempts to focus the mind of the bereaved, not on what he has lost, but on all that he still possesses; not on his circumstance, but his promise. Amid our need to thunder and rail

against the heavens for the appalling suffering that pervades our
world, the comforter still gives us the strength to carry on. But the
destruction of the Holocaust was so total, so complete, that it was
difficult to find solace at all. How would anyone have been distracted from the loss, in four years, of one out of every three Jews in
the world?

Each of Us Has an Obligation to Be a Messiah

Here we come to the most important aspect of messianism, namely,
the call to each of us to become a Messiah. Each of us has a portion
in the world that only we can redeem. To the young child waiting at
home for his father to arrive from work, that man is a Messiah. He
may not be able to redeem the entire world, but he can redeem that
tiny world that is his son. He is the person who plays with the child
and makes him feel loved. No one else can take his place. To a man
broken by the pain of the world, his wife is a Messiah; she comforts
him and makes him feel indispensable, even when his employers
have just fired him or when he finds himself racked with illness. To
the woman who has always dreamed of finding love, the man who
comes home to her every night and tells her that she is the most special person on the planet is a Messiah, redeeming her from ordinariness and constant comparison with other women. To the friend
whose relationship has just broken up and who desperately seeks
someone to talk to, you are a Messiah. Nobody else can take your
place. If you can't find the time to talk to your friend, you will leave
that part of the world in an unredeemed state.

Every American child believes that he can grow up to be president. Every Jewish child should grow up believing that he could be
the Messiah. He will then exert every effort to improve the lot of his
fellowman. If we each believe that we could be the Messiah, then we
will never pass up an opportunity to feed the hungry, comfort the
bereaved, uplift the helpless, and inspire the young. Nine hundred
years ago, Maimonides wrote that every individual has the capacity
to redeem the whole world. He wrote that one must always see the

world as being perfectly balanced between good and evil. If a single individual does even one good deed, that tips the earth's balance into righteousness and redemption. But careful, for the opposite is true as well. A single evil deed can make everyone else guilty.

Historically, messianic pretensions have been the scourge of the Jewish people. The rejection of the messiahship of Jesus has led to millions of Jewish deaths throughout the ages. Likewise, the embracing of false messiahs like Shabbatai Zevi, the seventeenth-century messianic pretender from Izmir, Turkey, led to global Jewish disillusionment. Thousands of Jews sold their properties in anticipation of the final redemption before they discovered that the man in whom they had placed all their hopes had converted to Islam. In the fifth century, Moses of Crete, promising the Jews that the millennium was at hand, encouraged his followers to jump into the sea, which he promised to part. Hundreds drowned.

These calamities came about when one person claimed to be *the* Messiah. The most dangerous human is the one who claims to have all the answers but has no proof of any divine appointment. What we need are millions of Messiahs, working in unison, to bring about the final redemption. Every doctor who fights disease or saves a life is a Messiah. Every man who loves a woman and makes her feel special is a Messiah. Every businessman who feeds the poor is a Messiah. Every individual who prays for a loved one's recovery from illness is a messiah. Every cleric who brings his congregants closer to God is a Messiah. And every child who shares with another child is a Messiah. The contribution of these millions of Messiahs and the cumulative effect of their efforts throughout time will one day produce the individual who will encourage the earth's inhabitants to deliver the final push.

So why do we need the Almighty to send a single individual to lead us out of the morass, rather than rely on the efforts of a united humanity? Because even as man endeavors to end pain, he is plagued by the fact that personal considerations often fuel social advance. The doctor who will one day cure AIDS labors strenuously not only out of a love for mankind, but also because he desires a

Nobel Prize. The businessman who builds hospitals insists that his name be placed over the front door. Man can never totally separate himself from his own selfish interests. Every act of altruism still generates a worthwhile feeling on the part of the doer. Only God can finally free man from selfish motivation, and therefore only God's chosen redeemer can liberate man from human shortcomings. One of the Messiah's most important functions will be to teach man how to do the right because it is right. We will then enjoy righteous action inspired by altruistic motivation. By so doing, the Messiah will bring about perfection of the world at large and the inner world of man, simultaneously.

Rabbis and Priests Are Human

People claim that they receive little or no inspiration from their Rabbis, ministers, or priests these days. I hear this complaint constantly. Part of the Rabbis' failure to truly connect with their congregants can be traced to communities' ignorance of or disregard for leadership. A leader is effective or challenging only when he or she is like you and me, that is, fully human. People today seem to expect the impossible from their clerics. They want them to be angelic and spiritual at the expense of their humanity. Clerics have to have an understanding of human dilemmas so that they can offer advice, but they are not permitted to experience the same dilemmas themselves. They have to be able to counsel people who are depressed, but their communities would respect them less if they too suffered from depression.

Of all the complaints that I have heard about Rabbis, and there are all too many, the one I hear most is that "they're just not sufficiently down to earth. They don't understand *my* problems." It plays itself out in a scenario that sounds something like this. "Hey, James, why don't you go discuss that problem that you and Jennifer are having with your Rabbi?" "Oh him! Great guy, but his head's in the clouds." Later, when James hears that his Rabbi is a beer guzzler and enjoys a night out bowling with the boys, instead of going out for a beer with him to get to know him better, he is appalled.

Here are some real-life stories that further illustrate the problem. I once published an essay that asked the question why we can never be totally in love, why it is that even after marriage and passionate intimacy with our spouse, we are still attracted to strangers. In the essay I went on to explain that it is this attraction to others that forces us constantly to choose our spouse anew, thereby guaranteeing that the marriage remains fresh and exciting. But an angry rabbinic colleague called me up and said that I sounded like the gynecologist who admits to being aroused by his patients! I felt his criticism was ludicrous and his comparison repugnant. So I said, "Is there anything untrue about the question I put?" His response: "It's certainly not true in *my* case. My wife is the only woman to whom I am attracted. To me any other woman is just the same as a block of wood." Now, he might have been telling the truth. But as another colleague with whom I discussed the issue remarked, he might also be a very bad carpenter. The mere fact that Rabbis feel the need to deny or obscure what is obvious to others is puzzling. Are the needs of any community really served when a Rabbi or priest is forced to become a liar? Would Catholics respect their priests less if the latter admitted that celibacy was particularly challenging?

I was quoted in an article in the London newspaper *The Independent* as saying, "People tell me that I am ego-driven. I take that as a backhanded compliment. By saying that clerics can have no ego, you end up getting people that are uninspired and unmotivated becoming rabbis and priests." This quote caused one woman in Glasgow to order me to leave the British Isles and return to the distant shores of America. "You're nothing but a braggart," she said, "you're not a real Rabbi." But does anyone know of even one Rabbi who doesn't wish for a small modicum of recognition for his efforts on behalf of his congregants? Does anyone really believe that Rabbis and Priests don't appreciate being appreciated?

Of course clerics have egos, and of course they have ambitions. But what should distinguish them from the rest of their communities is not their in-born natures, but rather *what each one does* with that nature: to what use it is deployed. The boy who dreams of being a priest one day is no less ego driven than the boy who dreams of being chairman of IBM. The difference is that the one who wishes to head IBM thinks mostly about how he can use his ambition to benefit himself, whereas the one who wants to be a cleric wants to use his gifts to benefit other people. Rabbis have the same blood and the same dreams as members of their communities. But the Rabbi has taken upon himself the commitment to employ his humanity—not forfeit it—in the service of a cause that is greater than himself, without ceasing to be himself.

Unrealistic expectations of Rabbis and ministers create an environment that might encourage them to become phonies. If they admit to the same cravings and yearnings as everyone else, their communities will stop respecting them. If you were to ask a Rabbi conducting the services on Yom Kippur, the Day of Atonement, on which we fast, whether he's hungry like the rest of his congregants, the proper response would be, "Hungry? How can I possibly feel pangs of hunger when my whole being is filled with the glory of God whom I praise and by whose heavenly mantle I worship on this glorious day of redemption and benediction." His real answer would be, "I'm so hungry that if you promise not to look, I'll run into McDonald's for a double-bacon cheeseburger." The fact that he refrains from doing so has nothing to do with his not being famished, and everything to do with the fact that he elevates his inclination to a higher purpose.

The real message of religion is that we should not subvert the nature with which we are born, but to channel it in the right direction. Judaism is not about repression but about sublimation. Don't fight your nature. Develop it! You're an ambitious person, you want to have your name up in lights? No problem! Do thousands of good deeds on behalf of thousands of people, and you will be loved and famous.

Clerics are no different from other people. They have the same natures, the same desires, and the same materialistic orientation.

The difference lies in how they channel that nature, and whether they will be consumed by ego and materialism. A cleric is just as human as everyone else, but he is distinguished by his attempt to live by the principles he preaches and to develop his humanity for the benefit of others. But the struggle is just the same for him as it is for anyone else. He's got to battle his nature, the same as his congregants.

In the final analysis, aren't you glad your Rabbi, Priest, or Minister is human? Wouldn't you rather be led by someone who possesses the very same constitution as you, rather than some angelic being with whom you have nothing in common? The relationship between leader and follower is most effective when the leader seems to transform his followers into leaders as well. He cannot be effective when the disciple feels that becoming a leader is outside his grasp. Ordinariness is the stuff of leadership so long as it is accompanied by a constant reach for something higher. To be *extra*ordinary, you first have to be ordinary. Our humanity is the very stuff of leadership, and never a hindrance to it.

13

The Supremacy of Action to Faith

Action is with the scholar subordinate, but it is essential. Without it, he is not yet man. Without it, thought can never ripen into truth.

—RALPH WALDO EMERSON,
in a speech, 31 August, 1837

Action is character.

—F. SCOTT FITZGERALD,
notes for *The Lost Tycoon*

Watch your thoughts; they become words.
Watch your words; they become actions.
Watch your actions; they become habits.
Watch your habits; they become character.
Watch your character; it becomes your destiny.

—FRANK OUTLAW

JUDAISM IS NOT A RELIGION OF DOGMA but of deed, not a collection of beliefs, but a way of life. The Jewish Bible is God's law concerning human behavior. If man seeks to live a life in accordance with God's will, and thereby be granted the great privilege of knowing God and being close to Him, then he must act in a Godly manner. To be a good Jew is not to have the right feelings or the right beliefs. Indeed, many observant Jews I have met are agnostics, a fact that I am sure puzzles Christians to no end. The Jewish faith consists mostly of laws pertaining to life, from the biggest things, like the obligation to save human life, to the smallest things, like knowing which blessing to recite upon seeing a rainbow.

Far from winning Judaism friends, Judaism's never-ending emphasis on action has made it one of the world's least popular religions. People prefer religions that can make them feel "spiritual." This, in my opinion, is the strongest reason that Judaism has attracted so few converts over the ages. There are other reasons as well, such as the Jews themselves discouraging converts and the persecution that being Jewish entailed. But the primary reason is that Judaism demands action. Emotions are simply not enough. And faith is subordinated to deed. This emphasis was bound to be unpopular with the majority of people for whom an emotional high is far more pleasurable than a moral imperative.

Every recent statistic pertaining to the place of religion in modern society shows that even in the secular West, the vast majority of people have a belief in God. So why is religion on the decline? The truth is that spiritualism—New Age spirituality, meditation, yoga, Eastern spirituality, New Age strains of the Kabbalah—are all on the rise. It is *organized* religion that is in steep decline. Western society seems to have overdosed for many decades on a suffocating selfishness, and people are now hungering for a spiritual transfusion. Spiritualist books top the best-seller lists all over the world, and people are running to spiritual healers and austere religious sects in larger numbers than ever before. And while there is an accompanying growth in greater mainstream participation in Judaism or Christianity, still, it lags far behind the popular pursuit of New Age spirituality. Even previously discredited belief systems like paganism and the worship of nature are gaining new adherents.

Not long ago a Jewish friend asked me to have a word with his son, who is utterly uninterested in Judaism. As I spoke to the boy, he told me that in his opinion there is no God in the synagogue. "Organized religion is a black hole for spirituality," he claimed. Instead, a spiritual experience for him, he told me, is watching a sunset or listening to the pattering rain outside his doorstep. Even smoking hash, he said, opens his mind to the ineffable far more than religion ever could. The organized and cloistered structure of the traditional synagogue service, he said, "just leaves me cold."

Young people everywhere complain that religion is encumbered with meaningless ritual and antiquated definitions of good works and righteousness. They reject a set prayer book, which stifles their creativity. Most of all, they resent religion's endless predictability and routine. They want spontaneity and excitement. Any time you go to the theater or cinema, you can see a new play or a new film. But at church or synagogue you can expect the same boring regularity week in and week out. This is one of the reasons that the cinemas are packed and the synagogues empty. The main precondition for excitement is the novelty of the unexpected, and religion just doesn't seem capable of offering that.

One student said to me that he cannot join us for the Sabbath evening prayers because he has no desire to recite someone *else's* prayer to God. "When I take out a woman on a date, I hardly ask my father how he wooed my mother and simply repeat his romantic chatter. To suggest I do that in my relationship to God is insulting. I want to offer my own prayer. Take back your prayer book."

Intelligent young Jews have always complained to me that the Rabbis, in their effort to regulate every facet of life to ensure that it is within the realm of holiness and the divine will, have missed the big picture. These young people accuse Judaism of being so obsessed with subtleties and trivialities—which shoelace to tie first, how large a piece of matzah one must eat in order to properly fulfill the obligation of retelling the story of the exodus of Egypt—that the truly important issues, such as fear and love of God, are often overlooked.

These complaints have some merit. Why indeed does religion in general, and Judaism in particular, remain so repetitive? The Siddur, the Jewish prayer book, though one of the great achievements of the

Jewish faith, has retained its basic structure for millennia. Why not jazz it up a bit? Why is it that organized Jewish spirituality will provide the same pattern in a man's old age as it did at his Bar Mitzvah? Wouldn't God prefer it if people served Him from the depths of their hearts? Likewise, there are many who believe that the great Jewish emphasis on action and ritual—as opposed to emotion and belief—only serves to make Judaism lifeless and cold. Is our faith nothing more than a dinosaur, obsolete in an age of personal participation and public confession?

Judaism: A Philosophy of Action

There are several responses to the ancient argument against the centrality of action, the minutiae of law, and the set patterns associated with Judaism. One response uses an analogy of romantic love. There are those who believe that marriage is an institution that stifles love and spontaneity. They point out that an obsession with taking out the garbage, discussions as to which school the kids should be sent to, and paying the mortgage is the enemy of real love, which involves the endless expression of passion. Such accusations are offered by those who cannot see that real love is measured not in how you kiss, but in the degree to which you are prepared to lovingly execute the everyday chores of a shared existence. This is not to say that passion is not essential. It is to say that we must be passionate about *all* aspects of love, from the mountain tops to the valleys. Is your love so pervasive that it even makes mundane chores feel like pleasures?

Judaism understood that real service of God involves two things: first, a wholehearted acceptance of the will of God and of His setting the agenda of how He wishes to be approached. Second, real service of God, and ultimately the measure of every relationship, is found in the details, rather than just the larger plan. A wife asks her husband to take her to the movies to see a romantic comedy for her birthday. Instead, he takes her to see the *Texas Chainsaw Massacre* and justifies his action by thinking that the important thing is that he made time for his wife on her birthday. The details aren't important. It's the thought that counts. But all she feels is anger and exploitation. The fact that he is inattentive to the details of her request shows her that he does not take her or her desires seriously. He leaves himself the latitude to interpret her requests, thereby treating her as if she were absent. What woman would agree to live with a man who tells her that he will determine how she should be loved?

The same is true of those who believe in worshiping God, but in no particular fashion. They will go to synagogue, but make up their own prayers. Or instead of going to synagogue, they prefer to play melancholy tunes on a harmonica or square-dance with their friends in a field. They consider these acts of personal pleasure far more spiritual than worship in a synagogue. They will eat, but not say a blessing over the food. They accept the need to love and fear God, but it is for *them* to define how love and fear are expressed. But such arbitrary and personalized forms of worship dismiss God's will as unimportant.

The analogy of husband and wife is particularly appropriate because it brings to the fore another important dimension to the God-man relationship. There are those who refuse to worship God in an unintelligible way. They will live by the Ten Commandments. They see the importance of religious belief, especially of refraining from murder and theft. They admit that adultery is hurtful and that unbridled covetousness is ultimately the destroyer of happiness. But they reject the other Jewish commandments, such as eating only kosher food or not driving on the Sabbath, thinking that these laws are archaic and irrational. What they unwittingly do, as a result of this attitude, is to create God in *their* image and force Him to fit into their limited human grasp. Their thinking is that whatever they value, God values. Whatever they find uninspiring would probably bore God as well.

Action is the essence of any relationship, but there is a deeper reason why Judaism puts action before dogma and belief. Some people come to religion because of the discipline it imposes. Others seek meaning and inspiration to live for more than money and material possessions. Still others embrace religion because they seek a moral compass. They are penitents who reject their past and want to learn the difference between right and wrong. These are all ancillary goals. The highest purpose of religion is to transform man and connect him to God. *It is specifically organized religion—with its regular demands and routines—that has the capacity to change the inner nature of man and make Him Godly.*

The Cult of the Natural

At the dawn of history, man worshiped nature. With the advent of monotheism, man was alerted to the presence of an omnipotent God. But paganism was never defeated, it just went into hibernation. Having slumbered thousands of years, it has reappeared, but with a twist. No longer does man worship plants and fire. He bows at the altar of *human* nature. Paganism has been inverted and teaches man to pay homage to himself.

The creed of this new paganism declares that anything that is natural is necessarily good. Since scientists seek a genetic basis for almost every human aberration, the new religion labels any attempt to try to change one's behavior as a crime against nature. Books like Robert Wright's best-seller, *The Moral Animal,* argue that adultery is not a crime because it is essential for the survival of the human species for the male of every group to seek the widest possible distribution of his gene pool. Men cannot help but stare at every woman; not to act on one's instincts is unhealthy and dangerous repression. Since adultery is natural, it cannot be labeled sinful. Evolutionary biologists have even shown that female birds secretly bear offspring from mates other than their partners because of the superiority of the infiltrator. If birds can do it, why not humans? After all, it's the law of nature.

There was a time when a man would memorize lines from Tennyson or Byron before going on a date so he could impress a woman with the depth and vibrancy of his personality, his sensitivity, and his fine education. Today, he goes to the gym so that he can impress her with his imposing biceps. Women spend an hour in front of a mirror getting ready for a date, but comparatively little time sprucing up their character. The body has supplanted the personality as the key to attraction. Painting one's face takes precedence over filling one's mind. Rather than forming an opinion, women are today encouraged to get breast implants. Modern society worships form at the expense of substance, the ephemeral body at the expense of the eternal spirit.

Judaism came into the world to uproot the worship of nature and focus human minds and hearts on the worship of God. Nature is neither inherently evil nor inherently good. It is man who chooses to utilize nature in conformity with, or in opposition to, the laws of morality.

Adolf Hitler repeatedly used nature as a justification for his race theory and the elimination of the weak in favor of the strong. "In nature there is no pity for the lesser creatures when they are destroyed so that the fittest may survive. Going against nature brings ruin to man. It is only Jewish impudence to demand that we overcome nature." To his accusation, we Jews must reply: Guilty as charged. Judaism has always goaded man to defy and transcend nature, elevating it to a higher purpose. For most people it would be more natural to sleep late rather than get up and go to work. It is natural for children to prefer watching television to doing their homework. It is also natural for parents to pacify their children with toys rather than give of their time. But are these actions good? The only real crime against human nature is not to channel our nature into actions that are life-affirming and holy. *It is a crime against human nature to leave it in an uncultivated state, one in which it is indistinguishable from animal nature.*

Right and Wrong Actions and Reasons

Religion is like a matchmaker who must prepare a slovenly and ill-attired young man for his first date. He has to be dressed up because only then can he make a favorable impression. Similarly, man cannot approach God with only himself on his mind. Religion begins with the premise that human nature must be weaned away from narcissism and selfishness to sacrifice and honesty. Man must forgo false relationships based on manipulation and approach God with sincerity. The question, then, is how is human nature best improved? How do we persuade people to change?

The answer to this question marks a principal difference between Christianity and Judaism. Both religions begin with the premise that man must be made better. But whereas Christianity argues that only *inner faith* and *divine grace* can change man, Judaism maintains that inner transformation comes about through *external action*. Rather than heart fashioning hands, here hands fashion heart. We can learn to love people by first treating them decently. And the more love we show, the more love we will feel. Correct action is superior to proper intention; given enough time, if the action is right, the intention will follow. What we do becomes an inextricable part of who we are. *Simply stated, in Judaism it is not the heart or indeed even the mind, but the hands that serve as the fundamental religious organ.* The Jew's first goal is to have the right actions before God rather than the correct beliefs or emotions.

Christianity, especially its Protestant denominations, maintains that man cannot achieve salvation through his own personal devices. He is entirely dependent on grace, which is given freely by the Deity. Man is too sinful, too removed from God, to save himself. Redemption is a product of faith. But unconditional faith and submission are the prerequisites for such grace being bestowed. Man must first have the right beliefs; he must embrace Jesus. Belief in Christ will lead to righteousness of action. Reversing the order is utterly useless. It is not enough to do the right thing. One must do the right thing for the right reasons.

A classic illustration of the divergent approaches adopted by both religions is their respective words for giving alms to the poor. The Christian word for helping the needy is *charity*, derived from the Latin word *caritas*, "dear." It is not enough to feed the poor. They must be dear to us. It is essential that one help the needy as a response to an inner feeling of compassion. Religion should be an inspiration rather than a duty. It must be a response to an inner emotion.

The act of assisting the needy is known in Judaism as *tzedakah*, which means *justice*. When a man knocks on your door and says that he is hungry, you must feed him, whether you feel like it or not. To do so is just and righteous, regardless of whether your heart participates in the mitzvah. Judaism does not concern itself with righteous intent, but righteous action. Ten to twenty percent of your income is simply not yours. It belongs to the poor. To deny the needy man what is his due is an act of *injustice* rather than a lack of compassion. Even if you consider him a lazy and irresponsible parasite, you still cannot withhold him assistance. A bank manager who hates his clients still must produce their funds upon demand.

A wealthy friend of mine once gradually lost everything in a series of bad business ventures. I went around collecting for him and his family to pay their mortgage so that they could continue to live in their beautiful house. (In Judaism, charity is as much about dignity as it is about feeding one's family. If a man is subject to the humiliation of being thrown out of his own home, he will probably never get on his feet again and become self-sufficient.) One wealthy man whom I approached told me that he would not contribute to the fund, "because he [the needy one] lives in a much larger home than me and I still see him walking around in Armani suits." I responded that I had not asked him for his opinion of the man in need, merely his support. Must a man don sackcloth and ashes to elicit our compassion? I didn't ask him to *feel* the man's pain, just to *end* it. Once you start to give, your actions will drag your heart along with them, and you will end up feeling compassion as well.

Habit Becomes Nature

Maimonides explains that there are two kinds of human nature. The first is our congenital nature, our in-born character traits. Modern science would call this genetic predisposition. Some people are born passive, with a kindly disposition; others are born aggressive, with a strong competitive streak. Still others are calm until provoked, and then their formidable, fiery temper shows itself.

The other kind of human nature is *acquired*. By practicing the same action again and again, the deed becomes ingrained into our personality, and its performance becomes instinctive. Repetitive behavior can rewrite our genetic programming and reprogram our nature. *What begins as something we do ends up as something we are.*

Take one who is born with a selfish, self-centered disposition. When he passes a beggar on the street, his natural reaction is to walk straight by and curse the "freeloader" under his breath. But one day, motivated by a sense of guilt or shame in the face of onlookers, he gives the beggar a few coins. The next day he also does it, again for external reasons, and the next day also. Soon it becomes a habit. Although he began as a selfish person who occasionally practiced kindness, he ended up as a compassionate person who *cannot help* but donate some coins whenever he walks by someone in need. He has gone from being one who *gives* charity to one who *is* charitable. If a few days go by and he hasn't run into anyone who needs charity, he will even feel uneasy.

This is the power of action in general, and repetitive action in particular. Thus, Judaism dictates that rather than man giving, say, one thousand dollars to charity once a year, he should distribute three dollars a day for the year. The same is true of prayer and every other religious ritual. Judaism has no desire for man to pray occasionally, but for man's life to become a living prayer. Prayer should become as integral a part of human life as having three meals a day, as intuitive as eating breakfast. Thus, Judaism ordains that humans pray three times daily at regular intervals, morning, afternoon, and evening. Likewise, Judaism has no desire for men and women to practice occasional hospitality, but to *become* hospitable. Inner transformation is our objective. Thus, Jewish law demands that every family have guests at its weekly Sabbath table. God must be built into our daily schedules so that He becomes an essential part of our lives.

A couple that had been married for sixteen years but recently experiencing severe problems in their marriage came to see me. The wife complained of a cold, inattentive, and distracted husband who could not shut off his business worries once he came home. The husband responded by describing his wife as insensitive and ungrateful. "I admit that I'm cold to her lately," he said, "because my business is in dire financial trouble. How can she expect me to be in a loving mood when everything I built is teetering on the brink of collapse? Haven't I always provided for her? Why isn't she more understanding? I can't talk to her about it because she would never understand." I told him that affection from husband to wife cannot be reserved for moments of financial prosperity. Life is filled with ups and downs and any man who sinks into a world of his own while walking through the valleys will not have a wife left to share the precious joy at the peaks. "Take your wife into your confidence, lean on her, and tell her of your woes. Married life must be shared throughout all times, especially life's most vulnerable moments."

The same behavior modification is true for evil deeds. The first time we cheat on our taxes, we feel guilty. "The state needs the money to build roads and finance social welfare, so why am I so selfish?" The second time, we rationalize it. "It's not so bad. It's not good either, but everyone does it." By the third time, we say to ourselves, "It's a good thing that I've not paid my full taxes. After all, just look at how the government wastes so much money on so many worthless projects."

The more we repeat a sin, the more it becomes embedded into our character, until it becomes difficult, sometimes nearly impossible, to purge the sin from our being. Contrary to popular opinion, we are not what we feel. Less so are we what we think. Judaism would have changed Descartes's declaration to: "I *act*, therefore I am." We are what we *do*. Of course, one can recant a sin and repent, washing away the sin and emerging sparkling again. But once man becomes inseparable from his sin—once the evil he commits becomes the person he is—it is far more difficult to achieve repentance.

Adolph Eichmann, the Nazi architect of the Final Solution, asked to address the Israeli Supreme Court on the forty-seventh day of his lengthy trial in Jerusalem in 1961. In a carefully worded petition, he requested clemency from the court and a pardon from the Israeli president. He acknowledged the hideous nature of the Holocaust, but still begged that his life be spared. Not surprisingly, his request was turned down, and he was later hanged and his ashes scattered on the Mediterranean Sea.

Assuming that he was completely sincere in his desire to reject his past and atone for his sins, why was he not forgiven? Does Judaism not believe profoundly in the idea of repentance? The reason for the rejection of Eichmann's appeal for clemency was not that he couldn't bring any of his victims back. Rather, *he could not bring himself back.* A man can only repent the bad things he has committed. As long as they remain in the realm of bad deeds, he can cleanse himself of the evil he has committed. But the evil that a man perpetrates cannot be exorcised from his person once it has sunk in and become a part of his essence. If Eichmann had murdered a single Jew in a bar brawl or in a crime of passion, we might have been able to forgive him, because we could have attributed his action to the loss of self-control. Perhaps he had a monstrous temper and killed on more than one occasion but was still a decent man when calm. But when you are responsible for the murder of six million Jews—as part of a cold and methodical program of genocide—there can be no repentance. You are no longer someone who murdered. Rather, *you are a murderer* and there can be no atonement. Eichman could not repent of his sin because he had become the sin. It was impossible to extricate his evil action from his evil nature.

This is how the ancient Rabbis answer the age-old question of how God could have punished Pharaoh so harshly after denying him the possibility of repentance by "hardening his heart." The question has confounded biblical commentators for generations. Why should God have continued to inflict plague after plague upon the Egyptians for not freeing the Jews when God had removed from Pharaoh the choice to free them? But prior to his decision to free the Jews, Pharaoh had murdered countless Israelite baby boys by having them thrown into the Nile River, fearing that one of them might grow to be the Jewish redeemer. Again, this was a calculated, calm, and rational program of murder. Pharaoh was beyond repentance.

More than two hundred years ago, a young Hassidic man traveled all the way across Russia to see the great Rabbi Levi Yitzchak of Berditchev, a sage noted for his great love of all God's creatures. In an age in which many Rabbis were known for fire-and-brimstone oratory, Rabbi Levi Yitzchak felt unconditional love for the righteous man and sinner alike. The young man was ushered into the great Rabbi's study. "Rebbe," he said, "I have sinned, and I have come to you for guidance about how to seek atonement. You see, there was a married woman after whom I lusted and she after me. To my eternal shame, we consummated our mutual attraction. I have come to you in guilt to expiate my sin. But before you tell me what penitence I may undertake, know that the sin was not so bad as it could have been. You see, before we acted on our desire, she went to the *mikveh* [the ritual bath in which a woman immerses herself after menstruation]. So at least she was ritually clean."

Upon hearing the man's confession, the Rabbi rose from behind his desk and commanded the young man to depart his office forthwith. "It is best that you go, for I cannot help you." The young man was perplexed. "I came to see *you* specifically. I could have been shunned by so many other Rabbis. But you have a reputation for tolerance and loving-kindness. Did I make a mistake traveling four days to see you?"

"I am tolerant and loving," replied the sage, "to most people. Because people on the whole are good. It's just that they sin and do foolish things which derail their lives, and I am here to help them on the difficult journey back to innocence. But you are different. You are not someone who sinned. You, my son, are a *sinner.* Had you told me that you found yourself in a room with a beautiful woman and you could not control yourself, I would have told you, *Nu, Gei veiter,* Get on with your life. Move forward. Put the sin behind you. Forget about it, and wash it away in a sea of good deeds. But this is not what happened. Rather, you said that she first went to the *mikveh.* In other words, this was not an act of passion. It was an act of premeditated sin. You planned your transgression. Both of you began your countdown after her period commenced. Five days till we sin, four days, three days, and so forth. So I cannot instruct you as to how to purge yourself of what you have done. Your attempt to whitewash your sin has relegated you to the ranks of the incorrigible. You and your sin are one."

All of us make mistakes. But we must ensure that our error never becomes so ingrained into our psyche that it is linked with who and what we are. Moreover, we must always be on the alert never to rationalize our mistakes. Between sin and sinner lies a barrier called the human conscience. A rationalization is a removal of the natural barrier that should separate our mistakes from our person. Although to err is human, to make peace with our errors is animalistic.

Pius XII

The danger of whitewashing our sins is something that our Catholic brothers and sisters should be mindful of. What can one say of the world's foremost religious leader who voiced no public condemnation of a genocide that claimed six million innocent lives, virtually in his backyard? The Vatican received detailed information about the murder of Jews in the concentration camps as early as 1942, but Pope Pius XII restricted all his public utterances to carefully phrased expressions of sympathy for the victims of injustice and to calls for a more humane conduct of hostilities. When the Nazis began rounding up the eight thousand Jews of Rome in autumn 1943, the pope remained silent, even though it happened right outside the Vatican's gates. Hundreds of them were transported straight to the Auschwitz death camp.

The pope could have saved numerous lives, perhaps even halted the machinery of destruction altogether, had he chosen to take a public stand and confront the Germans with the threat of an interdict or with the excommunication of Hitler, Goebbels, and other Catholic Nazis. At the very least, it has been suggested, a public denunciation of the mass murders by Pius XII broadcast widely over the Vatican radio station would have revealed to Jews and Christians alike what deportation to the east actually meant.

Many defend the pope's actions, saying that he mistakenly believed that communism—with its strong antireligious bias—was a greater threat than fascism and therefore felt that he had to remain neutral in the conflict for fear of emboldening the Communists. But the Bible states emphatically, "Do not stand idly by the blood of your neighbor." Biblical teaching brooks no compromises when it comes to murder. There is no excuse for remaining passive. When you see someone being murdered, you must do your utmost to halt the evil. It behooves all of us to come to terms with, and never rationalize, our shortcomings. This applies to mighty institutions like the Church as well. It is highly regrettable, therefore, that the Catholic church chose to defend, rather than assail, Pius XII's actions.

Breaking the Degenerative Cycle of Pain

A man who had just moved to Oxford with his three children knocked on my door and told me he had recently been divorced. I offered my sympathy. "No need," he told me. "You might even say that divorce is a tradition in my family. My grandparents were divorced, my parents were divorced. And now I am divorced."

Being a child of divorce myself, I know how difficult it is to overcome the sense of hopelessness and disillusionment it engenders. Indeed, studies show children of divorce are 50 percent more likely to divorce themselves. But the time comes in the life of an individual, a family, and a nation when a downward cycle must be reversed and put right.

In repairing the bridges of our broken lives, we must refrain from taking the shortcut of acting better only in moments of elation or triumph. Inner reorientation is a result of regular patterns wherein man submits to the good because it is right rather than because it is pleasurable or rewarding. Life is about prose that becomes poetry. Judaism conditions man to find the magic in the everyday. Displaying love to one's spouse only in moments of great passion or happiness is an illusion. One must submit to the beauty of simple, everyday married life. If you are a child of divorce, or if you are experiencing marital discord, don't wait for a moment of inspiration to tell your spouse that you love him or her and save your marriage. Rather, embrace the routine, however unpleasant initially. Wake up every morning and give your spouse a kiss, help tidy up the bedroom, clean the dishes, even if—especially if—you don't feel like it. And make that action the outgrowth of your unparalleled love for each other.

The same is true of our relationship with God. We must discard immature concepts of religion being about a crescendo of emotions. Rather, Judaism is about humans building a relationship with God by transforming themselves through everyday acts of kindness and holiness.

Personal Salvation and World Redemption

Action as opposed to emotion is emphasized in Judaism not only because our actions shape our inner character. The idea that world redemption, rather than personal salvation, is humankind's first calling is also part of the Jewish Weltanshauung.

Bertrand Russell, in his cogent and compelling essay "Why I Am Not a Christian," accuses Christianity of emphasizing the perfection of the self over the perfection of the world at large. Whereas the Christian faith once spoke of *collective* redemption, Russell says, it now speaks of *personal* salvation. Christianity is guilty "of adopting the belief that an individual can be perfect in an imperfect world." Hammering home his point, he writes with considerable ire that the Christian religion "leads to a conception of personal holiness as something completely independent of beneficent action. . . . I do not believe there is a single saint in the whole calendar whose saintship is due to work of public utility."

Some of the best insights into religion are offered by atheists. Working among young and idealistic students, I have often heard the refrain that righteous action that is not inspired by virtuous motivation is worthless. Love is the most important thing, and if you help someone but don't care about that person, you are a hypocrite. But this contention betrays the erroneous belief that the most important thing in life is to be a good person, one of those clichés that people accept without thinking. The most important thing in life is to make the world a better place—to rid it of pain and evil—even if *we* ourselves remain imperfect. In other words, our life goal is to practice goodness rather than merely to be good in our hearts. And by practicing goodness, we gradually become good on the inside as well as out.

Every action embodies two dimensions. The first is its *motivation*. The second is the action itself. There are the things we do, and there are the reasons that we do them. These two dimensions correspond to twin goals of personal perfection and perfection of the world. Why we do things speaks about the kind of people we are. If we give charity to get noticed, then we are selfish. If we give it because we love the poor, then we are kind. But as far as the consequences of our actions on the world at large, our motivation is of little consequence. The starving child in Sudan who eats the bread that we paid for rarely thinks about *why* we did it. The important thing is that he will live to see another day. Similarly, it does not matter to a bereaved parent if the drunken driver who killed her son had one too many because he was enjoying a romantic anniversary dinner with his wife. On the contrary, when it comes to the perfection of the world, our motivation is wholly inconsequential.

That is why Judaism insists that one must do a good deed even if it stems from improper or insincere motivation. Refraining from doing a good deed because we question our intention is the piety of fools. The ancient Rabbis taught that man's evil inclination is a wily fox and comes to us in many guises. Sometimes, it dons the robes of the scholar and approaches us as a learned and aged sage. "You can't help people when in your heart you know you are a hypocrite," the sage tells us. The key is to remember that any rationalization that obstructs us from doing a good deed emanates from the dark side of our personality. There are no exceptions.

Once a wealthy merchant came to the great Rabbi Shneur Zalman of Liadi. "Rabbi, I had an idea to endow an orphanage that can accommodate two hundred children. But I have since abandoned the project, for after careful examination of my intentions, I had to admit I was doing it as a means of receiving respect in the community."

The old master looked the merchant squarely in the eye and said sternly, "Build it anyway! You may not mean it sincerely. But those poor children who will eat hot food and go to sleep in a warm bed, *they* will do so sincerely."

There is, however, an important caveat. Although world redemption is mankind's first calling, individuals cannot ignore their own development as caring human beings who are sensitive to the suffering of other members of the human family. Motivation, intention, and the right incentive are highly significant in Jewish thought, albeit always of secondary importance. For even though the wrong reason will not negatively taint the good deeds we do, we have an obligation to improve first the macrocosm, the outer world at large, and then the microcosm, the inner world of man. Hence the Jewish religion always speaks of a *complete* mitzvah consisting of the Godly act coupled with the proper motivation.

The Bible encourages these two goals in the way it structures man's week. It commands: "Six days shall you work." For the overwhelming majority of the week, man focuses on world redemption. He builds hospitals and homes, schools and universities, studies ethics and science, and generally raises the world to higher levels of physical and spiritual development. "But the seventh day is one which is consecrated to God." On the Sabbath, man must turn his creative efforts inward toward introspection, Torah study, and spiritual refinement. He must examine his heart and ensure that the good things he will do in the coming week are all done for the right purpose. There is, therefore, a six to one ratio of works of public utility to introspection and personal growth.

Our first obligation in life is to do works of public utility, pursuing love and justice and enhancing the lot of our fellow man. But a significant proportion of our time must also be dedicated toward ensuring that we never forget that we too must be glorious human beings, on the inside as well as the outside. Thus, for thousands of years Judaism has insisted that even significant philanthropists, encumbered as they are with myriad business responsibilities, must still study Torah and pray with fervor and concentration. Likewise, scholars of the Law and the clergy must also give charity and assist their fellowman, even though the majority of their time is devoted to self-refinement and piety. In all our endeavors, we must seek wholesomeness, which involves, first, the performance of acts of loving-kindness and, second, refining our hearts and striving for spiritual enlightenment.

14

Chosenness

A History of Why the World Needed a Chosen People

I have set you for a light of the nations; to open the blind eyes, to bring out prisoners from the dungeon.

—ISAIAH 42:6–7

We Jews, you say, are proud and an elite because we reckon ourselves the chosen people of God, but for what were we chosen? To show all nations an example of a people who is not afraid to stand upright on the earth, to regard no man as God, to look even God in the face and not be overwhelmed. This is why we are the chosen people of God, for God does not want us human beings to be wretches and cowards who dare not stand on our own feet. And this is what makes us hated by all the nations on earth, who reckon that we are endangering their lifestyles, their saviours and demigods who save them from the effort of living like men. We are proud, yes, but we want all men to be proud. We were chosen, yes, but for what? For power? For happiness? For rest and security in our possessions? No. For pain and misery and persecution and wandering over the face of the earth. Do not say that we have not seen the abyss. We who are on the brink of it every day of our lives—we who began our journey by crossing the desert with only the pil-

*lar of fire to guide us—we have seen it. Yet we continue our
journey by the guidance of God's law, which was given for men,
not for angels or devils.*

—RABBI MOSES BEN NACHMAN
Disputation in Barcelona, 1263

THEOLOGIANS AND APOLOGISTS FOR RELIGION try hard to explain why God likes hiding. If God *is*, then why does he pretend that He *isn't*? Two centuries ago Rabbi Boruch of Medzebozh wrote, "Picture two children playing hide-and-seek. One hides but the other does not look for him. God is hiding and man is not seeking. Imagine his distress." Why shouldn't God plainly reveal Himself for all the earth to see? Why not show all the doubters and atheists some celestial fireworks and give the devout something to brag about? Millions of sincere spiritual seekers are prepared to take the religious package lock, stock, and barrel—if only God would give them a sign.

In Chapter 6, I explained that God's hiddenness provides man with the opportunity to exercise his free will. If God made Himself evident, so the argument goes, then people wouldn't have the choice not to obey Him. Nevertheless, we might respond, in order for man to have a free choice, he must also have the opportunity of appreciating the *presence* of God, and not just his absence. After all, a choice is only free if there is a reasonable option in both directions. God must somehow be both present and absent, visible and invisible, apparent and hidden.

According to the Bible, God does make Himself evident through having elected one nation to represent and proclaim Him in all places and all times. The earth's inhabitants find inspiration from other people more than from anything else. Rather than choosing the mountains or the stars to serve as a permanent reminder to the world of His omnipresence, God chose a nation of men and women, whose mission in turn would be to remind other nations of His permanent existence and His eternal moral demands. That nation is the Jewish people.

Proof That God Exists

Philosophy asks whether God exists, and humankind's ultimate quest is to find the hand of God in history. In our age, in which many affirm a belief only in those things that are immediately accessible to the senses, it becomes easy to deny the invisible God. We find ourselves crying out to God to heal our loneliness and suffering, but are not sure if that cry is worthwhile, or if our voice merely echoes in an endless and indifferent abyss.

However, the proof of God's existence is the miraculous survival of the Jewish people. No social scientist or historian can explain the continued existence of this most persecuted of all nations. The Jews have survived since antiquity, though other nations have bowed to the imperatives of historical decline and simply disappeared. Like a ghost that successive exorcists have tried in vain to expunge, the Jews continue to survive every torment and aggressor. This phenomenon is even more impressive when one considers that the Jews have not had armies or legions to protect them, and have not even had, until quite recently, a geographic location within which to define themselves.

To be sure, the Chinese and Indians are also ancient peoples. But their definition is dependent on geographic boundaries. Amid global dispersal on the one hand, and serving as targets for murder and oppression on the other, the Jew *alone* has survived as a relic of an ancient era. Mark Twain expressed it succinctly:

> If the statistics are right, the Jews constitute but one quarter of one percent of the human race. It suggests a nebulous dim puff of stardust lost in the blaze of the Milky Way. Properly, the Jew ought hardly to be heard of. . . .
>
> . . . The Egyptians, the Babylonians, and the Persians rose, filled the planet with sound and splendor, then faded to dream-stuff and passed away; the Greeks and Romans followed and made a vast noise, and they are gone; other peoples have sprung up and held their torch high for a time but it burnt out, and they sit in twilight now or have vanished.

The Jew saw them all, survived them all, and is now what he always was, exhibiting no decadence, no infirmities of age, no weakening of his parts, no slowing of his energies, no dulling of his alert and aggressive mind. (Mark Twain, "Concerning the Jews," *Harper's Magazine*, September 1899)

Tolstoy echoed a similar sentiment:

The Jew is the emblem of eternity. He whom neither slaughter nor torture of thousands of years could destroy, he whom neither fire nor sword nor inquisition was able to wipe off the face of the earth, he who was the first to produce the oracles of God, he who has been for so long the guardian of prophecy, and who transmitted it to the rest of the world—such a nation cannot be destroyed. The Jew is as everlasting as eternity itself. (L. N. Tolstoy, "What Is a Jew," *Jewish World*, 1908)

Aside from mere survival, the other miracle of the Jewish nation is the extraordinary impact it has had on the world and the myriad gifts it has bequeathed to civilization. As I write, fewer than three of every thousand people who currently walk the earth are Jews; historically, it has been even less. Yet, the Jews remain the most influential nation of all time. According to Alan Dershowitz, "Of America's Nobel Prize winners in science and economics, nearly 40 percent have been Jews. Of America's 200 most influential intellectuals, half are full Jews, and 76 percent have at least one Jewish parent" (*The Vanishing American Jew*, p. 11).

From any historical perspective, the survival of the Jewish people testifies to the existence of the Creator. In order to prove His stewardship of the world, the Almighty chose a single nation, one not known for its military tradition (a tradition the Bible refers to as the "hands of Esau"), but rather for its tradition of scholarship, the voice of Jacob, as the one to survive. Through this action God showed that it is not human prowess, the mightiness of the sword, or the ingenuity of politicians and generals that brings humans success and longevity. Rather, it is an unswerving and dedicated belief in God. It is Providence alone that determines the fortunes of nations.

Such a bold claim requires further elucidation. Everything in the world emanates from God and ultimately owes its existence to the Creator. Our universe was meant to serve as a showcase for divine unity. In the beginning there was heaven on earth. God created the world and was originally manifest within it. He was a friend and companion to Adam and Eve, from whom He did not hide. But then, little by little, He began to recede from creation. In the beginning He took an active managerial role in nature, bringing order to the primordial chaos and setting the sun as a luminary in the blackened sky. But once the work of creation was complete, God vanished and became a disembodied voice, speaking through holy men and prophets. Later He vanished even more and became a presence, animating all life from behind the scenes.

If one traces the events of the Bible, one will see how it is a history of God slowly reducing His overt presence. At first He speaks directly to Adam and Eve and then to Abraham. Later He communicates to the Jewish people through Moses and the subsequent prophets, until, by the end of the twenty-four books of the Bible and with the destruction of the First Temple and the exile of the Jews from the Land of Israel, He is hidden completely from immediate view. By the time we reach the story of Esther, God is controlling events and saving the Jews from the wicked Haman in Persia from behind the scenes. In fact, the Book of Esther does not mention God's name even once. Although His presence is felt, His voice is silent.

As time progressed, the Almighty established Himself as an all-enveloping, all-encompassing energy, draped behind the facade of nature. There are two reasons for God's disappearance. One involves sin. Man slowly pushed God away from the earth. It began with the sin of Adam and Eve and continued with the builders of the Tower of Babel and the subsequent rebellions of the emancipated Jewish slaves in the Wilderness of Sinai. The second reason is found in Jewish mystical sources. The Kabbalah says that had God continued to play with and order natural objects, to the observer it would have appeared that God and nature were two distinct entities. In other words, if we could look up at the night sky and see God suspending the earth in its orbit around the sun, we would naturally conclude that though God rules over the earth, He is not *part* of the earth. Man would have reasoned that God controls nature, just as a king rules over his people. This conception is what we call deism: It affirms God's creation of the world but detachment from it. But since God's unity is absolute, it became imperative for God to be perceived *through* nature, rather than as merely being above it. God serves as the fabric of our world and the matrix of existence. Nothing is independent of Him. Every cosmic force, every rainbow, every drop of dew, every leaf, and every beast of the field is ultimately designed to serve God and execute His divine will and plan for creation.

Man, too, is created and designed to dedicate his every movement and talent toward the service of the Creator. The first man and woman were placed in the Garden of Eden "to work it and protect it." Likewise, their descendants must till the earth and uncover the hidden divine spark that lurks within all created existence. Man is different from the animals in that he can choose to serve God or not. Although God acts *through* all the earth's forces and the laws of nature, He *speaks to* man. Man is the *subject* of God's attention, not just the *object* of His presence. God addresses man almost as an equal. The animals and nature, however, are treated as though they were nothing more than windows through which God's light can shine, though not clearly. Whereas animals are programmed to obey their instincts, man is capable of practicing love and justice, thereby living up to the highest purpose of creation, namely, that every mouth and every babe should declare the glory of God. By living in accordance with God's will rather than just pursuing his own self-serving appetites, man comes to acknowledge God as master.

The purpose of man, when he was created, was to recognize the mastery of God and to dedicate every human talent to the Creator. Man was meant to know what was worth living for. Everything God the Creator commands becomes good, since it helps man achieve the purpose of his creation, thereby maximizing his human potential. Men who live for money, pleasure, or clothes, though not evil, cannot be said to be fully human since they allow a vast panoply of their spiritual color to lie dormant. We would say of those who have not loved that they have not tasted fully of their humanity, and the same is true, and infinitely more so, of one who has not enjoyed a relationship with God. And God can only be approached through love and justice.

A Brief History of Trial and Error

In the beginning men and women were fully aware of the God who ruled creation through the mask of nature. But as time progressed, all man saw was the mask. Man began to forget God and thereby brought fragmentation to creation. At the very beginning of creation, Adam and Eve were given a single commandment: to refrain from eating from the tree of knowledge of good and evil. Although the reason for the commandment is not given explicitly, it showed them that their very being was contingent upon their acceptance of the sovereignty of the Creator. They failed. Since God was invisible, Adam and Eve assumed they could ignore His rules. Instead of living to fulfill His will, they began to live for the most destructive idol of all, namely, the satisfaction of their immediate desires and lust.

Since man found his ultimate joy in satiating his sensual pleasures, he began to worship the forces of nature that could bring him those pleasures. The sun was worshiped for its warmth, the oceans for their cool, refreshing waters, even animals for their meat. In worshiping the forces of nature, man dissolved the fragile unity that had governed all creation prior to his sin. Man's original calling was to serve as the gardener in Eden. A gardener is someone who orchestrates the variety of vegetation to create a striking, beautiful whole. In essence, he brings unity to what would otherwise be a far less attractive collection of individual flowers and trees. But since man began to use nature for his own purposes, he compromised his essential mission of making God one in the universe. In deifying that which was designed to express the splendor of the Creator, Adam and his descendants caused the light of creation to be dimmed, and God was removed even further.

The generations continued to deteriorate, each one successively indulging in the dual sin of idolatry—worshiping the forces of nature for their tangible and pleasure-giving properties—and pursuing immediate sensual gratification. Man began to live only for himself and was deaf to the still, silent voice that called out to him from beyond. Mankind became more and more obsessed with satiating the appetites; all restraint was lost; and anything was fair game in the pursuit of gratification—rape, adultery, theft, bestiality, and murder. It was for this reason that God was finally forced to destroy the generation of Noah, for mankind had become incorrigible.

After the flood, God gave humanity another chance to better its ways and recognize His presence through submission to His code of conduct. But the next generation built the Tower of Babel. Their sin, unlike their predecessors', was not the wanton pursuit of pleasure. Rather, they sought unbridled power and the ability to control their fellowman. They built the tower as a means by which to cast off the yoke of God, as well as to dominate their fellowman with a listening post from which all human affairs could be governed. The ancient Rabbis understood the Tower of Babel to have been a giant surveillance device. Furthermore, by centralizing all human authority in location, and because all humans were united by one language, it would be easy to control people. The Tower of Babel was the harbinger of all totalitarian regimes that would follow it. But mankind has only one master. The tower builders were attempting to overthrow the dominion of God. Their audacity could not be tolerated.

Rather than giving this criminal generation the opportunity of deteriorating into further moral decay—the Almighty had already promised Noah that never again would He destroy humanity—He dispersed them into many different nations and spread them out over the face of the earth. In the future, whenever one nation indulged in an orgy of immorality and self-seeking pleasure and power, it could be spun off and destroyed—like Sodom and Gomorrah—rather than infecting the rest of mankind.

Thereafter, the world entered into a period of trial and error, in which one nation after another would rise to prominence through its intellectual, cultural, and military achievements. All the while, God hoped that a nation would arise that would embrace His decree to pursue love and justice, and thereby reestablish His dominion over the earth. Inevitably, however, each nation displayed hubris and became victim of its own arrogance. Rather than ascribe their success to God and call upon their citizens to practice kindness and compassion, the people turned on their neighbors and exploited their weakness, bringing cruelty and further injustice to an already corrupted earth. Civilization itself eventually became the conduit for corruption. The more humans advanced in technology and the arts, the more they lauded their own powers of creativity, bringing further decay.

Rather than repeat this endless cycle of trial and error, after twenty generations had elapsed since the creation of the first man and woman, the Almighty elected to have one people serve as a standard-bearer to the other nations. Offspring of men and women whose lives were a model of dedication to love and justice, this nation would bear permanent witness to the invisible Creator through its longevity and survival amid persecution and oppression.

For this exalted mission, God chose the seed of Abraham—the individual who had rejected pagan idolatry and propagated the knowledge of God far and wide—as the conduit for reasserting His place in history. Here would be a nation lacking the overt greatness of other nations. Rather than by military might or its own ingenuity, it would survive entirely through God's providence. Indeed, after this weak nation was enslaved by Egypt, by far the most technologically advanced nation of its time, God brought its people into freedom amid miraculous events, thereby demonstrating that man was not master of the world and that God would ultimately seek vengeance against bullies and tyrants. Through the destruction of Egypt, the

Almighty showed that civilizations that undermined His authority were ultimately condemned to oblivion.

The Jews then set up their own nation-state, which was to serve as a light, illuminating God's ways to all other nations. Their homeland was located in the center of the world, a point connecting three vast continents, so that their example would spread far and wide—hence the eternal connection between God's chosen people and the Land of Israel. Solomon built God's Temple in the midst of the nation, on a high place (the Temple Mount) in Jerusalem, thereby demonstrating that God resided among humanity and filled all the earth, rather than merely inhabiting the heavens. The mission of the Jewish nation was to serve as "a nation of priests," a nation whose entire being would be devoted to the worship and service of God. Whereas the other nations of the world were given seven commandments—the Noahide covenant—by which to serve the one God, the Jews were given 613 commandments, which would govern their every waking moment so that their lives would serve as a model of total dedication to God the Creator.

Unfortunately, they too exhibited hubris. Having set up their own successful civilization after conquering the land through Joshua and established a monarchy like the other nations, they began to crumble under the weight of their own perceived self-importance. There were, however, a few righteous generations in which the Jews faithfully fulfilled their mission of disseminating ethical monotheism and practicing justice. Indeed, through their initial righteous example, the Jews established the Creator as a living presence among the earth's inhabitants. But Moses himself predicted that the Jews would forsake God and revert to the paganism of the nations that surrounded them.

After successive generations, the iniquity of the Jews having reached a crescendo, God sent against them the Babylonians, who destroyed the Temple and dispersed the nation. The Jews had been subverting their intended purpose, and their time on their land had therefore come to an end. There was to be a final sojourn of the Jewish people in the Land of Israel for four hundred years, during the time of the Second Temple and the Jewish Commonwealth. The primary purpose of that "family reunion" was to prepare them religiously and spiritually for the long, bitter exile that they were about to endure. After the destruction of the First Temple by Nebuchadrezzar (Nebuchadnezzar) in 586 B.C.E., the Persian emperor Cyrus the Great allowed them to return to their land and build the Second Temple in 515. The latter was destroyed in 70 C.E. by the Romans. But in the crucial centuries before the Temple's destruction, the Jewish religion was formally committed to writing down the Law, which had until then been only an oral tradition. This was to provide the next step in the development of the world and its reaching a higher state of Godly perfection.

Exile and Its Ramifications

The Jews, having lost their land, would henceforth be united, not by land and a *national* identity, but entirely through bonds of faith and religious practices. It would not be their common origin but their common values that bound them together. Their distinctive mode of divine service would be their principal unifying force. If the Jews could hold on to God through their long and torturous wanderings, this would be proof that belief in the Creator had permeated their collective consciousness. Then slowly the central tenets of their religious faith would make an impact on the Gentile nations.

Indeed, both tragically and heroically, the Jews far exceeded all expectations in their fidelity to God. For two thousand years, through crusades, pogroms, inquisitions, and the Holocaust, the Jews have never forfeited their belief in God and devotion to the covenant that He made with them at Mount Sinai. The tenacity with which the Jew clings to his identity defies all explanation. If the purpose of life is for man to learn to place his love for God before the pursuit of his own pleasure—to practice love and justice—then the Jews, over the past two thousand years, have sacrificed whatever meager pleasures they had for the sake of their Creator. Not even husbands, wives, or children—and certainly no material possession—have ever stood in the way of Jewish willingness to sanctify the name of God and to remain firmly attached to the Creator, even at the cost of life itself.

This unequaled devotion to God and the Jewish way of life has yielded substantial results. Directly through the propagation of ethical monotheism, and indirectly through Judaism's daughter religions, Christianity and Islam, the Jews have made God the most potent and important concept in the history of the world. Even in today's world, there is no one word that is as powerful and mysterious as the name of the deity. Nor is any other subject more discussed and debated. The influence of the Jews is astonishing. A nation that began as a small Middle Eastern tribe ended up becoming the most influential and longest-enduring nation in all history.

A Religion of Restraint

The primacy of this message of subjugation to the mastery of God is conveyed by the Jewish emphasis on obedience, restraint, and human submission to the divine will. The Hebrew Bible delivers 613 commandments incumbent upon the Jew. Of these, fully 365 are negative prohibitions. Indeed, the very first commandment to Adam was a prohibition, a divine injunction against eating the forbidden fruit. Man cannot simply do whatever his heart fancies. Worship of God is found in circumspection and in refraining from indulging every whim. Judaism, however, is not a religion of repression or denial. In fact, it is one of sensuality and celebration. Judaism allows, even obligates, man to engage in every earthly activity, but he must carry out all such matters in accordance with the divine will, through which he achieves holiness.

Nevertheless, Jewish observance consists principally of inaction rather than action, withdrawal rather than movement. Judaism instills within man an appreciation for the passive and a cultivation of the inner feminine energy. Negative commandments, prohibitions, are at the core of Judaism because they require greater devotion than positive ones. The greatest and first symbol of Judaism is circumcision. A Jew enters God's covenant when he accepts God's sign on his most impulsive organ. Only when man submits the random pursuit of sensual pleasure to divine dictate can he undo the sin of Adam. The beginning of religion is for man to learn to place God before him always. Restraint, discipline, and a commitment to self-mastery are the foundations of religious life.

Whereas William James saw happiness as the goal of religion, Judaism sees greatness and heroism as its goal. Most people today define greatness in terms of commercial, political, or professional success. But within Judaism greatness is defined in spiritual terms. The true test of moral courage lies in man's adhering to God's prescriptions, because they compel man to engage in moral restraint. As Rabbi Harold Kushner writes, "Judaism, done right, has the power to save your life from being spent entirely on the trivial" (*To Life! A Celebration of Jewish Being and Thinking*). This is also the reason that Judaism lays down myriad laws governing human sexuality. There is no other form of human activity that so reflects both man's Godly—in the human capacity for creation—and animalistic tendencies. Judaism bids man to refrain from behaving like an animal in the sexual areas and to raise all his human energies to spiritual heights. Whereas once a man and a woman were strangers, love draws them together, and sex sews them jointly as one flesh.

Heroism

There are two kinds of heroism. The first is the kind that the warrior exhibits on the battlefield, the glorious type of heroism that troubadours recount in the court. This heroism consists of bold, dramatic actions in which the hero displays valor by overcoming fear and vanquishing his enemies.

But there is a deeper dimension to heroism consisting of small acts of altruism and overcoming one's propensity to selfishness. This heroism may affect no one but oneself. Practiced in private chambers, this heroism will never reach the columns of the newspaper, and no memorable movie may ever be made to record it for posterity. Nobody is watching, save the Almighty Himself. Real heroism is displayed by the solitary man or woman of faith every time he or she resists an inner impulse for indulging lust and the desire for material gain, choosing to serve God and humanity instead. A married man or woman is on a business trip and meets a stranger. Nothing is stopping him or her from sinning, and no one will ever find out. Yet the person refrains because of love and the contractual bond with the Almighty and with their spouse. This is the type of heroism that the Rabbis were referring to when they said: "Who is a hero? He who gains mastery over him- or herself."

When Rabbi Yochanan ben Zakkai, the greatest sage of his generation, lay dying almost two thousand years ago, his students begged him to bless them before he expired. "I bless you," he said, "that all of you should learn to fear God as much as you fear your fellowman." His students were aghast. "Is that all you wish for us, great master?" they asked. "Yes," he replied. "Know that when a man is about to sin, and he sees a friend observing him, he refrains from doing so, for he does not wish to be thought of badly. May you learn to fear God just as much." And with these words he departed.

The task of the Jewish nation is to make God as tangible a reality as the person next door, and to influence the world to follow His dictates. Knowing that he is a member of the chosen nation imparts to the Jew a sense of strength to display moral heroism in a hostile world, which has always perceived him as its enemy. As Sigmund Freud writes:

> The Jewish people has met misfortune and ill-treatment with an unexampled capacity for resistance. It has developed special character-traits and incidentally has earned the hearty dislike of every other people. . . . We know the reason for this behaviour and what their secret treasure is. They really regard themselves as God's chosen people, they believe that they stand especially close to Him and this makes them proud and confident. (Freud, *Moses and Monotheism*)

To go from the sublime to the ridiculous, Courtney Love, widow of rock star Kurt Cobain, expressed this same idea slightly differently. Asked in an interview what it would have taken for her late husband to avoid suicide in 1995, she said, "He had a lot of German in him. Some Irish. But no Jew. I think that if he had a little Jew, he would have stuck it out."

Chosenness and an Egalitarian Generation

Whatever the virtue in being the chosen nation has conferred upon the Jews, it has also served as an endless cause of grief. It was the original cause of anti-Semitism: Many of the Jewish nation's enemies seemed intent on proving that the Jews were chosen only to be victimized. The ancient taunt of Joseph's brothers, "Come now, let us kill him and throw him into one of the pits . . . and we shall see what will become of his dreams" (Gen. 37:20), seems to have been adopted as the battle cry of those non-Jewish nations intent on undermining Jewish claims of chosenness. They chose to heap pain and suffering upon the Jew to show that he had no protector. Indeed, Jews themselves feel highly uncomfortable being called the chosen, arguing that if anything, they are chosen to suffer.

The idea of chosenness sits uncomfortably with modern Western egalitarian values, seeming elitist at best and racist at worst. Individuals hell-bent on the destruction of the Jewish nation, like Haj Amin el-Husseini, the mufti of Jerusalem who was a great admirer and supporter of Hitler, have used Jewish chosenness to foment anti-Semitism:

> The overwhelming egoism which lies in the character of the Jews, their unworthy belief that they are God's chosen nation and their assertion that all was created for them and that other people are animals . . . [makes them] incapable of being trusted. They cannot mix with any other nation but live as parasites among the nations, suck out their blood, embezzle their property, corrupt their morals. (quoted in Dennis Prager and Joseph Telushkin, *Why the Jews?*)

Claims to being chosen and special are not limited to Jews. The Japanese have a rising sun on their national flag, indicative of their belief that the sun rises primarily for them. The British once sang "Rule Britannia" with a firm conviction that their advanced civilization was divinely destined to conquer the earth. The United States has always seen itself as being an almost divinely appointed guardian and disseminator of democracy. As Herman Melville wrote, "We Americans are the peculiar chosen people—the Israel of our time; we bear the ark of the liberties of the world" (*White Jacket*, 1850, ch. 36). Yet, none of these nations was ever hated for its claims to chosenness, mostly because no one ever took the claims seriously. The Jews are the exception.

What exactly does chosenness connote? Does it mean that the Jews are a master race? Are they smarter than other nations? Does it infer a genetic superiority? Many years ago George Steiner was condemned for writing a provocative novel whose central plot had Hitler captured by the Allies after the war, imprisoned, and tried for his crimes against humanity. At the end of the novel, the prosecutor, tears streaming down his cheeks, excoriates Hitler for his fiendish genocide, pointing a finger at him and shouting the question how Hitler could have done this to the Jewish people. How was it possible for any human to have behaved in so cruel a fashion? Innocent men, women, and children were turned into ashes in the crematoria that he had ordered. Hitler then rises to his full height and points an accusing finger back at the prosecutor himself and says something to the effect of "Don't you dare accuse me. I am just a parody of you. It was you *Jews* who created me. Nazism is a Jewish invention. Who gave the world the original idea of a chosen people? Who taught the world that one nation was superior to another? All I did was translate the Jewish idea of a spiritual elect and a chosen nation to genetic superiority and a master race."

George Bernard Shaw expressed his belief that the Nazi proposition of Aryan racial superiority was merely mimicking the Jewish doctrine of chosenness. Similarly, the Methodist journal *Religion in Life* in 1971 included the statement, "It is not surprising that Hitler retaliated against the chosen race by decreeing that it was not the Jewish but the Aryan race that was chosen."

Are Jews guilty of arrogant pretensions to racial or at least spiritual superiority? Is this the reason that Jews have historically been so insular? Do they really believe themselves to be closer to God than all other nations? The answer is an emphatic no. Chosenness implies greater responsibility, with penalties as well as rewards: "You only have I singled out of all the families of the earth; therefore I will visit upon you all your iniquities" (Amos 3:2). The choice of the children of Israel as God's people was not because of their power or merit. Nor was it designed to isolate them from the other nations of the world. To say that the concept of chosenness is arrogant behavior on the part of the Jews is a gross misrepresentation. On the contrary, it is a humbling device.

The Jews were not merely chosen as God's special people, as if the Almighty was playing favorites. They were chosen *for a mission.* And that mission was to spread the knowledge of the Creator and His expectations of man to all nations. Thus, God's choosing the Jewish people would forever remind the Jews that alone they are insufficient. God is not satisfied with the contribution of the Jews alone but desires the service and participation of all nations. The Jewish mission, then, is to instruct the other nations of the world as to their centrality in God's plan for existence, is to educate them about how much God loves them and how all are equal in His eyes. How on earth could this be construed as divine favoritism or as a source of arrogance? What could be more humble than a nation whose existence is dedicated to teaching the other nations that God loves and desires them too?

The Bible never uses the word *chosen* in relation to the Jews as an adjective, but rather as a *verb,* thereby conveying the idea that they were chosen for a purpose. God has no favorite nations. Consider, "No, for I have chosen him, *that he may charge his children and his household after him to keep the way of the Lord by doing righteousness and justice;* so that the Lord may bring about for Abraham what he has promised him" (Gen. 18:19). Or again, "Happy is the nation whose God is the Lord, *the people whom he has chosen as his heritage"* (Ps. 33:12). The verse makes it clear that the Jews are chosen as God's witnesses to other nations to make Him known. The prophet Isaiah proclaims, "Here is my servant, whom I uphold, my chosen, in whom my soul delights; I have put my spirit upon him; he will bring forth justice to the nations" (Isa. 42:1). Here the word *chosen* is said in the context of being God's servant. The Jews are chosen to serve God's plan for the nations of the earth to come and recognize His presence and their corresponding moral obligations.

The same idea is reechoed in Isaiah: "You are my witnesses, says the Lord, and my servant whom I have chosen" (43:10). And yet again: "For I give water in the wilderness, rivers in the desert, to give drink to my chosen people, the people whom I formed for myself so that they might declare my praise" (43:20). All these verses attest to the fact that Jews are chosen as missionaries of ethical monotheism, rather than as a special race that possesses intrinsic superiority to the other nations of the world. In fact, racial superiority of the Jews is expressly dismissed by the Bible: "Are you not as the children of Ethiopia to me, children of Israel?" (Amos 9:7). As Dennis Prager and Joseph Telushkin write in *Why the Jews?* the Jews were chosen "simply because they are the offspring of the first ethical monotheist, Abraham. That is their single merit."

The Jews were chosen to serve as a light unto the nations—to reveal to the inhabitants of the world the hidden truth of the invisible God. "I have given you as a covenant to the people, a light to the nations" (Isa. 42:6). "I will give you as a light to the nations, that my salvation may reach to the end of the earth" (Isa. 49:6). In spawning the monotheistic faiths of Christianity and Islam, Judaism has largely fulfilled its mandate. As Louis Jacobs, a prominent Jewish theologian and thinker, writes, "It becomes obvious that [regarding the divine election of the Jews] we are not discussing a dogma incapable of verification but the recognition of sober historical fact. The world owes Israel the idea of the one God of righteousness and holiness. This is how God became known to mankind" (Jacobs, *The Jewish Religion: A Companion*).

Tolerance

Our inability today to appreciate the true definition of chosenness is based on misguided contemporary ideas of tolerance. The Jewish idea of tolerance is central to understanding chosenness, and I shall use a story of the great lawgiver Moses to explain it.

For over two hundred years the Jews were enslaved to the mighty empire of Egypt. The Almighty searched for a strong leader to deliver them. He would have to be noble, so that the Jews would respect him; compassionate, so that the Jews would esteem him; charismatic, so that the Jews would follow him; and wise, so that he could serve as an intermediary between the Jews and God. The selection of Moses was not based on his possession of any of these virtues. Rather, Jewish legend relates that one day Moses, when he served as shepherd to the flock of his father-in-law, Jethro, was bringing the flock back from pasture and noticed that a small straggler had been left behind because it could not keep up with the stronger, swifter sheep. Moses temporarily abandoned the entire flock and returned to gather in the straggler. It was at that moment that the Almighty declared, "This man shall be the leader of my people," and revealed Himself to Moses in the form of the burning bush.

Ostensibly, the story seems to indicate that Moses' care for each individual found favor in God's eyes. But this is a misunderstanding. Only a fool would have risked an entire flock for the sake of a single sheep. Rather, Moses did not return for just any sheep, but for the smallest and weakest. It was not because he believed that the straggler, if properly fed and cared for, could grow to be the pride of the flock, big and strong like its counterparts, that he collected it. Even this small sheep was an indispensable member of the flock. Moses recognized that without this straggler the *entire flock* was flawed and deficient.

In other words, the secret behind this seemingly straightforward story is this: Moses did not return for the sake of the *straggler*, but for the sake of the *flock*. Moses was, in the words of the *Zohar*, a *raayah mehemna*, a "trusted shepherd." He had been entrusted with an entire flock, not a collection of individuals. That flock included the little sheep. Had he returned from the pasture without the little sheep, he would not have brought back that with which he had been entrusted. Even replacing this sheep with another would not have served to compensate for its loss.

There is a profound lesson in this simple story. Moses was unlike the social worker who helps troubled members of society because, whether the world needs them or not, the social worker believes that every *individual* is significant. Rather, it was Moses' obligations to the *community* that made him understand the value of every component part.

The Almighty desired a leader who acknowledged that without the participation and contribution of every member, the nation would be deficient. He wanted a leader who saw that the diversity inherent in creation among nations, people, animals, and things—be they grand or small—was a blessing that made for a more colorful whole, a more glorious organization.

In today's society people pride themselves on their *tolerance*. They believe they have progressed beyond the prejudices of the past. They have learned to allow those opinions that do not necessarily accord with their own to be voiced. But is this progress?

I find this definition of tolerance repugnant. Rather than find enrichment or redemption in another's differences, one *tolerates*, or *stomachs*, their differences. One swallows hard, one suffers—tolerates—another's right to be different. This is hardly recognizing the virtue than can be extracted from another party's distinctiveness. This is a philosophy of segregation rather than mulitcultural enrichment. Tolerating another person implies that though one allows his opinions or differences today, if tomorrow he were to disappear from the face of the earth, one would hardly notice his absence. There is nothing to be learned from his conflicting opinion or uniqueness, and his absence in no way compromises or impairs one's own state of completion. Promoting or defending the modern definition of tolerance is really a license to indifference. It is not a call to harmony or multicultural enrichment.

Imagine a country in which all are pacifists. How long could it last? Would it not become prey to a belligerent neighbor? Conversely, imagine a country in which all citizens are hawks. What would prevent them from crossing the line of legitimate defense to inhuman aggression and even massacre? There is an inherent beauty and perfection in the divergence of human opinion. But in order for that beauty to be manifest, one must go beyond tolerating one's colleagues, and even one's rivals' existence, toward realizing that it is their existence and differences that allows us to maintain our own identity. Like Moses, we must adopt a commnal perspective.

This is a lesson that the Jewish people are fast forgetting. Israel today is quite fractured and internally divided. One camp would trade land for peace with the Arabs. The other contends that this would create indefensible borders and only invite further aggression. The sharp antagonism, even hatred, that divides these two camps shows that each group sees the other as a dangerous hindrance. Can none see that if they were all agreed, the country might degenerate into a totalitarian dictatorship, like many of its Arab neighbors, or weaken itself to the point where another Holocaust would be possible? The country's current political stalemate is a result, not of conflicting views, but rather of a lack of appreciation on the part of both groups for the necessity and redeeming features of the other.

Why can we not learn from our teacher Moses not merely to *tolerate* the existence of a different sheep in our flock, but to understand why that sheep is essential for the collective? What stultifying boredom would engulf the world if all were of the same mind or heart?

The ancient Sages declared, "Saving a single life is akin to saving the whole world." Why so? God created a complete world, one in which each individual, along with his or her intrinsic differences, was crucial to its perfection. When one individual is missing, there is suddenly a gross imbalance in creation, an imbalance that might serve to compromise the uniqueness of each of the earth's remaining inhabitants.

Here the magnitude of murder comes into perspective. The enormity of the offense is not confined to the violation of the sanctity of human life, but to adversely affecting the entire earth. When God created the world, this individual was an irreplaceable component of its perfection and equilibrium. The murderer chose to disrupt that fine tuning and throw the world into imbalance. Murder is thus the ultimate statement of arrogance. It is one man's actualization of his belief that another man serves no purpose. It is one man's arrogant affirmation that his view of life supercedes that of God.

The Bible teaches that the greatness of Moses and his ability to see the intrinsic worth of every individual lay in his unparalleled humility: "And the man Moses was the humblest of all the people that were on the earth" (Num. 12:3). How could a man who enjoyed constant and conscious intimacy with God, a man who split the Red Sea and brought the empire of mighty Pharaoh to its knees, remain humble? When looked at as an individual, Moses was far greater than other individuals, and should have felt arrogant. But Moses defined himself in reference to the nation as an organic entity. As every individual was essential to the integrity of the people, Moses was just one among equals. He was no more essential to the functioning of the people than the water carrier who executed his communal duties with honesty and rigor. Thus despite his elevated station, Moses remained the humblest of men.

I once met a prominent rabbi from Israel. Among other virtues, he had a reputation for being earthy and unassuming. Yet, he launched into a detailed account of his vast achievement over three decades and his world renown. I summoned the *chutzpah* to tell him I thought him a braggart. "I am, I am," he replied, without missing a beat. "But the difference between myself and other show-offs is that I leave room for you to be a show-off too."

Real humility is being fully aware of one's gifts, but still feeling an ability to learn from everyone else, indeed, a reliance on every other member of the community. Real humility is recognizing one's uniqueness, but also the specialness of everyone else. The contemporary mentality, born of a hypercompetitive and deficient mindset, would have us believe that the world is too small for all of us to be special.

The Other Nations and the Jews

In order for every nation to be special and every individual to feel indispensable, each must find its niche. There is a need for a guide, an instructor, to orchestrate the various contributions of all people to society, ensuring that each is life affirming and redeeming. Since every human group has something crucial to bring to the human family, a standard-bearer who would set up the rules of engagement was needed. This is the role of the Jews, a nation chosen to serve as the gardener in the reconstruction of Eden. The Jews gave the world the idea that man could reconstruct heaven on earth, that man could perfect the earth by ridding it of war, hatred, famine, and disease. All this could be achieved by submitting to God's authority and living life by His rules. Each nation was endowed with a special contribution to bring to the new garden, a fruit or plant that was uniquely theirs. The Jews were the recipients of a divine message as to how all these pieces of the puzzle could be assembled into one great whole.

For example, Christianity excels in the importance of faith. Islam excels in the importance of passion in all matters of religious endeavor. The Jews excel in the importance of law and its indispensability in maintaining a loving and just society. All three ideas are wonderful contributions to the world. Indeed, Judaism's greatest thinker of the past millennium, Maimonides, ascribes a divine purpose to Christianity and Islam. He writes that both of these religions have brought the knowledge of God and the Messiah to distant corners of the earth, so that there is now a universal familiarity with these concepts that there would not have been without them. And he wrote these lines 850 years ago as a victim of horrific Islamic Almohad persecution.

Who is to say that the thief, the bigot, or the Nazi doesn't make a positive contribution to his environment? Stalin approaches the community of nations and tells them that he has a contribution to make to the world. It's called the Gulag Archipelago. Hitler jumps in and says that he wants to build Auschwitz in the heart of the garden. Who will contradict them? Ultimately, it is the Almighty alone who can determine which contributions lead to the enhancement of society and which to its collapse. It was He who created all nations ethnically different, and it is He alone who knows what serves the public good. This is the essence of the Hebrew Bible and the message that the Jews must impart.

The world cannot be run at human whim. It needs an ultimate plan and a regulator who can determine whether it is progressing or regressing. This is the role of the Torah, the divine law, which puts each contribution into perspective. It organizes all human actions so that they coalesce into one supremely redeeming blueprint. It teaches that whereas contributions of compassion and justice by all peoples lead to the betterment of civilization, murder, bigotry, and racism lead to its rapid decay.

There had to be one people whose supreme purpose was to reveal this master plan to the world. History required a nation whose entire purpose was to teach the world Godly ethics and the contribution the nation could make toward the perfection of the earth. Thus, chosenness, far from implying any sense of Jewish superiority, conveys the idea that there is a family of nations and all of them must work together toward creating heaven on earth. Each is indispensable, and none is superior to the next. The task of the Jews is to be a light unto the nations. Light is an apt metaphor because it shows the way and provides guidance. It allows us to clean the room and arrange the furniture so that the home becomes fit for human habitation. God, too, desires to reside among man. But we must first make the earth fit to be a royal residence.

The Jews and the other nations of the world have different, albeit equal, roles. The Jews have the 613 commandments of the Torah to observe. Non-Jews have the Noahide commandments, included within which are prohibitions against idolatry, theft, murder, adultery and incest, cruelty to animals, blasphemy, and the responsibility to establish and maintain courts of justice in a just society. The extra commandments given to the Jews do not connote superiority or heightened spirituality. Indeed, two thousand years ago, well before egalitarian enlightenment would have caused the Rabbis to issue apologetics, the Sages of Israel went out of their way to dismiss any sense of Jewish spiritual or racial supremacy. Rather, everything was dependent on a person's deeds, regardless of nation or birth. In this vein, the Sages of the Talmud declared: "Even a Gentile who studies God's law is equal to the Jewish High Priest" (*Bava Kamah* 38a). Similarly, the Rabbis never reserved salvation only for Jews, declaring "the righteous of all nations have a share in the World to Come" (*Tosefta Sanhedrin* 13). And again, "I call heaven and earth as witnesses: Any individual, whether Gentile or Jew, man or woman, servant or maid, can bring the Divine Presence upon himself in accordance with his deeds" (*Tana Devei Eliahu Rabba* 9).

Since the Jews are entrusted with teaching and maintaining the divine message, they were given far more divine commandments to serve as a buffer against being affected by the lawlessness and un-Godliness that they are bound to encounter on their journey. To remain faithful to their mission they have to be extra vigilant. By way of analogy, in order for the rooms of a house to be a comfortable 70 degrees during winter, the boiler room must be 250 degrees. So too, in order for the world to have the light of God shine upon it, those who teach the world about that light must burn with an added intensity.

Dual Roles

The idea of dual, yet equal, roles in creation is exclusive to Judaism. The only one with a copyright on truth is the Almighty, and He designated different routes for different groups to maximize their individual potential. He even set out different avenues for men and women to realize their fullest spiritual potential and made it clear that it is harmful for women to choose men as role models. God gave women specific commandments that would serve to enhance their precious feminine gifts and mystique. Surely, if the entire world were female, it would be insufferable. And if it were only male, it would be even more insufferable. The same would apply if the entire world had been only Jews. If all people inhabiting the planet looked or thought the same, we would all die of boredom. The world achieves perfection through diversity.

It is for this reason that Judaism discourages conversion, which has nothing to do with Jews' being an elite club, as some have suggested. Quite the contrary. Judaism does not invite converts, because it is a fallacy to believe that one needs to be a Jew in order to enjoy proximity to God or lead a fulfilled life. The way God created each of us is the way in which He wishes for us to serve Him. By becoming a Jew, one might neglect to make to society the contributions that he or she was created for. The world needs him just the way he is, which is why God created him that way.

A Dislike of Differences

To our great misfortune, we live in an age that not only does not appreciate differences, but actively seeks to obliterate them. Equality in today's terms is synonymous with homogeneity. Multiculturalism is nothing more than a myth, as society sends the message that we should all melt into one big indiscriminate morass. The Pax Americana, or superimposition of a shallow American culture, which is supplanting indigenous cultures throughout the world, is just one expression of this development.

Why is diversity losing out? The first reason is a weakness of identity on the part of minority groups. Everybody wants to fit in. If an individual is not confident about who he is and what he represents, if he cannot answer the important question why his tradition should continue, then he will seek to be like everybody else. Nobody naturally likes being different. It takes conviction to swim against the tide. I believe that we fear diversity mainly because of the persecution it has led to throughout the ages. Jews were slaughtered by Christians, women were dominated by men, and Blacks were enslaved by whites.

In Judaism the word *holy* connotes "distinct" or "removed." Something is holy by virtue of its being dissimilar, aloof, and unique. Thus, a human being becomes holy when he acts differently from animals. Instead of eating from a trough, he preserves his dignity and eats only those foods that God has allowed. He does not merely tear apart and devour other animals, but has them slaughtered in the most painless way. When a person does eat without human etiquette, we say that he behaves like an animal. God is holy because He is not like man. He has no body or other corporal limitation. The Sabbath is holy because it is different from the other days of the week. To treat it like any other day of the week is to desecrate its holiness. Judaism teaches man to be sensitive and appreciative of differences.

Modern society, however, increasingly seeks to subtly obliterate all differences. Stores are open seven days a week, so that there is no day of rest. Men and women are encouraged to believe that aside from their plumbing, they are identical. And science and psychology have effectively demonstrated man's kinship with the animals.

With this kind of thinking rampant, the differences between nations and peoples are also being undermined. The Jewish people are gradually disintegrating through assimilation and intermarriage, and many young Jews feel alienated by parents who encourage them, with no rational explanation, to marry within the faith. To such young people, Judaism is just a guilt trip. It's about being made to feel bad for refusing to participate in a tradition that one finds uninspiring and vacuous.

A Jewish neighbor of mine who survived the Holocaust but converted to Catholicism after emigrating to England (explaining, "We did it because we were tired of being persecuted") visited Auschwitz with a Catholic group. They prayed in one corner, and a Jewish contingent that was also visiting prayed in another. My friend approached the Jewish worshipers and asked if they would join the Catholics in a joint prayer. They thanked him but declined. "Could you imagine," he said to me, "that even in a place like Auschwitz we are still divided and cannot get together for a joint prayer. Have we all become Nazis?"

"No," I replied. "The Nazis believed that everyone had to conform to a certain ideal. They believed in sameness. If you had brown eyes instead of blue, if you had black hair instead of blond, you were inferior. Thank God we live in a world where we can not only respect, but even thrive on each other's differences. The fact that we can pray in one corner and you in the other, and none derides the other for saying the wrong prayer or not having the right to pray at all, is proof that we have progressed beyond the Nazis." Why does the human mind see differences as a curse and not a blessing?

The Unholy Doctrine of a Single Race

A messianic world is one where all the people of the earth, while retaining their intrinsic identities, come together to create a better world. This is quite different from the doctrine of homogeneity usually found in the ideologies of secular Utopias. Marx and Lenin had visions of workers uniting to create a fairer, more just world. Hitler tried to achieve the same Utopia through other means. All three argued for a single race, a single class. This is what un-Godly and unjust ideologies have in common. They begin with suppressing the individual. They end with purges that kill millions or crematoria.

Judaism's conception of a messianic world is radically different. The epoch of the Messiah will be a time when the unity of God will be manifest. The world that God created will once again be reclaimed as His. But in Judaism, unity never means homogeneity; it means taking different parts and showing that together they constitute a greater whole. The glory of God is demonstrated through the orchestration of component parts into a more beautiful portrait, thereby giving witness to a single origin. Unity in marriage does not mean that a husband puts on his wife's dress, or that a wife joins her husband on a night out with the boys. It means that people who are essentially different join together and through loving each other prove that essentially they are one flesh. When they have a child to-gether, their unity is demonstrated in the form of a single, indivisible entity, which makes for an incredible equation: $1 + 1 = 1$. This equation sums up the messianic era: many different "ones," in the form of nations, people, and ideas, integrating together to serve and reunify the ultimate "One"—God almighty, whose infinite power and essence are reflected in the great diversity in creation, all of which emanates from Him.

Have the Jews Accomplished Their Mission?

For nearly two thousand years the Jewish people were unable to make an impact on the world. How could they? They were isolated from mainstream society and scorned by the Christian and Muslim world. The Jews had precious little chance to practice ethical monotheism among the nations.

While the world was fighting religious battles, popes were ordering crusades, imams were clamoring for holy war, and the world was going through a period of anti-intellectualism, the Jewish nation was not afforded an opportunity to influence the world with the words, "Thou shalt not kill," even in the name of God. Similarly, the Jewish teaching, "Who is rich? He who is satisfied with his lot," which could have prevented much bloodshed in the name of material acquisition, went unheard, as did the Jewish encouragement of study as the guide to a life of moral and ethical excellence. Medieval man could have learned much from Jews but, feeling threatened by their contrary way of life, chose to persecute and murder them instead.

This state of affairs changed drastically in the eighteenth and nineteenth centuries. After the French Revolution and with German emancipation, the Jews were effectively granted equal social and political rights, rights that enabled them to fully integrate into secular society. The Jews responded with great enthusiasm, the age-old fear of assimilation giving way to the pursuit of new opportunities. To be sure, certain groups responded with caution. "A new way of life is forbidden by the Torah" was the motto of the great Chief Rabbi of Hungary and champion of forced Jewish isolation, Rabbi Moshe Schreiber, the Hatam Sofer. But most Jews embraced the chance to rejoin the larger world.

Here at last was the opportunity to stamp a Jewish impression on the world, to contribute to a world that had been so dominated by the influence of other nations up to that time. How did the Jews respond? They largely failed. They made an impact, but not a *Jewish* impact. Already in the eighteenth century, Moses Mendelssohn had argued that "one should be a person in the street, and a Jew at home." A compartmentalized Jewish identity was favored. The world either was not ready for or could not appreciate an authentic Jewish imprint.

In the nineteenth century, others, notably Abraham Geiger, argued for the transformation of Judaism. The essence should be preserved, but repackaged in a way that would make it more appealing to the unenlightened masses. Traditional Judaism was out of date and out of touch. A more digestible Judaism, purged of antiquated ritual, was the answer. Of course, once one begins to tamper with age-old truths, it becomes difficult to distinguish between the inconsequential and the essential. It was not long before the new kind of Judaism, called Reform, bore little resemblance to the original. Later it was necessary to reembrace many of the discarded old rituals.

Still other Jewish thinkers maintained that there was no room for the Jew in Gentile society, even in the postemancipation enlightenment. Jews should all move to Israel. And though the Zionists and their hero, Theodor Herzl, justifiably argued that the Jews should reinhabit their homeland, they seemed oblivious to the important contributions the Jews could make in their native societies. Chosenness has both a passive and a proactive element. Living as a model society in Israel could never be as effective as actively promoting God and goodness in the midst of the nations. But the European continent and other adopted homes of the Jews were perceived as having soaked up too much Jewish blood; hence the Jewish hesitation to contribute anything to their benefit.

The result was a lost opportunity. Although Jews contributed to every major field—philosophy, science, the arts, and government—it was the mark of a Jew that they left, not a *Jewish* mark. And this neglect has largely continued to this day. The world learns of how the Greeks philosophized, the Romans conquered, how the English sailed and colonized, and how the Jews died.

The Jewish people must refocus their priorities. Although combating anti-Semitism is of great significance, it falls far short of the obligation to serve as a light unto the nations. We cannot shirk the responsibility of the prophets. For two thousand years the voice of Isaiah has been heard, his vision has inspired. He told of a world in which there would be no anti-Semitism, because there would be no hatred. No Jews would be killed, because there would be no war. No mother would be bereft of her child, because death would be uprooted from the earth. Jews are the bearers of these dreams, and it is the Jews who bear the principal responsibility of encouraging the nations to translate these ancient dreams into modern reality.

Non-Jewish fascination with the Jews continues to grow. In journalism's parlance, "Jews are news." While the Jews have the world's attention, they must seize the moment. Jews cannot know whether this opportunity will ever rise again. Judaism must emerge as a pivotal force influencing the public debate. The voice of the prophet Jeremiah lamenting the fall of Jerusalem and the burning of the Temple can still be heard: "How lonely sits the city that once was full of people! How like a widow she has become, she that was great among the nations! She that was a princess among the provinces has become a vassal" (Lam. 1:1).

The voice of doom, however, is today being superseded by the prophecy of the non-Jewish prophet Balaam, "A star shall rise forth from Jacob" (Num. 24:17). A new era is dawning upon the Jewish nation. The Jewish star is rising. Let us not be known principally for being captains of industry, savvy politicians, outstanding film directors, or great writers. Let us rather be known as the nation that for three and a half thousand years has kept the torch of Abraham burning brightly, welcoming strangers into our homes, and teaching them of the one true God, source of all life and light.

It is profoundly saddening that, in this age of egalitarian principle, so many Jews feel uncomfortable with being the chosen nation and actively deny it. The goodness that the Jewish faith has imparted the Jewish nation makes them uniquely qualified to serve as moral agents to the nations of the world. As Thomas Sowell, a noted Black economist writes:

> Even when the Jews lived in slums, they were slums with a difference—lower alcoholism, homicide, accidental death rates than other slums, or even the city as a whole. Their children had lower truancy rates, lower juvenile delinquency rates, and (by the 1930's) higher IQ's than other children. . . . Despite a voluminous literature claiming that slums shape people's values, the Jews had their own values, and they took those values into and out of the slums.

The Jewish penchant for study could do much to focus the modern world away from television and back to literacy and books. The Jews have always been the most charitable of all communities. Anti-Semites throughout the ages have charged the Jews with being excessively wealthy. This is preposterous. Until modern times, Jews were a despised and poor minority that had the semblance of wealth only because they looked after their poor; it appeared as though no Jews were in need of clothing or shoes. For example, among the few thousand Jews living in seventeenth-century Rome, seven charitable societies provided clothes, shoes, linen, and beds for the poor. Two other societies provided trousseaux for poor brides, another aided families struck by sudden death, and yet another was responsible for visiting the sick. One society collected charity for Jews in Israel, and another eleven groups raised money for Jewish educational and religious institutions. According to Chiam Bermant, one particularly dramatic, though not atypical, example of Jewish philanthropy was the situation in London in the early nineteenth century, when almost half the Jewish population was supported by the other half (cited in Prager and Telushkin, *Why the Jews?*). Large Jewish charities, like the United Jewish Communities (formerly United Jewish Appeal) in the United States and Great Britain's Jewish Care, rank among the top ten charities in their respective countries, even though the Jews make up less than 2 percent of the population in the United States and less than 1 percent in Britain.

In a world witnessing the highest divorce rates ever and the crumbling of the nuclear family, the Jews can show the world an outstanding example of family and marriage. Plato, in the *Republic*, advocated the abandonment of the nuclear family in favor of friendship, since "friends have all things in common." Similarly, Lycurgus, formulator of the Spartan constitution, decreed that Spartans should give "their wives to whom they should think fit, so that they might have children by them." Even Christianity idealized nonfamily life in the epistles of Paul: "It is well for a man not to touch a woman. But because of the temptation to immorality, each man should have his own wife. . . . I say this by way of confession, not of command. I wish that all were [celibate] as I myself am" (1 Cor. 7:1–7). By contrast, the ancient Rabbis of the Talmud taught that one of the first things asked of a soul in judgment after its time on the earth is, "Did you fulfill your duty with regard to establishing a family?" A man could not become the Jewish High Priest unless he was married (*Yoma* 2a), and a man could not be a judge of the Sanhedrin, the Jewish high court, unless he had children, "since they teach him compassion."

There are countless other examples of how much the Jews have to teach the world. The Jewish people have been chosen to educate the world about God and goodness and to serve as a light unto the nations. We must carry that responsibility with pride and humility and work with our non-Jewish brothers and sisters to create heaven on earth.

Jewish Contempt for the Other Nations

There is a final consideration for the Jewish people in fulfilling their ancient calling to serve as a light unto the nations. In fact, relatively few non-Jews know anything about Judaism, and the question is why. There aren't that many Jews in the world, but there aren't that many Tibetans, either, yet everyone seems to be familiar with the wisdom of the Dalai Lama. Why did Judaism, with its strong mystical tradition and celebration of everyday life, never become the Buddhism of the Western world, its spirituality embraced by millions of people the world over without becoming Jewish? Given the phenomenal influence that Jews exercise in so many fields, why have they done so poor a job at promoting Jewish values and teachings?

The main reason is Jewish insularity, and the cause of Jewish insularity is a basic, if unwitting, contempt for the outside world, especially among more observant Jews. *The Jews have not affected the world, because after centuries of persecution, they are not convinced about the possibility of its redemption.* Jews are anything but racists, but though they do not look down at non-Jews, they look down at non-Jewish living and non-Jewish society. After all, they argue, aren't these the elements that have been the cause of so much of our suffering over the centuries? They ask themselves how religions like Christianity, so committed to charity, could have been capable of such brutality. That is why the Jews have always insulated themselves from their neighbors. Wherever very observant Jews dwell, notwithstanding their success in commerce and the professions, they still lead mostly insular lives. Many Jews continue to live in self-imposed ghettos. The large Hassidic communities of Williamsburg, New Square, Flatbush, and many others demonstrate the point. Do these people feel that non-Jewish society is ultimately incapable of being redeemed or that the potential harm of exposing their children to non-Jewish influences is simply not worth the risk?

Jewish insularity and our shirking of our ancient responsibility is related to the negative Orthodox Jewish view of Gentile culture. There are a number of factors responsible for this negative appraisal. First, who could blame the Jews for being unimpressed with non-Jewish society when for two thousand years, societies that have invited the Jews in have later victimized them as scapegoats, murdered their children, raped their wives, and plundered their last remaining pennies. As the Jews witnessed the behavior of their non-Jewish neighbors toward them and others, they naturally withdrew in horror and cordoned themselves off.

Second, the Jews felt that, in Christianity, their core teachings had been perverted and abused. They read some of the New Testament's insidious attacks against them and wondered how a book claiming divine authorship can be so blatantly anti-Semitic. Although Christianity stemmed from Jewish origin, it took the concept of the Jewish God and associated it with a man; took the concept of sacrifice and associated it with a *human* sacrifice. Christianity took their cherished Torah and said that it had been superseded by a new testament. And finally, it took the concept of the chosen nation itself, claimed that the Jews had been abandoned by God, and called themselves the new Israel. Jews reacted with outrage. The Jews withdrew from mainstream Christian society. Christians' burning Jews at the stake as heretics would do little to make them draw closer.

Most important, the Jews were concerned that if they didn't isolate themselves from non-Jews, they would assimilate into oblivion. Their children would marry the children of their non-Jewish neighbors, and in a few generations there wouldn't remain a Jew in sight. The high rate of assimilation and intermarriage today confirms their worst fears. And today these fears have been legitimately heightened by an increasingly shallow and nefarious popular culture that idolizes celebrities, promotes commitment-free sex, and engages in an orgy of material consumption.

I am in a position to judge the nonmalicious contempt with which much of the observant Jewish world approaches the non-Jewish world. The L'Chaim Society, which I founded in 1988 in Oxford, England, became perhaps the first Jewish organization ever with significant non-Jewish membership. We have also had many non-Jewish officers, including African-Americans, Mormons, fundamentalist Christians, and Muslims. By the fourth year of its operation, the L'Chaim Society had over three thousand non-Jewish members. We were proud of this fact and welcomed our non-Jewish members as equals, which created an uproar in the Anglo-Jewish community and abroad. I was accosted by religious and secular Jewish parents wherever I went. "I won't let my daughter go to you. I didn't send her to Oxford to meet a non-Jewish husband over the Sabbath dinner table." "Why are you taking Jewish resources and giving them away to non-Jewish members? We support you because you cater to the needs of the *Jewish* students." Wherever I am invited to speak, irrespective of the subject, I am usually grilled by confused questioners who hammer home the same points.

But Jewish insularity will not safeguard the future of the Jewish people. On the contrary, in an open and egalitarian society, it will lead young Jewish men and women to want to rebel. The way that a wife ensures the fidelity of her husband is not by locking him in a closet, but by engendering within him a feeling of love and commitment. Similarly, the way that Jews ensure the future of the Jewish nation is by causing young Jews to internalize their Jewish commitment so that it accompanies them in every place and predicament. A Jewish man should seek to marry a Jewish woman because he wishes to perpetuate his people and their legacy, not because he only meets Jewish women. Faith should be a matter of conviction rather than convenience. And the strongest means by which to instill a sense of Jewishness in today's young is to give them pride in their tradition.

If young Jews today were to feel that they had an ancient calling as part of a Godly people to make the world a better place, they would rush to embrace their tradition with great passion because they would see its effects on the larger society. But when people are told only to insulate themselves on behalf of a meaningless tradition that benefits naught but them, when Judaism is portrayed as a tradition that demands limitless sacrifice with comparatively little social gain, the faith is sure to suffer.

I am a Jewish universalist. I believe that the Jewish nation has lost its way and its purpose whenever its highest objective becomes the preservation of its own heritage with no consideration as to how that heritage is influencing the wider world. I do not desire to preserve a nation that has no objective other than ensuring its own survival. Young Jews hear their parents pressuring them to "marry Jewish" because they want to have Jewish grandchildren. When the children ask what difference that makes to them, since they ignore every other tenet of the faith, they are stumped into silence. I still remember a young Jewish woman in Oxford telling me that she would not give up her non-Jewish boyfriend "because my mother is interested in my marrying a Jew. She just doesn't want me to marry a non-Jew." The emphasis was on the negative. Parents must lead by example. Insularity is a fundamental abrogation of the Jewish mission on this earth. Jews cannot adopt an attitude that what happens to the non-Jewish world is not important as long as the Jewish nation is still strong. We must overcome our collective scarring over thousands of years and learn that the time has come to open our hearts fully to our non-Jewish brethren while uncompromisingly retaining our own identity. Part of this is overcoming a belief that anti-Semitism is still rampant and is bound to break free at some undetermined time. Although we must be vigilant, this cannot be our raison d'être.

Although Christianity was the enemy of Jews and Judaism for nearly two millennia, times have changed. The Vatican, under the current pope, a true friend to the Jewish people, has granted diplomatic recognition to the State of Israel, and Christian fundamentalists in the United States are among the State of Israel's most trusted backers. Jews must reach out to their Christian brethren, especially to the attempts of many of the Christian clergy to pursue a policy of reconciliation with their Jewish brethren. The atrocities that have been inflicted upon the Jews by non-Jews must be remembered, but placed into the context of the past. To be sure, we must always be vigilant and protect ourselves from outbursts of anti-Semitism. But members of the post-Holocaust generation truly have an opportunity to establish the Jewish voice as a dynamic and influential force within society. It would be a tragedy to squander that opportunity because we are still haunted by the ghosts of an anti-Semitic past.

Like a country with an outdated foreign policy, the Jews continue to insist that combating anti-Semitism is the most important Jewish prerogative. Similarly, many Jews believe that a sigificant number of Gentiles in their heart of hearts harbor anti-Semitism. Raising Jewish children to believe that they will always be hated and to be on their guard is highly destructive. Not only will it undermine Jewish pride and self-confidence, it will also guarantee that these young Jews will hide their Jewishness and become ashamed of who they are. We must teach Jewish children to carry their heads high and celebrate their identity rather than remove their yarmulkes the same day that they arrive at universities, as I witnessed on all too many occasions at Oxford.

We continue to pour money and imagination into combating anti-Semitism at the expense of education and rebuilding the Jewish nation. It is true that only sixty years ago a "civilized" nation murdered the Jewish people with abandon, including one million Jewish children. But the world has changed. Anti-Semitism is on the decline. Jews today are fully integrated into Western society and can now travel freely even from Russia, which was forbidden only fifteen years ago. I believe that the Jewish people will be at the forefront of creating a family of nations—a community of countries that desire to work together for the good of the earth's inhabitants—if only we can first get over any disillusionment with the outside world. We must build a strong Jewish identity, fueled by the ancient Jewish aspiration to promote love and justice.

15

Dietary Laws

We Become What We Eat

Why does man kill? He kills for food. And not only food: frequently there must be a beverage.

—WOODY ALLEN

Motivation is like food for the brain. You cannot get enough in one sitting. It needs continual and regular top up's.

—PETER J. DAVIES

When I get a little money, I buy books. And if there is any left over, I buy food.

—DESIDERIUS ERASMUS

AS THE ARCHITECT OF MAN, God saw it necessary to incorporate within man an animal nature. Indeed, the ancient Rabbis said that without our animal nature—our lusts, passions, and instincts—no man would ever marry a woman or build a home. Furthermore, Proverbs, by tradition written by King Solomon, proclaims: "There is much wheat in the strength of an ox" (Prov. 14:4). That means that we should not repress our animal instincts, for they are responsible for our productive capacity. If man did not possess the brute strength and resolve of the animal, he could never have "subdued the earth," which is his divine mandate as given to Adam and Eve in Eden. Still, we need to harness our animal natures, ensuring that our passions are always channeled into Godly directions. The objective is not so much the repression of our passions and instincts as their sublimation.

Animals live by the law of the jungle. Man needs a code of conduct to purge him of his natural instinct for violence and to condition him to receive as great a thrill from altruistic action as he does from inflicting injury on others. Society has devised its own safety nets in the form of organized sports. Here the cheering populace can spur on its team to destroy a foe on the playing field, rather than hacking each other to death with machetes. Some social anthropologists even suggest that the vast amount of violence currently featured in television and films, far from being harmful, is actually of therapeutic value. It allows society to rid itself of its primal instinct for violence. Like many, however, I find this reasoning highly suspect. Long ago, Judaism devised a program of action that was to wean man away from his appetite for violence without indulging in it. This is the kashrut system, the highly misrepresented and misunderstood Jewish dietary laws.

Perhaps the most distinctive of all Jewish practices, kashrut, or the eating of kosher food and maintaining a kosher kitchen, is today still observed in one form or another by roughly half the Jews the world over. One of the most puzzling of all Jewish commandments, kashrut is often portrayed as having been legislated for hygienic reasons. Even today we hear that eating pork was banned because it can lead to trichinosis, and shellfish because of the dangerous bacteria they contain. Although there are definite health benefits to eating kosher food—because of the high standards of kosher meat, for instance, none has ever been found infected by mad cow disease (BSE)—they do not constitute the basic reason for the laws.

In essence, the laws of kashrut mandate that a Jew can consume only those animals that chew their cud and have split hooves. Furthermore, the only fish that may be consumed are those that have fins and scales. Among birds, the Torah lists twenty-four types that are prohibited, but the common denominator among them is that birds of prey are not kosher. In addition, the Jew is prohibited from eating blood and may only consume the flesh of an animal that has been slaughtered at the neck.

The Jewish laws of kashrut were established to wean man away from violence and to learn to abhor the sight of blood. The Jew must be taught to detest death, abhor blood, and recoil from unnecessarily hurting any of God's creatures. Love for sadistic pleasures must be utterly uprooted from the human heart. God is the Creator of life, and man is its guardian and protector.

Adam and Eve were commanded never to take the life of any animal, but to subsist on vegetation alone: "From all the *trees* of the Garden you may eat" (Gen. 2:16). A quandary arose after the flood, which decimated all living creatures, including plants and animals. Prior to that, the Almighty had never given man permission to consume animal flesh. Had God not permitted Noah and his family to partake of the animals, they would have perished. Moreover, since Noah had exerted strenuous efforts to save the animals as well as himself and his family, he was entitled to partake of their flesh in order to survive. God allowed Noah's descendants to eat meat as well, and since then there has been an acceptance of the human need to consume meat as a source of nutrition and sustenance.

The problem that arose was how to allow man to take animal life for food, while simultaneously suppressing his love for violence? Furthermore, how could man partake of the flesh of the animal without becoming one himself? The Almighty therefore gave the laws of kashrut, whose purpose was to regulate how man could take animal life, which animals he could slaughter, how he could put them to death, and which parts of the animal could then be consumed. Simultaneously with granting man the right to devour animal flesh, God insisted that he take life only in the most humane possible way, and even then never consume the animal's blood. Furthermore, man was permitted to partake only of nonaggressive, nonpredatory and servile animals like goats, cattle, and sheep. As the ancient Rabbis point out, all the permitted animals are herbivorous and therefore nearer the vegetable world. They spend a great deal of time in the process of digesting their food and show an almost plantlike passivity. The same applies to fowl. The only fowl allowed to the Jew are birds that survive on berries, worms, or bark, never scavengers or flesh eaters.

The rules of kashrut are based on the belief that meat eating is different from eating vegetables and requires a great deal of sensitivity to animals. Man must be weaned off the callous indifference to taking life—*any* life. Rabbi Joseph Albo, the great Spanish mystic, wrote that Adam and Eve and their progeny were originally forbidden to eat meat because of the cruelty involved in killing animals. In fifteenth-century Spain, Don Isaac Abravanel, one of the greatest biblical exegetes, endorsed the call for vegetarianism and taught that when the Messiah comes, everyone would return to this ideal state.

Contrary to the view that the main rationale for kashrut is hygiene, the fact that the laws of kashrut rule out all beasts of prey shows a different impetus. Animals that have split hooves cannot be predators, for the split hoof makes them slow moving and awkward. They cannot run and pursue other animals as the swifter hunters with paws can. The cloven hoof of the permitted animals seems to have been created more for the purpose of standing than for use as a weapon or tool. Furthermore, all animals that chew their cud are herbivores, unlike the flesh-eating omnivores and beasts of prey. Animals that chew their cud often have minimal teeth, but a rough palate, which allows them to eat grass and other foliage. They swallow a vegetable, but not having chewed it sufficiently, cannot digest it. The food is sent to the stomach, where the somatic acids break it down further. Animals that chew their cud and also have cloven hooves have four stomachs. After the food consumed has passed through two stomachs, it is driven up the gullet again, chewed for a second time, and then led through the other two stomachs. Thus, these animals spend a great deal of time in the absorption of food, or what may be termed *vegetative activity*.

In contrast to herbivorous animals, the nonkosher carnivorous animals have short intestines, and little time is wasted on digesting their food. It is quickly transformed into blood, the bearer of animal life. The permitted animals' plantlike passivity is best expressed in their ready submission to human domination. What the Torah was doing in limiting the Jews to these passive, vegetarian animals was, first, weaning them away from love of violence by causing them to slaughter animals humanely and, second, ensuring that they do not consume anything that would encourage their innate predatory streak by forbidding them to eat any omnivorous animals.

The founder of Christianity was insistent that "it is not what goes into the mouth that defiles a person, but it is what comes out of the mouth that defiles" (Matt. 15:11). Judaism rejects this belief, stressing that man can indeed be defiled by absorbing the wrong foods. Parents try to govern their children's television intake, convinced that violence and sex can have an adverse effect on the minds of their young. If this is true of mental material, why should physical sustenance be any different? The undeniable fact is that if you eat poison it can kill you. Judaism simply expands on this by applying it also to spiritual poison.

Long ago, Judaism taught that what we eat has a direct effect on how we behave. Consuming the flesh of violent, predatory animals can bring out these same instincts in man. In a book on dreams I published in 1990, I wrote of the effects of strong somatic stimuli on our mental processes. Studies show that people who eat hot and spicy foods often have violent dreams and nightmares, caused by toxins and the vapors of strong and acidic foods. The same has been proven true about thinking. The vapors arising from strong foods may impede or stimulate thought. Similarly, it has long been established that the effect of certain foods is an aphrodisiac. Why, then, should we not assume that foods affect our though processes?

We are what we eat. Therefore we must be careful of what we become when we consume. The Torah forbade the consumption of vicious animals and those that did not care for their young. Likewise, Judaism insists that the blood of an animal never be consumed "for the soul of the animal lies in the blood" (Deut. 12:23). The Almighty limited the negative effects that the consumption of animal meat could have on humans by restricting their consumption to passive, vegetarian beasts.

Man Was Originally Vegetarian

As we noted earlier, God's instructions to the first humans precluded the eating of meat. In slaughtering animals for food, man would be in danger of becoming immune to the shedding of blood as well as to the suffering of animals. God therefore declared that the Jews cannot eat any animal, even kosher, unless it has been slaughtered at the neck. The special method of slaughtering animals, called *shehitah*, consists of an incision made across the neck of the animal or fowl by a person especially trained for ritual slaughter. A special knife that is razor sharp and has a smooth edge with absolutely no nicks is used. The cutting must be made by moving the knife in a single swift and uninterrupted sweep, not by pressure or by stabbing. The cut severs the main arteries, rendering the animal unconscious and permitting the blood to drain from the body. The ritual slaughterer *(shohet)* recites a prayer before the act of *shehitah*.

According to scientific opinion, this method of slaughter results in immediate loss of consciousness, and any movement afterwards is muscle reflex only. In short, the animal does not suffer. Similarly, the Bible declares that right after the slaughter, the Jew must pour out all the blood into the earth and to salt the animal until all the blood is removed from the meat. Red meat filled with blood—even that of a kosher animal ritually killed—is forbidden to the Jew, since the Almighty insists that the Jew abhor blood in every form and manifestation. Indeed, the prohibition against eating blood constitutes one of the harshest and most often repeated commandments in the entire Bible.

Contempt for Hunting and Blood Sports

Hunting is anathema to a religion that will sanction the killing of an animal only for human survival and sustenance and finds it grotesque when used as a form of recreation. It is my Jewish up-bringing that made me feel so repulsed when I first came to live in Great Britain and observed highly cultured, civilized men and women taking obvious delight in shooting innocent animals, or when I saw foxes being torn to bits by wild dogs. One of the original seven laws given to the children of Noah, and thus to all mankind, was a severe prohibition against any sadistic treatment of animals.

In the Bible, the prevention of unnecessary pain to animals is one of the cornerstones of divine ethics. Man was given dominion over the animals in order to increase the quality of human life and to serve the Creator. Thus, man may affix a plow to an ox, or a saddle to a horse, in order to lessen his own burden and workload. But what does the Bible say about a society in which animals are mistreated and terrorized as a means of human amusement? The Rabbis referred to the severe prohibition against abusive treatment of animals as *tzaar baalei hayyim,* "distress to living creatures." The ancient Rabbis decreed that one must feed one's cattle before feeding oneself, and even the Ten Commandments include domestic animals in the Sabbath rest.

Hunting is severely forbidden within Jewish law and involves several prohibitions. Rabbi Norman Solomon, in his *Judaism and World Religion,* lists the following reasons, based on biblical and other Jewish sources:

1. Hunting is destructive and wasteful and thus transgresses the prohibition against waste.
2. It causes pain and distress to animals.
3. The hunter exposes himself unnecessarily to danger, which is strictly forbidden. The Bible enjoins, "and you shall guard your soul exceedingly well" (Deut. 4:9).
4. Hunting is an unproductive use of time.
5. The hunt is a "seat of the scornful" (Ps. 1:1).
6. Hunting is forbidden to the Jew in the verse "Do not follow their evil practices" (Lev. 18:3). Living under God's law, the Jew was

meant to set a moral example for the rest of the nations to follow, rather than imitate their bad example.

Fins and Scales

With respect to the biblical prohibition of not consuming fish without fins and scales, the great medieval scholar Nahmanides states:
"Now the reason for specifying fins and scales is that fish which have
fins and scales get nearer to the surface of the water and are found
more generally in freshwater areas. . . . Those without fins and scales
usually live in the lower muddy strata which are exceedingly moist
and where there is no heat. They breed in musty swamps and eating
them can be injurious to health." Shellfish, which are forbidden to a
Jew, live on the bottom of the sea, where they act as scavengers, consuming all the waste, debris, and refuse, deeply injurious to man,
both physically and spiritually and therefore forbidden to the Jew,
who is commanded to guard his life and his "soul exceedingly well."

Similarly, many modern scholars give hygienic reasons for the
dietary laws, since it is known now that bacteria and spores of infectious diseases circulate through the blood of many nonkosher
animals. No doubt the kosher laws do involve hygienic considerations, but there are even more valid spiritual and ethical reasons as
we have highlighted above. The Torah highlights the image of God
in man, a feat that can only be accomplished if man's animal nature does not overwhelm his higher self. Kosher food serves as the
strongest bulwark in the fight against man's carnality.

Separation of Milk and Meat

Another aspect of kashrut involves the prohibition against mixing,
eating, or cooking milk and meat together. A Jew may not eat a
cheeseburger or other mixture of dairy and meat products, nor may
he even cook the two together. In Judaism milk and meat are irrec-
oncilable opposites. There is a profound reason behind this seemingly obtuse rule.

Following from the principle of being weaned from a love of violence, the Jew is slowly conditioned to love life and abhor death.
More than anything else, Judaism is a religion of life, a celebration of
being. Man, as increasing misery overtakes him, may be led to believe that life is not an intrinsic blessing. Indeed in our own generation it is not life, but happiness, that is seen as the ultimate blessing.
And when happiness is not forthcoming—when life is riddled with
pain—life becomes a curse that we may wish to terminate. Judaism
teaches that though death is inevitable, it must be resisted with
every ounce of energy, irrespective of our happiness. Life is like having a child, always a blessing whatever the path. Life, even in its
most miserable manifestations, presents endless opportunity,
whereas death presents endless monotony, man's inability to change
and progress. In death man loses all uniqueness, becoming an object
like a stone.

Life in Judaism is everything that is Godly, everything that is
noble. In the Torah, God is referred to as the God of life, and the
Torah is described as the tree of life. As a river is connected to the
spring whence it stems, the living individual is connected with the
eternal source of life. Death comes about when the connection has
been severed. Death, rather than a state of being, is a void, a black
hole, a vacuum of meaning and existence. Death is the darkness that
ensues once the light has ceased to shine. There are no wakes in Judaism. The dead are buried quickly, with a quiet and solemn dignity,
and we await the time when all will be raised from the dust.

Therefore, Judaism always seeks to separate life from death. Although man may be overtaken by death, he must still run from it
with all his soul, with all his might. Jewish ritual is designed to rein-
force the light and restrain the darkness. Jewish observance establishes a perimeter into which death cannot infiltrate. Many
important Jewish rituals, therefore, revolve around symbols separating life from death. The mandatory period of sexual abstinence of
husband and wife during menstruation and for a week thereafter is
designed to separate life and death. Menstruation represents a lost
opportunity for life. Sex is the ultimate act of life because (in addi-

tion to the fact that it can cause life) it is the encounter in which a man and woman feel most intensely alive. It is also where their love for each other comes alive. It is therefore inappropriate that the pro-creative act of life be undertaken amid its simultaneous negation. Better for the couple to wait until after the wife has gone to the *mikveh*—a ritual pool of water connecting to a *living* spring—to pre-pare them both for an encounter of life. Likewise, a Kohen (member of the priestly class), who administers to the living God, is forbidden to come into contact with a dead body or attend a funeral, except that of a close relative. Since his being is dedicated toward the sacred service in the Holy Temple, bestowing life and blessing on the con-gregation of Israel, it is inappropriate that he should risk exposure to the antithesis of life.

Here we have the reason that Jews separate milk from meat. Milk is the ultimate symbol of life, the very elixir sustaining early exis-tence. Dead meat, however, is death incarnate. One represents at-tachment to the living God, the other His absence. Man must be weaned from a belief that life and death can coexist. Man must re-main firmly dedicated toward combating the darkness wherever it may appear. For this reason, the observant Jew even has separate dishes for meat and milk in the kitchen. His or her home and mate-rial possessions proclaim the line that divides the living from the dead, the eternal from the ephemeral. His or her very food supports a spiritual constitution that accepts his or her humanity while negat-ing their animal tendencies. And in this way, not only the soul, but even the body of man, can achieve sanctity and holiness.

16

Law Before Love

You must observe them diligently, for this will show your wisdom and discernment to the peoples, who, when they hear all these statutes, will say, "Surely this great nation is a wise and discerning people!"

—DEUTERONOMY 4:6

Power always thinks it has a great soul and vast views beyond the comprehension of the weak; and that it is doing God's service when it is violating all his laws.

—JOHN QUINCY ADAMS

Most married couples, even though they love each other very much in theory, tend to view each other in practice as large teeming flaw colonies, the result being that they get on each other's nerves and regularly erupt into vicious emotional shouting matches over such issues as toaster settings.

—DAVE BARRY

I HAVE OFTEN HEARD IT SAID THAT THE GOD of the Old Testament is vengeful, whereas Jesus' teachings are more humane; that the Old Testament is about law, whereas the New Testament is about love. There are endless comparisons between the Hebrew Bible's "eye for an eye" law (which has always been interpreted by the Jews to mean financial compensation rather than an eye itself) and Jesus' magnanimous philosophy of "turn the other cheek." It is undeniable that Judaism champions law above love, practice above faith, and religious service above theology and dogma, for which it has paid an enormous price in terms of popularity. Judaism maintains wholeheartedly that love without law is nothing more than meaningless sentimentalism, which will ultimately end in cruelty. As the popular saying goes, "He who is kind to those who are cruel will end up being cruel to those who are kind."

A bright student once walked into my office holding a book. "You just have to read this book," he said. "It's the most beautiful book about God." The book in question claimed to be a direct prophetic dialogue with God and promoted the idea of feelings as absolutely central to religion. In the quest for God, the book claims: "Ministers, Rabbis, Priests . . . even the Bible . . . are not authoritative sources. Then what is? Listen to your feelings. Listen to your highest thoughts. Listen to your experience. Whenever any of these differ from what you've been told by your teachers, or read in your books, forget the words. Words are the least reliable purveyor of Truth" (Neal Donald Walsh, *Conversations with God*).

Walsh's book, an international best-seller, speaks for a generation whose principal desire is to *feel* God rather than to *worship* Him. These opposing ways of relating to God actually go back to the origins of Christianity. Saint Paul in his letters continually upbraids Judaism for being weighed down by law at the expense of love. The two operative words in Christianity are *faith* and *love*, which were designed to undermine and replace the two central words in Judaism, *law* and *commandment*. "For sin will have no dominion over you, since you are not under law but under grace" (Rom. 6:14); and again, "But now we are discharged from the law, dead to that which held us captive, so that we are slaves not under the old written code but in the new life of the Spirit" (Rom. 7:6).

Paul's excoriation and condemnation of the law has directly influenced millions of people to see only oppression in the Torah. The celebrated English man of letters, Sir Edmund Goose, wrote in his autobiography that when his father was teaching him the Book of Hebrews, wherein Paul battles with those who still submit to the law of Moses, Sir Edmund suddenly exclaimed, "Oh, how I do hate that Law." He continued, "I took the Law to be a person of malignant temper from whose cruel bondage, and from whose intolerable tyranny and unfairness, some excellent person was crying out to be delivered. I wished to hit the Law with my fist, it being so mean and unreasonable." Even the great German moral philosopher Immanuel Kant could not resist attacking Jewish law: "The euthanasia of Judaism can only be achieved by means of a pure, moral religion, and the abandonment of all its old legal regulations."

Judaism rejects these attacks. Law is the ultimate safeguard for love. The separation of law and religion has proved to be a great calamity for human civilization. First, it means that atrocities can be perpetrated in the name of God and no one can say that religious law forbids it. Furthermore, the Christian rejection of law as a religious discipline would guarantee religion's divorce from the world and its realities. That religion has lost out to secularism as the mainstream guide to human life is a direct result of the detached role that religion began to play when Christianity abrogated the law. To say that religion cannot be about law is to say that religion is not designed to regulate human life. Governments must step into the breach with secular legislation. It comes as no surprise, therefore, that religion has had virtually no influence on the greatest social movements of our time, be they the rise of communism, the collapse of the Berlin Wall, or the gradual spread of liberal democracy. Even the influence of religion on Zionism was for the most part passive. The aloofness of organized religion from the problems of ordinary existence has alienated the great social reformers.

Likewise, purging law of religious association has robbed it of its sacred character and thereby of its strongest moral incentive. Law, rather than seen as an organic necessity springing from within man, has a coercive aspect, in which authority is something that ordinary citizens either resent or try to outsmart. Having been robbed of its

God-given origin, law today is perceived as artificial and as an invader, rather than welcomed as a partner, in the lives of young men and women. Worst of all, the Christian condemnation of law ultimately led to the unnatural division of life into two separate spheres, the religious and the secular. Today morality is not an active force in economics or foreign policy. Had Christianity preserved the rules of religion and its directives regarding every area of life, man would have perceived the need for law in all his ways, and the entire earth could have been made holy by attaching God to empirical phenomena. Instead, a religious dualism arose. Man worships God in the church, but abandons Him once in the street.

Even loving relationships need rules about how one party must treat the other. It is nonsense to say, as Walsh maintains, that God is found primarily in feelings. Why should we give our feelings free rein to govern our actions? Since when is love the supreme arbiter of right and wrong? Since when do feelings have any sense of permanence? Would anyone go before a judge who declared that he adjudicates his cases on how he feels that day? Is truth really as capricious as all that? Does this make it acceptable for a man to fall in love with a woman when he is married to someone else? If a man *feels* angry at his son for failing his expectations, does this justify not showing him love? And what marriage could possibly survive on feelings alone, without action? Judaism has always believed that actions, not feelings, are the surest way of determining the authenticity of love. Therefore, Judaism has always harbored an intense distrust of unguided emotions. The only way to preserve love is to preserve law. This is why the greatest revelation came in the form of the Ten Commandments, divine utterances that set forth a moral code by which man was assured of relating to God and his fellowman with love, decency, and justice.

Jewish insistence on the immutability of its laws and traditions exasperates a great many of its followers. Surely, if the purpose of religion is to guide man along a path, it must adapt to changing times and circumstances. If it does not, it runs the risk of becoming a dinosaur, an extinct relic of its former greatness. And yet, Judaism teaches that ultimately no law is worthwhile unless it is immutable. Moreover, in seeking to set forth a doctrine governing the God-man and man-man relationship, Judaism insists that every relationship must be predicated on a belief in immutable law. Indeed, no marriage will ever succeed if a man can cheat on his wife and rationalize it in thinking that lately his wife has been distant and neglectful. Truth has no expiration date or geographic constraints. It is operative at all times and in all places. It is a key ingredient in Judaism.

To understand the Jewish obsession with truth and law, one can focus on the Ten Commandments and reflect on their utter simplicity. I once saw a poster in London that said, "Life . . . Come and hear one man make sense of it." It was an advertisement for a lecture by Billy Graham. Now imagine that you are one of the eighty thousand people who cram into Wembley Stadium to hear him explicate the secret and meaning of life. Then the well-known evangelist gets up and says, in essence, "Be nice to your mother. Also, I say it's a bad idea to steal. And by the way, adultery can be very hurtful. Better do without it." Such simplistic teachings! The kind of lessons that parents teach their children, the kind of teachings that any government would have to legislate if it were to retain any semblance of order. Wouldn't you feel misled? Wouldn't you have come that night expecting something far more profound and far less obvious?

Imagine, then, how the Jews felt at Mount Sinai. For seven weeks they had spiritually prepared themselves for this great revelation. Moses had psyched them up. God Himself was to speak to them. And what did He say? Honor your father and your mother. Don't commit adultery. Don't be jealous of your friends. Don't covet your neighbor's wife. The Israelites' disappointment must have been enormous. One can imagine them asking, "For this we traveled fifty days in the desert?"

The importance of the Ten Commandments is not in their content—a human could have dictated these commandments—but the fact that *it was God who commanded them*. This concise and succinct code of conduct introduced immutable, divine law as the operating force in the universe. When mortals make laws, they become subject to human interpretation and, hence, manipulation. Ronald Reagan once said, "I have wondered at times what the Ten Commandments would have looked like if Moses had run it through a state legislature." Man has a knack for adapting laws to his own purposes and making them apply only to situations where it suits his fancy. When God gives commandments, however, they are universally applicable. The commandment not to steal is as relevant today as it was in ancient Mesopotamia, and as applicable here as it would be on Uranus or in some undiscovered galaxy.

It is notable that there are no rewards or punishments provided in the commandments. There are not even any rationalizations. God does not say, "Do not steal. After all, you would hate if it happened to you." The Almighty offers no possibility for argument or rebuttal. Rather, He simply says that these ten things must be observed. Period. This is My world and these are the rules. There is no other example in all of ancient literature of a code of conduct given so forcefully with no attempt even made to establish the credentials of the power making these demands. It is not because they make sense that the Ten Commandments are right. They are law because God ordained them. End of discussion.

Take for example the sort of theft often depicted in classic works of literature, like that of Jean Valjean in Victor Hugo's classic *Les Miserables*. Valjean, a poor man just released from prison, with no prospects of earning money, steals a loaf of bread from a bakery to sustain his life. The proprietor of the bakery wishes to prosecute even though the loss incurred is minimal. Is the starving man deserving of punishment? Has a crime been committed or not? If human conscience is the authority judging the validity of the act, then we could conclude that there was no transgression. Under the circumstances, the action of stealing the loaf of bread was justifiable, possibly even heroic. But stealing is forbidden by the Almighty, at all places and at all times. At Sinai we gave our assent. We will abide by His will, even if we don't understand why.

The poor man could have asked the bakery owner for the loaf. There is no excuse to steal.

A similar example can be cited with regard to murder. Man, no matter what persuasion, faith, or ideology, indignantly condemns the murderer and the act of murder. Yet, what about the situation that Dostoyevsky portrays so vividly in *Crime and Punishment?* The book depicts a cruel, miserly old woman, a pawnbroker sucking the blood of those unfortunates caught in her web. In sharp contrast is the brilliant young student who broods over his poverty and the hopeless situation of his sister and mother. The anguished young man decides to kill the pawnbroker so that he can take her money chest. He justifies the murder as ridding society of a parasite and intends to use the money for a noble cause. Should we consider the murder of the miser a crime? Again the answer is yes. The Almighty has forbidden murder, whatever the motive, and whatever the circumstances, aside from self-defense.

Morality and Divine Law

I believe that deep within every man and woman is the desire to do good. So why is there so much evil? Man harbors within his chest a survival instinct that always asserts his interests over that of others. A battle rages in the heart of everyone between altruism and selfishness, between a desire to give charity and a desire to hoard our resources for ourselves. But even when these values conflict, I believe that the desire to be good is much more powerful than selfishness. So why does goodness still lose out? The answer lies in the brilliance of the human mind. Infinitely clever, it can find endless justifications and rationalizations for immoral action. We might even say that for most people, rationalizing their bad behavior is the solution to their inner struggle. What do you do if you want to share some juicy gossip about someone, but know that it is wrong to stab someone in the back? Do you remain silent or speak up? Answer: You tell yourself that this is not gossip, since if you don't warn people about how bad a person that individual is, they will end up getting burned by him or her in business or in a relationship. Presto, problem solved! But immutable law removes all room for rationalization of sin.

The foremost aim of Judaism is to bring the world to ethical monotheism—the doctrine that there is one God, that He is the God of all people, and that God's primary demand upon humanity is to live ethical and compassionate lives, which means treating our fellow human beings decently. Because many religious people have adopted a belief in God without a concomitant belief in goodness, countless religious atrocities have been perpetrated throughout history. The error of those who commit such evil is that though they may be believers in God, they do not believe that God's primary demand is moral behavior.

Just as God without ethics leads to extreme evil, ethics that eliminates God as its basis culminates in moral depravity. It is not enough to have laws. All laws of morality must be rooted in an immutable, divine tradition. Morality that is not anchored in divine law leads to anarchy and a corrosive moral relativism.

Another problem that the earth's inhabitants face in their desire to be righteous is defining good and evil. Life is filled with moral dilemmas. How do we know which is the virtuous path? It is all too true that the road to Hell is paved with the best intentions. Life is a great labyrinth, and man needs more than intuition or intelligence to guide him through its vicissitudes. Judaism maintains that were there no God, good and evil would not exist. What remained would be subjective opinions regarding desired and undesired behavior. Good and evil would become nothing more than euphemisms for personal taste. Every culture, every civilization, would define the terms differently. When the Spanish conquered the Inca civilization in 1532, the Indians were immolating two hundred children every time a new Inca ruler assumed the royal fringe. Who is to say that this was wrong? After all, for the Inca it was a solemn religious ceremony.

We have seen it in the past century. Germany, a country known for its science and culture, was responsible for the systematic murder of millions of innocent people. The Nazis did have laws against murder—theirs was not an anarchist or lawless society—so how could they have murdered six million Jews? Simple. The law against murder that operated in Germany was man-made, thus subject to human interpretation. The law applied to humans. Hitler and Goebbels had identified the Jew as an inferior race, outside the law's protection. Murdering a Jew propelled society forward, just as exterminating smallpox was to society's advantage.

Gideon Hausner, in *Justice in Jerusalem,* his book about Adolf Eichmann's trial in Israel in 1961, writes that he was asked what was the scariest thing about coming face-to-face with the orchestrator of the Final Solution. Hausner, who served as chief prosecutor, answered that what terrified him most was that Eichmann was a *perfectly normal human being.* One could have found comfort had Eichmann behaved in his murders like Charles Manson, disemboweling his victims and writing Helter Skelter on the walls with their blood. We could have said he did it because he was crazy. But Eichmann was a highly educated and completely sane family man, who executed perfect control and manners throughout his trial. *Eichmann killed, not because his mind was bent, but because the rules were bent.*

In his monumental book, *Hitler's Willing Executioners,* historian Daniel Goldhagen echoes this point. Normal, rational, and otherwise decent Germans participated willingly in Hitler's plan to liquidate European Jewry. In a subsequent interview published on the Internet, Goldhagen developed this theme. When asked about the mental state of people involved in such killings, he said: "In no sense were they out of their minds. They thought they were doing the right thing. And the killings took place over a long time. Frenzies don't last for years at a stretch. This is a distinguishing difference between the Holocaust and other genocides. The regime took anyone available and discovered they were willing to kill."

The interviewer then asked whether the killers were typical of the German people at that time or constituted a criminal subculture, as seemingly happened in the former Yugoslavia. Goldhagen responded: "In no sense were many of the killers part of a criminal class. They were often chosen through a haphazard process used to get a cross-section of the population. And when you do the demographic work, you see they were representative of their age group. Members of the police battalions were not self-selected, as they were in the SS; they were haphazardly selected from German society." Such are the perils if we commute the prohibition against murder in the Ten Commandments to the Reichstag's law, which may sound the same but is radically different.

Science Without Law

Judaism's insistence on immutable law as the sole guarantor of society's decency applies not only to soldiers, but even to well-meaning scientists. Witness the similarity in the following two statements:

"The more civilised so-called Caucasian races have beaten the Turkish hollow in the struggle for existence. Looking to the world at no very distant date, what an endless number of the lower races will have been eliminated by the higher civilised races throughout the world."

"In nature there is no pity for the lesser creatures when they are destroyed so that the fittest may survive. Going against nature brings ruin to man . . . and is a sin against the will of the eternal Creator. It is only Jewish impudence that demands that we overcome nature."

The first quotation comes from the letters of Charles Darwin. The second were the words of a political leader who applied Darwin's evolutionary ideology to society. His name was Adolf Hitler (quote from *Hitler's Table Talk: 1941–1944*). Hitler was a spiritual and ideological student of Darwin and evolution. He developed his concept of the Aryan master race according to what he saw as the ethical implications of the theory of evolution. Once man was robbed of the dignity of having been created in God's image and identified instead with evolutionary development from the ape, race theory—a belief that certain human races are more highly developed than others—became inevitable. Hitler transmuted the survival of the fittest in the struggle for existence away from animals and applied it to peoples and races.

Sir Arthur Keith, Britain's leading mid-twentieth-century evolutionist, who endured with other Britons the suffering visited by Hitler on his country, cannot be said to have written the following statements out of any feeling of sympathy for the Nazi cause:

> To see evolutionary measures and tribal morality being applied vigorously to the affairs of a great modern nation, we must turn again to Germany of 1942. We see Hitler devoutly convinced that evolution produced the only real basis for a national policy. . . . The means he adopted to secure the destiny of his race and people were organised slaughter. . . . Such conduct is highly immoral. . . . Yet Germany justifies it; it is consonant with tribal or evolutionary morality. Germany has reverted to the tribal past, and is demonstrating to the world . . . the methods of evolution. . . . The German Fuhrer, as I have consistently maintained, is an evolutionist; he has consciously sought to make the practice of Germany conform to the theory of evolution. . . . It was often said in 1914 that Darwin's doctrine of evolution has bred war in Europe, particularly in Germany. . . . In 1935, a committee of psychologists representing thirty nations issued a manifesto in which it was stated that war is the *necessary outcome* of Darwin's theory.

In dealing with man strictly as a biological organism in a "great chain of being" with all other organisms, the human species, Homo sapiens, has been divided by evolutionary biologists into various "subspecies," or races, in the same way that other species are subdivided. Homo erectus, apelike man, may have evolved into Homo sapiens, and someday a particular superior race among the latter may evolve into, say, Homo supremus—superman. In such case, the ordinary man of today in relation to the superman of tomorrow will be labeled "subhuman" and not meriting preservation or, worse, suitable for annihilation. Just as today's humans feel it moral to experiment with apes for the benefit of mankind, Homo supremus may deem it necessary to experiment with Homo sapiens for his benefit. The Mengeles and Eichmanns of the past implemented experimentation on, what was to them, a lower species for the benefit of a higher species, the Aryan race.

Note the significance of Charles Darwin's giving his major work on evolution, *The Origin of Species by Natural Selection,* the provocative subtitle *The Preservation of Favoured Races in the Struggle for Life.* Though in his book Darwin was discussing races of plants and animals, it was clear that he also included the various races of men in the concept. Indeed today, the word *race* applies mainly to humans. If the criterion is mere power, and if men eat animals because men gained power by accidental evolution, then the murder of weak innocents "in the struggle for life" may be justified by an amoral scientific theory that can recognize no distinction between cattle slaughterhouses and the German murder factories, except the degree of "accidental evolutionary development." By identifying the Jew with the animals, highly educated German scientists could go about injecting dyes into the eyes of Jewish children with no pangs of conscience.

Consider the following statement made by a former president of the National Academy of Sciences: "We can, of course, be grateful to nature for the highly remarkable genetic gifts which we have inherited as a result of the very complex process of selection which our ancestors experienced. We must also keep in mind, however, that many of our most valued characteristics probably emerged out of inter-human competition." Without the Ten Commandments forbidding murder in any circumstance, people can even begin to believe that war is healthy for humanity, since it eliminates the weak and rids the world of genetic waste, conferring upon the survivors important gifts.

Race Theory

Thomas Huxley, the man most responsible for the widespread acceptance of evolutionary doctrine, remarked, "No rational man cognisant of the facts, believes that the average Negro is the equal, still less the superior, of the white man." A student of the Bible, who must acknowledge that we are all children of the one God, created in his image, could never support such a statement. But when evolutionary theory appeared in 1859, the question whether Blacks were of the same species as whites escalated to the question whether Africans could survive competition with their white relations. The answer was a resounding no. The African was the inferior because he represented the "missing link" between ape and man.

No wonder the concepts of race were so important in the development of the master race idea. Evolutionist George Gaylord Simpson wrote:

> Evolution does not necessarily proceed at the same rate in different populations, so that among many groups of animals it is possible to find some species that have evolved more slowly, hence are now more primitive, as regards some particular trait or even over-all. It is natural to ask—as many have asked—whether among human races there may not similarly be some that are more primitive in one way or another or in general. It is indeed possible to find single characteristics that are probably more advanced or more primitive in one race than in another.

What Hitler, unrestricted by compliance with the Ten Commandments, simply did was to take the ramifications of evolutionary thought and identify exactly who he thought these "more primitive" races were. He placed the Jew at the head of this list.

Social Darwinism, the term used to label the many collectivist systems resulting from evolutionary thought, has often been understood in this sense: a philosophy exalting competition, power, and violence over convention, ethics, and religion. Thus it has become the basis for nationalism, imperialism, militarism, and dictatorship of the cults of the hero, the superman, and the master race. From the "Preservation of Favoured Races in the Struggle for Life" it was a short step to the preservation of favored individuals, classes, or nations—and from their preservation to their glorification. A world that embraced the

creed of the Ten Commandments, and its concomitant unconditional acceptance of God as the Master of the Universe, could never
allow, or justify, the domination of one people by another.

The ancient Rabbis taught that at every moment a person must be
cognizant of "that which is above you; an Eye that sees, an Ear that
hears, and all your deeds are recorded." But once man discards the
Eye that sees and the Ear that hears and thus denies the ultimate
regulator of right and wrong, there is no telling what atrocities he
will perpetrate in an individual or collective framework. Without a
Supreme Judge, man is free to act according to animalistic whims
and the world becomes a jungle whereby right and wrong are determined solely by the vagaries like and dislike.

Scientific Definitions of Right and Wrong

What would the world be like without the Ten Commandments?
Man would feel the need to construct his own scale of values. Indeed, with God's demotion in favor of scientific theory, many modern scientists feel constrained to provide, in substitution, new
scientific ethics. Professor Bently Glass suggested a more natural definition of the concepts of good and evil whereby they would be
completely divorced from their moral connotations. His natural
guidelines would define "good" as what is good for the development
of the species; what is not good for the development of the species
would, by definition, be "evil." For example, if the species contains
the mentally ill, disease carriers, people of low intellect, or physically
repulsive people, the interbreeding of which would be bad for the
species, then these individuals could be eliminated. Already in Cuba,
AIDS sufferers have been incarcerated in order to prevent the con-
tamination of the citizenry. In 1996, I debated a famous humanist at
the Cambridge Union. When I asked my opponent whether a child
severely afflicted with Down's Syndrome should be put to death
right after birth, she shocked many students by responding "Yes. It
would be a mercy."

An equally horrific idea was proposed by Nobel laureate Francis Crick, one of England's greatest scientists, who suggested that it may be necessary to redefine the concepts of "birth" and "death." He recommended that the time of birth of an infant be redefined as two days after its parturition so that there would be time to examine it for defects. If its defects were sufficiently deleterious, the infant could presumably be eliminated with impunity because it had not yet become alive. Similarly, Crick proposed redefining death as occurring when a predetermined age, such as eighty or eighty-five, was achieved. At that time the person automatically would be declared dead and all of his property would pass to his heirs. Given that the world has limited resources, a finite number of hospital beds, why should we preserve those who will always be dependent, who will only take and never give?

The key in achieving a real appreciation of religion is to understand that it is counterintuitive. We who have grown up in the Judeo-Christian tradition forget that values are not intrinsic or self-evident. They must be inculcated through a system of law. And this is one of religion's foremost and most noble objectives. Murder and crime are normal, as we are assured by history. Values are abnormal and must be instilled. Only religion and the rule of divine law can safeguard humankind from the abyss.

This is not to say that religion is a guarantee against atrocities. Indeed, religion is responsible for numerous wars and much slaughter, all carried out in the name of the faith. For this reason, the Ten Commandments were delivered by God in the form of two separate tablets, each indispensable to the other. The first deals with laws concerning the belief in, and absolute respect for, God. The second deals with morality and proscriptions against indecent behavior. One safeguards our relationship with God, the other protects our relationship with our fellow humans. Both are indispensable. The message is that without both, the set is invalid. Without God, there can be no goodness. Without goodness, the belief in God becomes a farce.

Guardians of the Ten Commandments

The ancient Rabbis stated that the greatness of man, in contradis-
tinction to his animal counterparts, is his ability to recognize God,
to call Him master, and accept the yoke of His will. If we were to forget God and abrogate our divinely mandated responsibilities, we
would descend to the level of very clever animals and our fate would
be too horrible to contemplate. The only thing protecting the dignity of man is the belief in an all-powerful Creator who will exact
justice from those who destroy His creatures. Seen in this light, it
comes as no surprise that the man who sought to abolish God and
morality from the earth identified the Jews as his greatest enemies
and first target.

Historians often point out that Hitler's hatred of the Jews was so
great that he even abandoned his soldiers, leaving them without
food or ammunition while the railroads were continuing to ferry
Jews in boxcars to the gas chambers in the concentration camps.
This is no mystery. Hitler sought not only to win the war. His ambitions were far greater than that. He sought to establish an entirely
new world order. His greatest obstacle was the Jews: witnesses to God
in history, the nation who gave the world the rule of divine law,
guardians of the Ten Commandments. Hitler said as much about the
Jews and the carriers of their moral message, the Christians: "The
heaviest blow that ever struck humanity was the coming of Christianity. . . . The deliberate lie in the matter of religion was introduced into the world by Christianity" (Hitler's Table Talk:
1941–1944). And again, he stated of Christians:

> I'll make these damned persons feel the power of the state in a way
> they would have never believed possible. For the moment, I am just
> keeping my eye upon them: if I ever have the slightest suspicion that
> they are getting dangerous, I will shoot the lot of them. This filthy rep-
> tile raises its head whenever there is a sign of weakness in the State,
> and therefore it must be stamped on. We have no sort of use for a fairy
> story invented by the Jews. (Hitler's Table Talk: 1941–1944)

Humankind's desire to evade subjugation to divine law is predictable and understandable. With our shallow understanding of freedom, we view God as the party pooper in chief. Scientist and philosopher Aldous Huxley, who came from a family of avid supporters of the theory of evolution, wrote at the end of his life:

> I had reasons not to want the world to have meaning, and as a result I assumed the world had no meaning, and I was readily able to find satisfactory grounds for this assumption. . . . For me, as it undoubtedly was for most of my generation, the philosophy of meaninglessness was an instrument of liberation from a certain moral system. We were opposed to morality because it interfered with our sexual freedom.

Judaism's goal, however, is to empower man with real freedom, the freedom to reveal his Godly nature and liberate himself from the cage of animal instinct. The man and woman of faith must seek to create a loving and just society, in which one person approaches another with honesty, sincerity, and decency. This cannot be accomplished unless law is promoted above all else and unless morality is underpinned by immutable divine authority. To the critics who argue that Judaism is encumbered by too much law and too little emotion, the response is that we see law as the medium by which love is promoted, protected, and preserved. Where there is no law, there is no God. And where there is no God, there are no rules. And where there are no rules, there can be no way of safeguarding love or protecting those who most need it.

PART THREE

Festivals and Holy Days

17

Passover

Free at Last

People demand freedom of speech as a compensation for the freedom of thought which they seldom use.

—SOREN KIERKEGAARD

It is by the goodness of God that in our country we have those three unspeakably precious things: freedom of speech, freedom of conscience, and the prudence never to practice either.

—MARK TWAIN, (1835–1910)

Everything that is really great and inspiring is created by the individual who can labor in freedom.

—ALBERT EINSTEIN, *Out of My Later Years*, 1950

Freedom is nothing else but a chance to do better.

—ALBERT CAMUS, (1913–1960)

JUDAISM'S MAIN PERIODS OF CELEBRATION are known as the *shalosh regalim*, or three festivals, corresponding to three auspicious moments of the agricultural year. Each festival commemorates an earlier time in Jewish history and the miracles that God wrought on

329

behalf of the Jewish people on those occasions. Each festival also possesses its own unique theme and relevance to contemporary Jewish life. Many people make the mistake of thinking that the purpose of the pilgrim festivals and the many rituals associated with them— eating matzah on Passover, staying awake studying the Torah on the night of Shavuot, and sitting in a sukkah, a temporary outdoor dwelling that resembles a hut for the seven days of Sukkot—serve as a commemoration of an earlier period of Jewish history. But Judaism is not merely a collection of testimonials to an earlier time. It is a living faith, concerned with the present as much as with the past. Judaism is concerned with the past only insofar as it guides and informs our lives in the present.

Once I spoke with an intelligent young Jewish woman who felt passionately that Judaism had no relevance to her life. "You can live your life in the past," she said, "but I live in the present. I have no interest in reading of a man named Abraham who lived 3,500 years ago. That's the problem with all us Jews. We are forever living centuries ago instead of engaging the world today."

My response was that Abraham was not only a man who lived long ago. He was also the paragon of compassion and kindness, and as such his example is eternal. Moses was the Jewish redeemer in Egypt. But he also serves as the archetype of humility. King David was a great Jewish king who lived 3,000 years ago. But he also serves as the icon of valor—a great conqueror who attributed his successes to God, repented of serious sin, and wrote psalms that were melodious tributes to his Creator. I told her that although these men walked the earth physically thousands of years ago, all of them were alive today in that they all represent something glorious that can inspire us and that we can emulate. We don't read the Bible to learn that Abraham once walked the earth. Rather, we read the Bible to learn *how* Abraham walked the earth, and to emulate the same compassion with which Abraham made his footprints.

To recall or reflect upon some great event in Jewish history is not the purpose of the Jewish festivals. Their purpose is to *relive* that event in Jewish history as if it were happening now, today. We do not merely eat matzah on Passover. Rather, the rituals associated with the Passover Haggadah allow us to reexperience slavery and freedom, incarceration, and liberation, so that we are liberated anew each year as much as in the era of Moses. On Shavuot we do not merely remember the giving of the Torah at Sinai. Rather, in an inspirational ceremony, we stay up the entire night studying the Torah and read the Ten Commandments early in the morning so that we renew our commitment to the Torah's precepts and embrace our faith anew. None of this is a retelling of an ancient story. Rather, it is the reliving of a recurring event. The festival of Passover, with its timely message of freedom and liberation, is a classic case in point.

Today many of us, especially those who are privileged to enjoy the human rights safeguards of the West, believe ourselves to be free. Democracy continues to expand around the globe, and financial prosperity is creating lifestyles that are liberating. The most severe form of oppression we experience is perhaps paying taxes and getting pulled over by the police for speeding. And though the tragic events of September 11 changed much of this, we still enjoy civil liberties that were unknown anywhere in the world just a few hundred years ago. Therefore, demonstrating the contemporary relevance of Passover—the festival that celebrates Jewish liberation from Egypt—is fraught with difficulty. Why celebrate a festival that liberates us from bondage when indeed we are already free? When we Jews speak of incarceration, imprisonment, torture, or terror, our minds immediately flash back to our ancestors in the Spanish Inquisition and our fathers and mothers at Buchenwald and Auschwitz. But modern Jews living in the aftermath of the Holocaust are free. What message, therefore, does Passover have for our generation? Surely this seems to be an example of a festival that has lost its relevance.

We can indeed look at Passover as nothing more than the historical retelling of an ancient saga of bondage and liberation. The Jews were enslaved to their Egyptian taskmasters, and the Almighty, through spectacular acts of intervention—the ten plagues, the killing of the firstborn, the splitting of the Red Sea—redeemed them from servitude. Jews the world over may celebrate the Seder, or ritual

Passover supper, as a cultural celebration rather than a living commemoration. The ancient Rabbis stated, "in every generation, a Jew
is obligated to see him- or herself as having been *personally* liberated
from Egypt." Similarly, the Passover Seder night, highlight of the
Jewish calendar, is not merely about retelling, but reliving the exodus from Egypt. The Jew is enjoined to taste of saltwater and bitter
herbs, and thus to reexperience his forebears' tears and suffering in
Egypt; to eat matzah, the poor man's bread, thereby reexperiencing
a taste of servitude; and to drink four cups of wine, to experience the
elation of redemption. As the sages of the Talmud said: "In every
generation a man or a woman is obligated to see themselves as having been liberated from Egypt *today*." What possible relevance does
this message of bondage and servitude have for this, the freest, most
prosperous generation of all time?

Surely, it is the following: Although we think we are free, we are
still servants. In previous generations the body of the Jew was imprisoned. In this generation, the Jew's soul and identity are. There
are two great prisons of the modern world that present a much
greater challenge to liberty than the mightiest fortresses of yester-
year. They are social pressure and conformity and the cage of human
nature.

We who grow up in the West amid great pressures to conform to
Western ideals of success—to own a big house, to work long hours,
and thus have no time for family, community, or religion—are perhaps the most enslaved generation of all. We can't even bring ourselves to shut off the TV! Think of all the millions enslaved to a
superficial definition of prosperity, which cheers a man who becomes chairman of his company, even though he may have sacrificed his integrity and family in order to ascend this plateau. Man
today is enslaved to the pursuit of pleasure, considering it a sin to
sacrifice the indulgence of each and every lust.

Men and women today are enslaved by a sense of inadequacy.
They weigh their own self-worth against their neighbor's bank account; they are in the grips of their own ambition, as they aspire to
ever-greater heights of self-importance. Compelled by an inner

demon telling them all is for naught, since their neighbor has risen higher on the social ladder, men and women risk their health and happiness in the pursuit of a superficial self-esteem. Trapped in the dark abyss of insecurity, soon they begin to sell their very souls, as they will do almost anything to gain the recognition of their peers. If they are required to gossip about their neighbors, they will do so. If they are required to use Machiavellian manipulation to get ahead, slander their fellows, they will do that as well.

Then there are the millions of young women who diet constantly, slaves to an image of the "perfect woman" that makes them feel permanently inadequate. Millions more men and women are enslaved to an obsession with celebrity gossip. They cannot summon the willpower to close the tabloid magazines and pull out a wholesome book, which would bring them real knowledge and enlightenment. Every time George Clooney dates a new starlet, they cannot help but spend money to read about it. Is this not a cruel servitude?

Another manifestation of enslavement is the people losing their identities as they join the melting-pot morass of modern culture. Members of minority groups have assimilated in the hope of being accepted by mainstream society as insiders. Everybody wants to be a full member and to be loved. Young Jews who feel out of place in the majority Gentile society leave their Jewish identities imprisoned within their breast. I have witnessed many new Jewish students whose first action upon arriving at Oxford University is to remove their *kippot,* skullcaps, so that they may better blend into their new surroundings. One Orthodox student even told me that he would be far more effective denying his Judaism and removing his *kippa,* since he had never been afforded an opportunity to serve God amid temptation. "Besides, when I wear my *kippa,* the students in my year think I'm a Mossad agent." We offer every rationalization to justify our shame at being voluntarily incarcerated. And we wave and flail our hands, protesting that we are free, even while shackles dangle from our wrists.

The imprisonment of social conformity itself pales when compared to the cage of human nature. If an outside party superimposes its will upon us, we feel restrained and oppressed. If we are locked up in a metal cage, we seek to break free and reestablish our independence. If Jews cannot emigrate from a country like Syria or Russia, a clarion call goes out through the Jewish world: *Let my people go.* What we forget, however, is that the most ruthless form of duress is the one imposed upon us by our own inner nature. By virtue of being human, we are confined to our genetic constitutions. But though we possess an animal nature, we are not animals. The central message of Passover is that man, unlike the animals, is possessed of a Godly soul that is fully capable of liberating him from the cage of human nature. Man can transcend instinct and lead a glorious life suffused with altruism and love for his fellow human being. Man has an innate yearning to leave Egypt and be free.

But a slave mentality can be found even among politically liberated peoples. After Moses had redeemed the Jewish people from Egypt and sent a group of slaves to spy out the Promised Land and determine the most efficient way to conquer it, they returned with a dispiriting report: "The land is filled with giants . . . and we were in their sight as grasshoppers, and so we appeared to ourselves as well." Such feelings of inferiority would not have allowed the conquest of the land by the nation of Israel. Thus, God decided to wait forty more years—until that entire generation had died out—before allowing Jews to enter the land and attempt to acquire it. The Jews who came out of Egypt had internalized their enslavement. Only a new generation of free men and women could enter and conquer the Promised Land. A slave mentality would first have to be banished before the new generation could think and act as free men.

Exercising the Freedom to Choose

Judaism affirms that the defining characteristic of man is the consciousness of his existence and his concomitant ability to exercise choice. The principal difference between humans and animals is that the latter are ruled entirely by genetic programming and are thus amoral. Since animals have absolutely no choice about their behavior, it would be as foolish to speak of bad dogs as it would be to speak of bad computers.

Man's calling is to exercise his moral choice for goodness despite his compunction to act selfishly. Holocaust survivor Victor Frankl, founder of Logotherapy and author of *Man's Search for Meaning,* made the profound point that even in the depths of Hell in Auschwitz he still possessed the capacity for choice. The Nazis had robbed him of his physical freedom by incarcerating him in a concentration camp. They had stolen from him his human dignity by forcing him to defecate in public. They had robbed him of all joy and happiness by murdering his closest kin, and they had robbed him of his uniqueness by reducing him to the number tattooed on his arm. But there was one freedom that even the Nazis could not take away from him: the defining characteristic of his humanity, namely, the freedom to choose how he would react to the humiliations and horrors that were being visited upon him. Even in the cauldron of Auschwitz, Frankl found the wherewithal to exercise choice. While the Nazis would determine what Frankl would *do*, only Frankl could determine what he would *be*. That a Jewish prisoner in a Nazi death camp can still claim to be free is the ultimate testament to the ability of the human spirit to triumph.

But choice in the modern world is often misconstrued. By freedom of choice, Judaism means man's capacity to exercise his *moral* choice. Judaism would say that whereas man does not necessarily have the choice to *do* everything he wishes—a man cannot choose to fly like a bird or to become a pumpkin—he does have the choice of what to *be*, either good and evil. On the one hand, the Talmud maintains that forty days before a child is born, an angel named Ahzariel announces whether a child will be male or female, rich or poor, to whom he or she will be married, and how long the child will live. This would seem to suggest that the range of choice left to us humans is highly limited, and indeed, when we contemplate just what choices we can make in life, the arena is quite small. Most of us today would reject the belief that our choice of whom to marry is preordained, but when we think about it, the range of possible candidates is not that large.

We can only marry those persons whom we will (1) meet, (2) have an opportunity to get to know well, (3) are reasonably within our age group, (4) that consent to marry us, (5) are usually of the same religious or socioeconomic group, or nationality (so that there be something in common), and the list goes on and on. So too, in the area of riches, prosperity, and poverty, there is not great choice. Although democracy would like to promise equality of opportunity and distribution of wealth, in the world today these goals are too little realized. In what, then, do we have choice?

Judaism says that choice lies in our ability to deal with the circumstances that befall us, to choose to either be good or evil. To choose to complain or to be content with our lot. To choose to hoard what is ours or to be generous and share with our fellows. Those choices, which confront us every minute of our day, are totally undetermined. A poor child growing up in the slums of the inner city may indeed have little immediate choice to improve his economic standing. But he can certainly choose how he will respond to his poverty. Will he take and sell drugs and mug passersby, or will he strive to earn a decent living and be a good family man? Will a child growing up in such squalor choose to hate all humanity for his lack of privilege, or will he try to overcome the challenges imposed upon him and practice love for others? Will the one who is born into wealth be conceited, condescending, and arrogant, indulging every immoral desire and taking advantage of those who are lower on the social ladder, or will he share his wealth, practicing love, charity, and kindness?

Central to Jewish thought is an absolute belief in freedom of choice. Judaism rejects belief in Greek tragedy and fatalism. Humans are not subject to stars that govern their destiny. What people make of their lives depends entirely on their actions. Notwithstanding modern behavioral sciences', determinist psychology's, or genetics' rejection of the belief in choice, Judaism affirms that each of us possesses an infinite soul—an actual part of God, which cannot in any way be sullied or circumscribed. Human choice is limitless, and what we make of our lives depends entirely on how we exercise judgment and how we act.

When Man Becomes
Someone He Does Not Respect

There is a time in our lives when we open our eyes and discover that our existence resembles a thermometer rather than a thermostat. Rather than controlling our environment, we are shaped by external events. As a Rabbi and counselor, I have long noticed that the principal emotion governing people in their advanced years is regret. The Talmud says that most men and women only realize a small fraction of their ambitions in their lifetime. The saddest human realization is recognizing that we cannot summon the discipline to truly be whatever it is that we planned.

It is depressing when we reach midlife, look into a mirror, and discover that we have become people that we never planned to be. Often men and women see themselves repeating the very patterns that disillusioned them about their own parents. I remember promising myself on countless occasions that I would not make the same mistakes my parents made that undermined their marriage. Now, every time I find myself becoming upset over a trifle and unable for a short time to overcome my annoyance, I acknowledge just how imprisoned I am. But it is that confrontation with my incarceration that inspires me to struggle to break free and to approach my wife and apologize if my behavior has been inconsiderate. I have no desire to live my life as a prisoner.

Once I confronted two brothers who had been inseparable but had fallen out over a financial dispute. I beseeched the older of the two to apologize to his sibling so as to win back his love. "I simply cannot. *He* was wrong and *he* should apologize." "But that's not the point," I told him. "What is more important? To be right, or to have a brother? Here you have the opportunity to have your brother back. All it takes is a phone call. But you seem more interested in justice than you are in basking in the pleasure of sibling love, one of life's richest blessings. You are shortchanging yourself for the sake of your pride." I shall never forget how he then walked over to the telephone and lifted the receiver. He dialed his brother's home, but just as the phone was answered, he put the phone down. Looking up at me, he then said, "I want to do it! I want to call him. But I *can't*." He was imprisoned by his own stubbornness. I reminded him that Passover was approaching and that his goal this year in celebrating the festival should be to liberate himself of his incarcerating nature and become a better human being. One of the secrets to happiness in life is being prepared to lose the argument and win the relationship.

The Supremacy of Human Will over Human Nature

In the past two decades a nature craze has swept through the Western world. Everything natural is desirable and good. People run to the gym to become healthy and fit. They pay twice as much for organically grown fruit and vegetables. To be sure, there are many positive benefits from the trend, including a heightened appreciation for the environment. But an obsession with the natural can lead us to believe that it is a crime to do anything that violates nature, that human nature is intrinsically good, and that trying to suppress our nature is a sin leading to neurosis. From this was born the preposterous notion that whenever man attempts to transcend or act in contradiction to his nature, he scars himself internally. Freud, the high priest of this school of thought, convinced us that the suppression of our intrinsic natures leads to deep and sometimes irreversible mental harm. So if you're angry, don't bottle it in. It's unhealthy to repress natural emotion. And if you feel stifled in marriage, get out and be liberated. Man must accommodate, or at least find an outlet for, his every urge.

The festival of Passover, however, demands that we go out of *Mitzrayim*, Egypt. Egypt was the archetypal symbol of reliance on nature rather than God. Whereas most countries are directly dependent on rain for their crops and thus naturally look to the heavens for their sustenance, Egypt is a desert. Instead, the Nile River overflows its banks and irrigates the land. Thus, while other cultures looked to God for their sustenance, the Egyptians worshiped the Nile river.

Mitzrayim, however, may also be translated as *natural limitations.* Man is not a prisoner to his nature. Rather, far more powerful than human nature is human will. Each of us is endowed with the capacity to do whatever we wish to do, and to be whatever we wish to be. Scientists have recently identified a gene for promiscuity in men, but Passover dictates that this gene is not a license to cheat within a marriage. Man is capable of first transcending and later reorienting every inner urge. A husband is capable of focusing his libido on his wife, making her feel desirable and beautiful.

Whether man becomes an angel or an animal is completely dependent upon his choice and free will. We are all accountable for our actions. Nobody has the excuse that he cannot overcome his natural inclinations. Judaism is largely distinguished from other faiths by its doctrine of personal accountability. Man is held responsible for both his noble and his disreputable actions. Passions, however powerful, do not hold sway over us. We are sole arbiters over our own destinies, that is, so long as we are prepared to exit *Mitzrayim,* our instinctive constraints. Holiness transcends normative human experience, and man becomes holy when he acts in a fashion that is loftier than that to which his nature would have led him.

The Causes of Sin

Freud opposed religion because he believed it made unnatural demands on humans resulting in neurotic repression. Ever since Freud, religious man has been portrayed as repressed, weak, and unhealthy. The flimsy, flabby religious man—with his pale skin and pious demeanor—stands in stark contrast to the firm and robust Promethean man, who resembles Hercules. Society envisions the secular pumping iron in their gyms while men of faith are eating dry crusts of bread in quiet solitude. But are these stereotypes accurate? Is sin all it's cracked up to be?

The Bible insists that sin has a corrosive effect on the individual. Furthermore, the Bible attributes three specific origins to sin: Sin both results from and brings on madness, darkness, and boredom.

Sin creates a deep alienation between man and himself. It causes a disruption in the harmony of man's inner and outer world. What is it that we all desire from life? To be wealthy, powerful, influential, respected, and selfish? Or to be loving, kind, charitable, compassionate, honest, and selfless? Which of these competing human desires strikes deeper? To answer this question, Freud went back to man's beginning, to the child, and identified the child as selfish and narcissistic. Based on this insight, Freud saw an unruly unconscious, an uncontrollable and base id at the center of human consciousness. At heart, man is a beast.

Judaism sees things differently. To discover what it is we truly seek from life, we must go, not to the beginning, but to the end. What does man think of in his last moments of life? How does the individual wish to be remembered? If each of us could write our own eulogy, what would we include? It seems silly to examine man for what he is at the outset of his life rather than at the finish, since at the beginning of life he has not yet tasted of what life has to offer. He cannot decide what appeals to him most and identify what best accords with his innermost essence. Rabbinic statements abound entreating man to focus on the last day of his life, as well as on the grave, in order to bring about atonement.

Below are two versions of a eulogy. Which would you choose?

1. Harry Cohen was a phenomenally successful man. He worked himself to the bone, spending eighteen hours a day at the office, and was away from his family traveling for four days out of every week. He amassed a great fortune and spent much of it on himself. He was generous with his children and gave them many gifts, rather than love. He also gave money to charity, his contributions totaling 1 percent of his vast wealth. He owned a private jet and a yacht. Eventually he rose to be chairman of a multinational conglomerate and played golf with presidents and prime ministers. He had no friends who were worth less than fifty million dollars, was married three times, had a difficult relationship with his two children from two different marriages, and had the finest tailored, handmade Italian suits

that money could buy. When he died, his children and former wives sued each other over his will's contents.

2. Harry Cohen was a good and decent man. Throughout his life he struggled in business, never pulling off that big deal that he thought would finally put his financial troubles behind him. Yet, this made him neither indifferent to the plight of the poor or the less fortunate nor melancholy. Rather, he always retained his happy-go-lucky demeanor. He and his wife kept their home open, and guests of all economic backgrounds were often at his table. He put his children to bed every night and read them a story. He focused much attention on his wife of sixty years, always making her feel attractive and appreciated. He prayed and thanked God every day for his blessings, and he was heavily involved in many communal charities. When he left a room, no one had any bad thing to say about him. He led a life of humility and goodness for the length of his days. His children mourned him deeply and thought about him every day of their lives.

How many would seriously say that they would pick the first eulogy?

Fate Does Not Rule Our Destinies

In the Talmud, Rabbi Yehoshua ben Levi says, "There is no free man except one who occupies himself with the study of the Torah" (*Ethics of the Fathers*, chap. 6). Judaism is perhaps the most demanding and confining of all religions. It tells us what to do upon awakening and what our last utterances must be before retiring to bed. It dictates what we may eat and when we may engage in marital relations. It tells us when we must be joyous and when we must mourn. Is there any greater prison than this?

What the wise rabbi meant, however, was that only a life lived in accordance with God's law allows us to fulfill our innermost will, our deepest desire: to be good and decent people. The man or woman who occupies themselves with Torah is free because they are liberated from a suffocating selfishness. They do not spend their days catering endlessly to the rapacious needs of their insatiable ego. This is the point that Dale Carnegie makes on the first page of *How to Win Friends and Influence People,* noting that even a bank robber or murderer gets upset when described as *bad.* Deep down, every one of us would like to be a compassionate, kind, and caring human being. Despite our devoting our lives to the pursuit of money, power, or celebrity, we would like to have lofty and spiritual values in place of our materialistic ones. We crave to be the kind of individuals who, upon leaving a gathering of friends, can feel confident that their peers have only kind things to speak of them. We really want to be charitable, offering compliments freely and showing appreciation to family and friends rather than being envious of their success. We wish to learn forgiveness and forgo all bearing of grudges. We wish to be totally devoted to our spouses and the finest parents that the world has seen. We seek to be diplomatic and gracious in all social interactions, never losing our temper or offering an unkind word about others. Are there any of us whose aspirations do not include all the above? If we want this so badly, why doesn't it just happen? *Because we are slaves to our nature and our ambition.* It is not natural for man to put others before himself. Nor is it natural for someone to hear that a colleague has won the lottery and not experience a pang of jealousy. We cannot become what we truly desire, because we are fettered by our makeup. Genetic predisposition and material orientation dictate the direction of our lives rather than our conscience.

This is what makes religion liberating. When one is bound by the tenets of Jewish law that command sensitivity and love for the orphan and the poor; when one is forced to feed the hungry and clothe the naked; when one is enjoined into observing the Sabbath, thus putting family and friends before going to the beach; when one is commanded to start the day by praying to God in order to thank Him for all that we possess and to beg from Him our daily bread; when one is commanded to offer a blessing before and after every meal, thereby showing gratitude and appreciation for all we possess, then we live in accord with the desire of our irreducible essence, namely, to be good and righteous individuals who enjoy an unblemished relationship with God and our fellow humans.

Modern society caters to the satiation of man's external, thus ephemeral, needs. But Judaism caters to man's internal and eternal need: to feel that he has led a life of concern for his fellowman, suffused with meaning and purpose, a life in which he has engendered admiration and respect. The tenets of Judaism that direct him to dedicate his highest energies to both God and his fellowman lend his existence the meaning he most craves.

All this is symbolized in the matzah, the poor man's bread, which is eaten on Passover. The rich man is satiated with the symbols of his own success. He is enslaved to his possessions, which often impede his very ability to feel that he is spiritually deficient. As the ancient Rabbis said, "The more possessions one acquires, the more worries they create." His slavery is of the passive variety, and he has little cognition that he is even confined. His bread is bloated like himself, the yeast symbolizing his arrogance. But the poor man's bread is flat. He may not possess much, but his humanity is intact. He is not so puffed up with a sense of his own self-importance that he cannot see the needs of his fellowman. He has never sold his integrity in the acquisition of objects. He is free to serve his God and his fellowman. And not being chained to weighty material objects, he is free to rise and become holy. Living a life of religious virtue releases his truest self.

18

Rosh Hashanah

The Challenge of Renewal

Since nothing we intend is ever faultless, and nothing we attempt ever without error, and nothing we achieve without some measure of finitude and fallibility we call humanness, we are saved by forgiveness.

—DAVID AUGSBURGER

As we Jews now enter the High Holidays again, preparing ourselves to pray for a year of peace and happiness for our people and all people, let us make up, Master of the Universe. In spite of everything that happened? Yes, in spite. Let us make up: for the child in me, it is unbearable to be divorced from you so long.

—ELIE WIESEL,
New York Times, **October 2, 1997**

DEVELOPMENT AND CHANGE CONSTITUTE the very essence of life. Those things that are alive grow and move, and those that are dead stagnate and decay. Those who live without renewing themselves may be described more accurately as existing rather than living. The boredom of everyday routine can transform a life into a passive existence, one in which a man or a woman no longer looks forward to another day. Novelty is the very fabric of passion and excitement. We all need surprises if we are to remain fully engaged in life.

Every life form and every relationship is constantly challenged with obsolescence. This challenge of personal and collective renewal—and the threat of extinction in the absence of such renewal—is the essence of Rosh Hashanah, the Jewish New Year. Rosh Hashanah is the first day of the Jewish calendar, but the name of the festival means "head of the year." As the head of a body incorporates the body's functions—and a neurosurgeon's accidentally cutting the wrong tissue can permanently impair speech or eyesight—so does Rosh Hashanah incorporate the events of the year. How we behave on that day will have a permanent effect on the rest of our year. The ancient Rabbis therefore advise that we pray and remain constantly alert on Rosh Hashanah so that our soul remains alert through the coming months.

Balancing Tradition and Modernity

Identities are fragile. They require constant vigilance. By refusing to commit the energy to renewing who we are, we risk forgetting ourselves and seeing a previously robust personality slowly melt away. Both our public and our private identities require rejuvenation. If a movie star continues to play the same role in film after film, his or her fans will quickly become tired. Likewise, a comedian who tells the same jokes or a businessman who sells the same wares year in and year out will quickly lose his audience. The same, of course, is true in relationships. If a husband and wife pursue the same routine in their marriage, their union will grow stale and they will slowly drift apart.

Renewal is no easy task. It involves the careful balancing of extremes. One must renew oneself without becoming totally new and unidentifiable. To accomplish this task, one must first identity one's irreducible essence, answering the question, "What makes me, me?" When we speak of refreshing our identities, we mean that our core personalities must find newer, deeper, and more mature modes of expression. If individuals change completely, modifying their centers—if they clear out the very features of their souls and adopt identities wholly alien to who they were previously—then they are even worse off than before. If a man changes so much that his wife does not recognize him, she will not wish to remain married. The task in every act of renewal is to identify our immutable essence, then seek to reveal it in a refreshing and passionate manner without compromising that essence.

This same challenge confronts modern religion. How may we achieve the correct balance between the old and the new? At what stage do we modify accepted tradition in favor of more modern practices? Judaism and other world faiths are suffering today because they have failed to adapt to the needs of a changing world. And in the many instances in which Judaism has made strong adaptations—such as in the case of Reform or Reconstructionist Judaism—I believe that its essence as an immutable law has been unwittingly compromised and its passion lost. The question of renewing the faith pivots, therefore, on the far more fundamental question of the essence of Judaism. Once that is identified, newer methods of revealing that essence can be employed, thereby ensuring that the Jewish faith never becomes obsolete.

With respect to things like dinosaurs, we understand why renewal is essential. If the ecology and the climate change, then the organisms that depend on that ecology must change as well. If birds don't fly south for the winter, their wings will freeze and they will fall prey to predators. Similarly, if a Muscovite wears his thick Russian bearskin in the summer, he will die of heat stroke. But what about those of us who always live in the same environment? Why must we change? If things went well last year and there are no radical social or environmental changes, why is there a need to evolve?

The answer is provided in the second chapter of Genesis, where the Bible declares, "God created man in His image." Just as God is a creator, so is man. The nature of a creator is to be inventive always. We cannot just continue to do the same thing—repetition does not call forth our deepest selves. *Man only lives when he creates.* Every human being is an artist, and when we fail to originate and produce, when we pursue the same monotonous daily routine, our lives lose their most essential ingredient, namely, passion. And loss of passion transforms life into mere existence.

We must always change and evolve, to conform not with *external* modifications, but with *internal* ones. *In the same way that there are seasons of the sun, there are seasons of the soul.* Man is a dynamic creature, and he is constantly changing on the inside. The soul is a burning flame that flickers constantly. Man cannot stagnate on the outside, because he does not stagnate on the inside. Since renewal is part of us, it must be reflected in all that we do and in all that we undertake.

Failing to heed the call of Rosh Hashanah, the Jewish New Year, does not merely entail failing to perform repentance and failing in God's judgment. Rather, what is lost is the opportunity to be more passionate about everything we will do in the coming year.

Establishing the centrality of renewal to everyday life allows us to reach a completely new understanding of being human. I suggest that there are in general three ways to understand human existence:

1. Man is a boat floating on an ocean. Even if he makes no effort to swim, he will still always hover. He may be rocked a bit by the waves, but he will bob and survive. In this scenario, he need do little to make it through life, save get by. This view posits man as a *functional creature* whose principal preoccupation is the satiation of his needs and drives. As long as he has a warm bed and a hot meal, he is content and happy. This vision is man as intelligent animal.

2. Man is floating in the ocean, and he must always make an effort to remain afloat. Without treading water, he will quickly sink. In this scenario, man must constantly work in order to survive, but he need not invent. He can do the exact same thing throughout life. Just keep treading water: wake up, go to work, come home, watch television. According to this view, man is a guardian of existence, a keeper at the gates of Eden. His purpose is not to innovate but to protect. This is man as soldier and bureaucrat.

3. Man is a wave atop the ocean of existence, an excitation rising from the waters of life. Without seeking to redefine himself as a dis-

tinct and separate wave at all times, he will not only cease to exist, but it will be as if he never existed. He will just become another nondescript drop in the ocean of being. In this scenario, man must always change and rise in order to remain distinct and alive. This is a view of man as a creator who arises from the dust and who will one day return to the dust. But in that seventy- or eighty-year period, he can leave an indelible mark on creation.

Judaism's conception of man is the third scenario. The existence of man in relation to God is like the excitation of a wave from the ocean. Man springs up from the body of God. He is both a part of the Creator, yet remarkably, he is also an individual in his own right. He is distinct and identifiable. And without constantly remaining atop the crest of the wave, he quickly returns to the nothingness of being that was his original state. Hence, man must create and innovate as part of his very existence.

Einstein's theory of relativity demonstrated this to be true. We are all particles of congealed energy. "Dust are thou, and to dust shall thou return." We arise from nothingness, and return to nothingness. We spring forth from the mixing together of the elements and later decompose and return to those same elements whence we stem. The only question that needs to be answered when we return is How much impact did we make on our environment? Was there any trace left? We are not meant to grow hot and cold with the seasons, but rather to create light and warmth and brighten the earth.

In Judaism, life is defined as anything that changes its environment. The Talmudic Rabbis went as far as to declare that the patriarch Jacob was still alive even after his physical demise because the monotheism and commitment to a Godly lifestyle that he instilled within his children continues. Beyond the grave he continues to make an impact. Because his legacy lives on in the daily lives of the children of Israel, he is still relevant, still breathing.

Thus, renewal is essential to life because it is the very definition of life. Mankind is not a rock, and his destiny is not etched in stone. As we have seen, Judaism rejects any belief that man is born with a predetermined fate. Sophocles may have stated, "Awful is the mysterious power of fate" and "Pray not at all, since there is no release for mortals from predestined calamity," but the Jew responds with the triumphant words of King David, *"Lo amut ki echyeh va'asaper ma'asei kah"* (I shall not die, for I shall live and speak the glory of God) (Ps. 118:17).

Herein lies the dramatic message of Rosh Hashanah and the reason why the Jewish New Year is treated so reverentially. Rosh Hashanah is humanity's wake-up call. In the same way that hunger pangs remind the individual that he must eat or risk deterioration, Rosh Hashanah reminds the individual that he must recreate himself or hazard his own internal decline. The actual reminder that is employed on Rosh Hashanah is the shofar, or ram's horn, reminiscent of the ram that Abraham used as a replacement for his son Isaac after God rescinded his command to offer Isaac as a sacrifice. Every blast of the shofar, which resounds through the halls of the synagogue and the crevices of our souls, awakens humanity from its slumber and complacency, alerting us to the call of personal and collective renewal.

Horizontal and Vertical Renewal

Like previous generations, ours recognizes the importance of renewal, but we find it in shopping, going on vacation, and watching movies. People relieve their boredom in the acquisition of new possessions and tasting new experiences. For many, unfortunately, life has been reduced to the endless pursuit of meaningless distractions. Married men or women find illicit lovers rather than bringing their own marriages to a newer and deeper plane. This is horizontal, or lateral, renewal, not the kind of renewal we speak of.

There is, however, also vertical renewal, by which humans reach deep into themselves and unearth new and exciting dimensions of their personalities. Couples bring new facets to their shared lives. Having been created in the image of God, every human possesses infinite depth, and there is no limit to the store of meaning of which humans are capable. This is real renewal. Although renewal of this type is difficult to discover, like a limitless spring, once found, it lasts eternally. When we speak of a man or woman of greatness, we refer primarily to someone who has no deep reliance on material wealth, possessions, or consumption. Such a person has no time for these trifles. Life itself is an endless challenge. Such a person does not experience the kind of boredom to which the rest of us are so easily prone. A man or woman of greatness reaches vertically for renewal, toward the infinite expanse of God, and inwardly, toward the infinite depths of the human soul. Placing oneself at the center of an ever-expanding circle of possessions is meaningless to the man or woman of greatness, whose creative capacity is not fulfilled in acquisition, but in enlightenment and compassion.

The key words of the High Holy Day prayer liturgy are *teshuvah, tefillah,* and *tzedakah*, or repentance, prayer, and charity. In these three words is the essence of renewal. Renewal involves, first, repentance, or reaching more deeply *into* ourselves. Every man and woman possesses an innocence, a layer of pristine purity, that can never be tarnished or compromised. It is our ability to tap into this reservoir of blamelessness that facilitates our capacity to reinvent ourselves. In Judaism, *teshuvah* literally means, not repentance, but *return*. We are revisiting our pristine, primordial selves, our innermost essence, our true identity, that spark of God that animates every human life.

Next is *tefillah*, or prayer, whereby man cries *up* to God, the source of his salvation. Prayer represents the ladder that connects God and man, bridging the infinite chasm that separates mortals from the unknowable God. Last, there is *tzedakah,* or charity, wherein we reach *outside* ourselves to our fellowman. Now that we have tapped our innocence and joined in sanctity our source and Creator, we are able, indeed obligated, to share that bounty and blessing with our fellow creatures and experience collective salvation. We have then, as the Lubavitcher Rebbe said, renewal and growth in three essential dimensions: inward, upward, and outward. Deeper into ourselves, higher toward God, and across toward our fellow humans. And these three dimensions give us height (stature), width (presence), and breadth (depth).

Above all else, we find renewal in our compassion, drawing forth a sense of kinship and affinity with every creature of the earth. It is our ability to feel that most determines the intensity of our lives. The final and perhaps most important step within the process of renewal is not only to find and experience our inner Godliness but also to find God in every aspect of creation. Renewal means renewing our vision, seeing all those things that we may have glanced over in the previous year. We discover this mainly within the companionship of our fellow human beings. When man reaches within to the depths of his soul and heavenward toward the omnipotent Creator, he is overwhelmed by a feeling of God's abundant presence and he is humbled. He is then able to reach out to his human brothers and sisters as equals, and the human family ushers in a new year of light, joy, and blessing.

19

Yom Kippur

Rediscovering the Lost Father

All that is necessary for the forces of evil to win in the world is for enough good men to do nothing.

—EDMUND BURKE

When choosing between two evils, I always like to try the one I've never tried before.

—MAE WEST

Our greatest glory is not in never falling, but in rising every time we fall.

—CONFUCIUS

To sit alone with my conscience will be judgment enough for me.

—CHARLES WILLIAM STUBBS

YOM KIPPUR IS THE HOLIEST and most solemn day of the Jewish calendar. Legendary baseball pitcher Sandy Koufax refused to pitch in the World Series on Yom Kippur, and Wall Street virtually ceases to function on this day. Yom Kippur is the great celestial bath, a day in which the sins of the entire nation of Israel are washed away. A pristine and sparkling nation without taint or blemish emerges from twenty-five hours of fasting and prayers. Yom Kippur comes as the culmination of ten days of repentance, which begin with the two days of Rosh Hashanah, the Jewish New Year. Even now, when many Jews are assimilated, perhaps 90 percent of Jews go to synagogue on Yom Kippur. For many it constitutes their only annual Jewish observance. What is it about this most serious day that makes it Judaism's highest temporal shrine?

After the Jews sinned by building the golden calf in the Wilderness of Sinai, Moses ascended Mount Sinai a second time to beg God to forgive their sin. The enterprise took another forty days, and on the final day of his ascent, corresponding to the tenth day of the Jewish lunar month of Nissan, God proclaimed, "I have forgiven them as you have requested" (Num. 14:20). Ever since then, according to the Bible, all human sins are wiped away and cleansed on Yom Kippur, a day that became associated with atonement.

The Power of Innocence

Each of us has regrets. We may behave impulsively, without thinking of the consequences of our actions. We may embark upon a course of action that does not accord with our deepest desires. We may allow our passions to govern us and end up at a destination radically different from what we first envisaged. We have an innate desire to be better people, but many things stand in the way. Perhaps the greatest obstacle to sincere repentance is the feeling that the mistakes we made will stick with us forever, that we cannot undo our past. Most people feel that it is too late to start afresh, even when they are young and robust, and more so when they are advanced in age. There is a false belief that man is the product of his actions, that what we do is what we are. This is often taken to the extreme of believing that our professions and our wealth dictate our essential worth as human beings. Conversely, we feel that if we have done bad things, then we are necessarily bad people.

Judaism completely rejects this thinking, believing that actions are supremely important but not, in the final analysis, what define man. In the same way that possessions do not define our innate worth—thus the rich and the poor are socially equal—so too the errors we commit do not penetrate our spirit, and both the righteous and the sinner are worthy in God's eyes. There is always a hidden layer of innocence—of purity—that lies beneath our actions. Man's soul can never be adversely affected by human action. Although man's actions may be tarnished, his soul remains pure. Thus, it is always possible do undo wrongful action and start afresh by tapping into this layer of holiness, the soft virgin snow that lies just beneath our coarse exterior.

The belief in a Godly soul animating our bodies is central to most world religions. Deep within our character there is a shining Godly component, always pure and innocent, which remains impervious to human caprice and whim. It is not destroyed by death nor is its light diminished by sin. On Yom Kippur, the holiest day of the year, we summon forth that quintessential spark, that deepest part of ourselves, and utilize its immense power to renew our commitment to righteousness and goodness. The Hebrew word for repentance, *teshuvah,* means "return," literally. Repentance is a return to the path of honor, but more important, a return to our deepest, innermost selves.

The ancient Rabbis point out that unlike a mortal ruler, God treats each of our transgressions as if it is being committed for the first time, irrespective of how often the action occurred. Thus, our plea for forgiveness is treated as though we are beseeching Him for the very first time. No residue or grudge is ever built up. The human belief that we cannot undo our bad behavior has no basis in spiritual reality.

What would become of us if we thought that the nefarious actions we undertook in the past would always come back to haunt us? Tragically, the world that we inhabit today is extremely judgmental, so that people are reminded of their mistakes whenever they contemplate public office or try to undertake the common good. In Judaism, such actions would be highly illegal. Once a man has steered his life away from former sinful ways, it is unlawful to remind him of his former ways. Indeed, the ancient Rabbis taught that a penitent is a totally new person. Therefore, not only is it improper to remind him of his former ways, it is also inaccurate. The sinful man you speak of no longer exists.

In this lies the beauty of Yom Kippur, the Jewish Day of Atonement. It is a day in which we wipe the slate clean and begin our lives anew. Every year, man is given the opportunity to reestablish his relationship with his Creator. Whatever he did in the past is not just forgiven, but is forgotten. He need never be haunted by the goblins of his mistakes.

People are accustomed to thinking that the only essentials for human life are food, clothing, and shelter. But just as our body has minimum necessities for maintenance and preservation, the same is true of our spirit. The soul thrives on its own kind of nourishment. Faith, compassion, good deeds, prayer, time spent with family and friends, study, meditation, and reflection are all conduits to nurturing the health of the soul. Yet I am convinced that there is nothing more essential for sustaining the soul's well-being than innocence. Whereas a healthy diet and regular exercise make the body sparkle, the soul shines when it feels blameless. But the necessity of innocence by far transcends the needs of just the soul. Indeed, our innocence is essential to our spiritual, mental, physiological, and ultimately physical well-being.

The greatest cause of human misery and torment is internal dissension, or what we might call the strife of the spirit. It occurs when we feel as if we are being pulled apart from the inside, when our actions no longer reflect our convictions. If the individual feels fragmented and divided, he cannot approach his life with any sense of clarity. He begins to doubt his way and ends up doubting himself. As he spirals down through the abyss of uncertainty, he will undertake almost any action, however aberrant, to restore his self-confidence. If a woman who is not his wife praises his talents, he will find it impossible to resist her charms. When we lose our innocence, even the most basic decisions become major trials and we feel confounded at every turn. Thus another consequence of inner torment is unhappiness and depression.

Conversely, the source of the greatest human strength and happiness is internal harmony and personal cohesion. Contentment and cheerfulness are dependent on the integration of the human personality. Man needs to feel whole. He needs to feel that there is only one master of his mental household. There is nothing that synthesizes our personalities in one indivisible unit more than innocence, and there is nothing that compartmentalizes us more than sin. Whereas sin veils our innermost personality, innocence removes the veils and allows our essence to be manifest.

At the beginning of the creation story in the Bible, Adam and Eve frolicked in the Garden of Eden stark naked. Unacquainted with sin, Adam and Eve had nothing to hide. They lacked the kind of insecurities that need to be masked by designer labels. They had no tarnishing stains that need to be papered over with awards and degrees. In their innocence they found freedom, the freedom just to *be* rather than always having to *do*. Maimonides says that he was once asked by a wise man why Adam and Eve were seemingly rewarded for their sin, since after their transgression "they came to know their nakedness," a fact to which they were oblivious prior to the sin. It is almost as if they gained greater insight only after the sin had been committed. An adaptation of Maimonides' response to the wise man is this: The reason that Adam and Eve pranced around naked in the garden is that they had nothing to hide. They were totally *innocent*. They had done nothing wrong; they had no warts, no iniquity to conceal. So they needed no clothes. They felt that they were beautiful just the way they were born. They did not feel deficient and thus required no external embellishments such as those fancy clothes could provide. The light of their souls shined through their untarnished bodies.

But the moment they sinned, they had something to hide. They wanted to conceal their iniquity. Like a man who has a tattoo he has since grown ashamed of, they covered themselves with garments because they no longer felt innocent. They felt ugly, naked, and barren. Their newfound vulnerability resulted directly from their feeling that they were inadequate. And because they were no longer virtuous on the inside, they needed artificial enhancements to make them acceptable on the outside. Ever since then, humans have been dressing themselves in colorful raiment in order to hide their sense of deficiency.

This permanent feeling of inadequacy has many expressions. A man today feels he needs a good job in order to impress a woman, and he picks her up in a fancy car to confirm his high social status. Maybe the accoutrements he came with will cause her to accept him. A woman will spend hours painting her face, making her more attractive, and allowing her to feel more confident around a man.

The feeling of inadequacy also explains people's obsession with expensive clothing. Most of us do not dress in order to *enhance* our natural beauty so much as to *conceal* our external shortcomings. Using makeup is acceptable in Jewish thought, but a woman who overindulges in its use is probably not doing so to highlight her facial features, but to cover her perceived plainness.

Small children like to frolic naked. We assume that they do so because they are naive and immature. But in truth, the reason is that small children are blameless, spotless, virtuous, and pure. They feel no natural impulse to hide. They expect to be accepted in their natural state. The innocence of a child is also the principal reason for his or her beauty. There is nothing so immaculate as humankind's Godly soul, and in a child it radiates as in no other. This is also the reason that to play with a child is to be in the presence of something spiritual and to raise a child in one's home is to introduce Godliness into that home. By having children we invite God back into our lives.

The Peace of Innocence

The beginning of mental torment and illness is the development of a dual personality. When we are uncomfortable with who or what we are, or what we have become, we try to conceal the aspect of our personality that is base and pretend to be something different. If Sarah and Rachel are friends, but Sarah gossips behind Rachel's back, the next time they meet, Sarah will be uncomfortable around Rachel. She cannot be herself, because she has something to hide. The real her, the element of her personality that dislikes Rachel and is a treacherous friend, must now remain concealed in public. By developing this split persona, Sarah gradually becomes unhinged from herself. And all because she has betrayed a friendship and therefore has something to conceal.

This compartmentalization is a great waste. The best way to succeed in life and to create human friendships is to allow our fullest personality to be manifest. Confidence is essential to both personal and professional success. But how can one be confident when hiding something that one is ashamed of? Like a brilliant sun at high noon, the human personality is sufficiently warm, vibrant, and compelling to make every acquaintance into a friend, and even turn a foe into a comrade. But when partially concealed, it loses its potency. We simply are not every effective in creating loving relationships with half our personality tied behind our backs.

The same is true in marriage. A husband or wife who is unfaithful damages him- or herself and threatens their marriage. The damage will not occur because of the transgression. People are forgiving, and a couple must try to get beyond an act of faithlessness. Rather, the damage will occur because it takes all one's self to be successful in showing love to one's spouse. When a husband is hiding half his character because of wrongdoing, he will be an ineffective lover and companion. Rather than using his creativity to find new ways to be passionate with his wife, he will be using his intellectual faculties to hide his infidelity. The whole beauty of marriage is its naturalness. It is with one's marriage partner that we can be the most genuine and sincere at all times. Once there is a big secret that cannot be disclosed, we excavate part of ourselves in which to hide the infraction. But like a cancer, it grows, and slowly we become two different people. We cannot be ourselves with our spouse, and our informality and loss of constraints is forfeited. Soon petty irritations erode the foundations of the marriage. But the real issue is that the husband and wife have ceased to be each other's soul mates. They have forfeited the expression of vulnerability and emotional nakedness that is such an essential part of every marriage. In its place they now wear the garments of deception.

The ancient Rabbis declared that a man without a home is not a man. The only place where we all feel completely comfortable, where we can really be ourselves, is in the privacy of our own homes. When we are in the presence of strangers, we are always acting, never behaving completely naturally. The same is true to a more limited extent even when we are in the company of close friends. We wouldn't prance around naked in front of our colleagues. We still dress up somewhat for them. When we are guests at someone else's home, we don't have the same degree of comfort. The only time when humans behave in a real and honest fashion is when they are at home. But the man who has lost his innocence has no home. Everywhere he goes invites discomfort. There is no place left for him to let his hair down. Even in the presence of his wife he is always on his guard, trying to remember never to be himself because he might reveal his indiscretions.

Without innocence there can be no peace. Without peace, there can likewise be no happiness. We always find our inner and outer selves grating against each other. Since sin unhinges and separates our outer and inner selves there is always friction and an inner tension that grants us no rest. Soon we are at war with ourselves. A conflict is being waged between our inner Godliness and our outer selfishness.

A Spirit of Madness

A famous Talmudic dictum proclaims that "no man sins unless he has been consumed by a spirit of madness." Only madness would allow us to forfeit our most prized possession, our innocence. Our innocence is who we are; it is our deepest self. When we sin, we automatically develop a split personality, since we will always have something to bury. Sin destroys our sense of cohesion and gives us layers in the place of inner harmony.

In ancient Israel there was a ritual practiced every year in the Temple in Jerusalem on the day of Yom Kippur. The High Priest would enter the Holy of Holies and carry out a special program of sacrificial offerings designed to bring about atonement on behalf of the Children of Israel. If he were to make a single error in so holy a place, he might incur instant death. Thus, when he emerged in peace, a throng of thousands of the Jewish people who witnessed his service would accompany him, singing and dancing, to his home, where he would offer a celebratory feast. According to the Yom Kippur prayer liturgy, when he emerged from the Holy of Holies, he looked "like a bridegroom on the day of his wedding; this was the glow of the High Priest."

The common denominator of these two scenes is innocence. The glow of the bridegroom on the day of his wedding is owing to the fact that he is starting life anew. Any mistakes he may have made prior to embarking upon his life with his bride are forgotten. His bride embraces him completely and he feels wonderful and whole. They are a new unit and he is a new man. He is pure and innocent as on the day he was born. The same is true of the High Priest. His most important characteristic as he emerges from the Holy of Holies is his *glow*. He has been forgiven for sin, and therefore he shines. Any husk or impediment that separated his inner self from his outer self has been removed, and the light of his infinite soul is left to radiate unhindered.

The innocent person shines even as he or she walks down the street because the light of his or her soul illuminates the entire person. The body is translucent, not cloudy. It is clear, not a frosted glass. The guilty person has allowed his body to become opaque. Rather than his personality serving as a window to the soul, it is now an obstacle, a brick wall, that shuts in the soul's rays. Few people will ever discover the real person, and this is much to the guilty person's detriment. Only the radiation of the soul's inner fire can engender the warmth necessary to create lasting friendships and relationships. A cold personality makes a chilling impact.

Because reclaiming innocence is crucial to our mental health and our relationships, God in His infinite kindness provided the Yom Kippur day for men and women to reclaim their innocence and begin life anew. Yom Kippur is therefore a day for the soul's, rather than the body's, indulgence. Hence, on Yom Kippur we cater to all the needs of the soul and neglect the needs of the body. All sensual pleasures, like eating, lovemaking, and bathing, are prohibited and replaced by fasting, prayer, and basking in God's warmth.

Paternal Love

There is an even deeper understanding of why Yom Kippur can bring atonement and reestablish our innocence. Normally, our thoughts are that God is merciful and compassionate. Like a lover who cherishes his beloved, He is prepared to forgive our iniquity. So, whenever man repents his sin and asks forgiveness, his sins should be overlooked. Why the need for Yom Kippur? The ancient Rabbis stated that although man must sincerely repent on the Day of Atonement, it is not his repentance that actually brings about forgiveness but *the day of Yom Kippur itself.* This view is taken much further by Rabbi Judah the Prince, editor of the Mishnah and a highly influential figure, who maintained, even more astonishingly, that the power of the day of Yom Kippur is such that even if people do not repent, they are still forgiven for their sins!

Imagine a man who owns an electronics store that he has built up from scratch. He hires two new employees to help with sales. One is a stranger who applied off the street. The other is his own son, whom he has taken on board to teach him the business. Both turn out to be disasters. They are lazy and always late. He warns each to shape up, and when they don't, he fires them both. Months go by after he has replaced them with more competent staff. Father's Day arrives, and his son sends him an affectionate Father's Day card, telling him how much he loves him. The father is moved, and the very next day he rehires his son. Meanwhile, the other fired employee writes a letter apologizing for his negligence. But he is not rehired. What is the difference between the two? *Why is a sin for an employee not a sin for a son?* They are judged by two different standards. A son receives preferential treatment, whereas a stranger does not. When the father related to his son as an employee whose whole purpose was to run the shop responsibly and sell merchandise, his son was found negligent and given the boot. As an employee, he spoiled the relationship with his boss by virtue of his negligence and unaccountability.

But the moment Father's Day comes around and the son, through the simple gesture of sending a card, reminds the father that though an employee, the son was not a stranger, but his own flesh and blood, the father no longer construes his son's tardiness as a major infraction. After all, the whole reason the father works in the first place is for his family. How then can he fire his own son? Sometimes he needs a little reminder that his son is everything he lives for. So, the moment the son upgraded his relationship with his father and reminded that he is not just any employee, he is immediately forgiven of his sin. And not only is he forgiven, his action is not even viewed as having been sinful. His negligence is forgotten, treated as if it had never happened. In the face of the infinite bond that connects father and son, the boy's tardiness is utterly immaterial.

The same is true of man's relationship with God. In the Bible God is referred to both as the king and father of humanity. Similarly, humanity is referred to both as God's servants as well as His children. "You are children to the Lord your God." Throughout the year God relates to us as a master to a servant, as a boss to his worker. "We humans are all workers committed to spreading light," the Talmud declares. Humans are born to fulfill a mission: to pursue love and justice throughout their lives and serve the one, true God. We have a task to complete, and when we transgress the central tenets of our covenant with God, or when we fail to live up to our calling, we become like negligent employees who face the possibility of dismissal.

But on Yom Kippur, the most sacred day of the year, the whole world achieves elevation. God is closer to humanity, and humanity is closer to God. The special parent-child relationship between the Almighty and humanity is manifest. God no longer sees us as workers, but as His loving handiwork, who possess a fragment of Himself within us. At this exalted plane, what would have constituted a sin for a servant is simply nonexistent. The bad things we do during the year anger God only when he sees us as having been created to execute a divine mission. The moment that we show God our unbridled love for Him—through our passionate devotion in prayer and fasting—He embraces us as a loving parent. Suddenly, our transgressions and the sins that divided us are utterly inconsequential. If a Jew makes just a minimal effort, a minimal commitment of coming to synagogue and fasting and showing God that he cares, although he may ignore many of the precepts throughout the year, God sees that this is His child, and through this act of commitment all the bad is automatically forgotten. It's not that the sin is forgiven. Rather, it is as if it never happened. In the face of the infinite bond between God and His children, the infraction is utterly negligible.

By fasting on Yom Kippur and denying ourselves our usual daily pleasures, and by our willingness to sit in the synagogue the entire day in devotion and prayer, we affirm our deep desire to be close to our Creator. The Almighty is reminded of how much He cares for us, and He looks at us and says, "What sins are you talking about? You are My children. Why, the whole world was created for you! I created trees for you to bask in their shade, I created other human beings to comfort you and share your love, I created oceans for you to enjoy their refreshment, and birds to sing to you in the mornings." There are no sins. Hence, it is the *day* of Yom Kippur, like Father's Day, that brings about atonement. Our repentance is merely the catalyst reminding God of His unbreakable covenant with us. Blood, as they say, is thicker than water.

20

Sukkot

Nature and the Environment

My soul can find no staircase to Heaven unless it be through Earth's loveliness.

—MICHELANGELO

Every now and again take a good look at something not made with hands—a mountain, a star, the turn of a stream. There will come to you wisdom and patience and solace and, above all, the assurance that you are not alone in the world.

—SIDNEY LOVETT

SUKKOT IS THE HARVEST FESTIVAL IN JUDAISM, a time of great rejoicing. In Leviticus 23:42, the Jews are commanded "to live in booths for seven days," and indeed the central celebration of the festival is living and eating outdoors in a temporary, hutlike structure with a roof of leaves and branches through which the stars can be seen. The word *sukkot* means booths, or gazebos. A sukkah (singular) is like a mini-tabernacle.

When God brought the Jews out of Egypt, He sheltered them for forty years while they were traveling through the Wilderness of Sinai. The Bible relates that God provided seven protective clouds—one above, one below, four for north, south, east, and west, and one to lead the way—which shielded the Jews from the elements. Not the scorching sun, freezing winds, or even scorpions or snakes harmed the Jews while they were traversing the difficult terrain. The clouds protected them from every danger.

These protective enclosures and God's sheltering of the Jewish people are the principal focus of commemoration in the Festival of Sukkot. In the same way that Shavuot celebrates the preservation of the Jewish soul—a time when God gave the Jewish people a spiritual heritage that would distinguish them from the nations of the world—Sukkot celebrates the preservation of the Jewish body. God preserved the Jewish people from certain destruction at the hands of the elements. His setting up visible shields to shelter them in the desert foreshadowed the invisible shield that the Almighty would hold above the heads of the Jewish people throughout history to protect them from endless assailants. This is the source for the great joy and celebration traditionally associated with the harvest festival, Sukkot. We rejoice in the fact that our nation survives and flourishes. Although other nations have succumbed to the imperatives of historical decline, the Jewish people continues to strengthen because God still nurtures us in His protective embrace, His invisible sukkah. God's providence spreads like a canopy over the Jewish people to protect them from trouble and sorrow.

The Sukkah is a temporary structure that must be big enough to accommodate one person, but is usually built large enough to fit the entire family. It must have at least two and a half walls, but usually ends up resembling a small room closed on all sides, with a single door. Its roof, made only from branches, leaves, and twigs, does not provide protection from the rain, thereby emphasizing its temporary nature. It must be constructed of material that can withstand the wind. The roof must be made of plants that cannot be used for food. These plants must be in their natural state and detached from the ground.

In addition to the overall symbolism inherent in Sukkot as a festival celebrating the continued physical survival of the Jewish people, the sukkah itself has four important associations.

1. The Sukkah Represents Our Reliance on God Rather Than on Human Ingenuity. One of the worst sins according to Judaism is hubris. With the strong structures in which we dwell throughout the year, and with the technological advances of the modern era that are the product of the human mind, men and women can begin to see themselves as their own protectors. Even those who profess belief in God do not necessarily rely on Him, but rather on their own skills. They pray to God out of habit, rather than a sincere belief that God is the rock of their salvation. If the modern man of faith truly believed in God as his protector and source of all sustenance, he would pray with heartfelt devotion rather than out of a sense of ritual obligation. If we stood before a king or philanthropist who could grant our every wish, we would not simply mumble some words that had little meaning to us.

The purpose of dwelling in a sukkah is to inculcate within us once again a sense of total reliance on God as the Master of the Universe. By reliving the experiences of our ancestors in the wilderness, by living in the outdoors in a flimsy hut in which we are exposed to the elements, we once again perceive God as our light and the source of our salvation. We move outside the security of our brick homes and into the vulnerability of nature. Just as King David speaks of God "hiding me in His sukkah in the day of trouble . . . under the cover of His tent" (Ps. 27:5), so too we come to rely on the God who is veiled behind nature rather than on men or women who delude themselves into thinking that they are the masters of nature.

2. The Sukkah Resembles a Divine Embrace. Each of God's commandments involves the performance of some action. A mitzvah is something we do, and it is usually connected with one or more human functions. The tefillin are placed upon head and heart. Eating kosher food involves our gastronomy. Lighting Shabbat candles requires hands and eyes.

The sukkah is unique among God's commandments in that it involves a divine embrace. Whereas all other mitzvot involve a human undertaking, eating in a sukkah involves stepping into, and being totally enveloped by, a divine commandment. For seven days, the Jew eats and sleeps within the sukkah, which encompasses him completely. Sukkah, therefore, rather than something we do, is something we enter. It is a divine commandment into which the Jew is immersed. It is a mitzvah that encompasses the Jew with Godliness from head to toe, as if he is being embraced by the divinity.

After the solemn days of Rosh Hashanah and Yom Kippur, in which God evaluates our actions, the individual might draw the conclusion that God loves us only for our righteous deeds. Rather than loving what we *are*, God loves what we *do*. Rather than loving our being, the Almighty loves only our virtue. And when we are not blameless, when we are sinful, then He dismisses us like so many unworthy scoundrels. The High Holy Days can make man feel that he has no intrinsic value to God, that he is special only when he behaves in a prescribed fashion. This can lead to despondency, like that of a wife who feels that if she is not fit and thin, she will not be desirable to her husband. Permanent insecurity may ensue. Therefore, to counteract this misguided notion of divine love, the Almighty provides a festival in which He hugs us, as it were, to show unconditional love and total acceptance. When you hug someone, you embrace all of them, even their back. The statement inherent in the embrace is this: I adore all of you. Not only your beautiful and distinctive features—your eyes, face, intelligence, and warmth—but even those aspects of you that are not at all distinctive, like your back. I love the highest parts of you, and I love the lowest parts of you. Similarly, God is telling us on Sukkot that he admires every one of our features, from the part of us that is righteous and faithful, to the part that is sometimes rebellious and selfish. Belief in God involves our highest intellectual faculties. Prayer involves the lofty components of lips and tongue. But into the sukkah go even our heels and our shoes.

This statement of unconditional love is the source of the great joy that characterizes the Sukkot festival. Whereas joy is a staple of the other three festivals, with the Bible stating emphatically *"vesamachta bechagecha*—you must rejoice on your festival" (Deut. 16:14), on Sukkot this joy is especially pronounced and is celebrated by wild dancing and singing throughout the seven-day period. Our joy comes from our reconciliation with God after the somber High Holy Days and our relief at having been acquitted in God's judgment. Like two lovers who ecstatically celebrate their reunion after geographic or emotional dislocation, we rejoice with God and are heartened by His embrace. The Midrash declares that the shaking of the palm branch in the direction of the four winds during the harvest festival is like the waving of a flag, symbolizing our victory in judgment.

3. The Sukkah Represents Man's Reentry into Nature.   Another powerful meaning of the sukkah is man's reentry into nature. Judaism attempts to prepare man for a discovery of the ineffable. Man's purpose is to find the God who is cloaked behind nature. Religion teaches us to find the awe and wonder in creation. The Hebrew word for nature—*tevah*—also means sunken and submerged. Likewise, the gematria (numerical value of the letters) of the word *Elokim*, "Lord," is eighty-six, the same as that of the word *hatevah*, "nature." These statements mean that there is no Mother Nature. Rather, nature is merely a cloak that God wears. The Almighty is *submerged* in nature. The objective of the man of faith is to seek God out, to be guided by the grandeur and awe that he or she feels upon encountering the majesty of nature and discovering the Creator who lies behind it. Similarly, in every area of life, man must remove the outer husks, the facade, and appreciate the spiritual layer that lies underneath.

For man to reexperience the sublimity of creation, he must reimmerse himself in the awe-inspiring beauty of nature. The brick and concrete structures of modern-day life often stifle our affinity with the natural. Man becomes blinded by his carpets and his walls, his electric lights and his fireplace. As he gazes at them, he sees only objects that he himself has crafted. He focuses on the splendor of human ingenuity rather than on the magnificence of God's handiwork. He begins to lose sight of the glory and majesty of all that surrounds him. Once a year, during Sukkot, we get out of our artificial, man-made boxes and reexperience the soul of God, which is to be found in nature. The Jewish Kabbalists, like the great Ari and Rabbi Haim Vital, all migrated to Safed in the north of Israel because of its immaculate natural surroundings. Being immersed in nature revealed to them the mysteries of the universe.

It is clear that Judaism, with its mystical orientation and insistence that God is found in all things, is profoundly concerned with the environment, ecology, and all living things. Several times in the creation story in Genesis we read that "God saw that it was good."

Central to Jewish thought is the idea that man, as the jewel of creation, was placed by God as custodian over the garden of creation. God's commandment to Adam and Eve when He placed them in the Garden of Eden was to protect the garden. "The Lord God took the man and put him in the Garden of Eden to work it and care for it" (Gen. 2:15). Man therefore is held accountable for the state of the world.

Furthermore, the Bible refers to man as a tree of the field. The Jewish philosophers recognize a hierarchy of four types within creation. In ascending order, they are mineral, vegetable, animal, and intellectual. Since man incorporates elements of each within his person—when he sleeps he is inanimate, like a tree he grows, he has animal tendencies, and he possesses cognitive functions—he can therefore find it within himself to have empathy with and protect every element of creation.

Thus, the Jews are commanded never to cut down a fruit-bearing tree, even when they must build siege engines during war. Likewise, the Jews are forbidden to waste anything within creation. Rabbi Aaron Halevi of Barcelona concluded, "The Jews never destroy even a grain of mustard, and are upset at any destruction they see. If only they can save anything from being spoilt they spare no effort to do so." Furthermore, when the Jews inhabit the Land of Israel they must strictly obey the laws of the Sabbatical year. The land must rest, be refreshed, and recapture its capacity for production. The Bible strictly warns against overuse of the land.

Throughout the Bible, the concept of the Jews as a chosen nation is always linked to the Land of Israel as a chosen land. The Jews must always be in harmony with the land. The biblical pilgrim festivals revolve around the land and its crops. Through the joyful experience of the people with these festivals, the Jews learned to cherish the land. This joy was also greatly enhanced through the fulfillment of the divine commandments to share the bounty of the land with the Levites, who had no personal share in the land, the stranger, the orphan, and the widow.

The Bible specifically commands the Jewish people to put all their refuse "outside the camp" (Deut. 23:13–14). It had to be collected and removed to a location where it would not interfere with the quality of human life. The ancient Rabbis extended this prohibition to not dumping refuse in a place where it would pollute the environment or harm the crops. The Talmud also discusses extensively where odoriferous commercial operations, like tanneries, could be located, since odor was regarded as a particular nuisance. The Rabbis always accorded priority to environmental over commercial concerns.

Preempting naturalist thinkers like Rousseau, the Bible was profoundly concerned that man should not become so consumed by his own creation that he is desensitized to the beauty of nature. Thus there are laws that govern the building of cities, ensuring that they never grow to become concrete jungles, where man cannot see grass or flowers in bloom. The Bible spells out how all the Levite cities were to look. There was to be a double surround to each town. First a green belt of 1,000 cubits, and exterior to that, a 2,000-cubit-wide belt for "fields and vineyards" (Num. 35:2–5). Although some exegetes maintain that the 1,000-cubit band was for pasture, Rashi explains that it was not for use, but "for the beauty of the town, to give it space." Maimonides reflects this idea by legislating that there be a certain distance between trees and residences, and that a strict proportion of each be maintained so that residences are not constructed to the detriment of the environment.

4. The Sukkah Represents Man's Vulnerability.   Locked behind his strong wooden doors, surrounded by his strong brick walls, man feels invincible and impregnable. He feels immune from danger as he relaxes in his man-made abode. He feels secure, knowing that he has worked hard to achieve his social position. He feels that his security is the money in his bank account and the investments in his equities portfolio. He carefully monitors his pension fund and feels confident that he is doing the best for his family. He feels untroubled by existential longing or suffering.

But all that security is insubstantial and easily lost. The man who sits on top of the world today may find himself at the bottom tomorrow. Shares rise and fall, and there is no such thing as true job security. Even if our material assets last us a lifetime, our health situation is always precarious: We may find ourselves dependent on God rather than any doctor.

The only real security man has is his love for God and the blessing that God bestows upon him in all his endeavors. When we enter the Sukkah every year, with its unsound roof and the wind howling through the walls, we experience our vulnerability and see that ultimately security stems only from the protection of the Creator. It is essential, once a year at the very least, for men and women to be exposed to the elements, the torrential downpour and the terrifying tempest. By encountering our mortality we remove the protective layers and artificial barriers that wall us off from one another and from God. Once a year, a husband must take his wife into his mud hut. So many men want to show women that they are kings who live in castles. They relate to their women only through shining body armor. They misguidedly believe that it is strength and honor that are respected. So they hide their emotions and never speak of their fears. They are strong and invulnerable and have no trepidation or fright. But a wife really wants to know that her husband needs her, relies on her, confides in her, confesses to her. And that's what Sukkah is all about. It is about men and women moving out of their protective enclosures and dependency. It is about overcoming the fear of relying on God and our fellow humans. Being within the shaky walls and leaky roof of the Sukkah allows us to experience our emotional vulnerability. A man and a woman fall in love with each other when they get emotionally naked. For that to happen, we must sometimes expose the leaks in our hearts and the cracks in our egos.

Sukkot is described in the Torah as "the time of our rejoicing." On the final day of Sukkot, the final section of the Torah scroll—Moses' blessing of the Jewish people just prior to his death—is read and completed. This last day, known as Simchat Torah, ranks as the most joyous day of the Jewish calendar, and the synagogue comes alive with children waving flags and congregants dancing and singing in the aisles with the Torah scrolls. On the same day, a new one-year cycle of reading the ancient scroll is commenced, and the Jews immediately begin the Book of Genesis. In this way, the cycle of renewal and joy is revisited, leading to another year of blessing and abundance.

PART FOUR

The World at Large

21

"A Stranger and a Resident"

Jews, Non-Jews, and Anti-Semitism

As long as Nazi violence was unleashed only, or mainly, against the Jews, the rest of the world looked on passively and even treaties and agreements were made with the patently criminal government of the Third Reich. . . . The doors of Palestine were closed to Jewish immigrants, and no country could be found that would admit those forsaken people. They were left to perish like their brothers and sisters in the occupied countries. We shall never forget the heroic efforts of the small countries, of the Scandinavian, the Dutch, the Swiss nations, and of individuals in the occupied part of Europe who did all in their power to protect Jewish lives.

—**ALBERT EINSTEIN**

I know who caused the war [First World War]—the German-Jewish bankers! . . . I have the evidence here. Facts! The German-Jewish bankers caused the war. I can't give out the facts now, because I haven't got them all yet, but I'll have them soon.

—**HENRY FORD**, letter to a friend

ONE OF THE SADDEST MOMENTS IN THE BOOK OF GENESIS is the death of the matriarch Sarah. Throughout Genesis, Abraham is portrayed as a loner. Armed with the courage of his convictions, he is prepared to risk social censure and estrangement in order to promote the truth of monotheism against the pagan mores of his time. His only and constant confidant is his wife, Sarah. With her loss, he is left all alone. He finds a suitable burial ground for her in the form of the two-tiered cave belonging to Ephron the Hittite in the ancient city of Hebron. He addresses the Hittites in a famous soliloquy. "I am both a stranger and a resident in your midst," he tells them (Gen. 23:4).

This paradox of the first Jew foreshadowed later Jewish existence. Even today, Jews are both residents—equal citizens of their adopted lands—and strangers. Jews in the United States are Americans, Jews in the United Kingdom are British, Jews in South Africa are South African. But they are also distinctively recognized as Jews. Wherever they are, the Jews represent what is almost a subnation within a nation. An American Jew and a British Jew often have more in common with each other than with their American and British counterparts. The Jews have a different New Year from the rest of the world's, are circumcised, don't celebrate some of the most important national holidays of their adopted lands, like Easter and Christmas, and are staunch supporters of the State of Israel. They are both residents and aliens, a people within a people.

But in what sense are the Jews a people? Are they a race, like Black Africans and Native Americans? Or is their distinctiveness defined through their having common cultural practices? Are they a nation the way that the Irish are a nation, identified through common history, a common land, and common cultural heritage? Or are they a people defined by religious affiliation? Indeed, can they survive without their religion and only through language, culture, and national will? And if Jews are defined primarily through having a common faith, if they possess only a religious identity, then why is the notion of a national territory and national distinctiveness necessary to their religious identity? And if they do need a common homeland called Israel, then why should religion be intrinsic to their identity? Can one only be born a Jew? Is a convert a full Jew? Are Jews distinctive from other nations or races? The questions go on and on.

The Jews as a People

Contrary to popular opinion, the Jews are not a race. The proof is that there are Black Jews and white Jews. Indeed, the Jewish nation includes people of all races. Although the Jews are bound by a common faith, they constitute far more than a mere faith community. After all, there are religious Jews and secular Jews. Some Jews claim to be atheists, whereas others are passionately devoted to God. Yet, nearly all Jews, regardless of degree of religious affiliation and/or belief in God, care deeply about their Jewishness. This has forever been one of the great riddles of history. Isaac Bashevis Singer liked to say: "I met a Jew who had grown up in a Yeshiva and knew large sections of the Talmud by heart. I met a Jew who was an atheist. I met a Jew who owned a large clothing store with hundreds of employees, and I met a Jew who was an ardent Communist. . . . It was all the same man."

Even Jews who have forsaken every trace of religious or nationalist identity still refuse to relinquish the title *Jew*. Throughout history some extremely secular Jews have suffered martyrdom and terrible deprivations rather than convert to another faith or adopt an identity foreign to their Jewishness. A catholic priest once described this phenomenon by claiming, "The Jews are a people who are religious without even knowing it." They have a Jewish identity even when they don't work on it or consciously work against it. A classic case in point is that of Sigmund Freud, the founder of psychoanalysis. An affirmed atheist, he was still a proud Jew, and on several occasions he attempted to understand his latent Jewish identity. In his preface to the Hebrew translation of *Totem and Taboo*, Freud wrote:

No reader of the Hebrew version of this book will find it easy to put himself into the emotional position of an author who is ignorant of the language of holy writ, who is completely estranged from the religion of his fathers, as well as from every other religion, and who cannot take a share in nationalist ideas, but who has yet never repudiated his people, who feels that he is, in his essential nature, a Jew, and who has no desire to alter that nature. If the question were put to him: Since you have abandoned all these common characteristics of your countrymen, what is there left to you that is Jewish? He would reply: A very great deal, and probably its essence. He could not now express that essence clearly in words: But someday, no doubt, it will become accessible to the scientific mind.

In an address to the B'nai B'rith society, Freud, speaking as if he were a Jewish mystic, defined Judaism as being "not the faith, not even the national pride . . . but many dark emotional powers, all the stronger the less they could be expressed in words, as well as the clear consciousness of an inner identity." Is it not amazing that this most eloquent of men, who could identify and give expression to the hidden workings of the human psyche, could find no words to express his own Jewishness?

But the answer to the eternal question of what the Jews are is the following: The Jews are not a race, religion, cultural, or ethnic group. Rather, the Jews are a people sharing common ancestry, common history, and a common destiny. The Jews are one because they all stem from the same source, and they are all headed to the same destination. The Jews are a family consisting of the children of Abraham, Isaac, and Jacob; Sarah, Rebekah, Rachel, and Leah; and the righteous converts who have adopted, and in turn been adopted by, the extended Jewish family. In fact, the Jews are the world's oldest people, sharing a single covenant made between their patriarchs and God and binding on every Jew from now until the end of time. The Jews constitute both a nation and a religion, a collection of individuals scattered throughout the world but united by both a common ancestry and a common faith. In essence, we are one family with one faith, but it is the familial component that is the most pronounced.

Outsiders approaching the Jewish religion and the Jewish people often make the mistake of treating Judaism like other world religions. They define the Jewish people as a faith community, a group of individuals who subscribe to a particular way of life governed by time-honored religious rituals and faith. Being Jewish, however, is not a state of *belief*, but a state of *being*. It is not a state of practice, but a state of existence. Whereas a nonbelieving Christian is a contradiction in terms, there are atheist, Marxist, and even Christian Jews. Nor is Judaism a strictly cultural heritage, because indeed there are vast cultural discrepancies between Ashkenazi and Sefardi Jews. Rather, the Jews are a large family, all stemming from the same parentage. Their historical destiny was revealed to them at the birth of their nationhood.

Philosophers like Spinoza and Jean-Paul Sartre have argued that the Jews are defined by the hatred that surrounds them. It is only because other nations refuse to absorb them that the Jews endure. This, however, is ludicrous. The Jews do not carry on because of the animosity of the nations, just as men of principle do not endure because they are not admitted to nightclubs and gambling parlors. Rather, the Jews have internalized a Godly identity. They are bound by a common destiny and a common mission. The Jewish people are possessed of a natural disposition toward God and a natural orientation toward compassion for their fellowman, both of which are a heritage from Abraham, who served God and humanity with all his heart.

To be sure, there are Jewish atheists, but atheism is an unnatural state for Jews. As Elie Wiesel once said, "A Jew can love God, or a Jew can hate God. But a Jew can never ignore God." Find the Jew who is indifferent on the subject of God. The Jew's natural relationship with God is described in the Kabbalah as the natural gravitation of a flame to a torch. Light a small candle near a large flame, and the small flame bends toward the larger one. The Jews who are atheists are by and large *aggressive* atheists, as they are consciously struggling against a natural gravitation towards theism.

The Impossibility of Escaping Jewish Identity

One who affirms a belief in Christ can rightfully call himself a Christian. One who was raised as "a nice Catholic" but rejects a belief in

Christ must abandon the title of Christian. But the Jews can never lose their title. If you are born a Jew, you will die a Jew, even if you do not live as a Jew. It is much like being a son. Even if you hate your father and mother and have nothing to do with them, you shall forever be their child. A child of Abraham is always a child of Abraham, no matter the lengths he or she goes to distance themselves from the Jewish heritage. There is no escape. It is not a question of affiliation but existence.

Thus, the Jews do not recognize the act of conversion to another faith. Once a Jew, always a Jew. All the baptism water in the world will not wash away a Jew's indestructible and millennia-old identity. Nor can the Jews effectively hide or conceal their identity. History has shown time and again that despite the most strenuous efforts to blend in with the nations, the Jews are noticeable. A historical calling follows them everywhere. The God of history will always hunt the Jews down and summon them to His service. As Job said, "Thou dost pursue me like a lion" (Job 10:16).

A parable of Rabbi Nachman of Bratslav describes the inability of the Jew to escape his Jewishness. A king once had a son who thought he was a turkey. That the crown prince of the nation behaved so bizarrely was a source of great shame to the king and his kingdom. His father sought every wise man to cure the young prince, to no avail. The future ruler continued to prance around the palace stark naked on all fours, saying, "Gobble, gobble."

One day a Rabbi came and claimed to be able to cure the prince. The prince was scrounging around on the floor, unclothed, eating scraps. The Rabbi removed his own clothing and joined the prince, who was curious at the sight. "Who are you?" asked the prince.

"Why me? I'm a turkey."

"That's amazing," said the prince. "Why, I'm a turkey too, and I am so happy to have company."

The next day, the Rabbi scrounged on the floor, this time fully clad.

"I thought you were a turkey," inquired the prince.

"I am," responded the Rabbi. "But even turkeys can wear fine clothes."

"You're right," said the prince, and he promptly put on his finest royal robes.

The next day the Rabbi appeared eating at the table with knife and fork.

"I thought you were a turkey," said the prince.

"I am," said the Rabbi, "but even turkeys can be cultured and eat at a table with proper manners."

"You're right," said the prince and promptly joined him.

After a few weeks, the prince was dressing splendidly, adhering to all royal protocols, and conducting himself with the finest etiquette. All the while, he believed that he was a turkey. The moral of the story is that you may believe you are a turkey, but you are still a human being. Therefore, it didn't make any difference what the prince thought. He could not change his status. What the wise Rabbi understood was that it was never important to persuade the prince that he was human. Rather, it was important to influence him to *act* like a human. Just as no person can change his status of human being, neither can the Jew. The Jew can assimilate, acculturate, and strongly deny his Jewishness. But that will change nothing. Even the most assimilated or nonpracticing Jew is still adamantly Jewish, and his or her Jewish identity is usually central to his entire being.

The best way then to understand the Jewish nation is as an extended family, a people, who were also given a special religion and mission in life. But the former always precedes and even supersedes the latter. Even those Jews who do not actively affiliate in the faith community are still as Jewish as Abraham, Sarah, and Moses.

Historically, the Jewish nation was first a people; later the Jews as a nation were chosen by God for a specific divine mission and given a religion uniquely suited to that mission. Their nationhood preceded their divine election. An Israelite is someone who is a descendant of Jacob, to whom the Almighty gave the name Israel, after he had wrestled with and prevailed against an angel. After the dispersion of the ten tribes, the Israelites were referred to as Jews because the remainder of the Jewish nation—those that today form the bulk of the Jewish people—all stem from the tribe of Judah.

It can be clearly seen from this that the definition of a Jew has little to do with the Jewish faith and everything to do with the fact that all Jews are either direct descendants of the original house of Abraham or righteous converts who adopted, and were adopted by, the Jewish nation. Parents who build a family may have biological children or they may adopt children. But once these adopted children have been fully assimilated into the family, they are equal members and are indistinguishable from their biological siblings.

In Judaism, a convert to the faith is as Jewish as the prophet Moses, and there are several injunctions in the Torah forbidding the Jews from ever treating a convert as anything less than fully Jewish or as a stranger. I have found that there is some apprehension among potential converts, fearing that they will never be treated as equals. This is certainly not the case. The only criterion for a convert to be fully embraced and accepted by the Jewish community is that their conversion be sincere and incorporate the following three requirements:

1. The convert must choose to join the Jewish nation for no reason other than his or her love for the God of Israel, His will as revealed in the Torah, and a desire to share the fate of the Jewish nation, for better or for worse. Conversions that are undertaken for external reasons—such as the most common reason today, whereby someone converts to Judaism because he or she wishes to marry a Jew—are not valid. Ulterior motives impede the authenticity of the conversion. Although a desire to marry a Jew can serve as an impetus for conversion, it cannot be its sole motivating force. Rather, one must seek conversion out of a sincere and deep appreciation of Judaism. Marriage may therefore serve as the catalyst to study Judaism, but not to convert.

2. The convert must be knowledgeable about the fundamentals of the faith and undertake to carry out that knowledge in a life suffused with Jewish observance and commitment. Most rabbinical courts today that perform the conversions would insist on the candidate's demonstrating a thorough knowledge and observance of the Sab-

bath, all the Jewish festivals, keeping a strictly kosher diet both inside and outside the home, and following the Jewish laws of family
purity, which mandate a period of sexual abstinence in marriage for
the five days of menstruation and seven days thereafter.

3. The candidate must go to the *mikveh*, the Jewish ritual pool of
immersion. And if the candidate is a man, he must also be circumcised. If the candidate is already circumcised, then he need only have
a drop of blood drawn in accordance with the circumcision ritual.

Nevertheless, Judaism discourages conversion, but not for reasons
of its being an elite club that does not allow new members. Rather,
Judaism sees all people as being inherently holy and Godly, just the
way they are born. The manner in which the Almighty created us is
the way in which He wants us to develop our fullest spiritual and
material potential. Judaism does not advocate the idea that converts
upgrade their existence by becoming Jewish, and indeed the ancient
Rabbis declare that a righteous Gentile who leads a moral and ethical life has an equal share in the immortal hereafter.

Circumcision and Holiness

The most important identifying symbol for male Jews, which is also
the symbol of the covenant that God made with the seed of Abraham, is circumcision. In contemporary times, circumcision has come
under severe attack as a barbaric ritual of bloodletting. From my ex-
tensive exposure to interfaith couples, I have discovered that a non-
Jewish father usually has no objection to his children being raised
Jewish—with the one exception of the circumcision ritual. As one
Gentile father said to me, "My son was born perfect. Why do we
need to cut him and tamper with his perfection?"

The story goes that Moses looked up to the heavens quizzically
and said, "Now God, let me get this straight. The Arabs get all the
oil, and we get to cut the tips off our what?" I know of many young
men who have contemplated conversion until they discovered that
an essential part of their anatomy—what Woody Allen refers to as

his second-favorite organ—would be diminished, literally, by the experience. What could the Creator have been thinking in commanding so strange a ritual? And although Jews overall remain highly devoted toward the practice of circumcision—with a recent statistic showing that over 98 percent of Jewish boys are circumcised—nevertheless, there is an increasing sense of discomfort, both figurative and literal, toward the practice in a rationalist age that demands explanations.

In the twentieth century, the Jew came to be identified with ugly signs, such as the yellow star that an enemy who sought to humiliate him ordered placed upon his breast. But the Jew has age-old symbols of external identification, which have great meaning for him. Foremost among them is the covenant of circumcision. At the tender age of eight days a male Jew's foreskin is cut away from his reproductive organ. The first explanation we may offer for this most famous of all Jewish symbol is the recognition on the part of the Jew from the earliest age that everything he has belongs to God, especially his body, his natural gifts, his aspirations and goals. Therefore, the very first thing he must know is that his sexual desire, representing the human life force itself and the desire to perpetuate the species, is no more than a means to a higher end, namely, to love and serve God for the length of his days. It must therefore be sublimated toward a higher goal. The circumcision on the male member enjoins man to turn his lust into love, his passion into marital pleasure, and his desire for sexual conquest into a monogamous union wherein man and woman become one flesh.

There is, however, a deeper explanation. When God created the world, he used a special hylic, or formless, substance that could assume any shape. This special substance derived from His infinite potential. Later, God shaped the world into its present form, thus using His finite energy to give definition and limits to creation. In man too there exists both an infinite and a finite energy. Possessed of an infinite power for creativity, man is a creator, but he must also know when to stop creating. He must be expansive and loving, but he must also learn when to put on the brakes. He must be compassionate and show pity, but this too must know limits. He must show severity when the occasion calls for it; a parent who cannot discipline his children does not truly love them. Indeed, the art of leading a fulfilling life is finding the fine balance between love and severity, between creativity and actualization, between love and discipline, between indulgence and restraint.

When we speak of someone with an artistic temperament, we mean someone who is gifted with creativity, but who unfortunately finds this as great a curse as a blessing. Such an individual finds it difficult to manage the more mundane aspects of life. An absentminded professor exhibits the same tendencies. This is why God commanded that on the reproductive organ—man's greatest symbol of his creative energy and his infinite capacity for Godly emulation—there must be a sign of God to teach man discipline. What shakes and destroys our contemporary world is that people love, but they don't know when to stop loving or how to love with discipline. A man marries, but he does not learn the art of fidelity or how to channel his love and make it potent by focusing it endlessly on one woman. Conversely, there are women who continue to love abusive men and who remain in relationships when they should have long left them.

The sign of circumcision embedded on man's reproductive organ is a symbol to him that the essence of holiness is the knowledge of when to refrain. Through the covenant of circumcision, God gave man a symbol of the need to rein in illicit desires. It is specifically in sexuality, the strongest of all human desires, that such control is most necessary and where such a symbol has the strongest impact. Circumcision is a symbol of the human ability to master our passions and guide our pleasures. The sign of circumcision for the Jew is the equivalent of a heavenly "Congressional Medal of Honor." It is the acknowledgment that its bearer is an individual capable of reaching the heights of moral excellence. Circumcision is a mark of moral heroism, enjoining its bearer to be the master of his passions, channeling them into an erotic relationship with his wife rather than diffusing them in casual relationships that lack permanence.

The first ritual undertaking of every Jewish male, therefore, is a commitment to moderation and finding a healthy balance, surely the most difficult task in life. The secret to understanding and mastering human nature is to know that people are all naturally extremists. Striking a balance is difficult and counterintuitive. Judaism maintains that evil and harm lie in extremes. Man must exercise his rational judgment, amid an overall submission to God's laws, in achieving a temperate and moderate nature. Circumcision teaches us that man is not an animal, that we should not be ruled by our emotions or instincts. Sex is a beautiful and Godly undertaking, but only as long as it is practiced with restraint and focus. Maimonides even maintained that circumcision weakened the sex drive in man, making it more accessible to his control. And though his is a minority opinion, it conveys the same sentiment. Man is capable of transforming sex into an act of love. He is capable of controlling his desires and directing them toward life-affirming goals rather than being their prisoner.

There is a further consideration. The first ten generations of mankind, culminating in the flood of Noah, which decimated the world's population, emphasized the pleasure principle, the unbridled pursuit of sensual pleasures, as the primary goal of life. According to Maimonides, this sensuality constituted the sin of the first couple in partaking of the tree that the Bible says was "good for food and a delight to the eyes." They ate from the forbidden tree because they could not control their lust for sensual gratification. The pleasure experience is boundless, reaching out without restraint or discipline. One does not seek, but indulges, in pleasure. To the man or woman intent on satisfying the craving for pleasure, ethics are irrelevant and all barriers or authority become oppressive. The fleeting sensation of the moment is primary. Future consequences are dismissed.

Surely, the pursuit of happiness is one of modern society's greatest idols. Undoubtedly, such a value system, which comes at the expense of duty to God and one's fellowman, invites moral decay. Cain killed Abel, Lamech boasted of his crimes, and the aristocratic sons de-

scribed as having fallen in the Book of Genesis flouted all morality by
appropriating for sensual pleasure the wives of the common folk and
indulging in pederasty and bestiality. Ruthlessness and moral anarchy ensued, as society became perverted and the land was filled with
violence. "All flesh had perverted its ways on earth" (Gen. 6:12). The
flood was inevitable. The very earth upon which these men trod
called out for cleansing. Just think about the September 11 tragedy at
the World Trade Center. It was undertaken by a group of men who
were promised seventy virgins apiece in Paradise if they martyred
themselves for their faith. So there again, unbridled sexual longing
leads to tragedy and murder.

When Abraham, who lived a life in a different manner from that
of his contemporaries, came along, he offered a new vision of man's
purpose and destiny. Not wallowing in pleasure or the arrogance of
power, but clinging to God, to find Him, to please Him, and to love
all His creatures—these were man's primary purpose. Abraham introduced the concept of holiness into the world. As God is holy, so
should we be holy, even if this effort involves discipline, withdrawal,
and sacrifice, even if it circumscribes one's range of permissible behavior. A person is said to be saintly or holy if through his or her
deeds the person has attained a close proximity with the Creator. But
to achieve this lofty state involves placing God first, even at the expense of our personal pleasures. As the Psalmist chanted, "I have always placed the Lord before me." Likewise, a place or thing is holy
by virtue of the Deity's open association with and revealed attachment to the object or place in question. Holiness is attained only
when man opens his heart and mind to the possibility of God resid-
ing within.

In Judaism, the meaning of holiness is separateness. When something is treated in a distinct and separate fashion, it is holy by virtue
of its being different. If no one remembers your birthday, or if a couple treats their anniversary like any other day, it can hardly be said
to have been special. God is holy because he is aloof, distinct, and removed from the realm of man. A man becomes holy when he refuses
to be carried away with social trends that run contrary to the divine

will. He is holy because he is aloof, distinct, and removed from the realm of the animal. There are many ways to summarize the essence of Judaism and the religious responsibilities incumbent upon man. But perhaps none is as powerful as this: Man is not an animal, and the purpose of religion is to teach man how to express the uniqueness of his own humanity. Religion is the press that releases the oil from the olive, the clamp that squeezes the wine from the grape. Religion is designed to train man to raise his activities above that of the beast and to realize the full potential of his human heart. When human beings behave like animals, they forfeit the *tzelem elokim*, the "divine image," which is imprinted on the visage of every man and woman.

Circumcision, therefore, is holy because it makes the Jew distinct. It consecrates his procreative capacity to a higher purpose, so that he is not ruled by his passions, but uses his passions to bring pleasure to his spouse. Whereas others may engage in sex for sensual gratification only and because of hormonal compulsion, the Jew engages in intimate human contact in order to become one flesh with his marriage partner and to draw fragments of the divine being into an earthly body. By bringing discipline to the realm of the animal within us, man becomes sanctified. In this sense, circumcision, more than any other commandment, brings holiness to man. It is specifically in the impulse that most craves selfish satisfaction that man is granted the opportunity to consecrate the divine name. It is specifically in the realm of sex, where men especially are impatient, that they must put the needs of their wives before them and focus on their wives' pleasure before their own.

There Is No One Great Truth

In what other ways are Jews and Judaism distinguished from other peoples and faiths? I have had many public debates with secular humanists and confirmed atheists. At each occasion a similar argument against religion has been proposed. If religion is true, then why are there so many different ones? How could so many religions claim to be the absolute truth and still be right? Especially when they all seem so contradictory?

Judaism is unique among the world's religions in that it claims no copyright on, or exclusivity to, truth. It does not denounce other faiths as misguided or heretical. It is adamant that there are many paths to the one God. Judaism is *a* path, not *the* path. There is no *one* way. There is no one great truth, but rather a series of truths possessed by each nation that, when brought together, creates *the* truth. And this is what makes every nation indispensable. Jews, Christians, and Muslims could learn much from one another if they would only just stop and listen. As long as any religion leads to humility and worship of the one God, to passionate religious rituals and compassion and loving-kindness, then it has created a legitimate path to the source of the universe.

how Jews interpret/see other religions?

Take the sexes as an example. The world is possessed of masculine and feminine virtues. But it would be a mistake for either gender to assume its superiority over the other because of its inherent gifts. On the contrary, femininity is truth for a woman and best accords with her personality, psychology, and unique spiritual energy. Masculinity is truth for a man, and if a man were to lead a completely feminine life, it would not accord with his deepest nature. By itself, neither of these truths is capable of generating life, and each is incomplete without the other. Similarly, for a man to want to have a baby or for a woman to want to grow a beard is a case of mistaken potential and misguided identity. What is needed is for each gender to accept its individual identity amid a commitment toward mutually enriching the other through shared experience and goals.

The same is true of Judaism. Judaism does not constitute ultimate truth. Rather, it constitutes ultimate truth *for the Jew.* Judaism is a science of living by which the Jew—with his distinct spiritual constitution—can actualize his Godly potential to the fullest. The Jewish people were given a special mission in this world, to educate and teach the other nations of the world to love God, pursue justice, and spread compassion on earth. Judaism accomplishes these goals through an emphasis on law as the cornerstone of liv-

SHMULEY BOTEACH

ing. That is not to say that Judaism has nothing to learn from Christian love or Muslim passion. On the contrary, the fact that each of the great monotheistic faiths shines in one important category shows how much they can enrich one another. The same is not true, however—and here I apologize if I sound intolerant—of those religions that are polytheistic in nature. There is one, true God. Any religion whose destination is not God is a false doctrine that cannot enrich the monotheistic believer. This is not to say that there is not much good in these religions. Rather, it just means that their *fundamental* premise is false. Religions that lead to no God or to many gods steer man away from the truth and back into darkness.

Because there are many paths to the one God, Judaism is not a proselytizing religion. Jews are not closer to God than Gentiles, and no man or woman achieves instant salvation by becoming Jewish. Rather, God judges each man or woman according to the righteousness of his or her actions. It is righteousness that brings redemption, not the title of one's faith. Nine hundred years ago, Maimonides wrote that non-Jews who live by the seven Noahide commandments would inherit the same place in heaven as a Jew.

If Jews have a holy destiny as a nation, what does Judaism say about the relevance of other nations' aspirations? Is there any genius for religiosity in non-Jewish nations or individuals? Can they commune with God, and furthermore, do they transmit any genuine messages from God?

Jews believe that the righteous nations of the world will inherit everlasting life. We have already noted (chapter 14) that the Rabbis saw God's love as available to all people, not only to Jews: "The righteous of all nations have a share in the World to Come" (*Tosefta Sanhedrin* 13). An even stronger statement, which we quoted above, is found in Midrashic literature: "I call heaven and earth as witnesses: Any individual, whether Gentile or Jew, man or woman, servant or maid, can bring the Divine Presence upon him- or herself in accordance with his deeds" (*Tana Devei Eliahu Rabba* 9).

The Jewish attitude toward non-Jews is most clearly expressed in the words of King Solomon: "When a stranger, who is not of Your people Israel, but comes from a distant land . . . turns in prayer toward this Temple, then listen to his prayers" (1 Kings 8:41–43). Indeed, King David proclaims beautifully in the Book of Psalms, "God is good to all, and his love extends over all His works" (Ps. 145:9). No distinction is made between Jew and Gentile. Indeed, two thousand years ago the ancient Rabbis legislated that a Jew is as obligated to assist a needy Gentile as a Jew: "We are obliged to feed the Gentile poor in exactly the same manner as we feed the Jewish poor (Talmud Bavli, *Gittin,* 61a).

The Rabbis of the Talmud also taught: "Do not despise any man" (*Ethics of the Fathers,* chap. 4). Hence, racism and the hatred of other tolerant faiths is an unforgivable sin in Judaism. Likewise the Rabbis declared, "Even a Gentile who studies God's law is equal to a High Priest" (*Bava Kamah* 38a). These Rabbis saw God's salvation freely available to all men and women. Contrast this with this proclamation in the name of Jesus, "He who does not abide in me is thrown away like a withered branch. Such withered branches are gathered together, cast into the fire and burned" (John 15:6). This statement was later used by the Catholic church to justify its practice of burning nonbelievers at the stake.

Tolerance is an important lesson that Judaism can teach all world religions. Despite Judaism's being the world's oldest monotheistic faith, the Jews have never insisted that their beliefs are superior to others. Nor have the Jews ever persecuted another nation for not adopting Judaism. Coercion is as foreign to Judaism as Christmas. A close friend of mine adopted a twelve-year-old Christian girl whose parents had been killed in a car crash. Although the girl lived in a devoutly religious Jewish home, her foster parents insisted that she be raised a Christian, which is what her parents would have wanted. The girl went on to marry a vicar and is a devout Christian to this day, although always being treated as an equal member of her Orthodox Jewish family.

Anti-Semitism

Jewish tolerance toward other monotheistic religions has unfortunately not been reciprocated by the nations of the world toward the
Jewish people. In one of those supreme ironies of history, the nation
whose raison d'être was to teach the world about God, love, ethics,
and values became most known for having been mankind's eternal
victims of hatred, persecution, rejection, and wholesale slaughter.
Indeed, anti-Semitism remains today a great mystery, reappearing
throughout the ages amid diverse social conditions, both in countries with and in countries without Jews. Many think that anti-Semitism is confined to the lower, less literate classes. But some of the
world's most respected thinkers have been rabid anti-Semites. Even
supposed moralists, like Voltaire, father of the Enlightenment, could
not overcome their Jew hatred. Voltaire hated the Jews with an intensity that is difficult to comprehend. He called Jews "the most
abominable people in the world" and assessed them in the following
way: "In short, they are a totally ignorant nation who, for many
years, have combined contemptible miserliness and the most revolt-
ing superstition with a violent hatred of all those nations that have
tolerated them." Voltaire even accused Jews of engaging in ritual
murder: "Their priests have always sacrificed human victims with
their sacred hands."

Jews have also, of course, been hated by other Jews, like Karl
Marx, a lifelong and rabid anti-Semite who often resorted to Nazi-
like invective against the Jews: "What is the secular cult of the Jew? Haggling. What is his secular god? Money. Well then! Emancipation
from haggling and money, from practical, real Judaism would be the
self-emancipation of our time."

Traditional academic and social anthropological explanations as
to the origin of anti-Semitism—such as the ghost theory, that nobody likes a ghost of a nation that should have died out when it was
expelled from its land, or that the Jews have been used as scapegoats
by totalitarian rulers—seem weak and cannot account for the linger-
ing hatred of Jews in every corner of the earth and among people of

all social and religious persuasions, for thousands of years. As David
Lloyd George, the British statesman and prime minister, wrote in his
1938 article "What Has the Jew Done?":

> Of all the bigotries that savage the human temper there is none so stu-
> pid as anti-Semitism. In the sight of these fanatics, the Jews can do
> nothing right. If they are rich, they are birds of prey. If they are poor,
> they are vermin. If they are in favour of war, that is because they want
> to exploit the bloody feuds of Gentiles to their own profit. It they are
> anxious for peace, they are either instinctive cowards or traitors. If
> they give generously—and there are no more liberal givers than the
> Jews—they are doing it for some selfish purpose of their own. If they
> don't give, then what would one expect of a Jew?

How can we possibly explain this kind of irrational hatred?

The Talmud itself provides the deeper reason for anti-Semitism.
Prior to the election of the Jews at Mount Sinai as the world's moral
standard-bearers, nations behaved in any fashion they saw fit. God
and his laws were unknown. Tyrants ruled, and the inhabitants of
the world were exploited by the strong and the wealthy. But with the
advent of the Jewish nation and its message of an invisible God who
watched and scrutinized the actions of all men, and who gave rec-
ompense according to man's actions, the party was suddenly over.
No longer could the strong oppress the weak without fear of divine
retribution and those of noble birth claim the right to preside over
those of lesser social standing. With the revolution in social ethics
heralded by the Jews, it makes sense that they would immediately
become the most hated nation in the world. The wrath of those who
had most benefited from the law of the jungle would be poured on
the divine messengers who sought to instill justice in the world.

Asked how anti-Semitism could be curbed, German philosopher
Johann Fichte wrote in 1793, "I see no other way of doing this except to cut off all their heads one night and substitute other heads
without a single Jewish thought in them. How shall we defend ourselves against them?"

The More Wicked the Man,
the More He Hates the Jews

Among those who have hated the Jewish nation were the world's great villains: Hitler, Stalin, Chmielnicki, Torquemada, and Hadrian. Each of these ogres had to first uproot the legacy of the Jews in order to perpetrate his evil. The unequivocal voice of Sinai condemned their evil work with the authority of a divine calling. In this sense, the Jew, with his message of the equality of all mankind, a loving and personal God, a God of justice who avenges the blood of innocents, has always been the eternal enemy and the scourge of tyrants and bullies.

Hitler treated the war effort against the Allies as secondary to the war against the Jews. As noted earlier, even while his soldiers were languishing on the Eastern and Western Fronts, bereft of food, fuel, and ammunition, the railroads continued to ferry Jews to the crematoria of Auschwitz rather than resupplying German troops. Holocaust historian Lucy Dawidowicz writes in *The War Against the Jews:* "Serious people, responsible people, thought that Hitler's notions about the Jews were, at best, merely political bait for disgruntled masses, no more than ideological window dressing to cloak a naked drive for power. Yet precisely the reverse was true. Racial imperialism and the fanatic plan to destroy the Jews were the dominant passions behind the drive for power."

The reason for this priority given to slaughter of the Jews is straightforward. The Allies represented a temporal problem for Hitler. Today they were his enemies, but tomorrow they might sue for peace and become his allies, as was the case at first with the Soviet Union. Hitler's real adversaries were not Churchill and Roosevelt, but Moses and Isaiah. The Jews represented Hitler's eternal nemesis, and with them there could only be a struggle to the death. Hitler sought not only to win the war but also to impose a completely new world order. He sought the complete overturning of the Judeo-Christian ethic. Hitler wanted a world in which race theory supplanted the idea of all man having been created in the image of God. He wished to make the world a place where theft, murder, and the evolutionary doctrine of the survival of the fittest replaced the Godly ideals of the sanctity of life and the brotherhood of all mankind. Hitler's first plan, therefore, was to destroy the people who were witnesses to God in history. If the messengers of good and evil could be removed from the earth, then their message would atrophy, and the countries fighting Hitler might see the good sense of compromise and cease-fire.

Even today, we see that evolutionary ethicists have declared war on Judeo-Christian values. These "ethicists" promote the opposite of the Bible's message. They believe, not in an ethic of goodness, but in an ethic of survival of the fittest, and that the strong have earned the right to survive at the expense of the weak. Humanity and other species are moved forward by the removal of the genetically inferior. Anti-Semitism is far more than simply a continuing war against the Jews. Rather, it is a war against God and His eternal, revealed values. But since man cannot fight God, he instead fights His messengers.

In contrast, regimes based on justice and egalitarian virtues have always treated their Jewish citizens with compassion and benevolence. The Jews, far from posing a threat to the regime, help strengthen it by leading lives that accord with the state's democratic values.

Reversing Anti-Semitism

The greatest paradox of anti-Semitism is that it can only be eradicated when the Jews fully live up to their ancient calling and become a light unto the nations. Rabbi Abraham Joshua Heschel, one of the twentieth century's foremost Jewish thinkers, wrote, "The Jews are a messenger who forgot his message." Only when the Jews impart ethical monotheism to the world, teaching the nations values and ethics—repugnance of violence and brotherhood of all mankind—will the earth be rid of senseless, irrational hatred. Although the Jews may be despised by some for promulgating this message of morality and ethics, they will be appreciated by many more nations for imparting these eternal values. This is probably the strongest argument against Jewish insularity. Jewish aloofness is bound to provoke hostility. The Jews must live among the nations of the world and be fully integrated into the family of nations, while always retaining their unique heritage and never becoming assimilated. This is a daunting task.

When I was a young boy, I was a poor student and the ringleader of our class's troublemakers. We all used to bully the class genius, Marc. We hated him because he thought he was better than us. And he was. But rather than trying to be like him, it was easier just to ridicule him and make him regret the challenge he posed.

One day, he made an effort to befriend me. There was a big exam, and I was told by the teacher in front of the whole class that if I failed I would have to repeat the school year. As I sat cramming for an exam that I was almost certain to flunk, Marc called my house and asked if he could come over and study with me. He said that he also needed to prepare for the exam, so why not do it together? I passed that exam and became his best friend and constant defender.

The Jewish nation must likewise join together with the nations of the world to teach and impart goodness, but not in a condescending manner. We will then engender the love and appreciation of a world that is crying out for light and guidance.

22

Judaism and Christianity

Science has done more for the development of western civilization in one hundred years than Christianity did in eighteen hundred years.

—JOHN BURROUGHS

He who begins by loving Christianity better than truth will proceed by loving his own sect or church better than Christianity, and end in loving himself better than all.

—SAMUEL TAYLOR COLERIDGE

The Christian cannot be satisfied so long as any human activity is either opposed to Christianity or out of connection with Christianity. Christianity must pervade not merely all nations but also all of human thought.

—J. GRESHAM MACHEN

CENTRAL TO ANY DISCUSSION OF JUDAISM and world religion is a consideration of Judaism's relationship with Christianity. Judaism gave rise to Christianity, yet has had a tortured and sometimes tragic relationship with its much larger daughter religion. That relationship has not been helped by repeated Christian efforts to proselytize and convert Jews. Indeed, to some it seems that Christians are obsessed with that goal. To be sure, Judaism's relationship with Christianity today is far healthier than it was in the past. One might say that Judaism and Christianity are now great and effective partners in attempting to promote and safeguard religious convictions amid a torrential secular onslaught. Indeed, some of the prime builders of the L'Chaim Society at Oxford over the eleven years I ran it there were highly dedicated Christian students who shared L'Chaim's passion for bringing spiritual values to an ancient and increasingly secular university. They remain my loving and devoted friends until this very day. There is much that unites the two great world religions, among which are the belief in one God, the pursuit of righteousness and social welfare, and, of course, the belief in the Messiah and directional history. Nevertheless, their sharp differences must be understood as well.

Why Jews Are
Uncomfortable with Christianity

For the Jews, respect for another faith, especially Christianity, is not confined to modern society or enlightened liberalism. Maimonides, a man who suffered all his life from religious persecution at the hands of both Muslims and Christians, wrote almost a millennium ago that Christianity had significantly assisted in "perfecting the world and facilitating the religious worship of God on the part of the earth's inhabitants." Christianity, he argued, had filled the world with the concept of a messianic redemption and with God's laws, and "these ideas have now become widespread and have been broadcast to the farthest isles, even amongst pagan peoples, so that they now debate and discuss Godly ideas and the words of the Bible." The Jews have always credited Christianity with familiarizing the world with the central concepts of the Bible and the belief in God. Indeed, there can be no doubt that Christianity has had far greater success in bringing the knowledge of God to the distant corners of the globe than Judaism.

viding line separating God and man is immutable and eternal, and for us there can be no greater heresy than for a man to declare himself to be, or ever be revered as, a deity. This is not to say that Jews do not have a profound respect for Christian belief. But it does serve to explain the uncompromising nature of the Jewish rejection of Jesus.

Another reason for the Jewish feeling of discomfort with the deity of Jesus lies in Judaism's pride in its rationalist tradition. Tertullian, the early Church Father, in a famous paradox proclaimed *"Credo quia impossible"* (I believe because it is impossible)—that because certain fundamental Christian beliefs, such as the son of God dying on a cross and then being resurrected, were absurd and impossible (how could the infinite die?), they necessitated belief as opposed to rational affirmation. To be sure, there are many tenets of the Jewish faith that we do not completely understand, such as the obligation to have a mezuzah (scroll of parchment from the Torah) affixed to our doorposts, or the need for the daily donning of tefillin (leather boxes with scrolls of the Torah inside). Nevertheless, whereas the ultimate reason for these commandments may *transcend* logic, they do not *contradict* logic. There is nothing inherently irrational about not lighting fire on the Sabbath. But the belief that a man who is born and who dies is the Eternal incarnate is for the Jew a supreme contradiction to rational thinking. And though God may transcend logic, He is not *il*logical.

Ten Essential Differences

There are several forms of Christianity, but the differences between classical Judaism and classical Christianity may be summarized in the following ten points.

1. Judaism Conceives of God as an Absolute Unity. In Judaism, there are no internal distinctions within the deity. Indeed, the very first portion of Scripture studied by Jewish children when they first learn to read Hebrew is the Shema, the quintessential statement of Jewish faith, which reads: "Hear O Israel, the Lord is our God, the Lord is One" (Deut. 6:4). The Kabbalists speak of God's essence as indivisible. Although God has chosen to reveal Himself in many different ways throughout history—as a warrior in Egypt, as a lawgiver at Sinai, as a stern parent during the deterioration of the First Temple period, and as a comforter after its destruction—these are all modes of expression, and never a change in essence. Furthermore, there is no real existence outside that of God. The universe is not a real, but a dependent, entity, relying entirely on God for its continuity. Furthermore, it is sustained at all times through God's providence and would cease to exist if God were to remove that providence for even a moment.

There is a Hassidic story about a teacher who asked a clever child what God would have to do if He wished to destroy the world. The child responded that He would immolate the world with fire. "What would become of the ashes?" inquired the teacher. "God would wash them away with water." "And what would He then do with the water?" "He would evaporate it with a giant flame." "And what would he do with the fire?" "He would send a wind to blow it out." "And what would he do with the wind?" asked the teacher. And here the child was stumped. The teacher looked into the child's eyes and responded, "If God wished to destroy the world, He would simply *stop creating it.*" The unity of God, both with Himself and with His creation, is absolute, and the world exists by God's grace only through a constant act of re-creation.

Christianity, however, maintains a divine Trinity of three Persons, the Father, the Son, and the Holy Spirit, which together form the *mysterium tremendum* (overwhelming mystery) of Christian beliefs. And though each of the three is God, it was the Father who generated the Son, and the Father and Son together who, according to Western Christianity, caused the procession, or emanation, of the Holy Spirit. Christianity thus affirms a belief in a tripartite God, which to Judaism is illogical and unacceptable.

2. For Jews, the Belief That God Can Be Human Is the Ultimate Heresy. Judaism operates firmly on the belief that there is a fundamental order in creation, and that the dichotomy between God and man is infinitely greater than even the division between man and beast. God is incorporeal. He may be experienced in the spirit, but can never be visible in human form or apprehended by the human senses. The belief that God could have been born of a human womb, or could once have walked the earth, is so foreign to Judaism that it is rejected even by the most assimilated Jews. Judaism brings many scriptural proofs to substantiate this cardinal tenet of its faith. "He who is the Glory of Israel does not lie or change his mind; for He is not a man, that he should change his mind" (1 Sam. 15:29). "You saw no form of any kind the day the Lord spoke to you at Horeb out of the fire. Therefore watch yourselves very carefully, so that you do not become corrupt and make for yourselves an idol, an image of any shape, whether formed like a man or a woman" (Deut. 4:15–16).

Christianity, however, sees in Jesus the incarnation and embodiment of the Second Person of the Trinity, the Son. Images and icons—the image of the crucifix foremost among them—are absolutely central to Catholicism and figure prominently in Protestantism as well. The Jew (as well as the Muslim) is confused by homage and worship offered to an image, dismissing it as an unlawful representation of God. Although Judaism wholeheartedly accepts that visual and concrete images assist religious man in his attempt to apprehend an otherwise abstract God—indeed the Rabbis explain that many of the mitzvot, such as tefillin and *tzitzit,* serve this purpose by offering man a concrete area of focus—God Himself is utterly off limits in such representations. From the outset Judaism aimed to destroy the idols and false Gods that ancient man was wont to worship. Therefore, no visual images can ever be employed in prayer and religious devotions.

3. Jews Do Not Believe in Original Sin and the Fall of Man, a Cornerstone of Christian Faith. According to Christianity, all mankind is damned because of Adam's sin and therefore any human effort at self-redemption through righteous action is an exercise in futility. The Torah cannot save man, since its many commandments make it

too difficult to keep. The only thing that can prevent man's utter
damnation in Hell is faith in Christ. After Adam and Eve transgressed God's commandment and partook of the tree of knowledge,
they were damned eternally and died a spiritual death. No good
works could ever compensate for their iniquity. God therefore sent
his son to die on a cross as the only cure for man's sinful nature. The
suffering of Jesus, coupled with the faith of the believer, is the only
road to personal salvation.

Judaism does not promote the idea that people are born either meritorious or sinful. Rather, the individual is born innocent, with predis-
positions toward both good and evil, compassion and selfishness,
enlightenment and self-destruction. Furthermore, in Judaism there is
the idea that man is created in the "image of God." Man therefore
does not have to go very far to discover the Divine, both within himself and in others. There is always the opportunity to awaken the
Divine within one's person by obeying God's commandments. Ultimately, Judaism judges people by their actions and believes that people have the ability to achieve salvation by virtue of their good deeds,
in accordance with God's law rather than their faith.

Christianity holds that the sinful nature of humanity, caused by the
original sin of Adam, prevents salvation without the intermediacy of
the sacrifice of the divine-human Messiah. It is arrogance on the part
of man to believe that by virtue of acts alone, he can lift himself out
of the swamp of human sinfulness. But Judaism compares faith that is
not allied to action to a ghost, or disembodied spirit, that has far
greater potential for harm than good. Witness abuses of faith such as
the Spanish Inquisition and the Christian Crusades, in which the zeal
for the true faith was not tempered with an emphasis on good deeds
and righteous action. Countless horrors were carried out against those
who refused to accept Jesus as their savior. Judaism insists that the true
measure of faith is to be found specifically in how it shapes and molds
the behavior of the believer. The Talmud demonstrates the inadequacies of faith with the story of a thief who tunnels under a house to rob
its inhabitants, yet prays to God that he not be caught. Faith alone is

insufficient. It is specifically the employment of faith to lead a right-eous life that is desirable.

The Torah does speak of Adam's sin. But it teaches that man can rise above it. Righteousness may be challenging, but it was for this reason that God gave humankind the Torah. It is absurd to think that God would give a Torah that is impossible or too difficult to fol-low. In no place does Judaism teach that one can be saved from damnation by faith alone. Any true belief in God must lead a person to follow His commandments also.

These differences between Christianity and Judaism with respect to their emphases on faith and action find philosophical underpinnings in the two religions' approach to the question of mind/matter dual-ism. Christianity embraced the ancient Zoroastrian and Greek posi-tion of dualism, separating the world into heaven and earth, mind and matter, soul and body, and, ultimately, good and evil, with the former always taking precedence over the latter. Thus, the ethereal realm of faith and cerebral domain of theology are the natural superi-ors to the tangible realm of action and the concrete domain of law.

Judaism, however, chooses as its starting point the first verse of the Bible: "In the beginning the Lord created the heaven and the earth." Both heaven and earth are creations of God, and one is not superior to the other. God inhabits both equally. Judaism utterly re-jects any belief in dualism, offering instead a strict insistence on monism, according to which everything emanates from one source, the indivisible Creator. There is no devil in Judaism. There is an all-encompassing unity within creation with God as its locus. There-fore, action is as much a way of serving God as prayer and faith. Action is in fact superior to the latter because it makes Godly tenets a tangible reality and demonstrates His living presence within our world.

4. In Judaism, the Messiah Has a Political and Physical Role, Not a Spir-itual One. The Jewish Messiah is to be a human descendant of David who restores the monarchy, establishes Jewish political autonomy, rebuilds the Temple, and gathers in the Jewish exiles from the Diaspora. The Jewish Messiah is a mortal man, endowed with great wisdom, holiness, and charismatic leadership skills. His primary task is to reestablish Jewish temporal sovereignty and an era of peace and brotherhood on earth. The Messiah will bring about the ingathering of Jewish exiles and rebuild the destroyed Temple after which there will be the resurrection of the dead.

For Christians, the task of the Messiah is entirely spiritual, rather than physical, redemption and is primarily geared at humanity's redemption from the original sin of Adam. And the Messiah has already come.

To the Jews, the ultimate test of whether the Messiah has come, and indeed whether someone is the Messiah, is the fulfillment of the messianic prophecies.

5. *To Christians, Jesus was the Messiah, or Christ, Predicted by the Prophets of the Bible and Awaited by the Jews.*   To Jews, Jesus could not have been the Messiah, because the prophets predicted a world of peace and love and an end to war and conflict after the Messiah's coming, which did not come to pass. Furthermore, talk of the Messiah's being the son of God is utterly heretical to Jews. In no place do the prophets say that he will be anything but a remarkable leader and teacher who will turn humanity's hearts back to their Father in heaven.

6. *Jews Believe the Covenant Between God and the People of Israel Embodied in the Hebrew Scriptures to Be Eternally Valid.*   In many places the Bible clearly states that God's covenant with the Jewish people will be forever. The prophets speak of God's "eternal love for Israel" (1 Kings 10:9). Similarly, God made an eternal pact with Abraham and his descendants: "I will establish my covenant as an everlasting covenant between me and you and your descendants after you for the generations to come, to be your God and the God of your descendants after you. The whole land of Canaan, where you are now an alien, I will give as an everlasting possession to you and your de-

scendants after you; and I will be their God" (Gen. 17:7–8). Again, in the Prophets: "Is not my house right with God? Has he not made with me an everlasting covenant, arranged and secured in every part? Will he not bring to fruition my salvation and grant me my every desire?" (2 Sam. 23:5). And in the Writings, "He confirmed it to Jacob as a decree, to Israel as an everlasting covenant" (1 Chron. 16:17).

Christians, however, believe that the Torah was superseded by the teachings of Jesus in the New Testament. Therefore, although the authenticity of the Hebrew Bible is accepted and still studied by Christians, it is classified as the "Old" Testament, as opposed to the "New" Testament, which incorporates the Gospels, describing Jesus' life and works, the letters of Saint Paul elucidating Christian principles, as well as the apocalyptic Book of Revelation. Since Christianity dismissed the supremacy of the Old Testament, it also abrogated the observance of Old Testament law and the law of Moses.

To the Jews, the laws of the Torah are as binding today as they were in Temple times. The covenant that God established with the Jews in the Torah entailed the observance of the commandments, as understood through Talmudic legislation, as the ultimate means by which man would connect with God. The Torah's jurisdiction is eternal and can never be cancelled. The Jews remain God's chosen nation to spread ethical monotheism to the other nations of the world for all eternity.

For a Christian, there has been only one law since Christ came, and that is love. One must follow the example of Christ's sacrifice and patiently hope that God will be gracious in return: "Therefore no one will be declared righteous in his sight by observing the law; rather, through the law we become conscious of sin. But now a righteousness from God, apart from law, has been made known, to which the Law and the Prophets testify. This righteousness from God comes through faith in Jesus Christ to all who believe. There is no difference, for all have sinned and fall short of the glory of God, and are justified freely by his grace through the redemption that came by Christ Jesus" (Rom. 3:20–24). The new covenant, recorded in the New Testament and announced by the mission of the divine-human person of Jesus, states that salvation can be achieved only through belief in Jesus as the Messiah, not through observance of the commandments. Christianity therefore speaks of Christians as the new Israel. The Jews were rejected when they refused to accept Jesus as God's son. According to Christianity, the name *Israel* is today carried only by those who accept Jesus as the Messiah. Everyone else is damned to Hell.

7. Christianity Is Oriented Toward the Next World, Judaism Toward This World. Christianity posits that the purpose of man is to achieve the salvation of his soul and to attain everlasting life in Paradise. Monasticism, asceticism, and celibacy have therefore always been central to Christianity, since any attachment to this world impedes a closer relationship with heaven. Man is bidden to remove himself from day-to-day involvement with the world and concentrate instead on building heaven on earth. Indulgence of the flesh is sinful, and the needs of the soul must always take precedence over those of the body.

Judaism is oriented toward this world and steadfastly promotes the idea that man's purpose is to perfect the world and bring Godliness into an otherwise un-Godly planet. Celibacy is a sin in Judaism; marriage its ultimate happiness. The purpose of Jewish life is the consecration of physical existence by bringing God down into our world and making Him an active partner in our lives. Jewish festivals are celebrated through merriment, food, and drink. Joy is an essential precondition to closeness with God. In Judaism the purpose of man is to uncover and make manifest for all to see the underlying spiritual character of the world.

8. In Contrast to Judaism, Christianity Advocates an Intermediary Between God and Man. Jesus, in bringing about the salvation of souls, is the ultimate intermediary between God and man, but priests too serve as middlemen. Communion must be performed by a priest, and confession can only come about through the agency of the clergy.

In Judaism, however, there is no religious function that a Rabbi performs that an ordinary Jew cannot perform. A Rabbi is a position of scholarship and moral instruction rather than any particular divine agency. The idea of a man confessing his sins to a human is anathema in Judaism and breaches all Jewish laws of modesty and privacy. It is proper for man to confess his sins to God alone. The role of the Messiah is not to serve as intermediary for the people, bringing about their salvation, but rather as the one who uplifts the people and reminds them of their innate ability to bring about their own redemption through Godly acts. The Messiah teaches man to cultivate the inherent Godliness from within. His role is one of universal inspiration rather than one of spiritual salvation.

9. Historically, Jews Have Been the Objects of Christian Missionary Activities. Christianity is a supremely proselytizing faith. Since Christianity affirms that none shall come unto the Father except through the Son, it takes the view that there is only one road to truth, one path to salvation.

Judaism, however, is a supremely universalist religion, teaching that there are several paths to the one, true God. A non-Jew does not enhance his existence by becoming Jewish, and indeed a righteous Gentile who leads a Godly and moral life will inherit the same place in the world-to-come as a Jew. Indeed, the only kind of proselytizing that Judaism has pursued throughout history is to convert the world to ethical monotheism, which involves a belief in God coupled with a belief in goodness. Jews actively discourage non-Jews from conversion because of the Jewish belief that one is not closer to God as a Jew than as a righteous Gentile.

10. Judaism Is Based on God's Revelation to and Covenant with the People. Judaism is predicated on the belief of a collective divine revelation at the foot of Mount Sinai to the entire assembled House of Israel. God revealed Himself and gave the Torah to every member of the Jewish nation in a single display of divine might and power 3,300 years ago at Mount Sinai. Since the Sinaitic covenant was binding upon all Jews and their descendants, it was important for all the people to be present.

Christianity, in contrast, is predicated on the teachings of a single man/deity as revealed to the apostles.

Contrary to popular belief, Judaism repudiates martyrdom. The purpose of the Jew is to exert every effort toward making this earth a worthy dwelling for the King of Kings by exposing its inner and latent spiritual character. This is a task for the living, not for the dead. Moreover, because of its "this-world orientation," Judaism would never contend that God is more easily found in the heavens than on earth. Seeking death, therefore, so that one might bask under the heavenly divine throne, is a misguided effort. Although it is true that Jews are the most martyred people of all time, the Jew is given specific instruction to violate all but three tenets of his faith—idolatry, sexual immorality, and murder—rather than die for his beliefs. To be sure, those who have been martyred for their faith are accorded a special place in the religion and are said to directly enter the gates of Eden. But this is a de facto acceptance after the martyrdom has occurred. Judaism has no tradition of saints who exalted their position through their deaths. All the giants of Jewish history attained their lofty status through their example and teachings while alive. With very few exceptions, Judaism does not triumph the example of its martyrs. Martyrdom is something to be endured if necessary, not something to be sought.

In its attitude to martyrdom, Judaism is radically different from religions like early Christianity and especially Islam, which encourage their followers to seek martyrdom. From Jesus on to many of the great saints, martyrdom is glorified in Christianity, and its very symbol is the cross of the Son of God martyred for his beliefs.

Judaism is profoundly a religion of life. L'Chaim, "To life," is the quintessential Jewish toast. Not even good life, or happy life, but just life—because life itself is an unconditional blessing. Churches traditionally are ringed with cemeteries. Similarly, the treasures of the great European cathedrals consist of relics of the saints—their fingers, hands, and vials of blood. One great medieval cathedral that I visited even contains the head of Saint Catherine of Siena, displayed for all visitors to see. But for a Jew, the opposite is the case. No cemetery is allowed anywhere near the synagogue. Judaism celebrates life to the full and its greatest promise, by the ancient prophets, is that one day all death shall be defeated: "And he will destroy on this mountain the shroud that is cast over all peoples, the sheet that is spread over all nations; he will swallow up death forever" (Isa. 25:7).

PART FIVE

The Future of Judaism

23

The Way Forward and
the Holocaust

The danger is that if nothing but the Holocaust exists in Jewish life, we'll become a morbid people, a sick people. We shouldn't do that. There is a statute of limitations on morbidity. . . . But without it, Jewish life would also be false. How can one lead a Jewish life today and not learn something about it?

—ELIE WIESEL,
New York Times, March 5, 1997

We who lived in concentration camps can remember the men who walked through the huts comforting others, giving away their last piece of bread. They may have been few in number, but they offer sufficient proof that everything can be taken from a man but one thing: the last of the human freedoms—to choose one's attitude in any given set of circumstances, to choose one's own way.

—VICTOR FRANKL,
Man's Search for Meaning

WHERE DO WE GO FROM HERE? What is the way forward for the Jewish people, and what does the future hold? Less than three out of every thousand people in the world are Jewish, and out of that number only about half are in some way observant. Jews continue to be

417

a tiny dot immersed within a huge majority of Christians, Muslims, Hindus, Buddhists, and atheists. We have survived this long, but how much longer?

The most ancient and influential of all nations is today at a crossroads. The Jews have mastered every test. We survived the destruction of both of our Temples and the exiles imposed upon us first by the Babylonians and subsequently by the Romans. We survived nearly two thousand years of Christian anti-Judaism and almost three hundred years of racial anti-Semitism. We survived the slaughters of the crusaders and the thousands of pogroms that followed. We survived the Spanish Inquisition and countless other religious persecutions for our refusal to adopt a faith foreign to the covenant of Abraham and the law of Moses. We survived the Chmielnicki and Cossack pogroms, which wiped away one-third our number in the years 1648–1649, and the Holocaust, which killed one of every three Jews in the world. Through every adversity the Jews not only survived, but emerged triumphant. Those who survived the Nazi German atrocities did not merely sit and mourn the loss of parents, wives, and children. Rather, they built the flourishing State of Israel which has miraculously survived five decades of ferocious Arab aggression and war.

After all this, it is now, paradoxically, in the modern world, where Jews are accepted as equals, that the Jews seem in danger of annihilation. Although the Jews survived persecution and hatred, the question today is whether they can survive acceptance and success. Everywhere we turn, rampant assimilation and intermarriage seem to engulf the Jewish people. Apathy and boredom among the young have made the synagogues empty and the Friday night nightclubs full. Secular culture seems to entice young Jews to abandon, or never explore, their 3,500-year-old heritage.

To be sure, there are many points of light. More Jewish day schools and yeshivas than ever before are opening around the globe, and kosher restaurants and Jewish bookstores now dot the Western landscape in numbers that fifty years ago would have been unthinkable. In the State of Israel there is a strong religious revival that has created a mass movement of hundreds of thousands who are returning to the faith. In the Diaspora there are highly successful outreach organizations, with Chabad-Lubavitch foremost among them, that have brought huge numbers back to Judaism. Nevertheless, these beacons flicker in the darkness of the continued abandonment of Judaism by millions of Jews the world over. Even with a Jewish renaissance taking shape, there can be no question that we are losing the numbers war. How can this be reversed? Can the Jewish people surmount the trial of acceptance and success in the same way that they have always overcome the trial by fire and suffering? Or are we destined to witness the gradual demise of the world's most ancient people?

Identifying Through Fear

For half a century now, the Jewish people have largely identified through negative compulsion. Rabbis and Jewish lay leaders have felt that one of their roles is to act as scaremongers, inducing commitment among the world's Jews by painting a picture of their imminent demise. In so doing, they have inculcated a Jewish identity focused on the Holocaust. Interwoven with more positive messages, Jewish leaders have tried to instill guilt, telling Jews that if they assimilate, then all the martyrs of the years of 1939–1945 died for nothing.

The Jews are understandably Holocaust-obsessed and rightly so. Eminent Jewish thinkers like Emil Fackenheim have even argued that in the wake of the Holocaust a 614th commandment has come into being, namely, that we must make sure that we never lose another Jew, so as not to grant Hitler a posthumous victory. Others, like Spinoza and Jean-Paul Sartre, have even taken this concept further and argued that without anti-Semitism there would be no Jewish people.

Nevertheless, I do not believe that the necessity of perpetuating the legacy of the Holocaust, or combating anti-Semitism, will ever serve as the principal means by which Jews identify. The world Jewish community must fine-tune its approach toward engendering commitment. Because Jews today have lost confidence in the power of their ancient faith, the community is resorting to guilt and fear in order to persuade young Jews to identify with what would otherwise be a dying tradition.

Resorting to panic and alarm is wrong because fear has a shelf life. Fear is one of the two emotions that motivate people. The other is love. Rather than teaching young Jews of their glorious heritage, rather than exposing them to the great giants of Jewish history—like Moses and Abraham—whose lives and legacy shook the whole earth— we instead teach them to affirm their identity because we are the most despised of all nations and must therefore be vigilant. Indeed, fear is the worst possible way to sustain long-term commitment. Where is the Soviet Union today? Its vast secret police apparatus and the fear it induced among their citizenry were insufficient to sustain the loyalty of their people. History has demonstrated in every circumstance that with time people grow immune to fear. In stark contrast, democratic countries like the United States that reward their citizens with good lives for their efforts rather than scaring them to death have flourished. Fear always leads to rebellion. The power of fear can last a generation or two, but then people decide that enough is enough. Their attitude becomes, "Go ahead and kill me already. I'm tired of being afraid." But people never tire of love and pride. Increasingly, therefore, people are realizing that only positive reinforcement has the capacity to rebuild the Jewish nation and attract the young. Only a program of educating the world's Jews about the nobility of their heritage has the capacity to reawaken a sleeping nation.

An outsider who studies modern world Jewry and its educational institutions would be forgiven if he concluded that before the Holocaust nothing of significance ever took place in Jewish history. The Jewish obsession with the Holocaust is understandable. Our innocent martyrs must always be remembered, but we must likewise be wary of a holocaust—consciousness pervading the complete fabric of the national consciousness. Most Jews know far more about the life of Adolf Hitler than they do about prophecies of Jeremiah or Isaiah.

The Holocaust pervades every Jewish educational curriculum, every national celebration of the State of Israel, a significant percentage of rabbinical sermons, and certainly the Jewish youth movements of virtually every denomination. In the area of Jewish fund-raising, collecting money to build a Holocaust museum or memorial is often given precedence over building more Jewish day schools or other educational establishments. To be sure, both are necessary, but the consequences for the Jewish people in highlighting the negative over the positive is tragic.

The Jews have always been the nation of life, and the Jewish religion has always been the faith of the living. Through countless persecutions, the Jews never became morbid or obsessed with death. In stark contrast to Christianity, with its icons of a martyred god dripping with blood adorning the world's churches, the Jews always focused on life. Though death and mortality were their constant companions, the Jews still pulled out the best bottle of wine they could every Friday night and festival eve and toasted to life, *L'Chaim*. The fixation with the Holocaust risks making Judaism into a religion like Christianity, focused on death and absorbed in tragedy and the redemption brought about by suffering. Judaism has never been a religion of cemeteries, tombs, and mass graves. Rather, it has always been the religion of young children, families, communities, and the living Torah, which has sustained and animated this most ancient people through every trial.

The Holocaust must be seen as an important event in Jewish history rather than its defining moment. The Jews did not become a nation in Auschwitz, but at Sinai. Their defining moment was rising to the challenge of living according to the highest moral code, not succumbing to the world's greatest brutes. This is not to say that we should not teach our children of the world about the Holocaust. Indeed, we must familiarize every earthly inhabitant with the Holocaust and with the stark lesson of man's brutality to his fellow man. But the Holocaust must be taught in the context of the overall triumph of the Jewish people, who have successfully served as a beacon and light unto the nations.

Young Jews must learn that their great heroes were those who responded to the call of God and changed the world rather than only those who were victims of other nations' brutality. The Jewish places of pilgrimage must continue to be first the Holy Land of Israel and only afterward the death camps of Poland, Germany, and Austria. Jews must pray at the last remnants of the Temple Mount, the Western Wall, where David sang his sweet tunes to the Lord and where Solomon exercised wise counsel in judging the nation; where Yochanan ben Zakkai entreated the Roman emperor Vespasian to allow a city dedicated to Torah to survive his onslaught against Jerusalem, and where a group of survivors who had just endured the Holocaust somehow mustered the courage to fend off eight Arab nations and set up an independent Jewish state for the first time in two millennia. The story of the Jews is a story of hope and victory, not death and morbidity.

Primo Levi was perhaps the Holocaust's most famous survivor, although one hesitates to call him a survivor, since his suicide many years after Auschwitz is believed to have resulted from his horrific experiences there. He wrote that the only truly original contribution of the Third Reich to civilization was the *Muselmänn*, concentration camp slang for a prisoner near death—the skin-and-bone walking corpse, or living dead. The vast "anonymous mass, continuously renewed and always identical, of non-men who march and labour in silence, the divine spark dead within them, already too empty really to suffer. One hesitates to call their death, death" (Levi, *Survival in Auschwitz*, p. 82). But by using fear and guilt to induce Jewish commitment and perpetuate Jewish tradition, we risk creating an entire generation of Jewish religious *Muselmänner*, young Jews who feel too guilty to abandon their Judaism. Therefore, they keep it out of a sense of guilt, fear, and habit. We cannot have a generation of Jews who, though identifying with their Judaism, do it with little life. The Jews who witnessed the revelation of the living God of history at Sinai must once again embrace their tree of life—the Torah—in order to ensure that their children continue to be written in the book of *Jewish* life.

Faith and the Jewish People

Neither an obsession with the Holocaust nor a redirection of attention toward Jewish culture will point the way forward. Rather, we must draw on the distinction of our incomparable God, religion, and values. The goodness and holiness that we have brought to the world has no parallel. We have given the world a personal God of history who is attentive to human suffering; the idea that all men and women are created in the image of God and are therefore holy and equal; the notion of a world run on the principles of law and justice and that man's highest calling is to serve as an agent for their establishment and maintenance. Judaism has taught the world that history is directional and that humankind is slowly progressing toward a world of peace and global fraternity. Our religion is what is truly beautiful; its influence has no parallel in the annals of any nation, either ancient or modern.

The Jews have given the world a day of meditation, prayer, and family every seven days, thereby affording man an awareness that he is more than just an ox that pulls a plow. He is a contemplative, spiritual being who must cater to the needs of his soul. We have given the world the concept of the nuclear family as the mainstay of society, as well as the idea of holiness and fidelity in marriage. Judaism gave husbands and wives the *mikveh*, which I wrote about extensively in *Kosher Sex;* no better secret for retaining passion in marriage has ever been found. We don our tefillin every morning, thereby integrating mind and heart in the service of the divine calling. We affix mezuzot to our doors and invite strangers into our homes, transforming them into miniature sanctuaries for the communal good instead of private dwellings designed to keep people out. And because of the compassion taught us by Judaism, we are the most charitable community on earth.

Our religion has served as a great light to ourselves and other nations throughout time. The Bible declares, "Moses charged us with the law, as an inheritance for the assembly of Jacob" (Deut. 33:4). Jewish faith is the rightful possession of every Jew, and it is incumbent upon Jewish parents to impart this living spring of inspiration to their young. By doing so they will ensure not only that their child remains the next link in an unbroken chain of Jewish existence, but also that he or she continues the job of serving as a light in a world suffering from darkness.

Rediscovering Awe and Wonder

The Jewish man of faith will not cease to be an anachronism and will not assume his rightful place in society until his contribution to modern life is reevaluated and its necessity reestablished. There are three principal categories where the man of faith can contribute invaluably toward a world that is fast losing its moral compass.

The first is in the field of depth and transcendence. Modern man is so consumed by the satiation of his desires and material consumption that he looks at the world in an entirely utilitarian way. In seeing a beautiful mountain range, he is not overcome by a feeling of awe or wonder. Rather, his first thought is how he can develop the site for his own advantage. Perhaps he will build a ski resort or summer retreat. When modern man meets someone new, his first thought is how he might exploit the new relationship to his advantage. Perhaps his new acquaintance has useful business contacts. When a man meets an attractive woman, his first thought is how she might eventually service his physical needs. Modern-day man seems concerned exclusively with improving his position relative to his environment. The first thing, therefore, that the man of faith can do is to reintroduce to the earth's inhabitants a sense of majesty and grandeur, a sensitivity to awe and wonder. The religious man of faith can teach the modern man of technology how to simply stand back and behold the world in all its color, to learn how to appreciate rather than to manipulate. The divine nature of religion today loses out to its social dimension, and its covenantal role is superseded by its aesthetic value. Here the man of faith can reintroduce humanity to God in an honest and loving relationship, so that religion becomes something experiential rather than just ceremonial. We get to enjoy God as a vibrant part of our lives rather than just another social accoutrement.

The second contribution of the man of faith lies in the area of ethics. Without God, good and evil become nothing more than euphemisms for personal or collective tastes. In an age that longs for guidance and a path out of worldly entanglement, the man and woman of faith can provide a beacon for the rest of humanity.

The third contribution of religious man lies in the realm of crisis. Technological man feels triumphant through his conquest of disease and his ability to travel long distances in hours rather than months. In moments of insecurity and fright, however, when he is confronted with a situation that he cannot master, he finds himself spinning out of control, crying out for a comforting presence who is always attuned to his pain. As the architect of man, God is the only Being capable of understanding man's greatest fears and alleviating his deepest pain. Without God, modern-day man remains a ship tossing in the wind, his cry deafened by the howling tempest, as he becomes lost at sea.

The Jews are carriers of the religious flame that is the source of all three blessings. The light of their faith can impart the inspiration to the rest of humanity to translate these precious gifts into a meaningful program of action.

Jewish Religious Influence

For two thousand years the Jews were cut off from making any direct contribution to, or having any direct impact on, wider society. Christianity and Islam were the dominant religions, and both either persecuted and subdued the Jews directly or at the very least shut them behind ghetto walls. The Jews reacted by cowering in fear and developing a subtle and understandable contempt for their Gentile tormentors. Indeed, the immorality and lawlessness that they witnessed and to which they were subject made them despise wider society, and they protected their children from its nefarious influences by electing to remain cut off and isolated. Thus was born the idea of a self-imposed ghetto, where Jews voluntarily disengaged from Gentile culture by living among themselves and having little to do with the outside world.

But since the French Revolution and the emancipation of European Jewry, all that has changed. Jews are treated as equals of every major society in which they dwell. In the United States, the most tolerant nation that the Jews have ever had the good fortune to become citizens of, they exert influence and have justly earned great respect. Either this acceptance will swallow them whole and lead to their total disappearance, or it will finally present the long-awaited opportunity for the Jews to influence the world directly with Jewish light. Modernity has afforded Judaism its first opportunity since the age of Christ to shape and mold the public debate and participate directly in the marketplace of ideas. Today, immersed into a democratic and largely secular society that has become disenchanted with religion, the Jewish faith can rise and make an impact on mainstream civilization. Judaism, with its strong ethical emphasis, can serve as an inspiration for modern-day men and women who long for a spirituality that will make them into better people— teaching them how to be more happily married, raise more secure children, channel their ambition into purposeful actions—and transform the world into a kinder, gentler place. Judaism should be promoted, not as a truer religion than any other, but as a model of faith uniquely suited to the twin goals of material prosperity amid spiritual growth. The world cries out for leadership. Judaism is mankind's oldest monotheistic faith. Its light is finally being granted an opportunity to shine without obstruction. May its rays illuminate the distant corners of the blessed earth as well as the smallest crevices of the human heart.

Books Cited

Books that are referred to or quoted from in the text are listed here.

Birnbaum, David. *God and Evil.* Hoboken, N.J.: KTAV Publishing House, 1989.

Carnegie, Dale. *How to Win Friends and Influence People.* New York: Simon & Schuster, 1937.

Dawidowicz, Lucy. *The War Against the Jews.* New York: Bantam Books, 1986.

Dershowitz, Alan. *The Vanishing American Jew.* Boston: Little, Brown, 1997.

Frankl, Victor Emil. *Man's Search for Meaning.* Boston: Beacon Press, 1963.

Freud, Sigmund. *Moses and Monotheism.* New York: Knopf, 1939.

Gibbon, Edward. *Decline and Fall of the Roman Empire.* New York: Washington Square Press, 1963.

Goldhagen, Daniel. *Hitler's Willing Executioners.* New York: Knopf, 1996.

Hausner, Gideon. *Justice in Jerusalem.* New York: Harper & Row, 1966.

Heschel, Abraham Joshua. *Who Is Man?* Stanford: Stanford University Press, 1965.

Hirsch, Samson Raphael. *Horeb: A Philosophy of Jewish Laws and Observances.* New York: Soncino Press, 1994.

Hitler, Adolf. *Hitler's Table Talk.* Collected by Martin Bormann. Enigma Books, 2000.

Jacob, Louis. *The Jewish Religion: A Companion.* Oxford: Oxford University Press, 1995.

Johnson, Paul. *History of the Jews.* New York: Harper & Row, 1987.

Kafka, Franz. *Letters to Friends, Family and Editors.* Translated by Richard and Clara Winston. New York: Schocken, 1990.

Kamenetz, Rodger. *The Jew in the Lotus.* San Francisco: Harper San Francisco, 1994.

Kushner, Harold. *To Life! A Celebration of Jewish Being and Thinking.* Boston: Warner Books, 1993.

_____. *When Bad Things Happen to Good People.* New York: Avon, 1983.

Lamm, Norman. *Faith and Doubt.* New York: KTAV Publishing House, 1972.

Levi, Primo. *Survival in Auschwitz.* New York: Scribner, 1995.

Maimonides. *Guide for the Perplexed.* New York: Dover Publications, 1956.

Patterson, James. *The Day America Told the Truth.* New York: Prentice Hall, 1991.

Prager, Dennis, and Joseph Telushkin. *Why the Jews?* New York: Simon and Schuster, 1983.

Russell, Bertrand. *Why I Am Not a Christian and Other Essays on Religion and Related Subjects.* New York: Simon & Schuster, 1957.

Soloveitchik, Joseph. *The Lonely Man of Faith.* New York: Doubleday, 1992.

_____. *Man of Faith in the Modern World.* Hoboken, N.J.: KTAV Publishing House, 1989.

Spengler, Oswald. *Decline of the West.* 1926–1928. Reprint, New York: Knopf, 1980.

Steinsaltz, Adin. *The Strife of the Spirit.* Northvale, N.J.: J. Aronson, 1988.

Toynbee, Arnold. *A Study of History.* Oxford: Oxford University Press, 1961.

Walsh, Neal Donald. *Conversations with God.* Putnam Publishing Group, 1996.

Wiesel, Elie. *The Town Beyond the Wall.* New York: Holt, Rinehart and Winston, 1967.

Wright, Robert. *The Moral Animal.* New York: Pantheon Books, 1994.

Index

Children, 215
  behavior of, 158
  and Holocaust, 297
  requirement for Sanhedrin to
    have, 293
  spiritual quality of, 358
  time spent with, 158–59
Chmielnicki and Cossack pogroms,
  418
Chosen people and nation, 261–98
  accomplishment of mission of,
    289–93
  and anti-Semitism, 275
  to bring world together, 19
  and egalitarian generation,
    275–78
  and establishment of ancient
    Jewish nation, 270
  and God's inequities towards, 277
  as guide and instructor to other
    nations, 283–85
  and heroism, 273–75
  history of, 267–71
  and humility, 277, 282–83
  idea of and other peoples, 275–76
  and land of Israel, 371
  as light unto the nations, 37,
    284, 291, 397, 423–24
  as mission rather than
    superiority, 277
  as nation of priests, 270
  and necessity of commandments
    to keep aligned, 284–85
  and other nations, 283–85
  and survival through God's
    providence, 270
  and tolerance, 279–80
  uncomfortableness of Jews
    regarding, 292
  See also Mission of Jews
Christianity
  and Adam and Eve, 67, 68–69,
    201
  asceticism in, 44

  as decisive factor in world
    history, 13
  and efforts to convert Jews,
    399–400, 411
  everlasting life in Paradise in, 410
  fall of man in, 50
  fear of human existence in, 44–45
  heavenward flight in, 49
  and Hitler, 324
  idealization of nonfamily life in,
    293
  incarnation of Deity on earth in,
    93, 401–2, 405
  and intermediary between God
    and man, 410–11
  and Lewinsky affair, 3–4
  love in, 391–92, 409
  martyrdom in, 412
  necessity of grace in, 248
  negation of self in, 52
  original sin in, 405–7
  personal salvation in, 256
  as perversion of Jewish ideas,
    295
  and Pope Pius XII, 254–55
  primacy of faith in, 50–51, 52,
    301–11
  redemption through suffering in,
    196–97
  rejection of law in, 311–12
  rejection of world in, 47
  renouncing of, 382–83
  spiritual role of Messiah in, 406,
    408
  spreading idea of God in, 400–7
  Torah superceded by teachings
    of Jesus in, 409–10
  Trinity and, 404, 405
  See also Judaism and
    Christianity, differences
    between
Christian Right, 118
Churchill, Winston, 202
Circumcision, 272–73, 385–90

Civilization, corrosion of when no challenge, 59–60
Clinton, Bill, 3, 31, 37
Cobain, Kurt, 275
Coleridge, Samuel Taylor, 399
Columbine High School shootings, 58
Comforter, 230, 232, 233–34
Commandments, 97, 120–22, 367
 and gender, 174, 183–84
 include action and motivation, 258–59
 to keep Jewish peoples aligned, 285
 Noahide, 284–85
 six hundred thirteen of, 190, 270, 272
 and sukkah, 367–68
 See also Mitzvot
Communism, 225, 255
Community, 280, 281
Compassion, 352
Complaints against God, 193
Compromise, 141
Conception of God
 and ancient man, 77
 Biblical, 76–79
 Christian, 81
 Israel's vs. ancient man's, 77
 Jewish contrasted with previous, 79–81
Confucius, 353
Contempt for non-Jews, 293–98, 425
 and Christians, 295
 previous Jewish persecution and, 294
Conversations with God (Walsh), 310
Conversion
 Christian attempts with Jews, 399–400, 411
 criterion regarding those who have converted, 384–85
 Jewish non-recognition of, 382–83
 non-encouragement of, 286, 385

Cooley, Mason, 187
Covenants
 between God and Jews as eternally valid, 408–10
 patriarchal, 64
 Sinaitic, 64, 411–12
Covey, Stephen, 32
Creation story, 85
Creativity
 knowing limits of and circumcision, 386–87
 and man making idol of himself, 162–63
 necessity for, 347–48
 physical, rest from on Sabbath, 162–65
Creator, God as, 76–77, 190–91, 264–65, 266–67
 allowance of suffering and, 192–93
 and Darwin, 191
 establishment of by Jews, 271
 and incarnation in body, 402
 man in His image, 15–16, 347, 406, 423
Crick, Francis, 323
Crime and Punishment (Dostoyevsky), 315
Crisis, 138–39, 425
Crowe, Russell, 108
Crucifix, 402, 412
Cultural malaise, 14
Cyclical history
 dominating ancient world, 221–22
 Jewish vs. Eastern attitudes towards, 219
Cyrus the Great, 271

Dalai Lama, 4, 229, 294
Darwin, Charles, 191, 318–19
David, King, 94, 156, 228, 330, 350, 367
Davies, Peter J., 299

questioning existence of, 75–76
reducing of overt presence over
time, 265–66
and slaughter of twentieth
century, 192
subjugation to, 272–73
transcendence and immanence
and, 87–88, 179
unity and, 81–84
vs. religion, 113–14
wrestling with, 18
See also Conception of God;
Creator, God as; Existence of;
Hiding of God; Love, for God;
Prayer; Relationship to God;
Sefirot; Suffering
God and Evil (Birnbaum), 193–95
Goebbels, Joseph, 254, 317
Golden calf, 29, 208, 354
Golden Rule, 11
Goldhagen, Daniel, 317
Goodness, 315–16, 323
Good people suffer along with
wicked, 194
Good works. *See* Mitzvot
Goose, Edmund, 311
Graham, Billy, 111, 313
Greek mythological gods, 79
Greeks
and fate, 221–22, 336
use of leisure, 170–71
Guilt, 422

Ha'am, Ahad, 153
Halakhah, 116
Halevi, Rabbi Judah, 45, 97, 99,
153
Halevi of Barcelona, Rabbi Aaron,
370
Handicapped skiing
championships, 231
Hannah, 137–38
Hare Krishnas, 44
Hassidism, 215
Hausner, Gideon, 317

Hedgehog and the Fox, The (Berlin),
82–83
Hegel, Friedrich, 27–28, 85
He-Hasid, Rabbi Judah, 157–58
Heine, Heinrich, 57
Heroism, 30–31, 273–75
Herzl, Theodor, 134, 290
Heschel, Abraham Joshua, 126, 397
Hiding of God, 75–76, 194, 262
Hillel, 214, 228
Hinduism, 52
Hirsch, Rabbi Samson Raphael,
44–45, 47
History
directional, 16, 221–23, 423
and Jewish contributions, 10–11
of Jews as chosen people, 269–72
past dominated by Christianity
and Islamic, 13
prior to Jews as chosen people,
267–69
History of the Jews (Johnson), 11
Hitler, Adolf, 247, 254, 276, 288
attitude towards Christianity,
324
intention to establish new world
order, 324, 396
and murder of Jews, 316–18,
396–97
race theories of and evolution,
318–19, 321, 396–97
Hitler's Willing Executioners
(Goldhagen), 317
Holocaust, 188
abandonment of God and
Judaism and, 233–34
building of State of Israel and,
212, 225
creation of Jewish identity and,
419–20
domination of Jewish
consciousness and, 420–21
freedom of choice and, 335
"normality" of perpetrators of,
317